RWBY
THE
OFFICIAL
MANGA

VOLUME

2

STORY AND ART
BUNTA KINAMI

BASED ON THE ROOSTER TEETH SERIES CREATED BY MONTY OUM

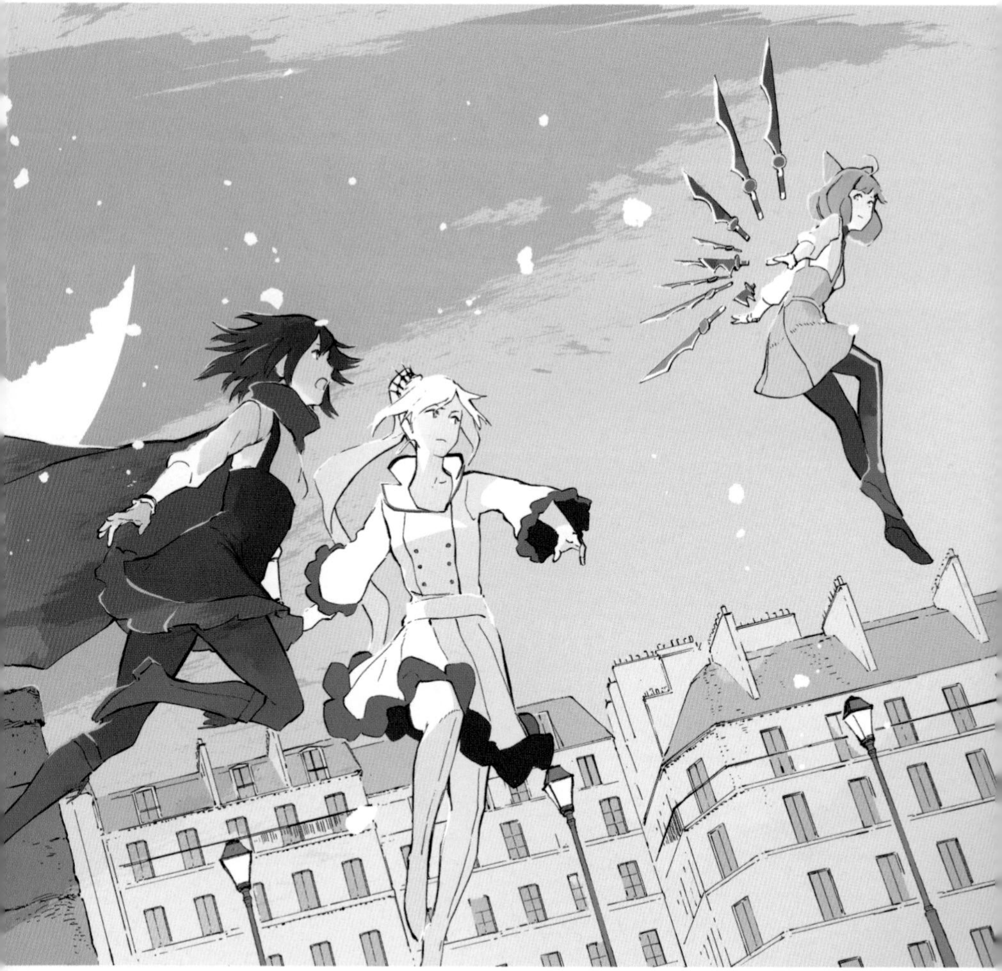

CONTENTS

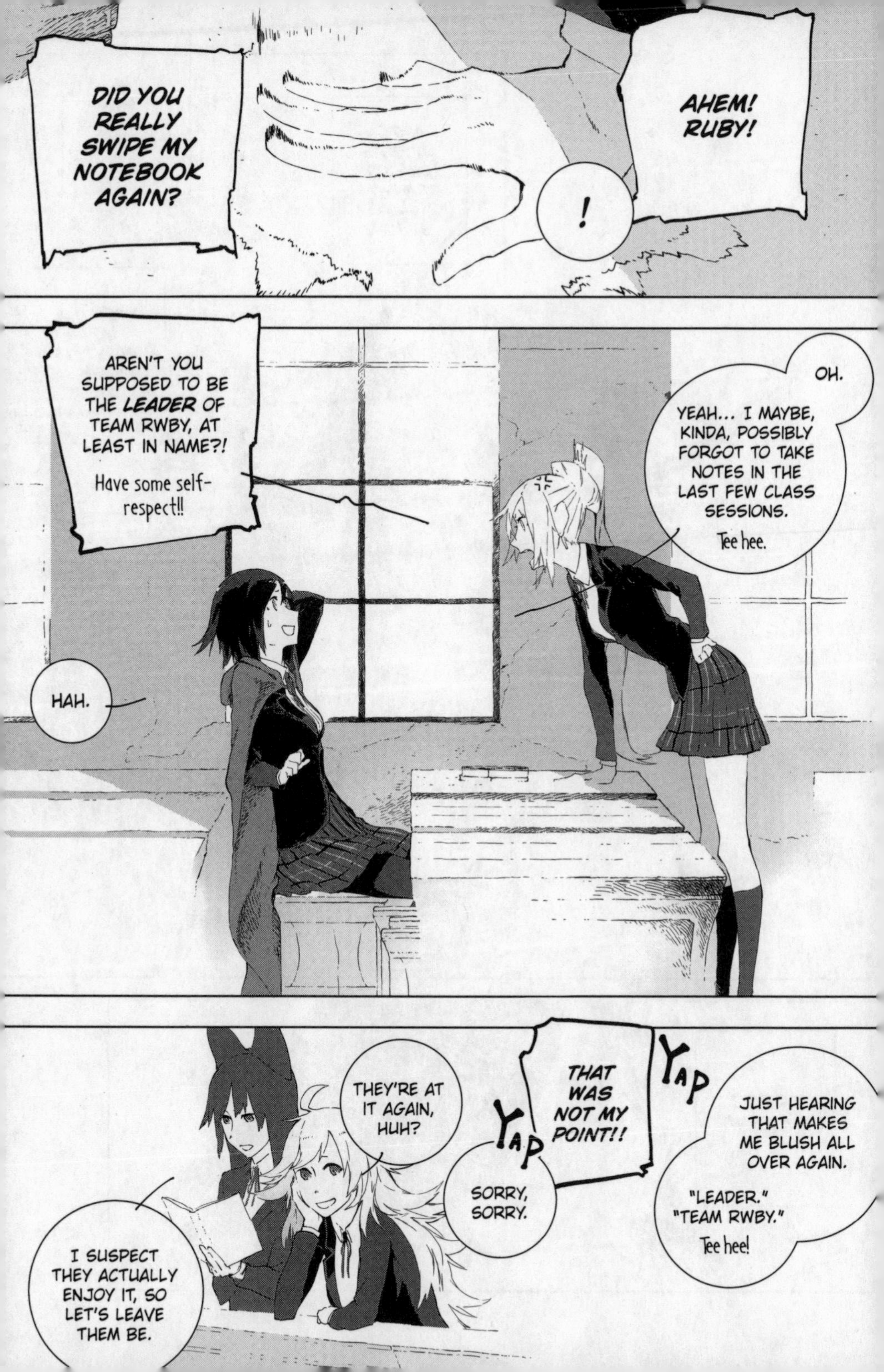
AHEM! RUBY!
!
DID YOU REALLY SWIPE MY NOTEBOOK AGAIN?
OH.
YEAH... I MAYBE, KINDA, POSSIBLY FORGOT TO TAKE NOTES IN THE LAST FEW CLASS SESSIONS.
Tee hee.
AREN'T YOU SUPPOSED TO BE THE LEADER OF TEAM RWBY, AT LEAST IN NAME?!
Have some self-respect!!
HAH.
JUST HEARING THAT MAKES ME BLUSH ALL OVER AGAIN.
"LEADER." "TEAM RWBY."
Tee hee!
YAP
THAT WAS NOT MY POINT!!
YAP
SORRY, SORRY.
THEY'RE AT IT AGAIN, HUH?
I SUSPECT THEY ACTUALLY ENJOY IT, SO LET'S LEAVE THEM BE.

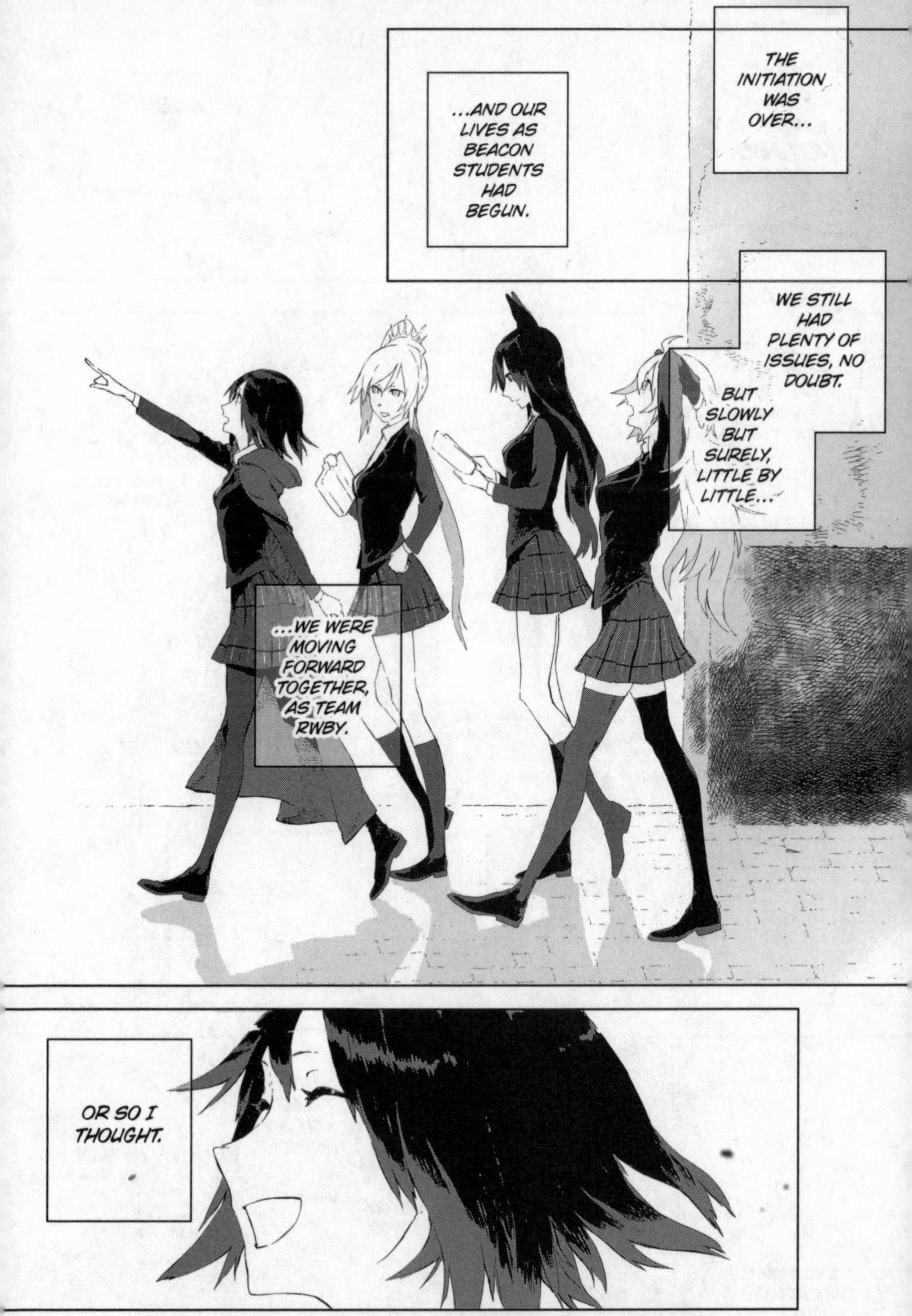
THE INITIATION WAS OVER...
...AND OUR LIVES AS BEACON STUDENTS HAD BEGUN.
WE STILL HAD PLENTY OF ISSUES, NO DOUBT.
BUT SLOWLY BUT SURELY, LITTLE BY LITTLE...
...WE WERE MOVING FORWARD TOGETHER, AS TEAM RWBY.
OR SO I THOUGHT.

Episode 06

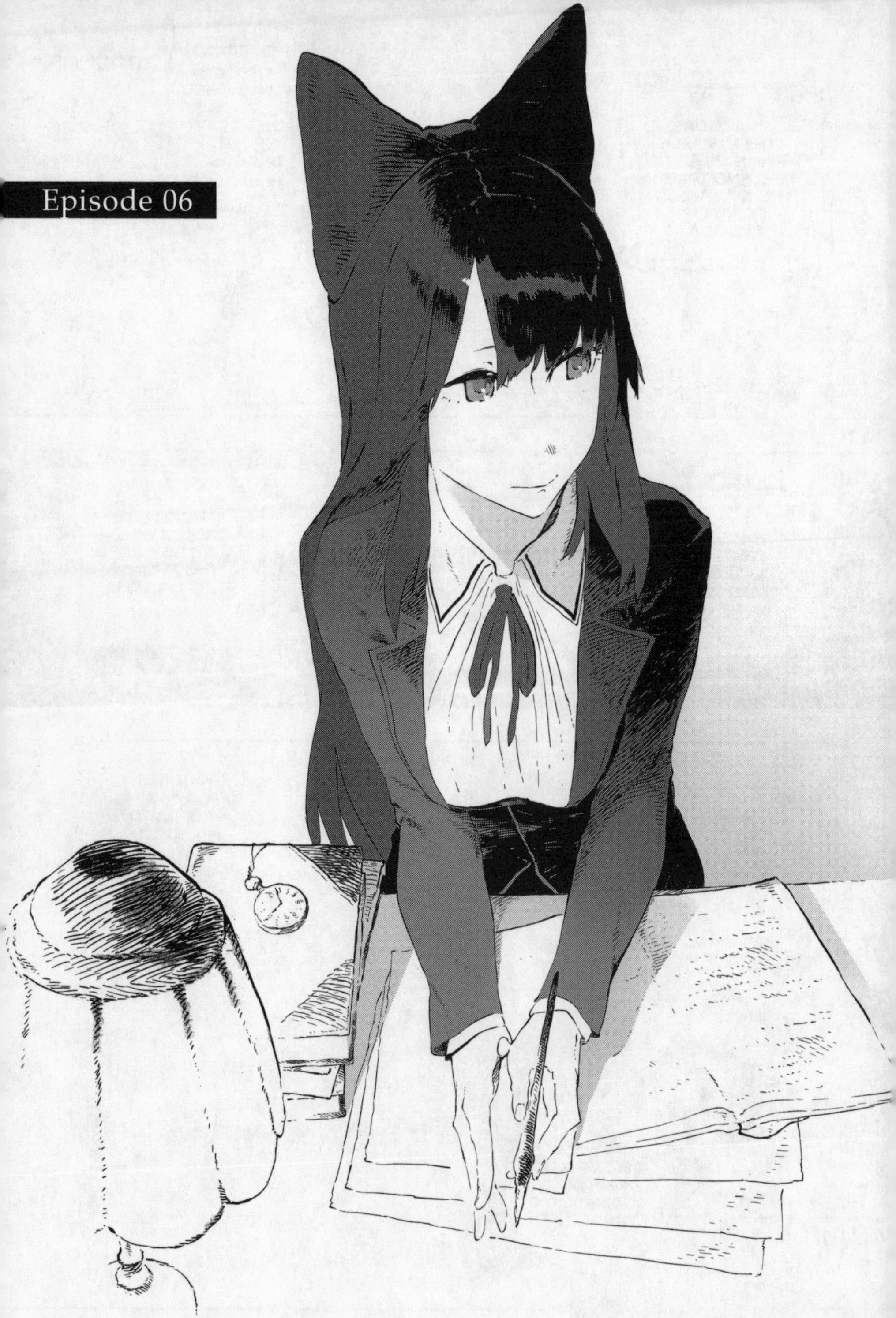

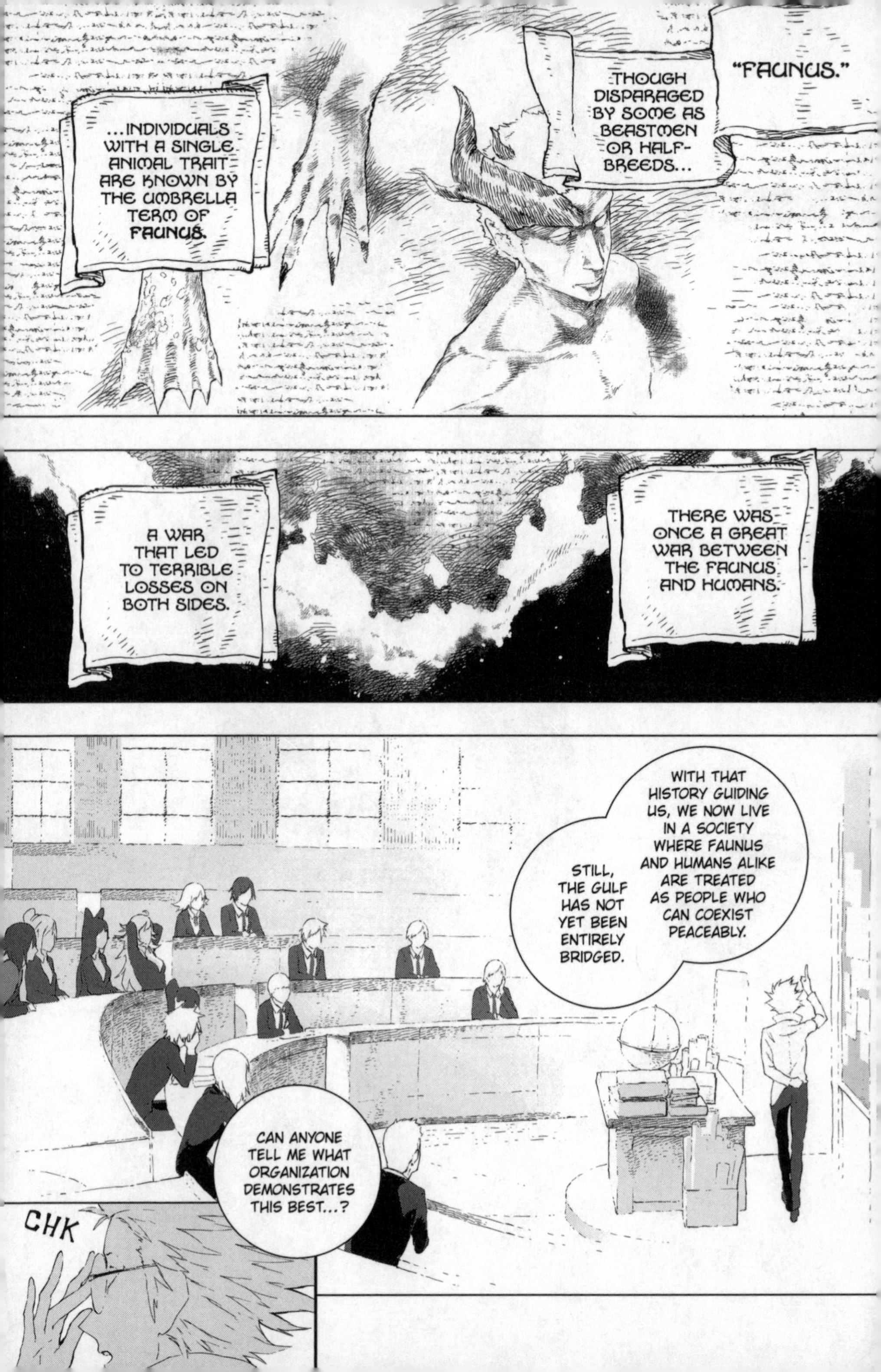
"FAUNUS."
THOUGH DISPARAGED BY SOME AS BEASTMEN OR HALF-BREEDS...
...INDIVIDUALS WITH A SINGLE ANIMAL TRAIT ARE KNOWN BY THE UMBRELLA TERM OF FAUNUS.
THERE WAS ONCE A GREAT WAR BETWEEN THE FAUNUS AND HUMANS.
A WAR THAT LED TO TERRIBLE LOSSES ON BOTH SIDES.
WITH THAT HISTORY GUIDING US, WE NOW LIVE IN A SOCIETY WHERE FAUNUS AND HUMANS ALIKE ARE TREATED AS PEOPLE WHO CAN COEXIST PEACEABLY.
STILL, THE GULF HAS NOT YET BEEN ENTIRELY BRIDGED.
CAN ANYONE TELL ME WHAT ORGANIZATION DEMONSTRATES THIS BEST...?
CHK

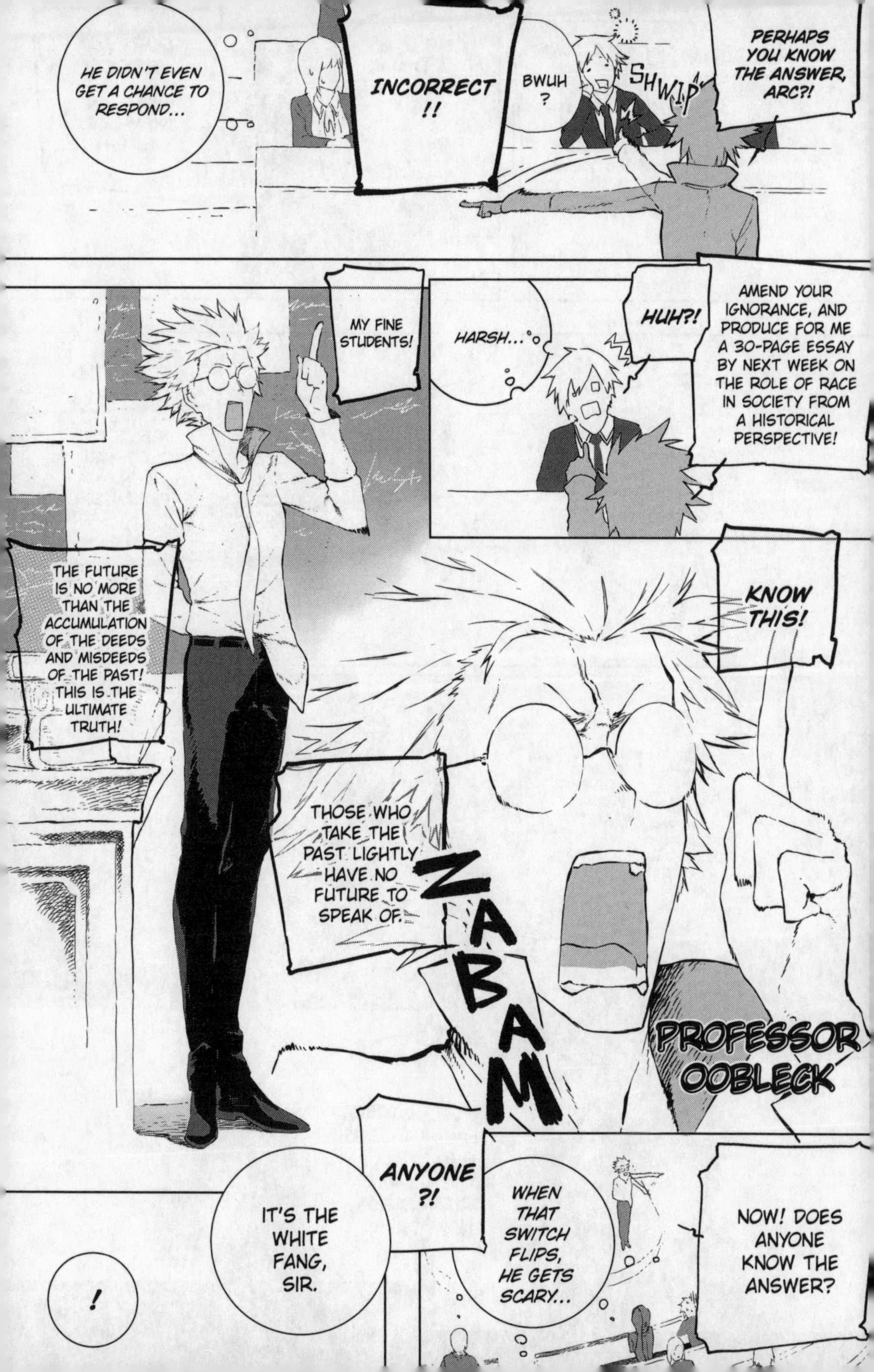
PERHAPS YOU KNOW THE ANSWER, ARC?!
SHWIP
BWUH ?
INCORRECT !!
HE DIDN'T EVEN GET A CHANCE TO RESPOND...
AMEND YOUR IGNORANCE, AND PRODUCE FOR ME A 30-PAGE ESSAY BY NEXT WEEK ON THE ROLE OF RACE IN SOCIETY FROM A HISTORICAL PERSPECTIVE!
HUH?!
HARSH...
KNOW THIS!
THOSE WHO TAKE THE PAST LIGHTLY HAVE NO FUTURE TO SPEAK OF.
ZABAM
PROFESSOR OOBLECK
MY FINE STUDENTS!
THE FUTURE IS NO MORE THAN THE ACCUMULATION OF THE DEEDS AND MISDEEDS OF THE PAST! THIS IS THE ULTIMATE TRUTH!
NOW! DOES ANYONE KNOW THE ANSWER?
WHEN THAT SWITCH FLIPS, HE GETS SCARY...
ANYONE ?!
IT'S THE WHITE FANG, SIR.
!

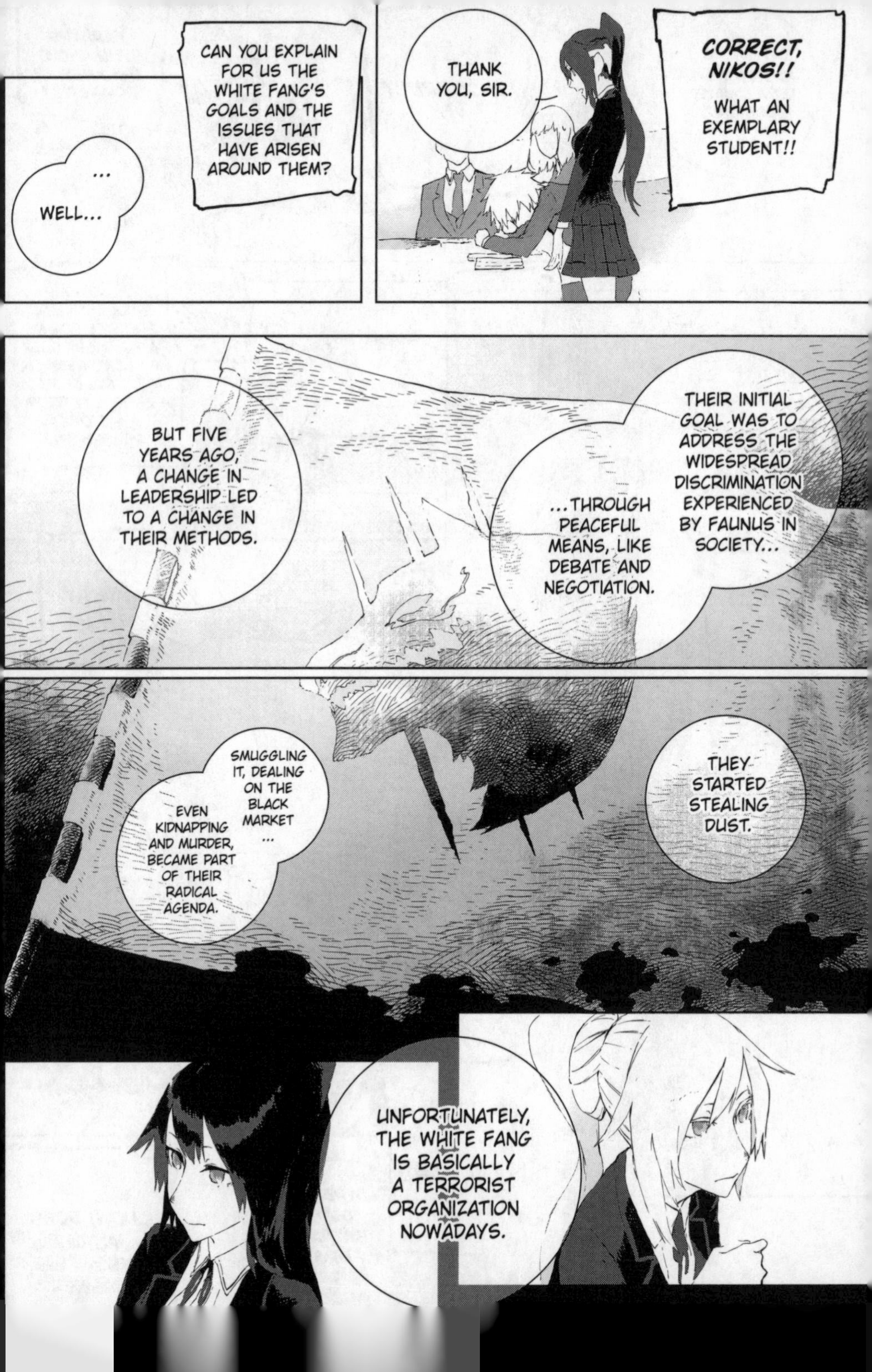
CORRECT, NIKOS!! WHAT AN EXEMPLARY STUDENT!!
THANK YOU, SIR.
CAN YOU EXPLAIN FOR US THE WHITE FANG'S GOALS AND THE ISSUES THAT HAVE ARISEN AROUND THEM?
... WELL...
THEIR INITIAL GOAL WAS TO ADDRESS THE WIDESPREAD DISCRIMINATION EXPERIENCED BY FAUNUS IN SOCIETY...
...THROUGH PEACEFUL MEANS, LIKE DEBATE AND NEGOTIATION.
BUT FIVE YEARS AGO, A CHANGE IN LEADERSHIP LED TO A CHANGE IN THEIR METHODS.
THEY STARTED STEALING DUST.
SMUGGLING IT, DEALING ON THE BLACK MARKET...
EVEN KIDNAPPING AND MURDER, BECAME PART OF THEIR RADICAL AGENDA.
UNFORTUNATELY, THE WHITE FANG IS BASICALLY A TERRORIST ORGANIZATION NOWADAYS.

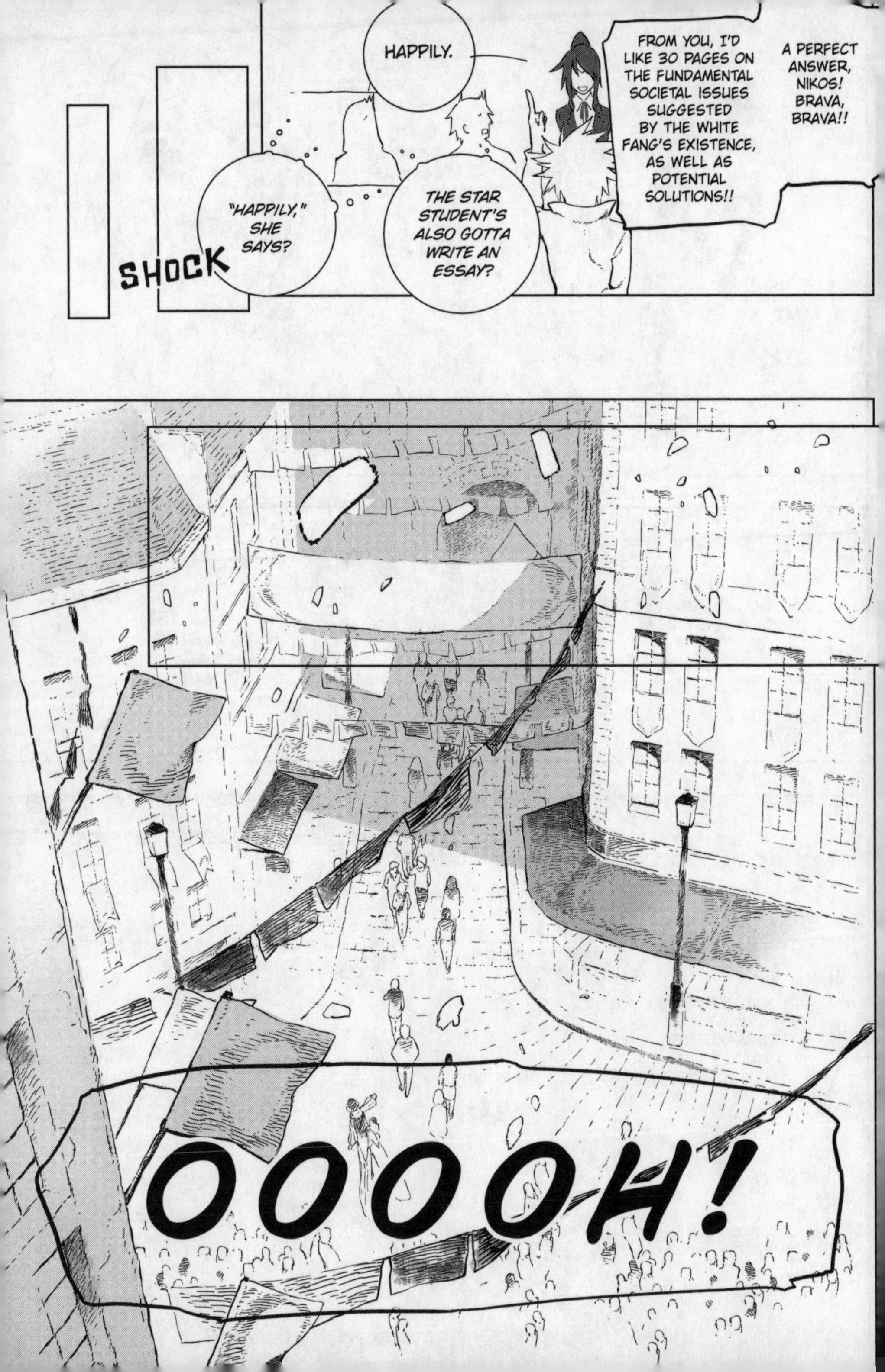
A PERFECT ANSWER, NIKOS! BRAVA, BRAVA!!
FROM YOU, I'D LIKE 30 PAGES ON THE FUNDAMENTAL SOCIETAL ISSUES SUGGESTED BY THE WHITE FANG'S EXISTENCE, AS WELL AS POTENTIAL SOLUTIONS!!
HAPPILY.
THE STAR STUDENT'S ALSO GOTTA WRITE AN ESSAY?
"HAPPILY," SHE SAYS?
SHOCK
OOOOH!

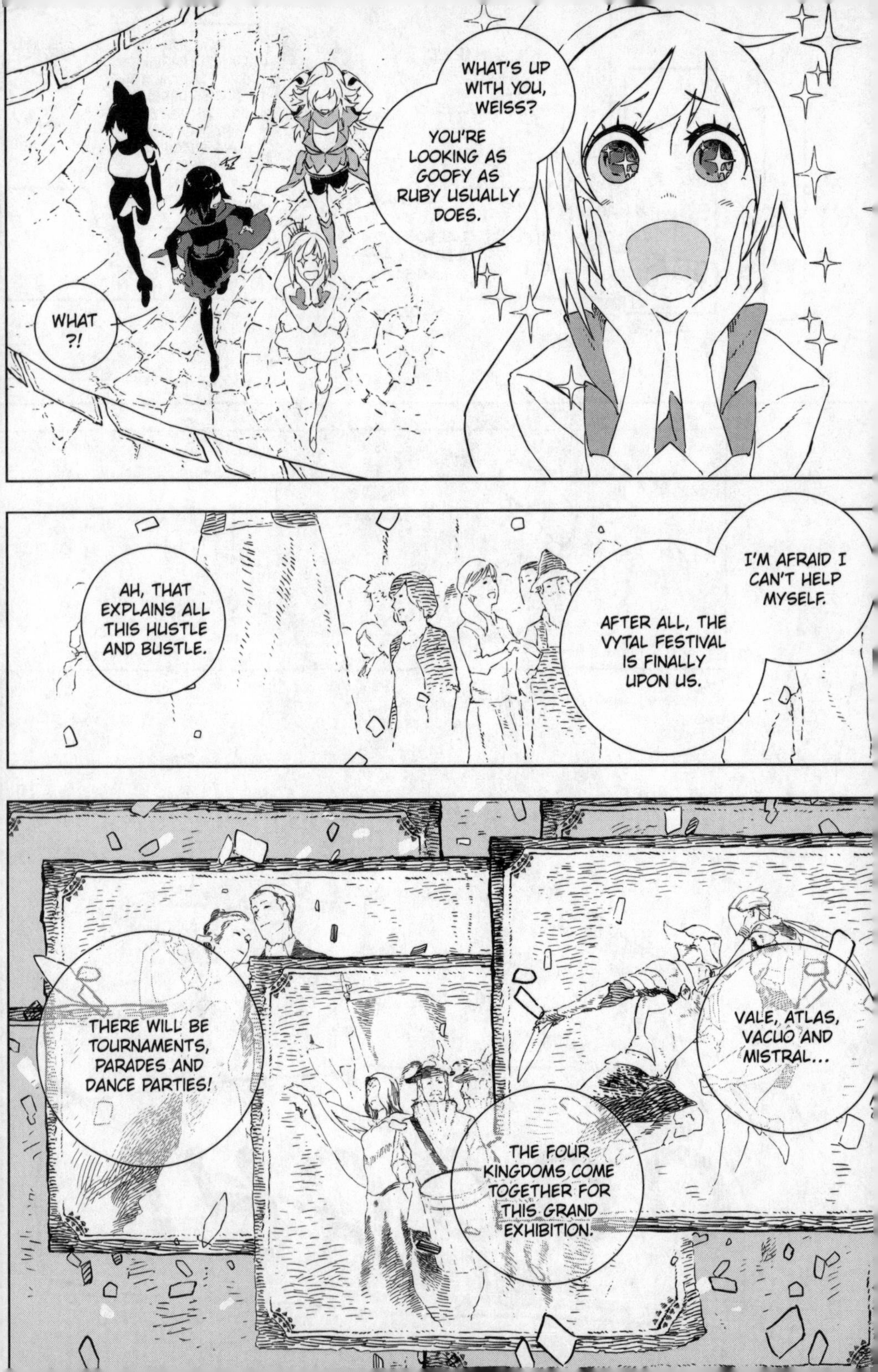
WHAT'S UP WITH YOU, WEISS? YOU'RE LOOKING AS GOOFY AS RUBY USUALLY DOES.
WHAT?!
I'M AFRAID I CAN'T HELP MYSELF. AFTER ALL, THE VYTAL FESTIVAL IS FINALLY UPON US.
AH, THAT EXPLAINS ALL THIS HUSTLE AND BUSTLE.
VALE, ATLAS, VACUO AND MISTRAL...
THE FOUR KINGDOMS COME TOGETHER FOR THIS GRAND EXHIBITION.
THERE WILL BE TOURNAMENTS, PARADES AND DANCE PARTIES!

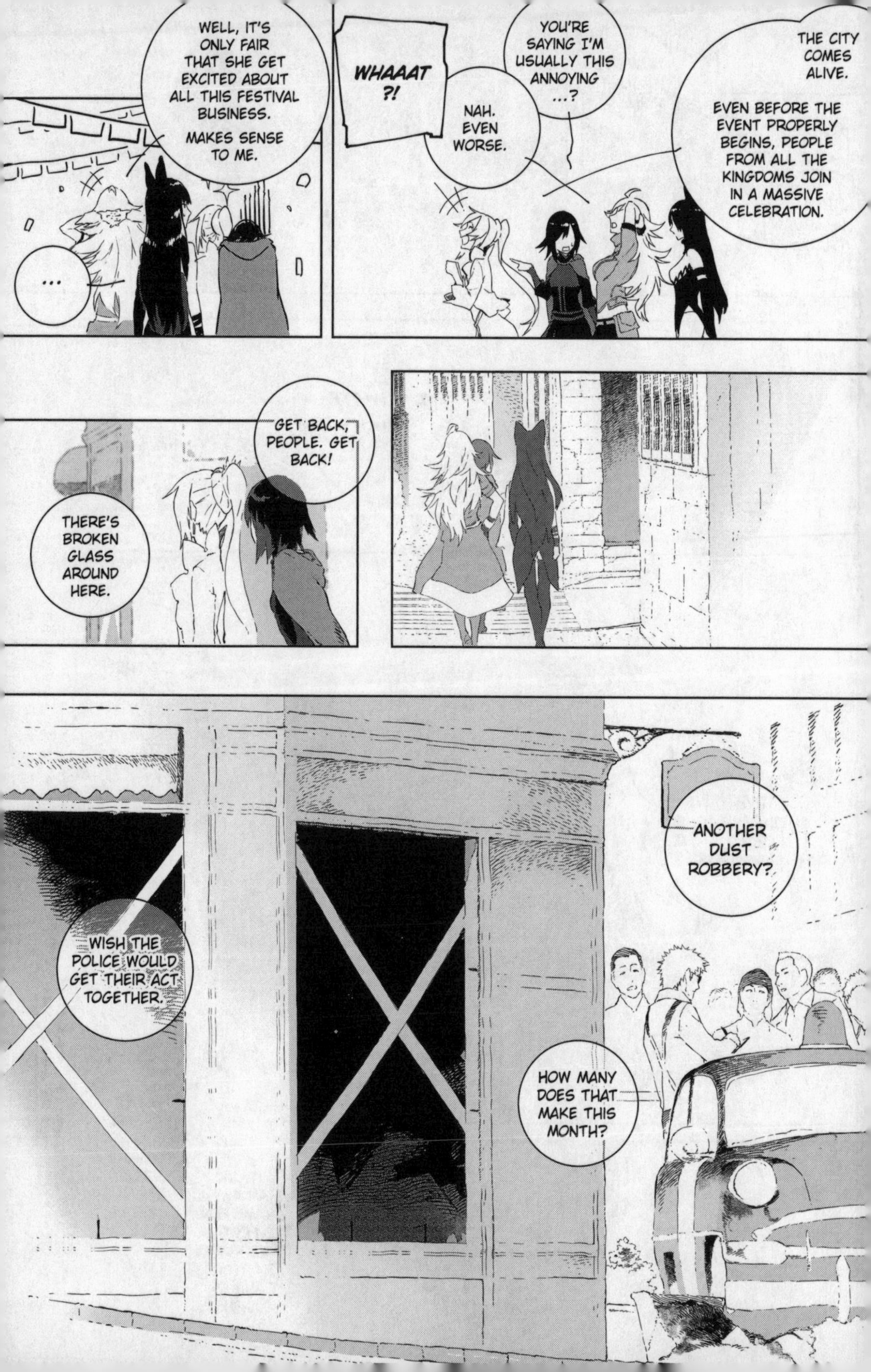
THE CITY COMES ALIVE.
EVEN BEFORE THE EVENT PROPERLY BEGINS, PEOPLE FROM ALL THE KINGDOMS JOIN IN A MASSIVE CELEBRATION.
YOU'RE SAYING I'M USUALLY THIS ANNOYING ...?
NAH. EVEN WORSE.
WHAAAT ?!
WELL, IT'S ONLY FAIR THAT SHE GET EXCITED ABOUT ALL THIS FESTIVAL BUSINESS.
MAKES SENSE TO ME.
...
GET BACK, PEOPLE. GET BACK!
THERE'S BROKEN GLASS AROUND HERE.
ANOTHER DUST ROBBERY?
HOW MANY DOES THAT MAKE THIS MONTH?
WISH THE POLICE WOULD GET THEIR ACT TOGETHER.

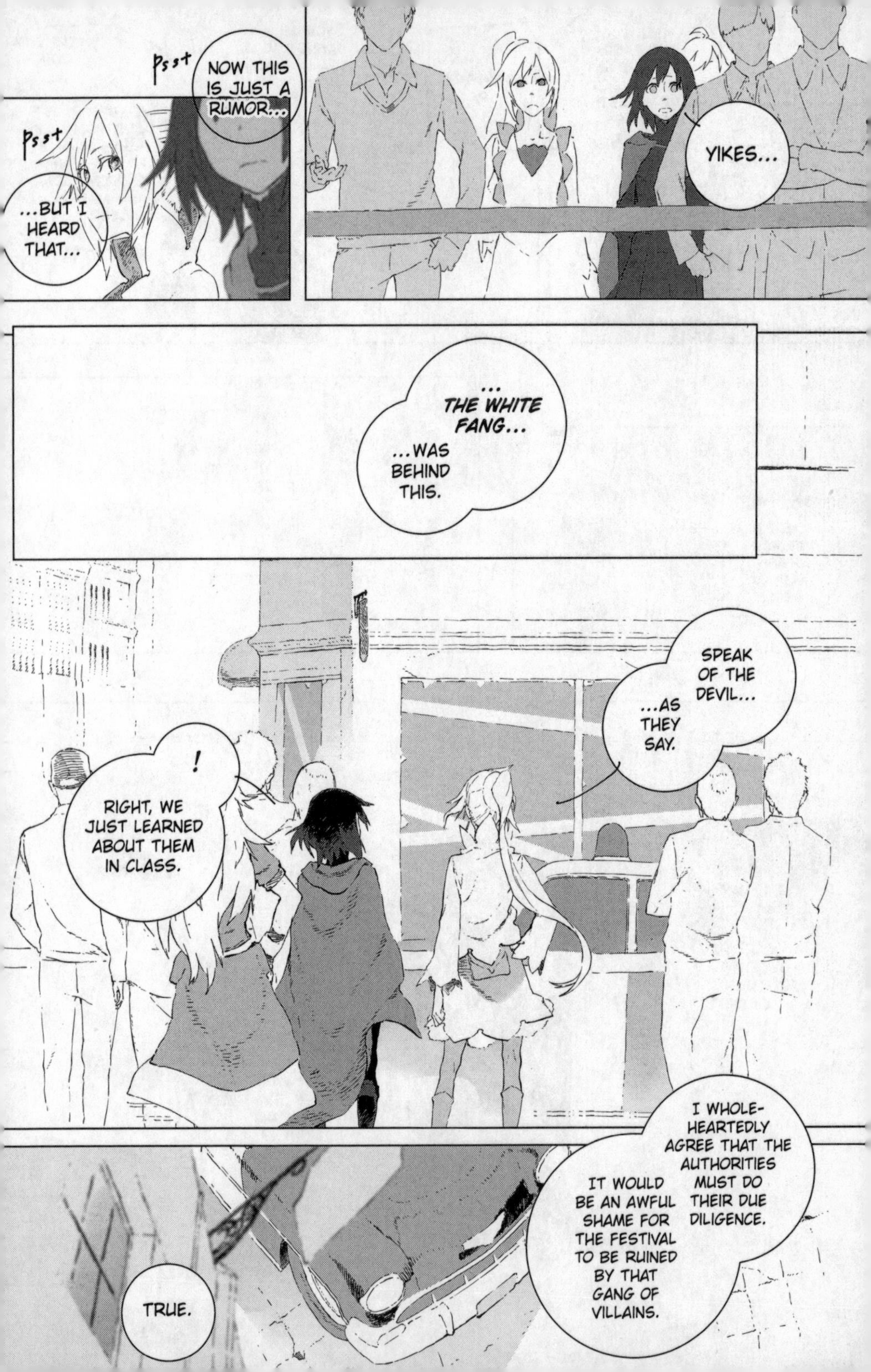
YIKES...
Psst
NOW THIS IS JUST A RUMOR...
Psst
...BUT I HEARD THAT...
... *THE WHITE FANG...*
...WAS BEHIND THIS.
SPEAK OF THE DEVIL...
...AS THEY SAY.
!
RIGHT, WE JUST LEARNED ABOUT THEM IN CLASS.
I WHOLE-HEARTEDLY AGREE THAT THE AUTHORITIES MUST DO THEIR DUE DILIGENCE.
IT WOULD BE AN AWFUL SHAME FOR THE FESTIVAL TO BE RUINED BY THAT GANG OF VILLAINS.
TRUE.

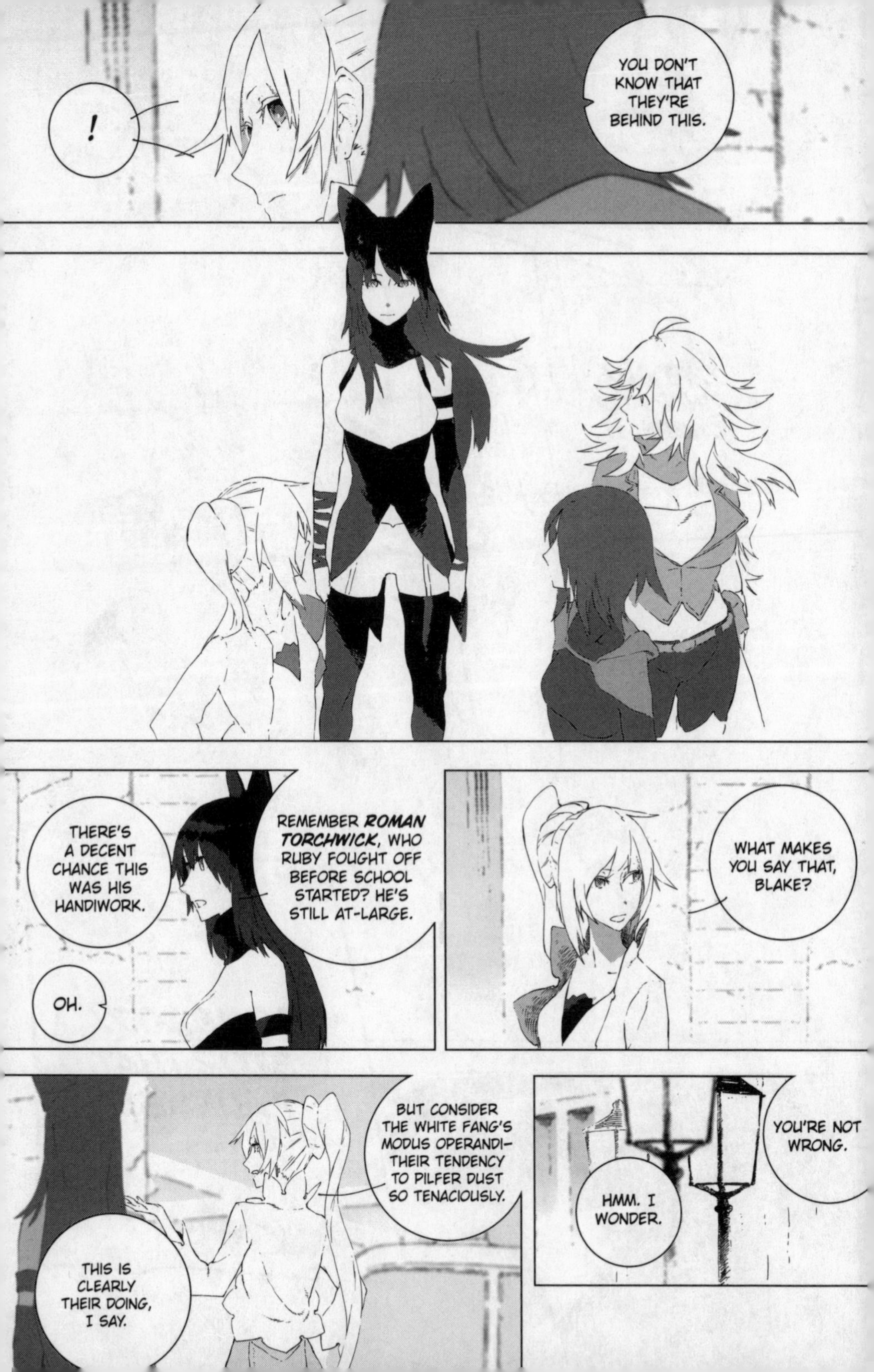
YOU DON'T KNOW THAT THEY'RE BEHIND THIS.
!
WHAT MAKES YOU SAY THAT, BLAKE?
REMEMBER ROMAN TORCHWICK, WHO RUBY FOUGHT OFF BEFORE SCHOOL STARTED? HE'S STILL AT-LARGE.
THERE'S A DECENT CHANCE THIS WAS HIS HANDIWORK.
OH.
YOU'RE NOT WRONG.
HMM. I WONDER.
BUT CONSIDER THE WHITE FANG'S MODUS OPERANDI–THEIR TENDENCY TO PILFER DUST SO TENACIOUSLY.
THIS IS CLEARLY THEIR DOING, I SAY.

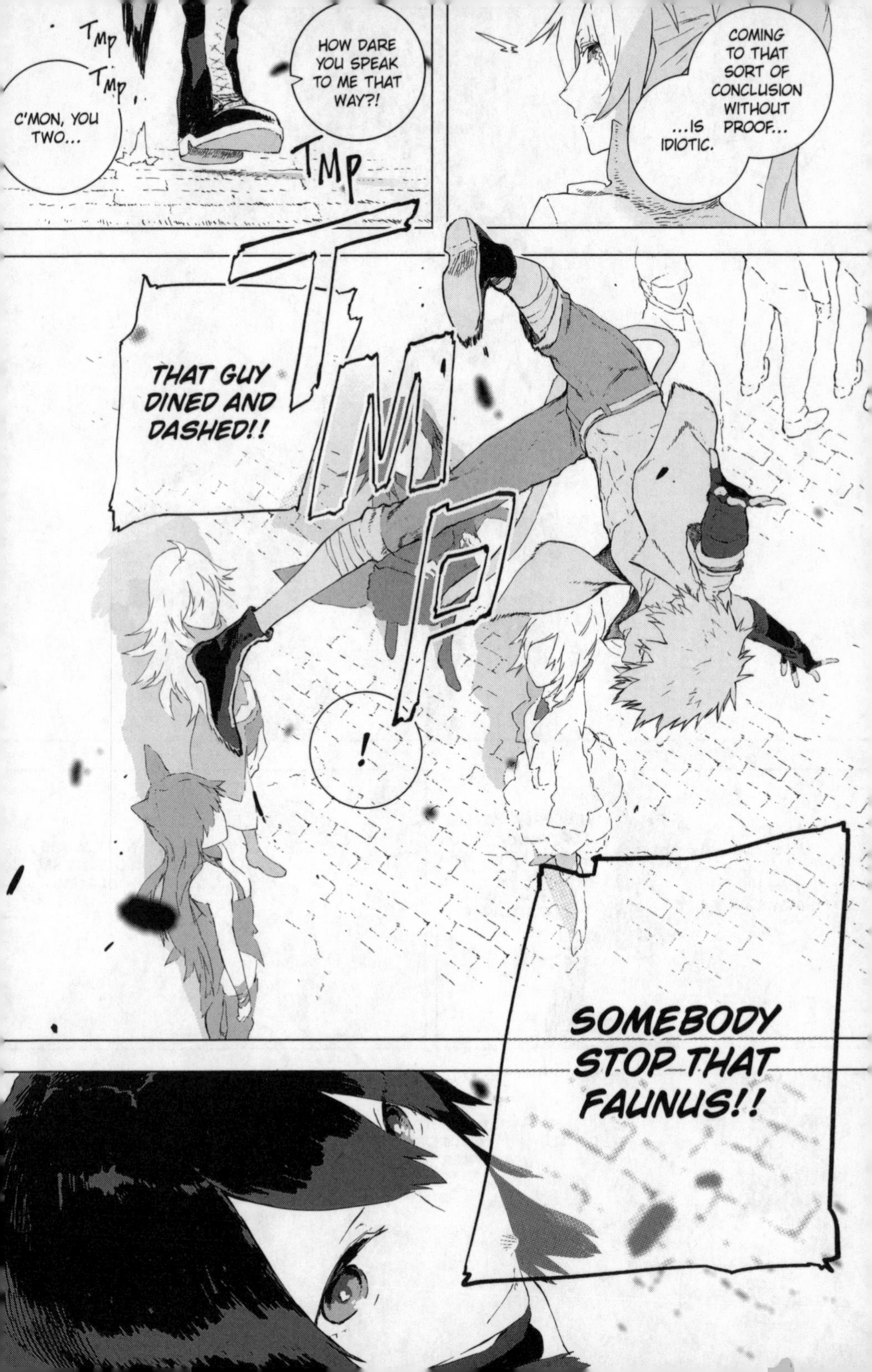
COMING TO THAT SORT OF CONCLUSION WITHOUT PROOF...
...IS IDIOTIC.
HOW DARE YOU SPEAK TO ME THAT WAY?!
TMP
TMP
C'MON, YOU TWO...
TMP
TMP
THAT GUY DINED AND DASHED!!
!
SOMEBODY STOP THAT FAUNUS!!

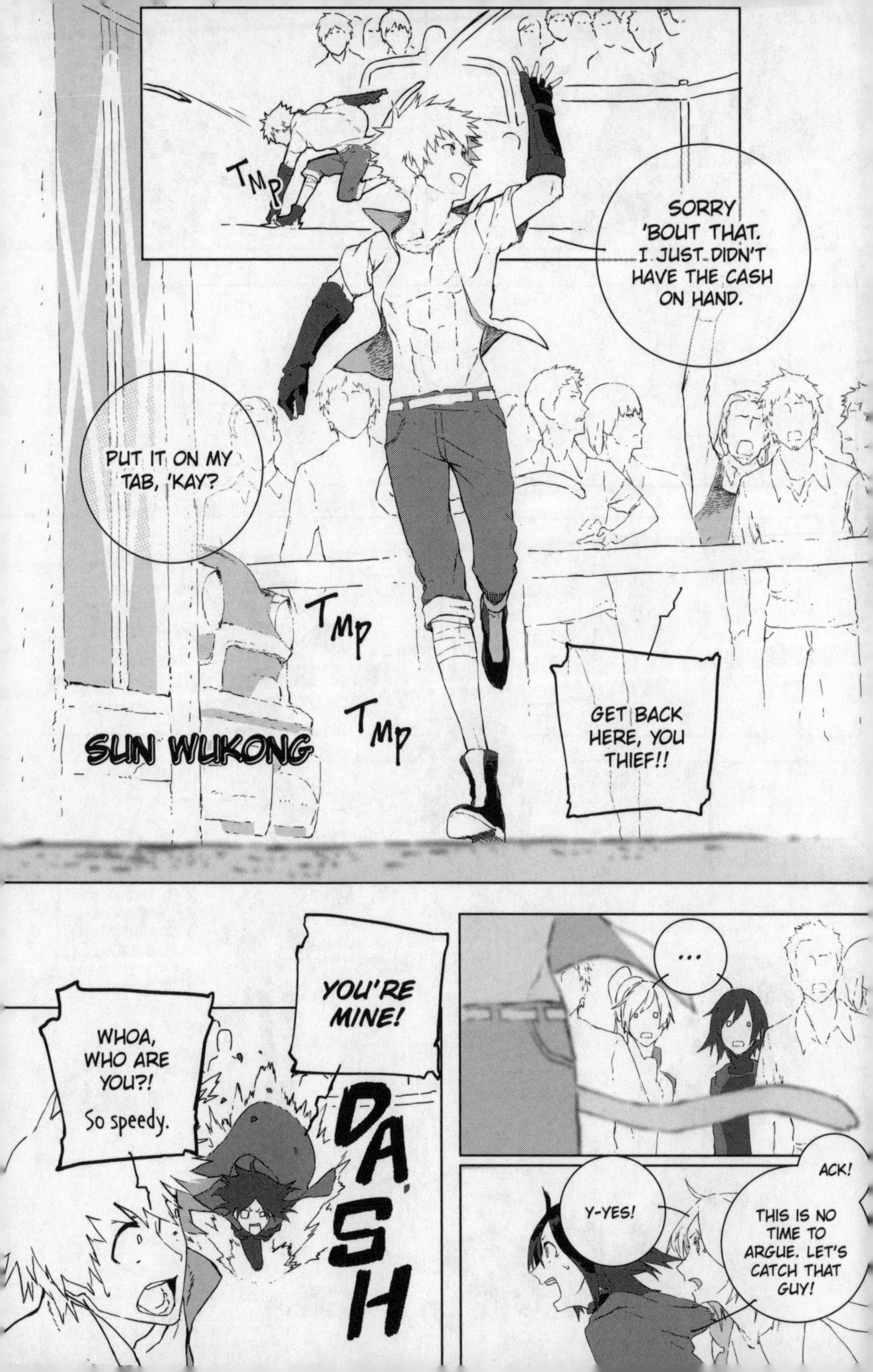
SORRY 'BOUT THAT. I JUST DIDN'T HAVE THE CASH ON HAND.
TMP
PUT IT ON MY TAB, 'KAY?
TMP
GET BACK HERE, YOU THIEF!!
TMP
SUN WUKONG
...
ACK!
THIS IS NO TIME TO ARGUE. LET'S CATCH THAT GUY!
Y-YES!
YOU'RE MINE!
DASH
WHOA, WHO ARE YOU?!
So speedy.

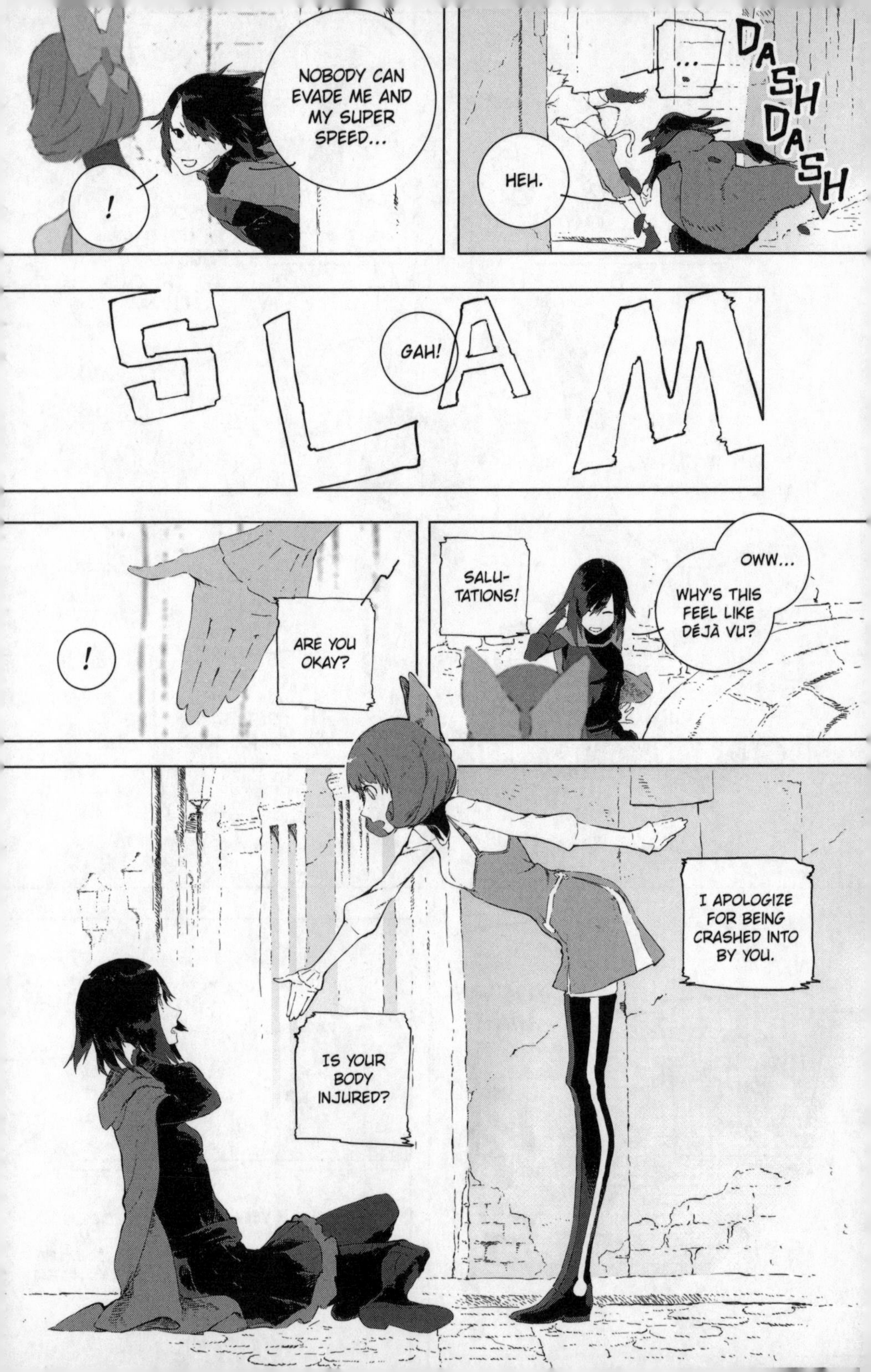
DASH DASH
...
HEH.
NOBODY CAN EVADE ME AND MY SUPER SPEED...
!
SLAM
GAH!
OWW...
WHY'S THIS FEEL LIKE DÉJÀ VU?
SALU-TATIONS!
ARE YOU OKAY?
!
I APOLOGIZE FOR BEING CRASHED INTO BY YOU.
IS YOUR BODY INJURED?

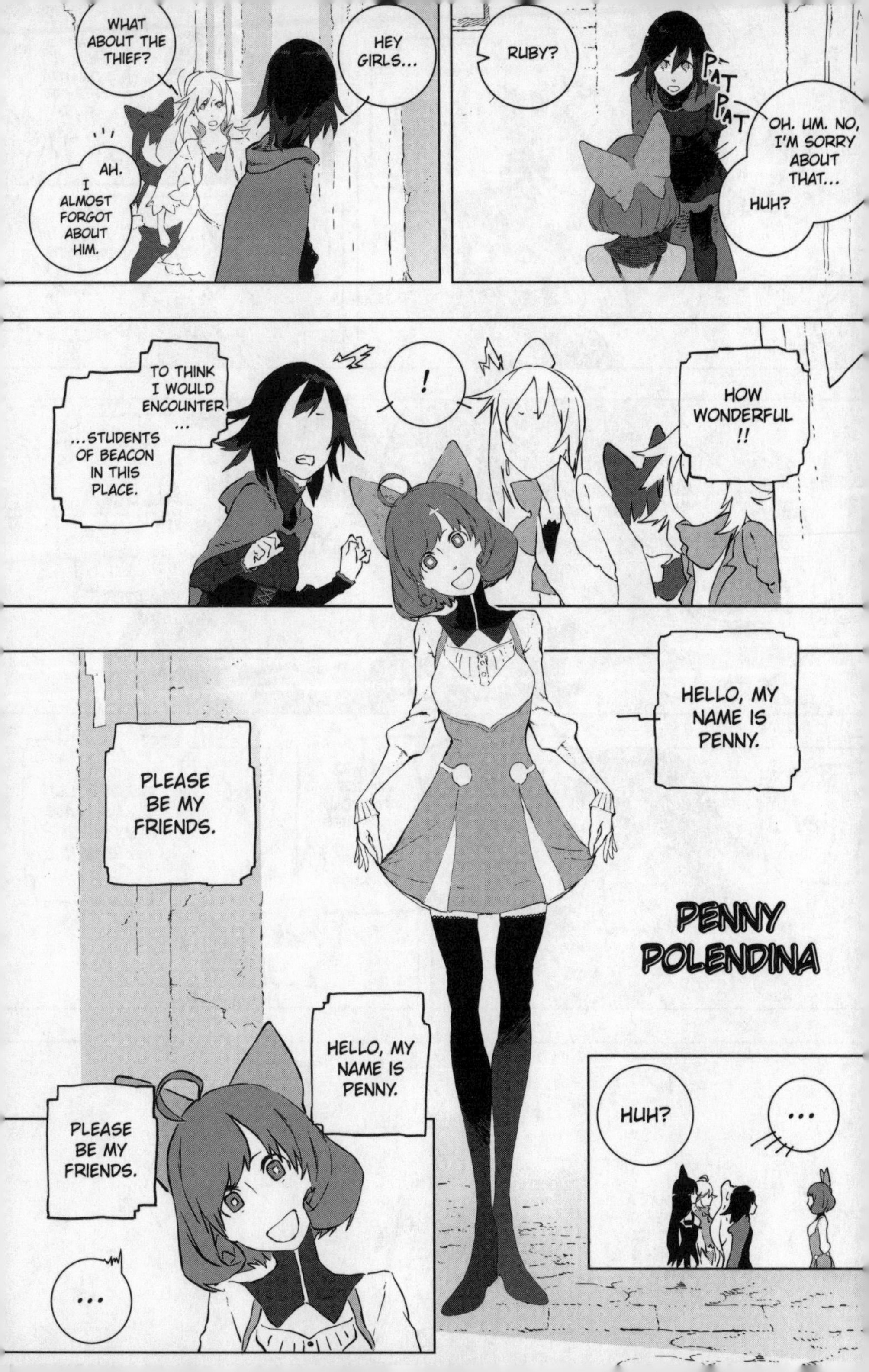
RUBY?
PAT PAT
OH. UM. NO, I'M SORRY ABOUT THAT...
HUH?
HEY GIRLS...
WHAT ABOUT THE THIEF?
AH. I ALMOST FORGOT ABOUT HIM.
HOW WONDERFUL !!
!
TO THINK I WOULD ENCOUNTER ...
...STUDENTS OF BEACON IN THIS PLACE.
HELLO, MY NAME IS PENNY.
PENNY POLENDINA
PLEASE BE MY FRIENDS.
HUH?
...
HELLO, MY NAME IS PENNY.
PLEASE BE MY FRIENDS.
...

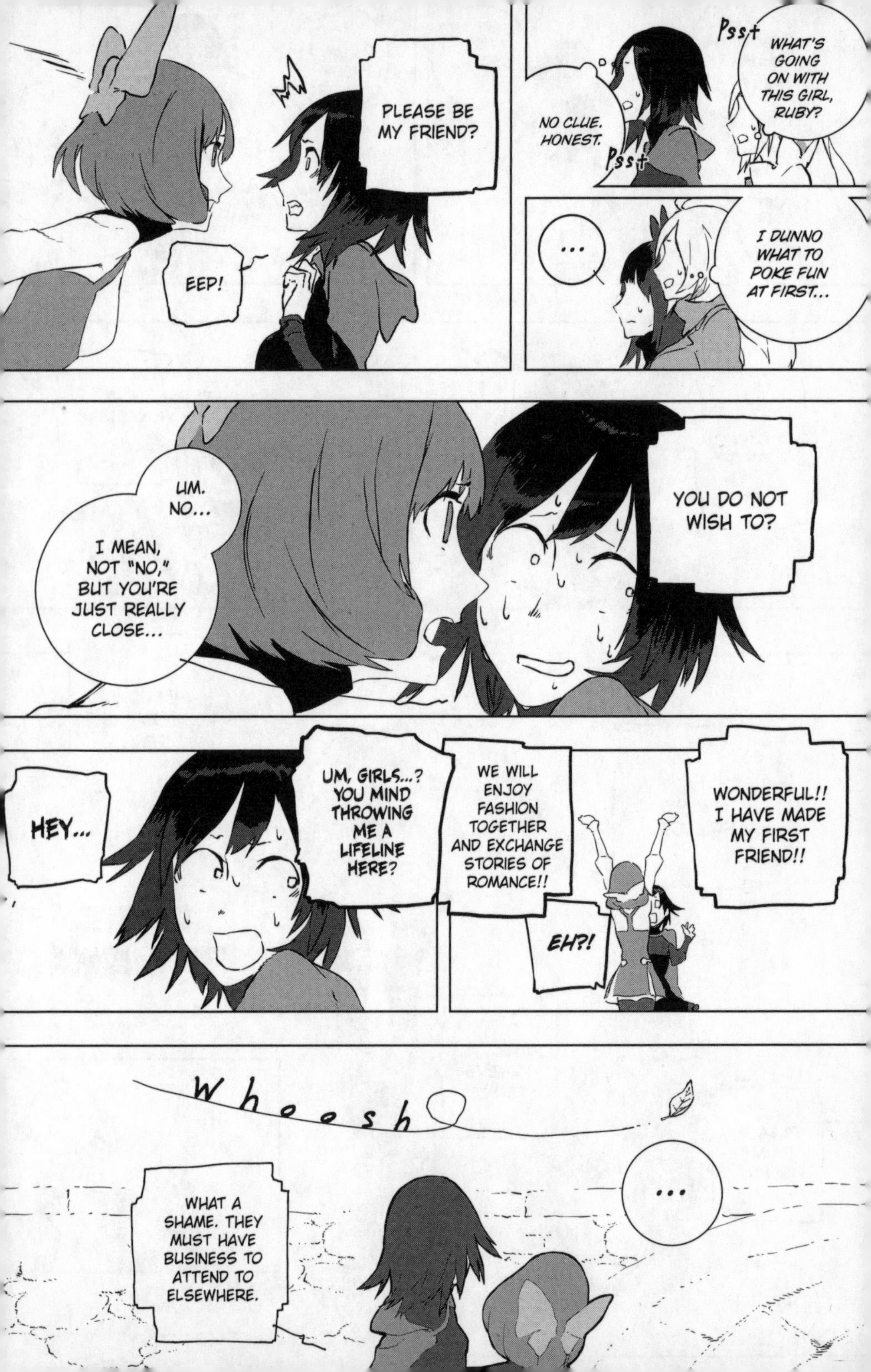
Psst
WHAT'S GOING ON WITH THIS GIRL, RUBY?
NO CLUE. HONEST.
Psst
I DUNNO WHAT TO POKE FUN AT FIRST...
...
PLEASE BE MY FRIEND?
EEP!
YOU DO NOT WISH TO?
UM. NO...
I MEAN, NOT "NO," BUT YOU'RE JUST REALLY CLOSE...
WONDERFUL!! I HAVE MADE MY FIRST FRIEND!!
WE WILL ENJOY FASHION TOGETHER AND EXCHANGE STORIES OF ROMANCE!!
EH?!
UM, GIRLS...? YOU MIND THROWING ME A LIFELINE HERE?
HEY...
Whoosh
...
WHAT A SHAME. THEY MUST HAVE BUSINESS TO ATTEND TO ELSEWHERE.

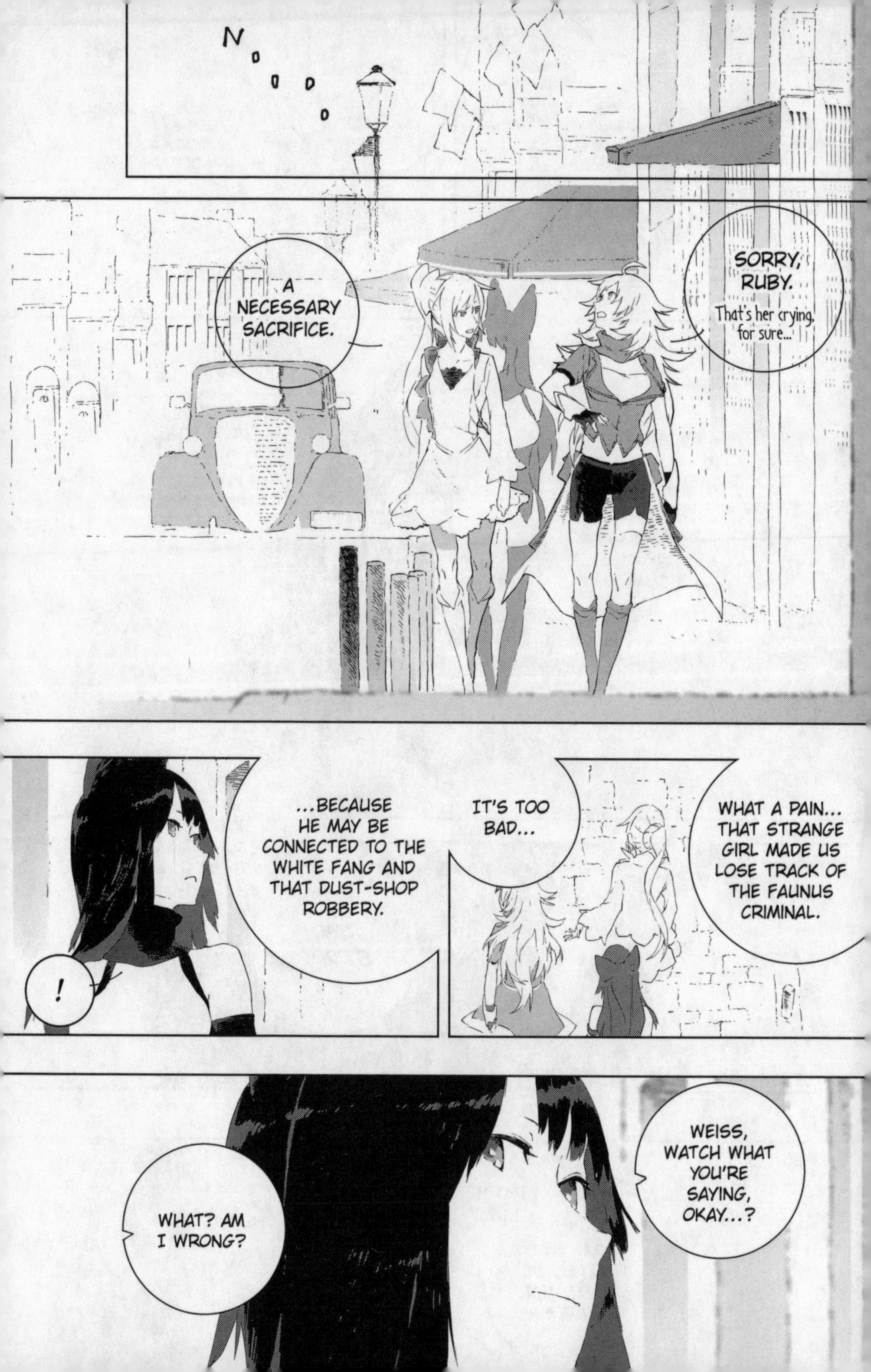
Noooo
SORRY, RUBY.
That's her crying, for sure...
A NECESSARY SACRIFICE.
WHAT A PAIN... THAT STRANGE GIRL MADE US LOSE TRACK OF THE FAUNUS CRIMINAL.
IT'S TOO BAD...
...BECAUSE HE MAY BE CONNECTED TO THE WHITE FANG AND THAT DUST-SHOP ROBBERY.
!
WEISS, WATCH WHAT YOU'RE SAYING, OKAY...?
WHAT? AM I WRONG?

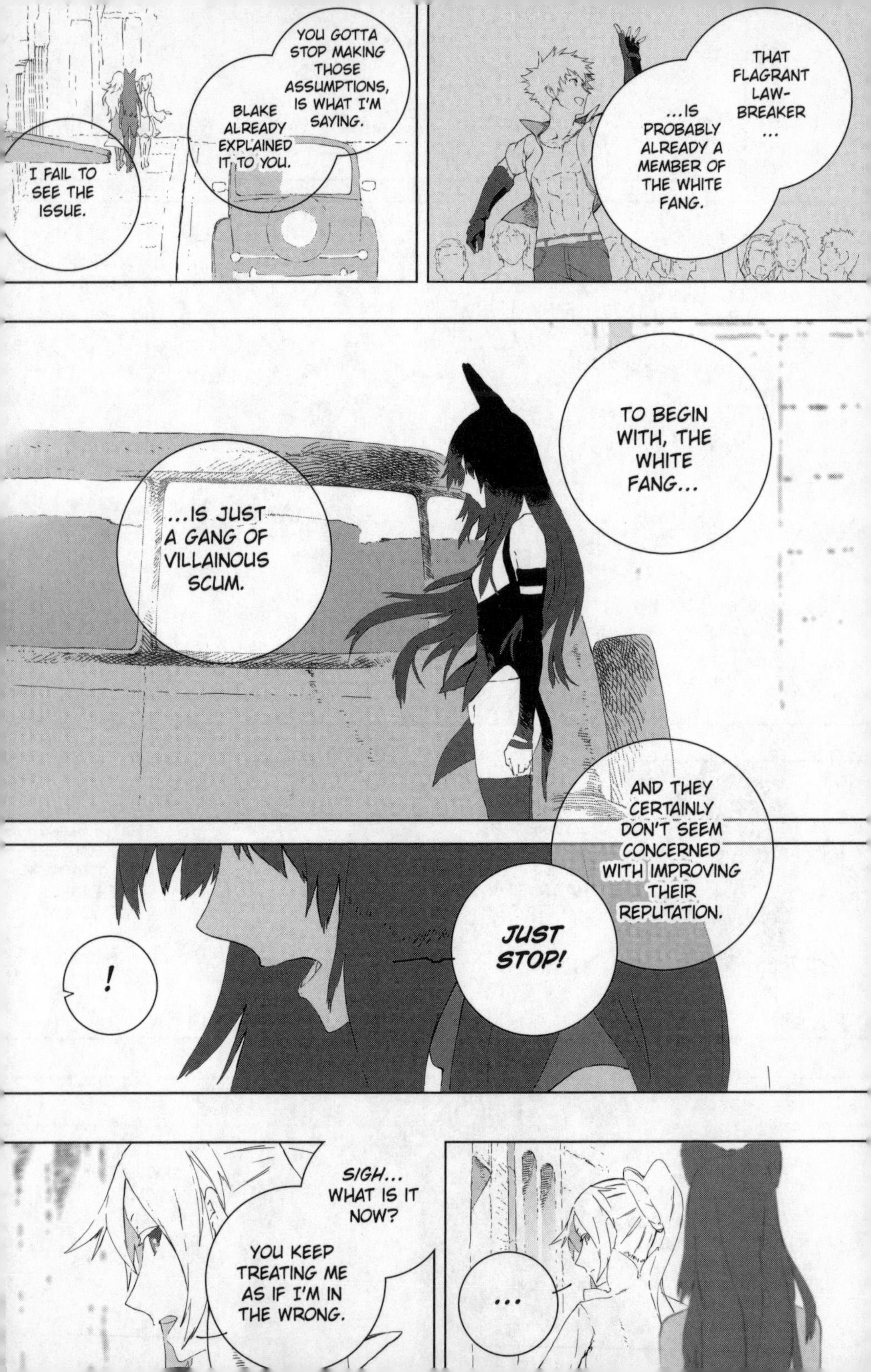
THAT FLAGRANT LAW-BREAKER ...
...IS PROBABLY ALREADY A MEMBER OF THE WHITE FANG.
YOU GOTTA STOP MAKING THOSE ASSUMPTIONS, IS WHAT I'M SAYING.
BLAKE ALREADY EXPLAINED IT TO YOU.
I FAIL TO SEE THE ISSUE.
TO BEGIN WITH, THE WHITE FANG...
...IS JUST A GANG OF VILLAINOUS SCUM.
AND THEY CERTAINLY DON'T SEEM CONCERNED WITH IMPROVING THEIR REPUTATION.
JUST STOP!
!
...
SIGH... WHAT IS IT NOW?
YOU KEEP TREATING ME AS IF I'M IN THE WRONG.

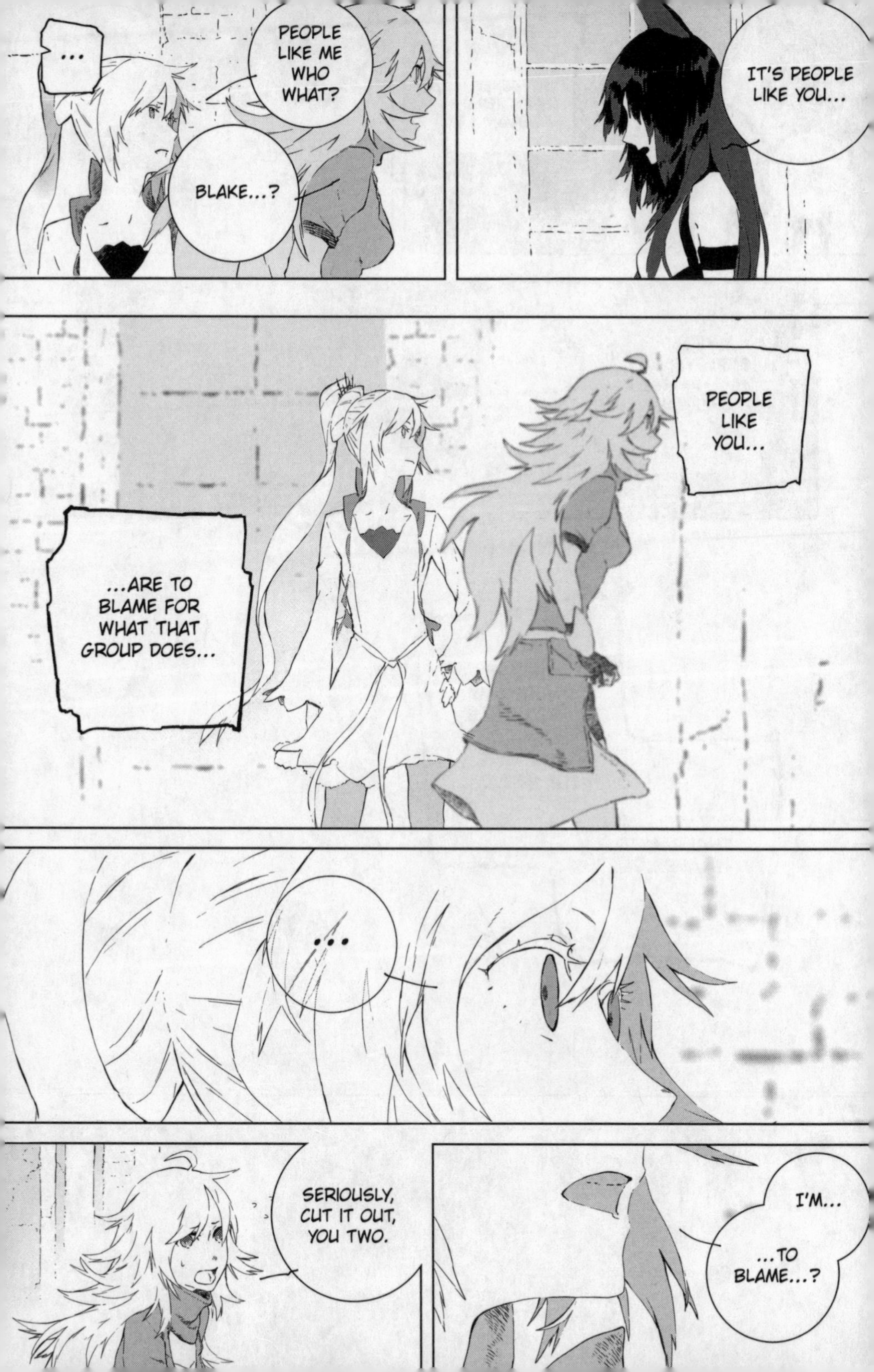
IT'S PEOPLE LIKE YOU...
PEOPLE LIKE ME WHO WHAT?
...
BLAKE...?
PEOPLE LIKE YOU...
...ARE TO BLAME FOR WHAT THAT GROUP DOES...
...
I'M...
...TO BLAME...?
SERIOUSLY, CUT IT OUT, YOU TWO.

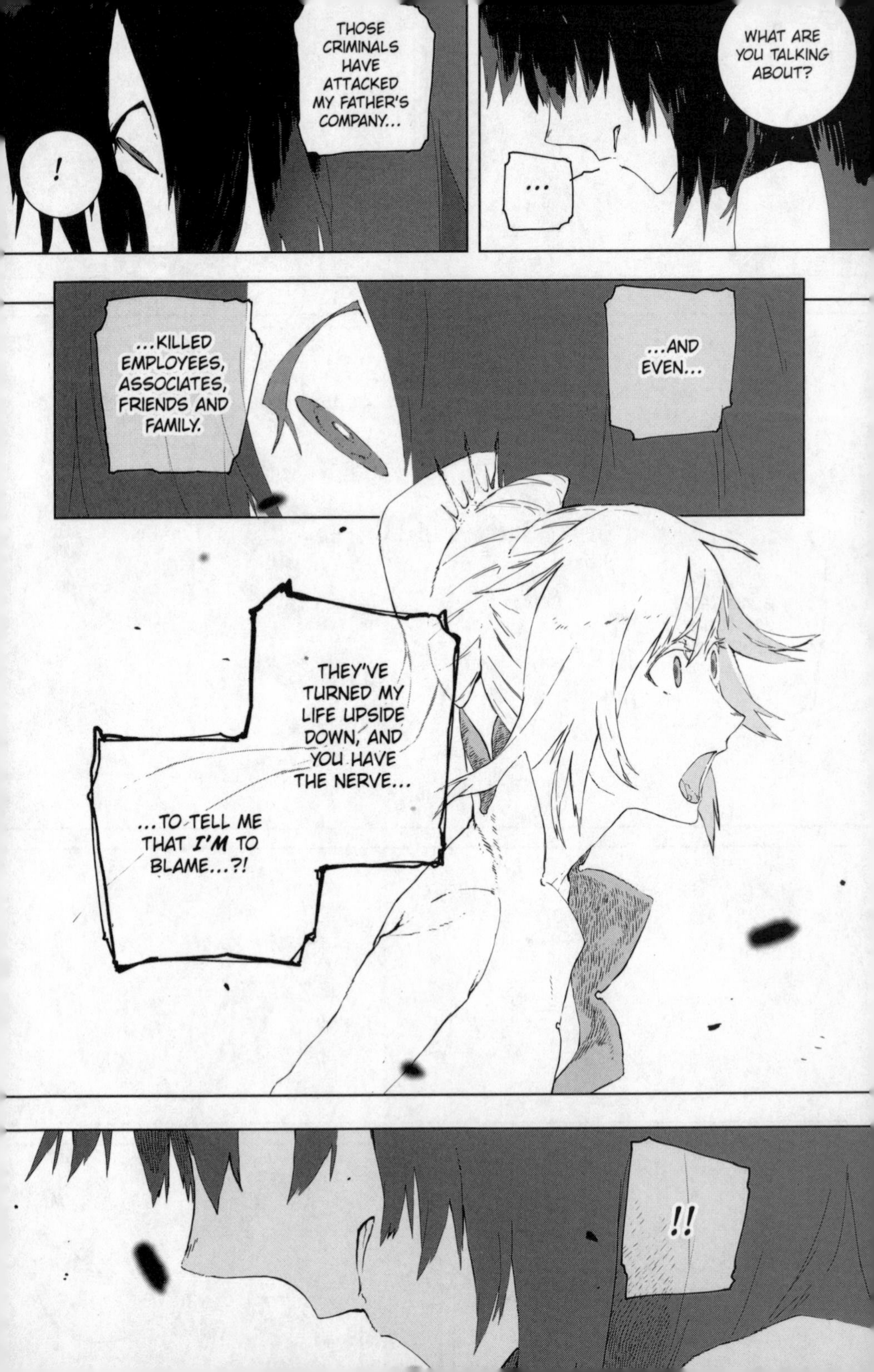
WHAT ARE YOU TALKING ABOUT?
...
THOSE CRIMINALS HAVE ATTACKED MY FATHER'S COMPANY...
!
...AND EVEN...
...KILLED EMPLOYEES, ASSOCIATES, FRIENDS AND FAMILY.
THEY'VE TURNED MY LIFE UPSIDE DOWN, AND YOU HAVE THE NERVE...
...TO TELL ME THAT *I'M* TO BLAME...?!
!!

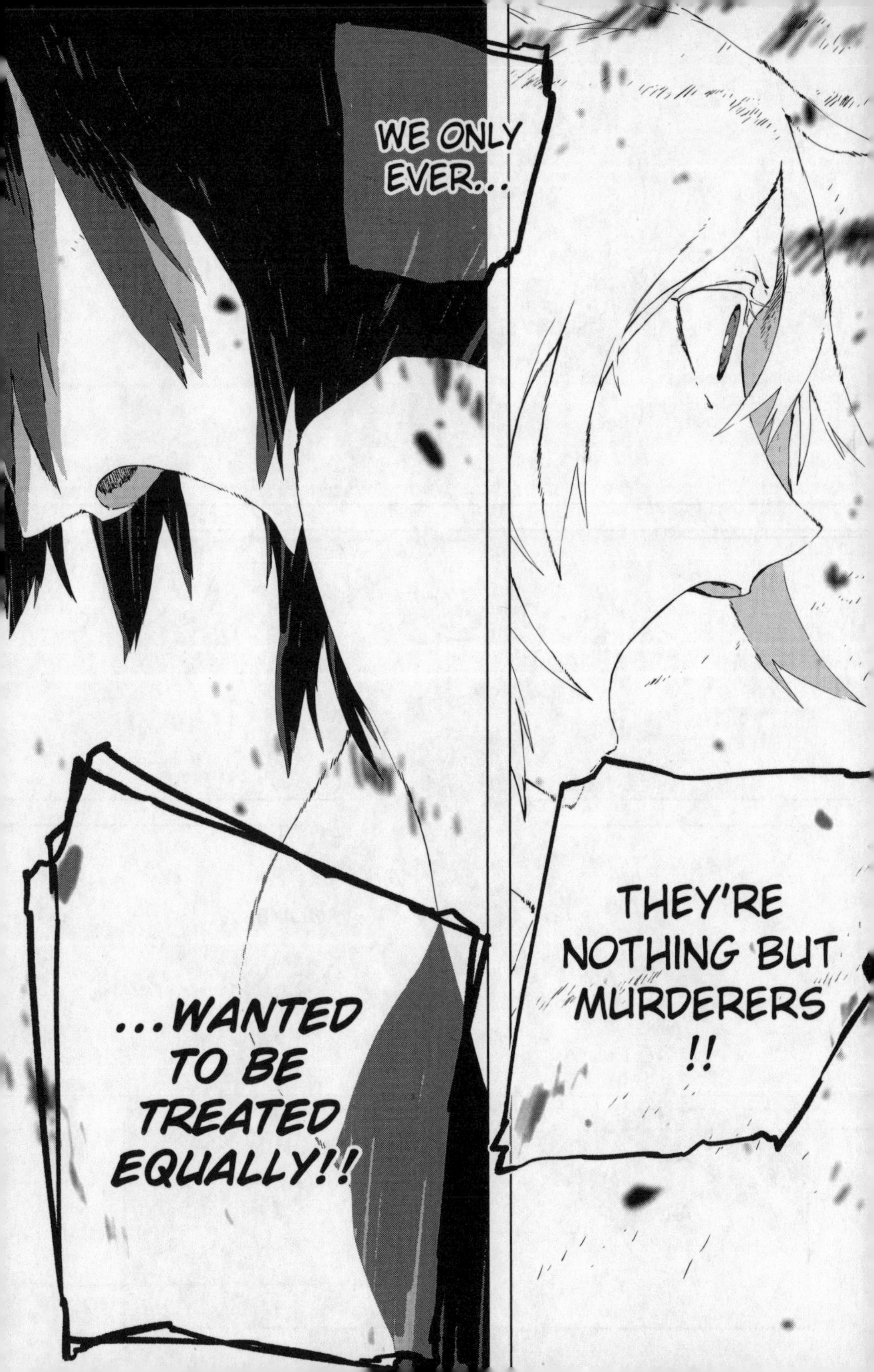
THEY'RE NOTHING BUT MURDERERS !!
WE ONLY EVER...
...WANTED TO BE TREATED EQUALLY!!

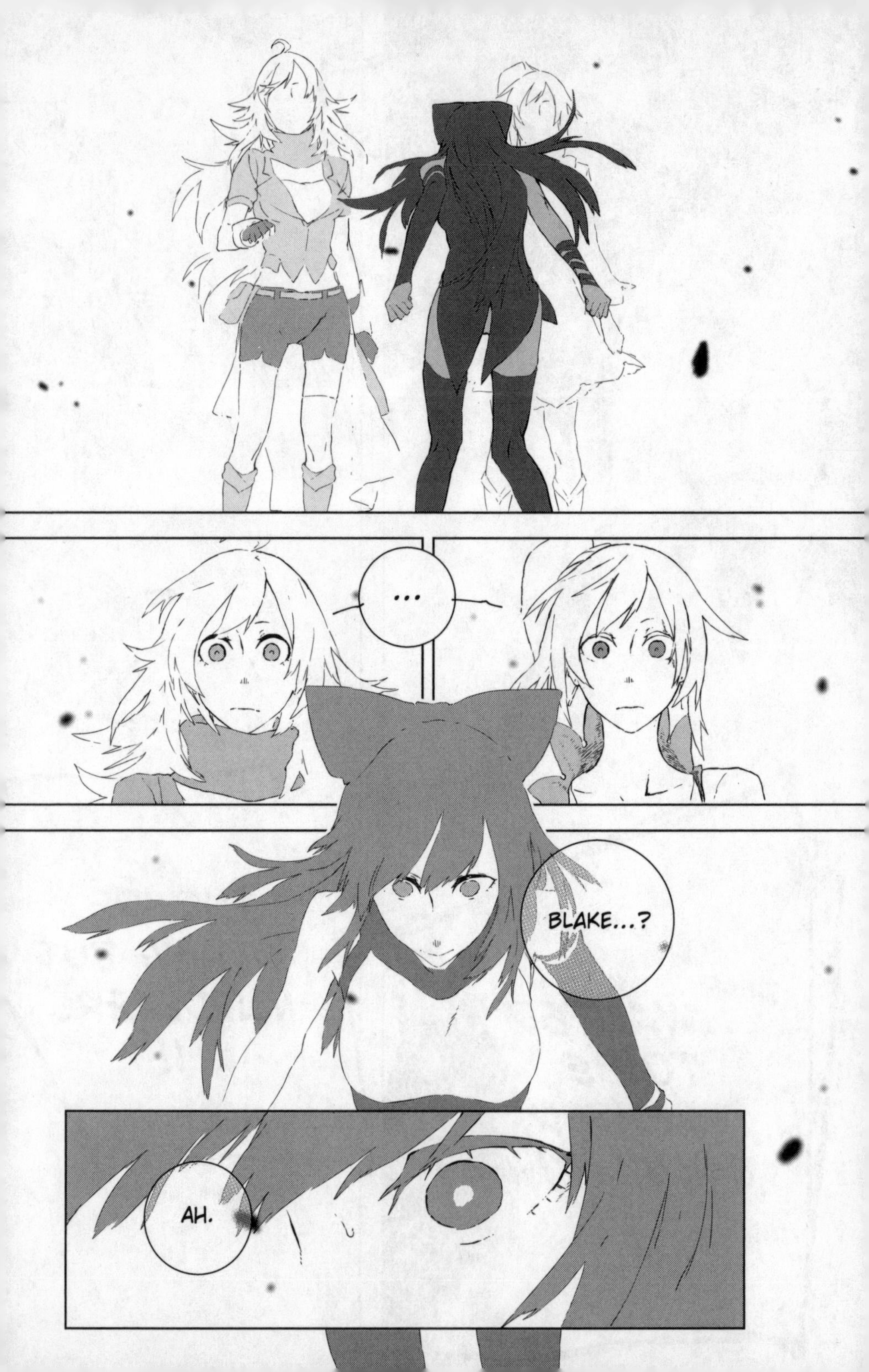
...
BLAKE...?
AH.

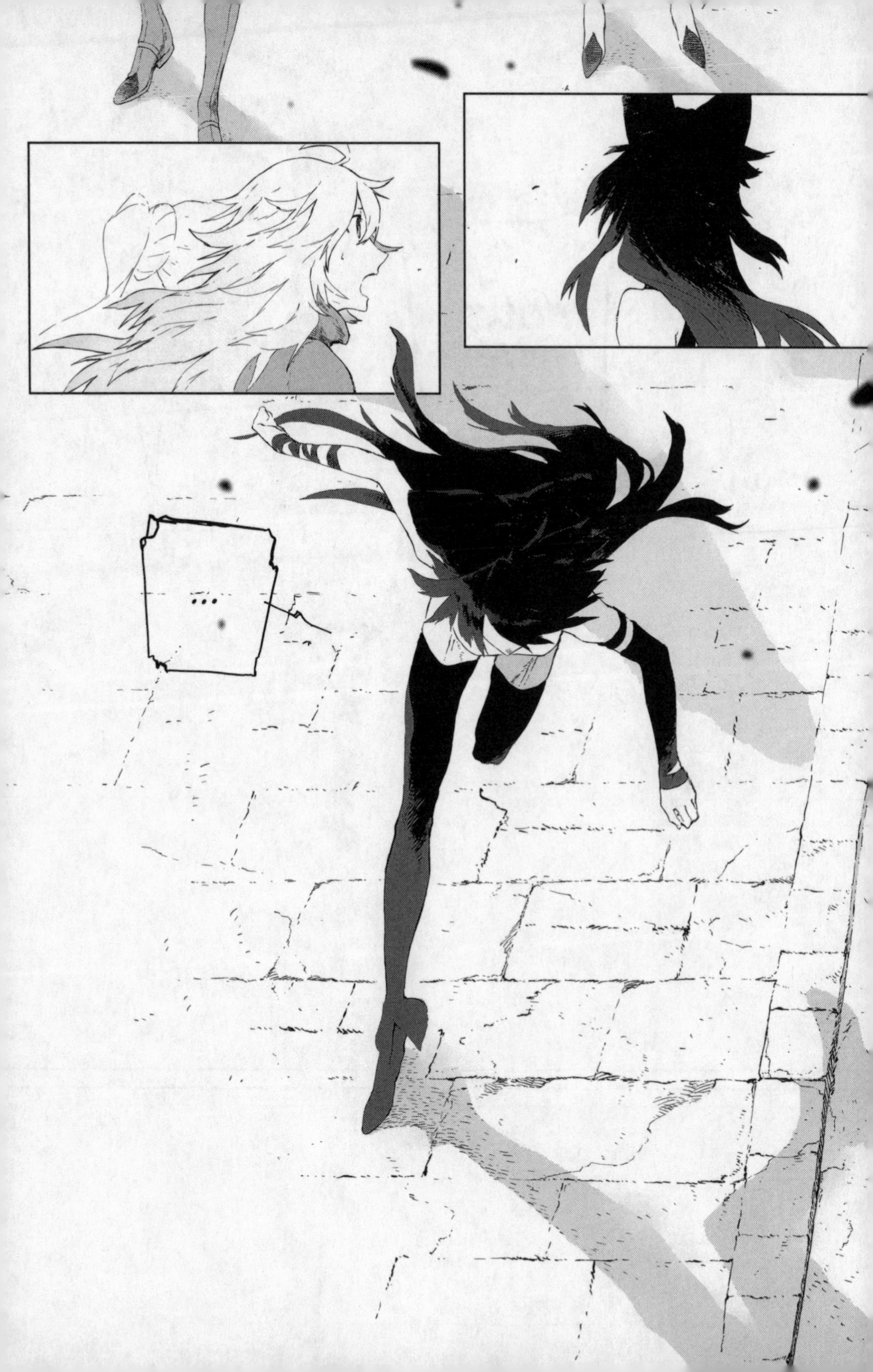
...

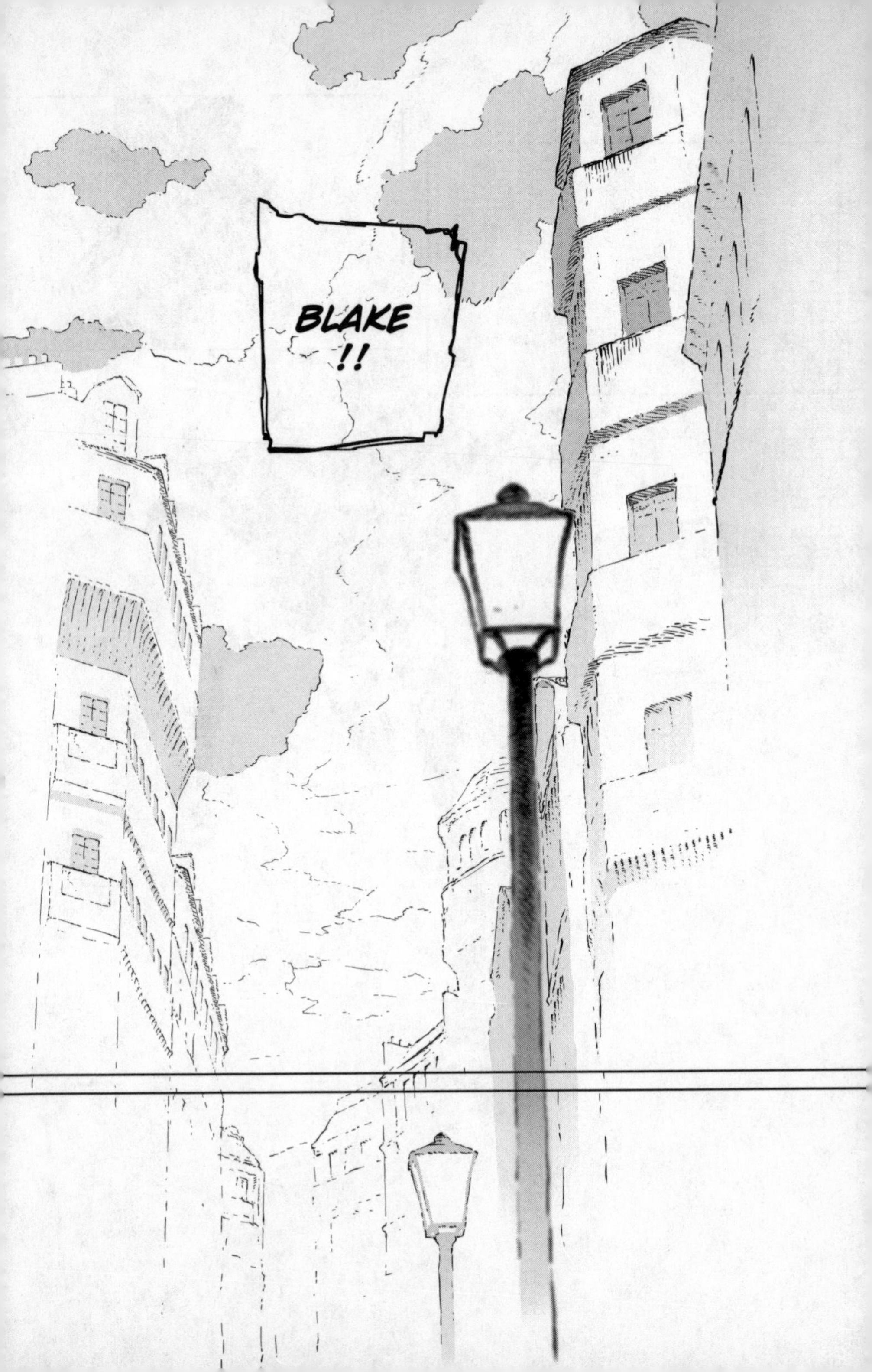
BLAKE !!

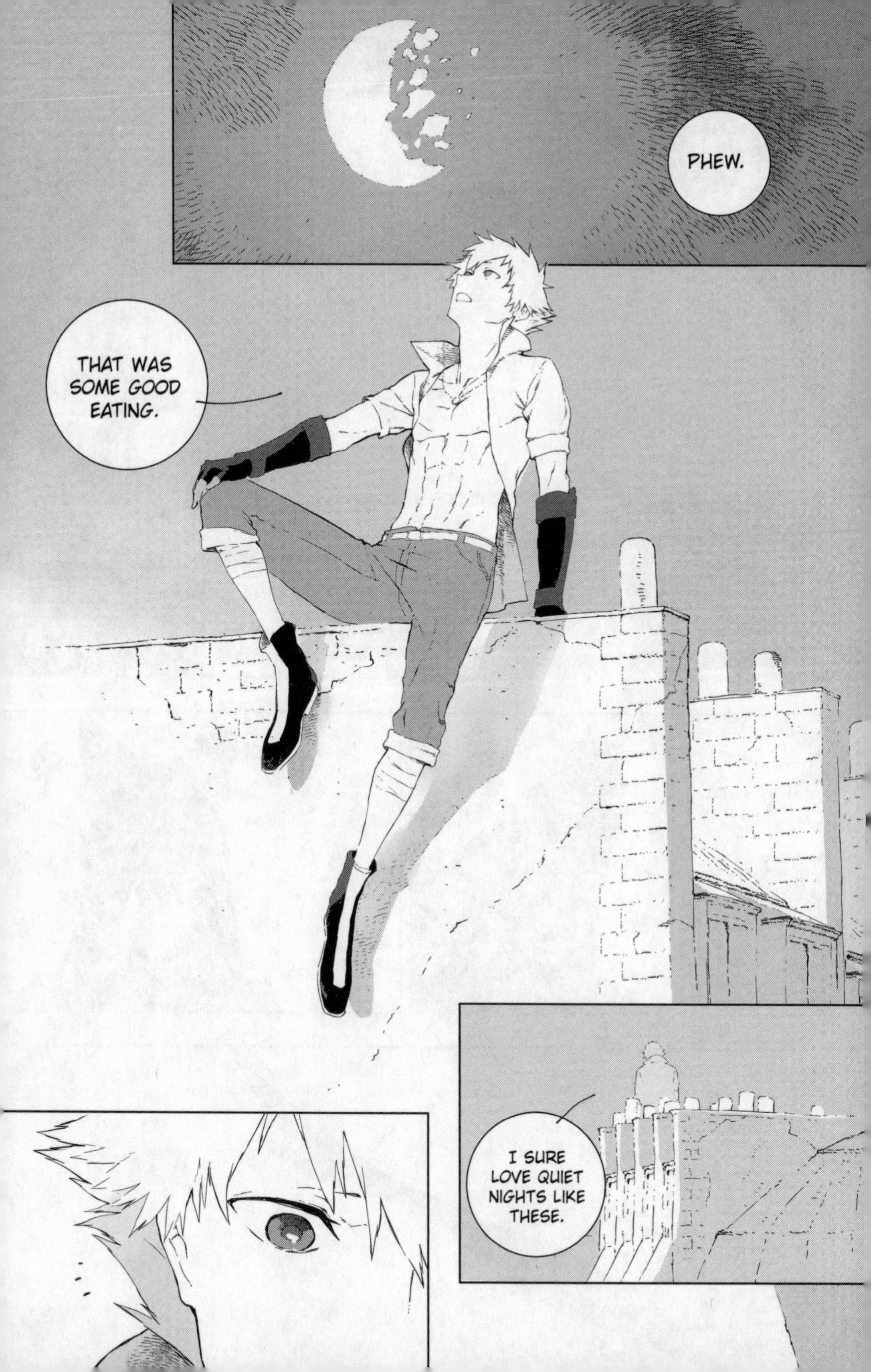
PHEW.
THAT WAS SOME GOOD EATING.
I SURE LOVE QUIET NIGHTS LIKE THESE.

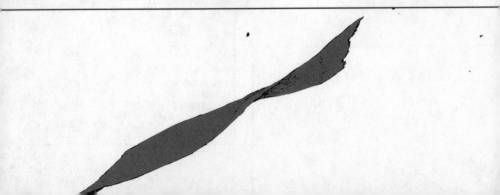

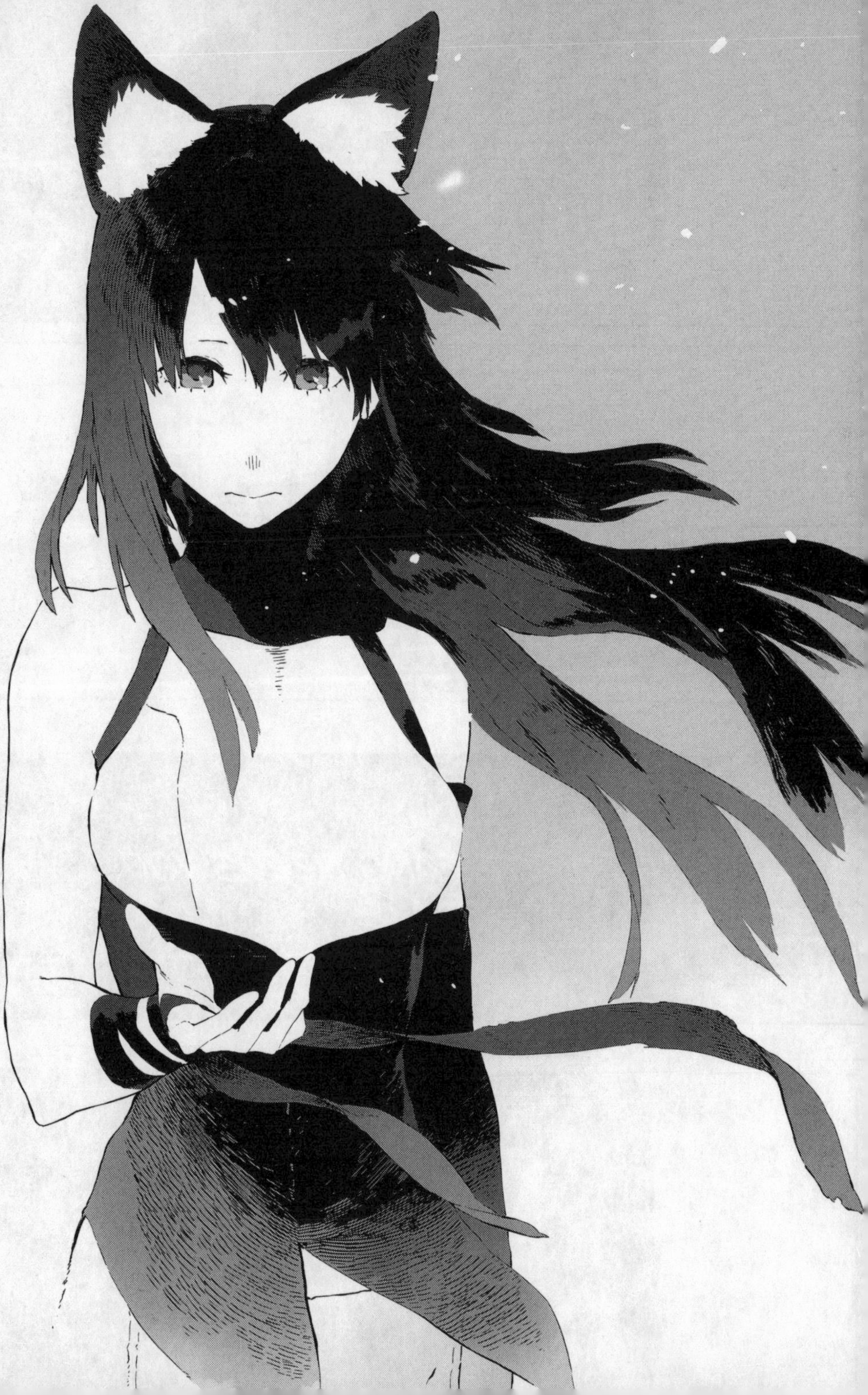

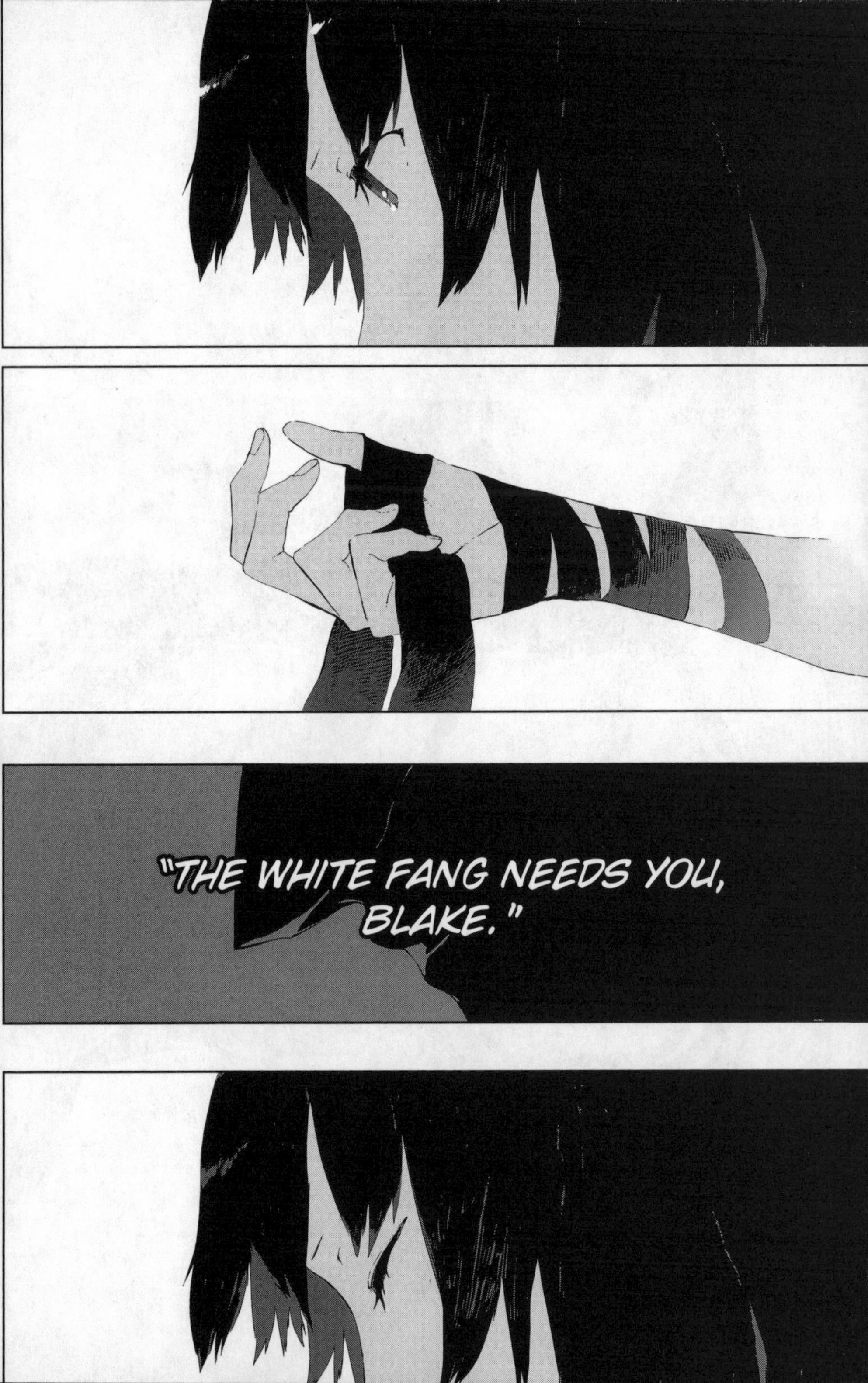
"THE WHITE FANG NEEDS YOU, BLAKE."

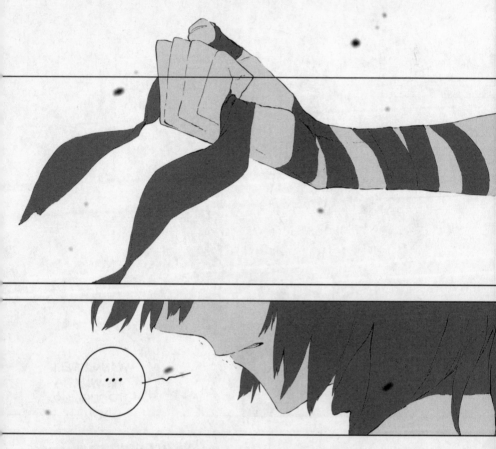

"THEY'RE NOTHING BUT MURDERERS!"

...

I SAY YOU LOOK BETTER WITHOUT THE RIBBON.

!

Tmp

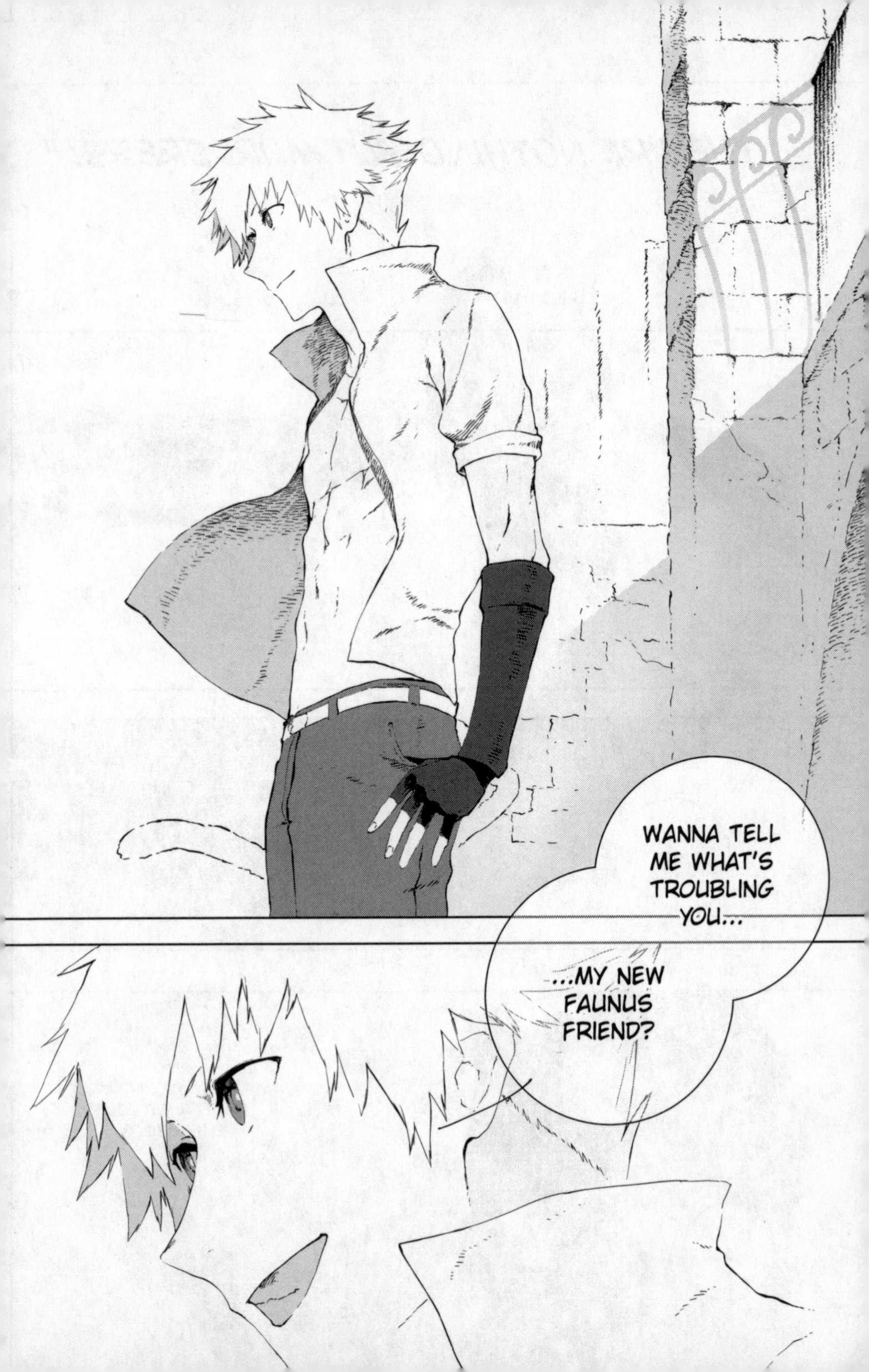
WANNA TELL ME WHAT'S TROUBLING YOU...
...MY NEW FAUNUS FRIEND?

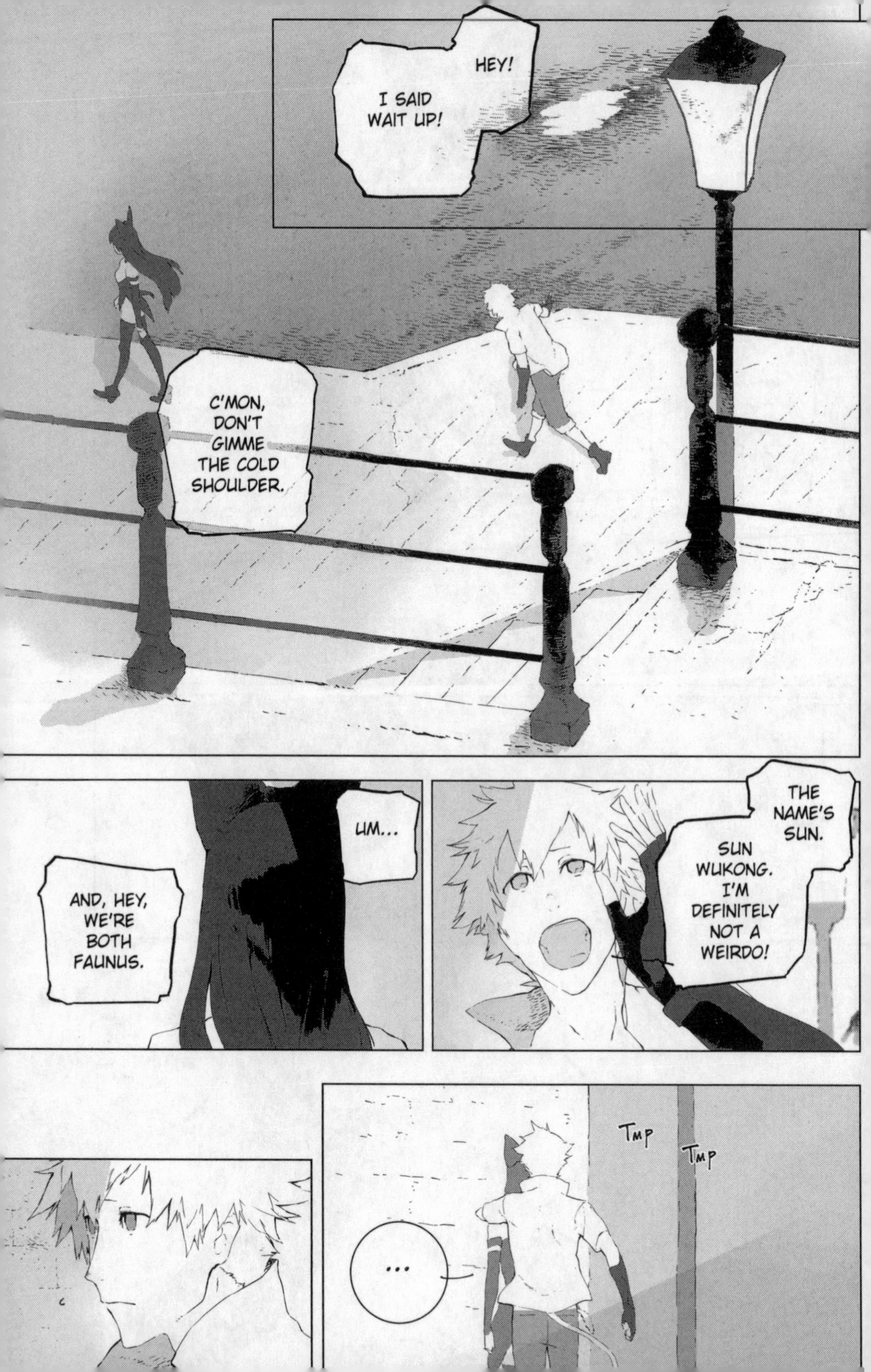
HEY!
I SAID WAIT UP!
C'MON, DON'T GIMME THE COLD SHOULDER.
THE NAME'S SUN.
SUN WUKONG. I'M DEFINITELY NOT A WEIRDO!
UM...
AND, HEY, WE'RE BOTH FAUNUS.
TMP
TMP
...

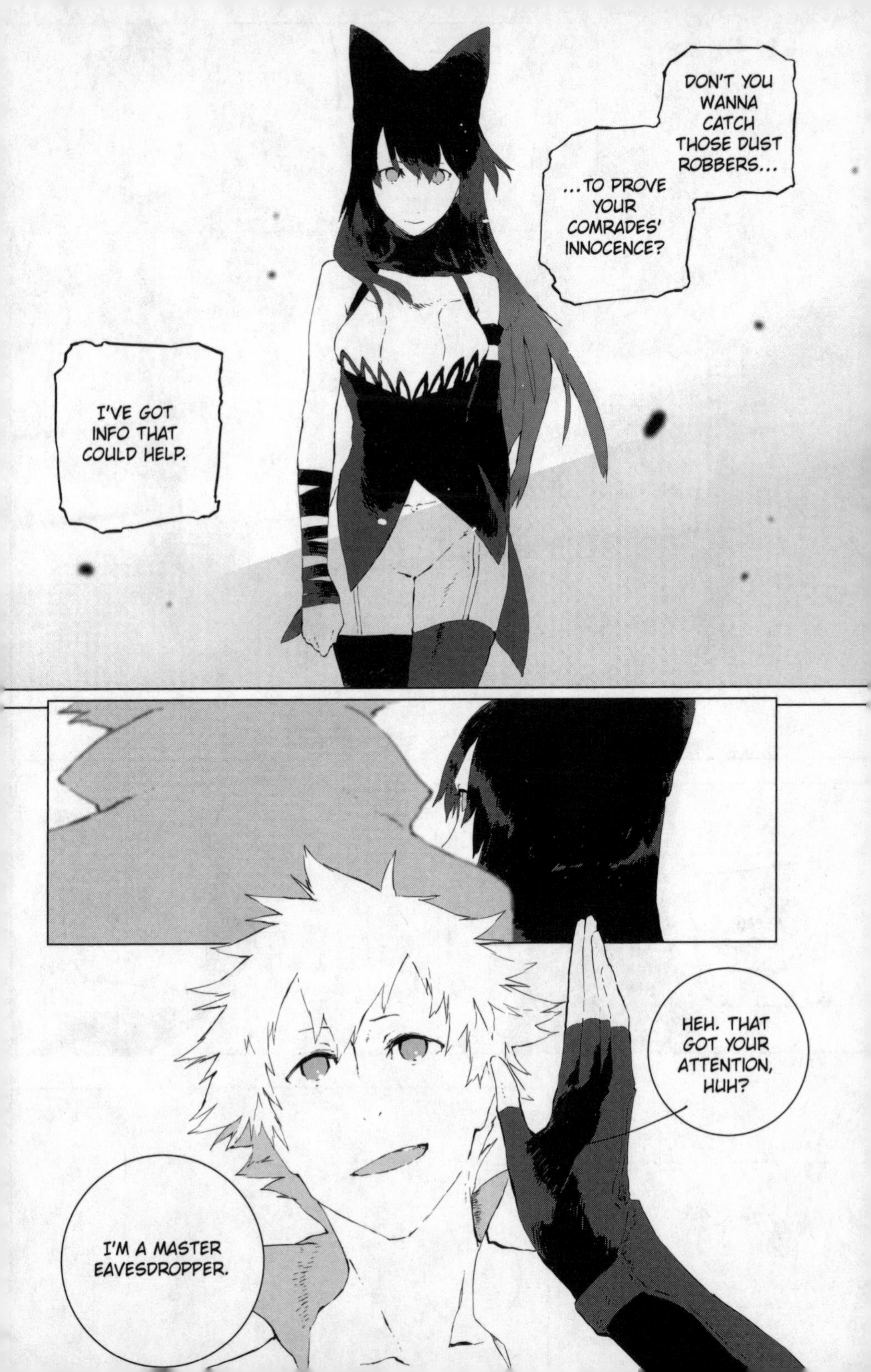
DON'T YOU WANNA CATCH THOSE DUST ROBBERS...
...TO PROVE YOUR COMRADES' INNOCENCE?
I'VE GOT INFO THAT COULD HELP.
HEH. THAT GOT YOUR ATTENTION, HUH?
I'M A MASTER EAVESDROPPER.

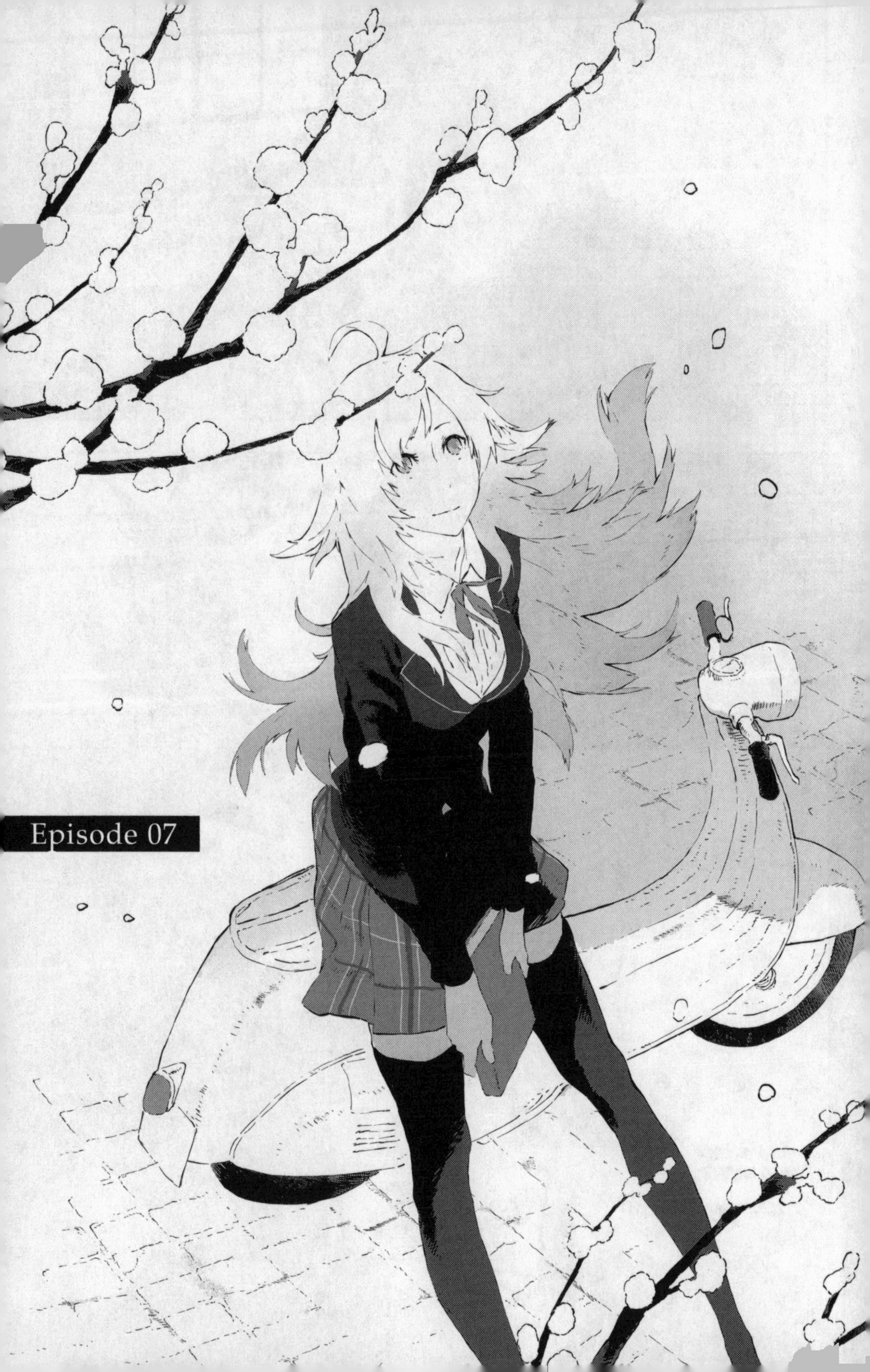
Episode 07

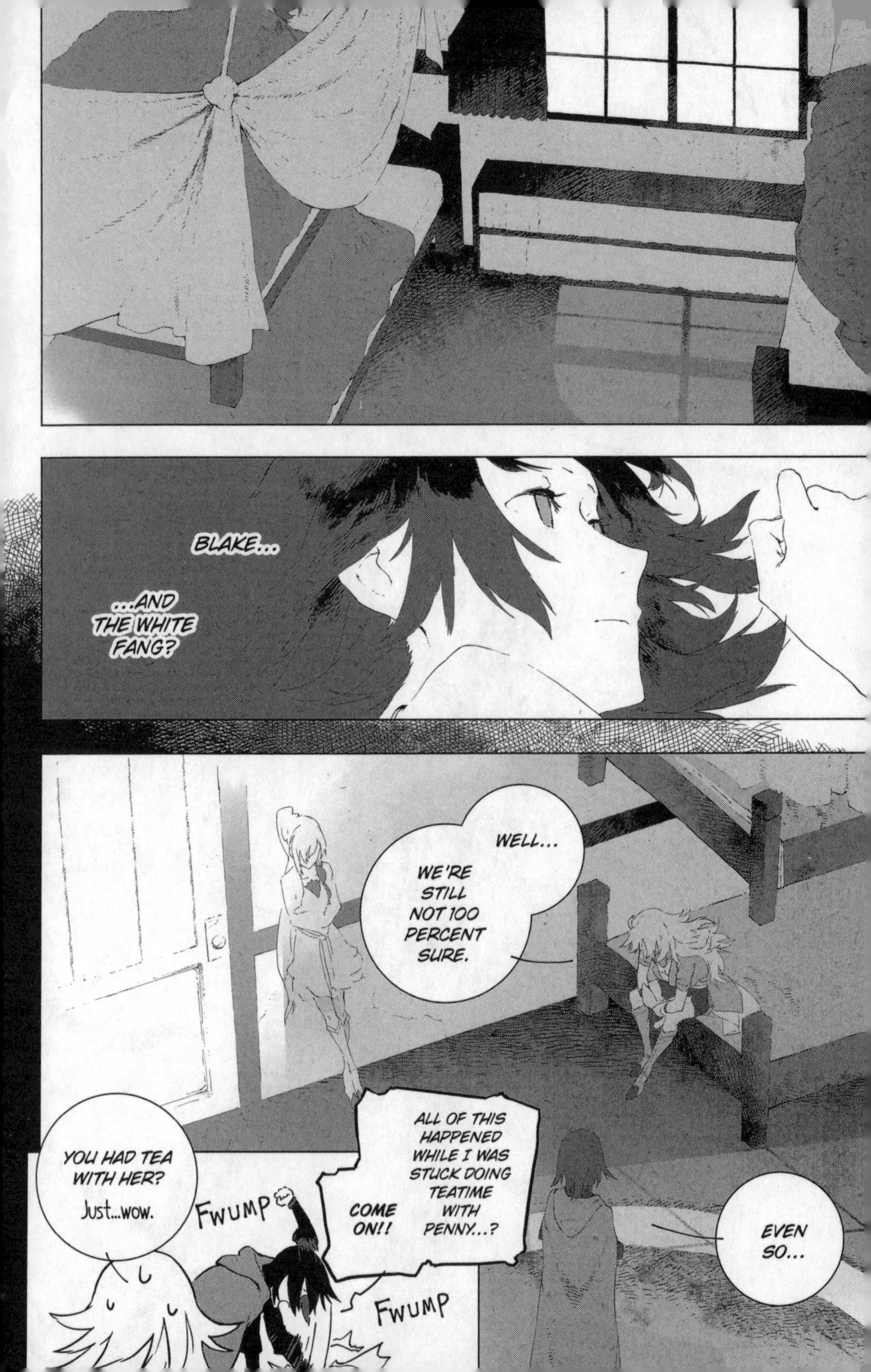
BLAKE...
...AND THE WHITE FANG?
WELL...
WE'RE STILL NOT 100 PERCENT SURE.
EVEN SO...
ALL OF THIS HAPPENED WHILE I WAS STUCK DOING TEATIME WITH PENNY...?
COME ON!!
FWUMP
YOU HAD TEA WITH HER? Just...wow.
FWUMP

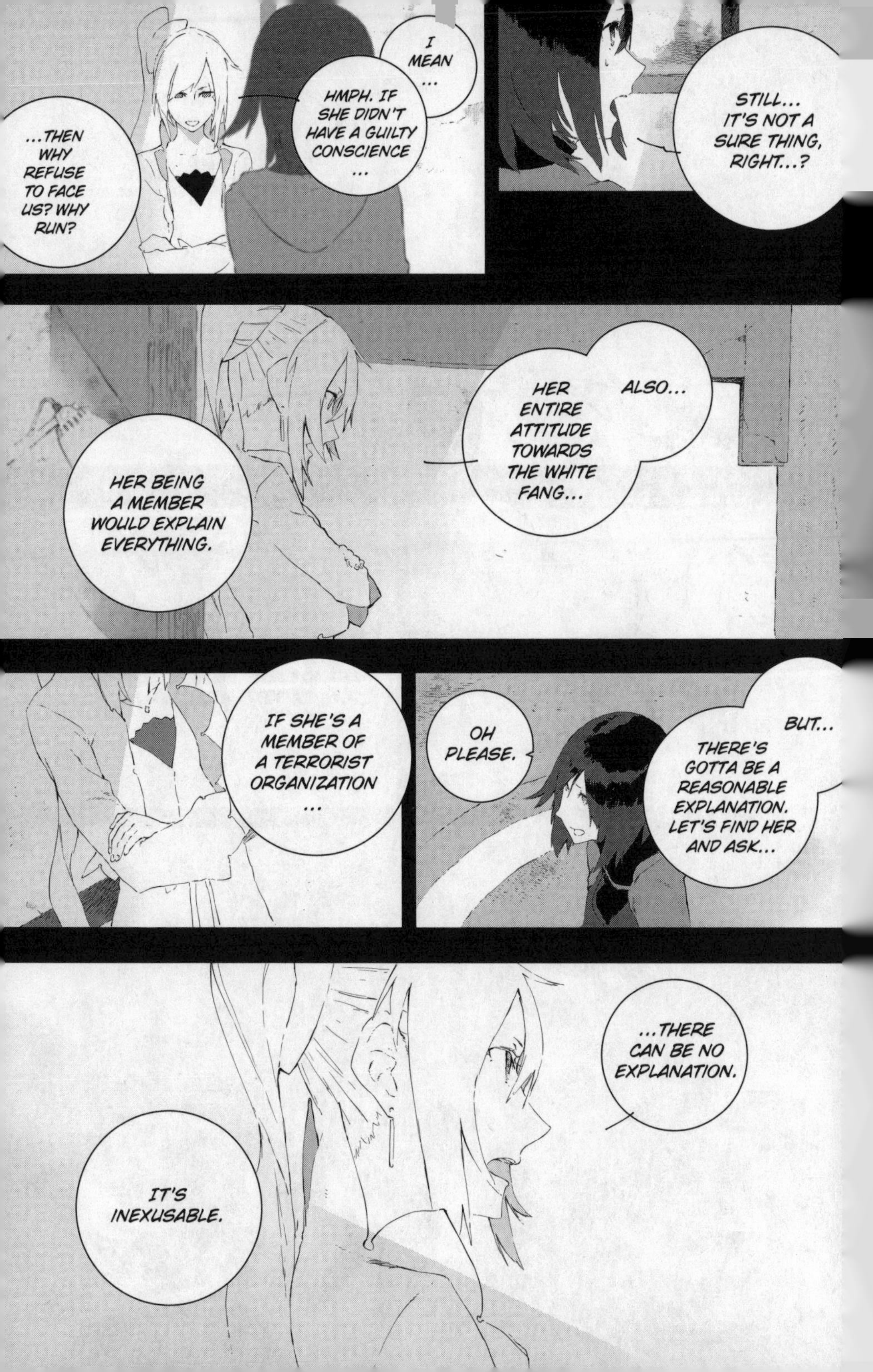
STILL... IT'S NOT A SURE THING, RIGHT...?
I MEAN...
HMPH. IF SHE DIDN'T HAVE A GUILTY CONSCIENCE...
...THEN WHY REFUSE TO FACE US? WHY RUN?
ALSO... HER ENTIRE ATTITUDE TOWARDS THE WHITE FANG...
HER BEING A MEMBER WOULD EXPLAIN EVERYTHING.
BUT... THERE'S GOTTA BE A REASONABLE EXPLANATION. LET'S FIND HER AND ASK...
OH PLEASE.
IF SHE'S A MEMBER OF A TERRORIST ORGANIZATION...
...THERE CAN BE NO EXPLANATION.
IT'S INEXUSABLE.

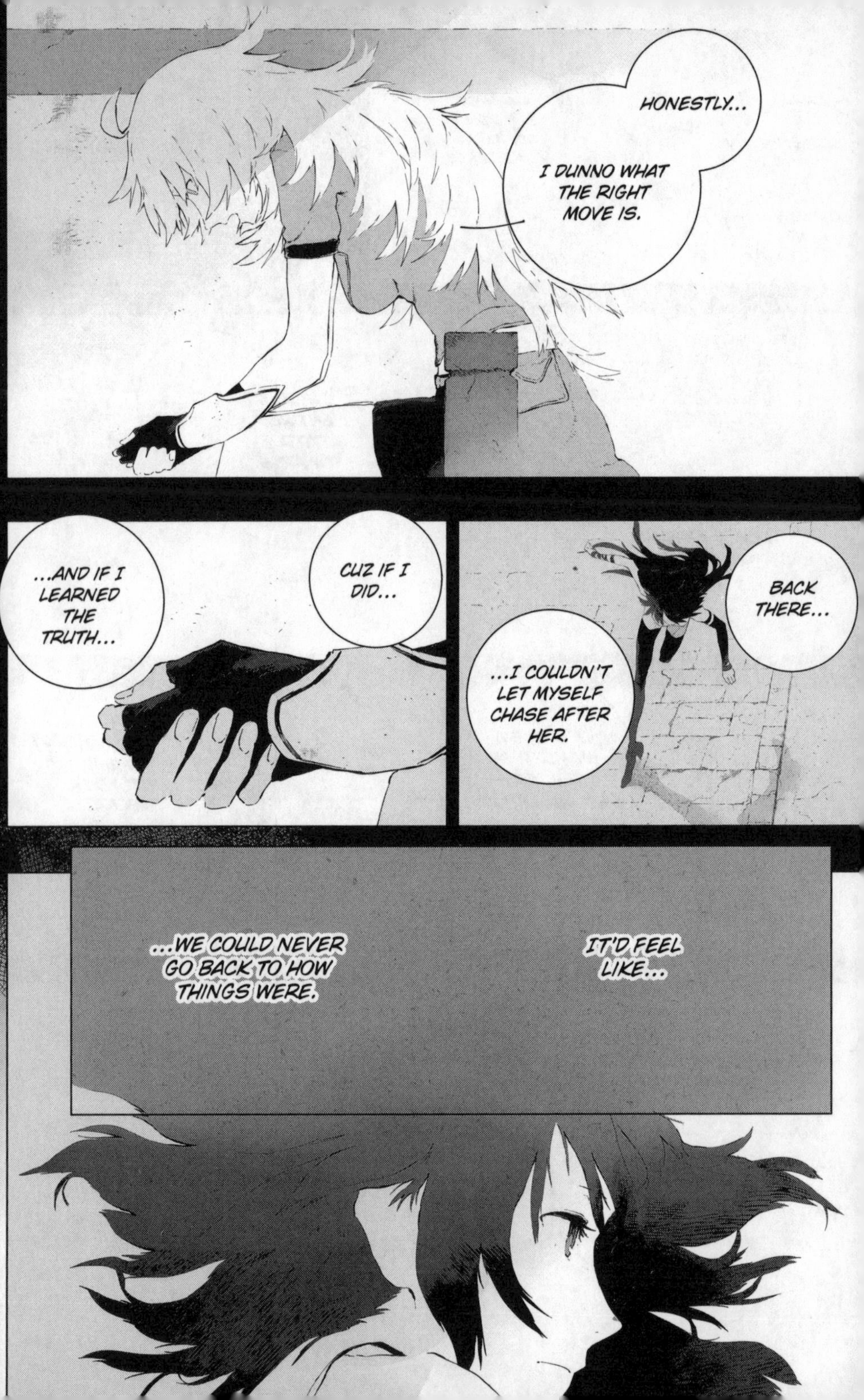
HONESTLY...
I DUNNO WHAT THE RIGHT MOVE IS.
BACK THERE...
...I COULDN'T LET MYSELF CHASE AFTER HER.
CUZ IF I DID...
...AND IF I LEARNED THE TRUTH...
IT'D FEEL LIKE...
...WE COULD NEVER GO BACK TO HOW THINGS WERE.

Kree

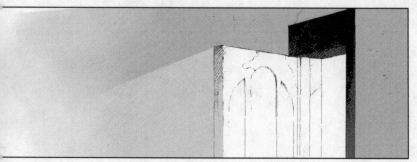

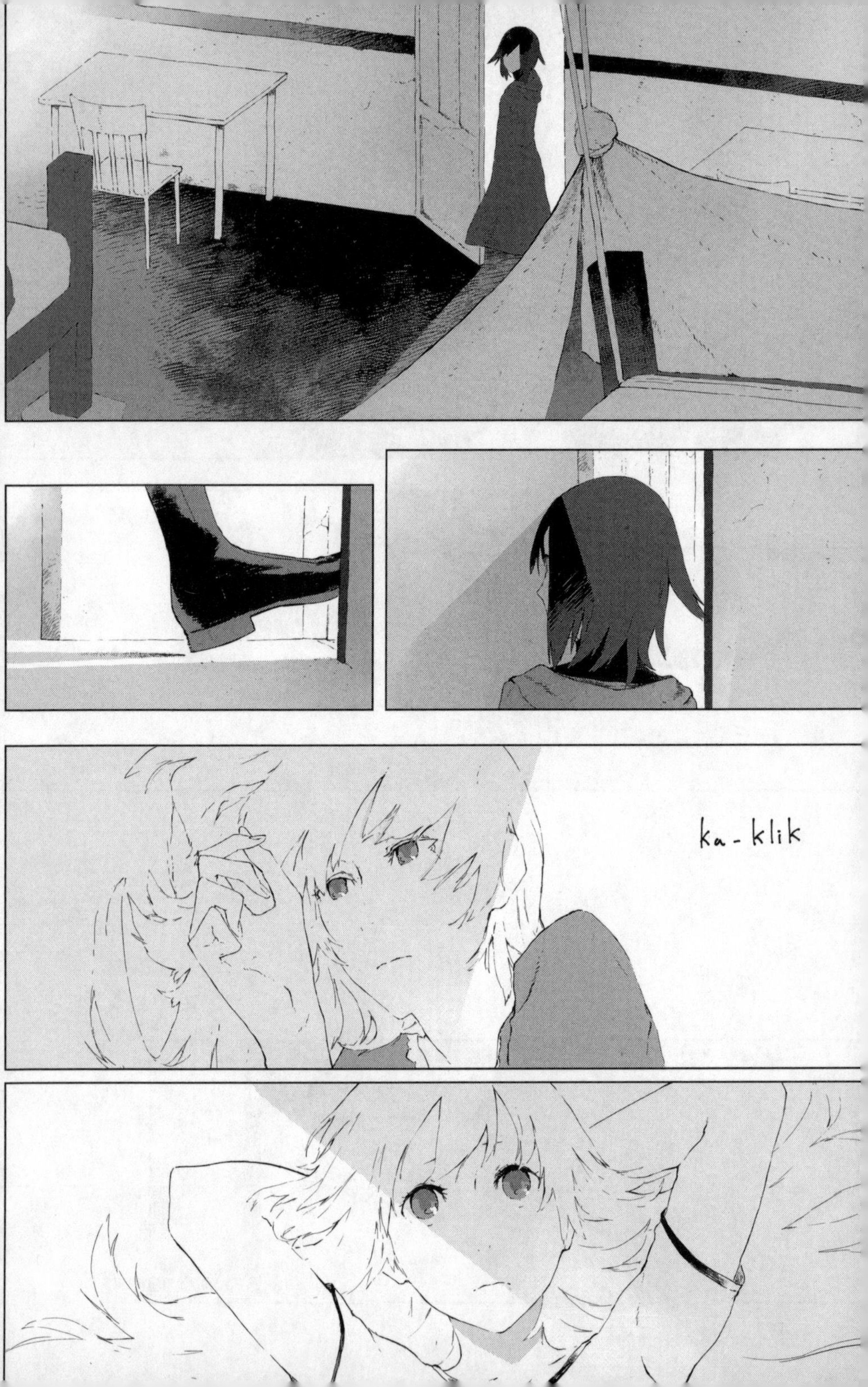
ka-klik

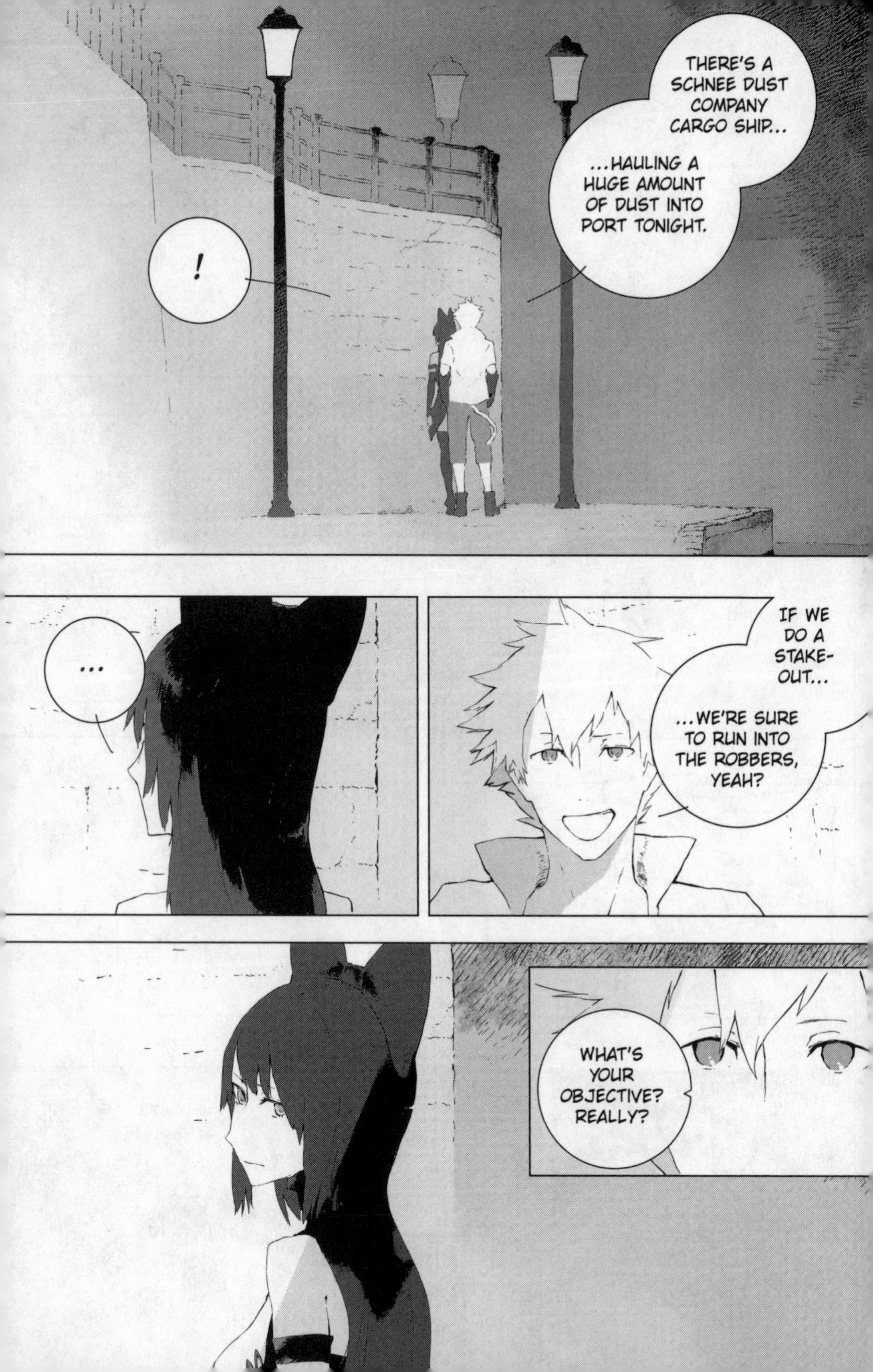
THERE'S A SCHNEE DUST COMPANY CARGO SHIP...
...HAULING A HUGE AMOUNT OF DUST INTO PORT TONIGHT.
!
IF WE DO A STAKE-OUT...
...WE'RE SURE TO RUN INTO THE ROBBERS, YEAH?
...
WHAT'S YOUR OBJECTIVE? REALLY?

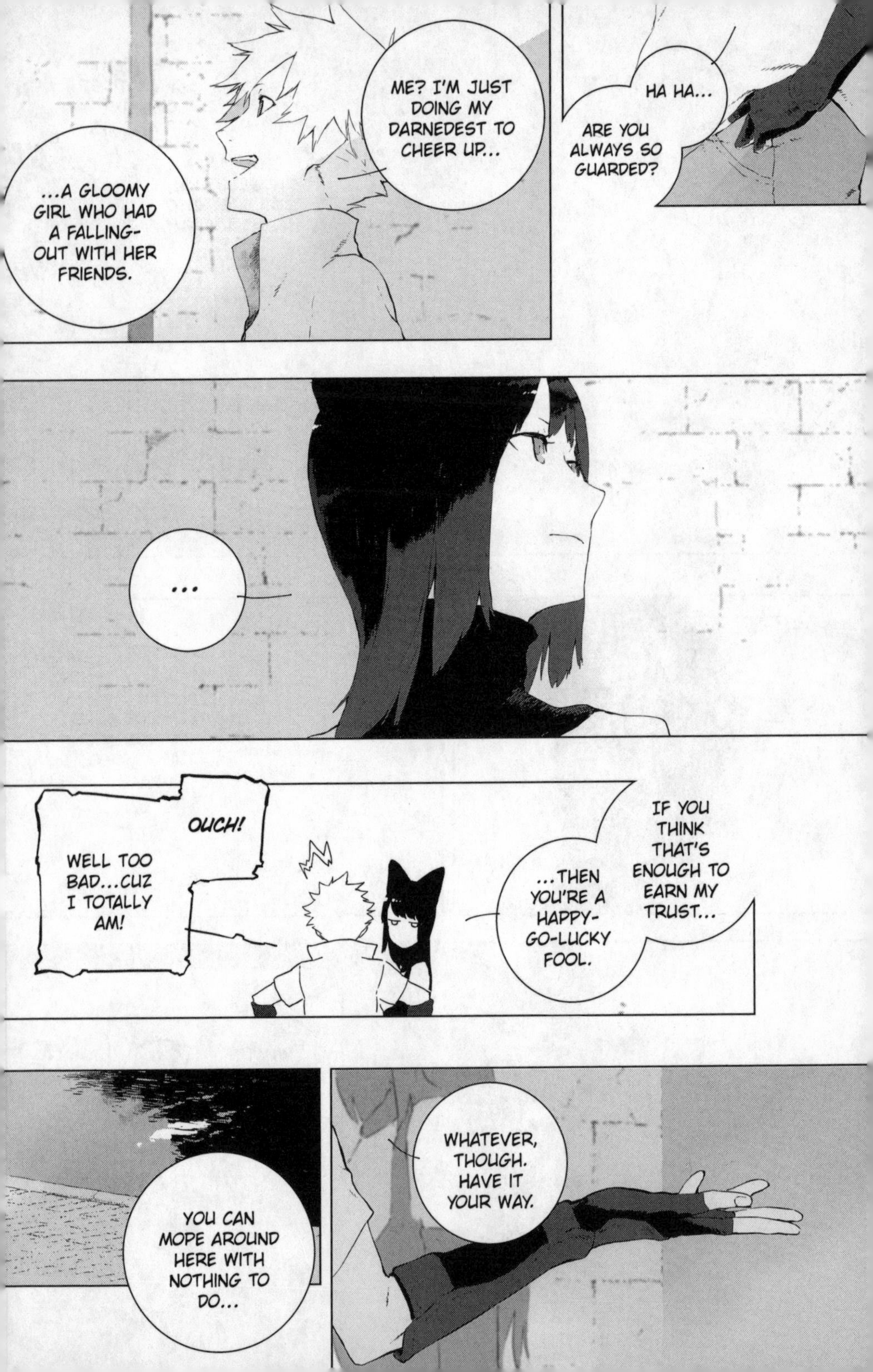
HA HA...
ARE YOU ALWAYS SO GUARDED?
ME? I'M JUST DOING MY DARNEDEST TO CHEER UP...
...A GLOOMY GIRL WHO HAD A FALLING-OUT WITH HER FRIENDS.
...
IF YOU THINK THAT'S ENOUGH TO EARN MY TRUST...
...THEN YOU'RE A HAPPY-GO-LUCKY FOOL.
OUCH!
WELL TOO BAD...CUZ I TOTALLY AM!
WHATEVER, THOUGH. HAVE IT YOUR WAY.
YOU CAN MOPE AROUND HERE WITH NOTHING TO DO...

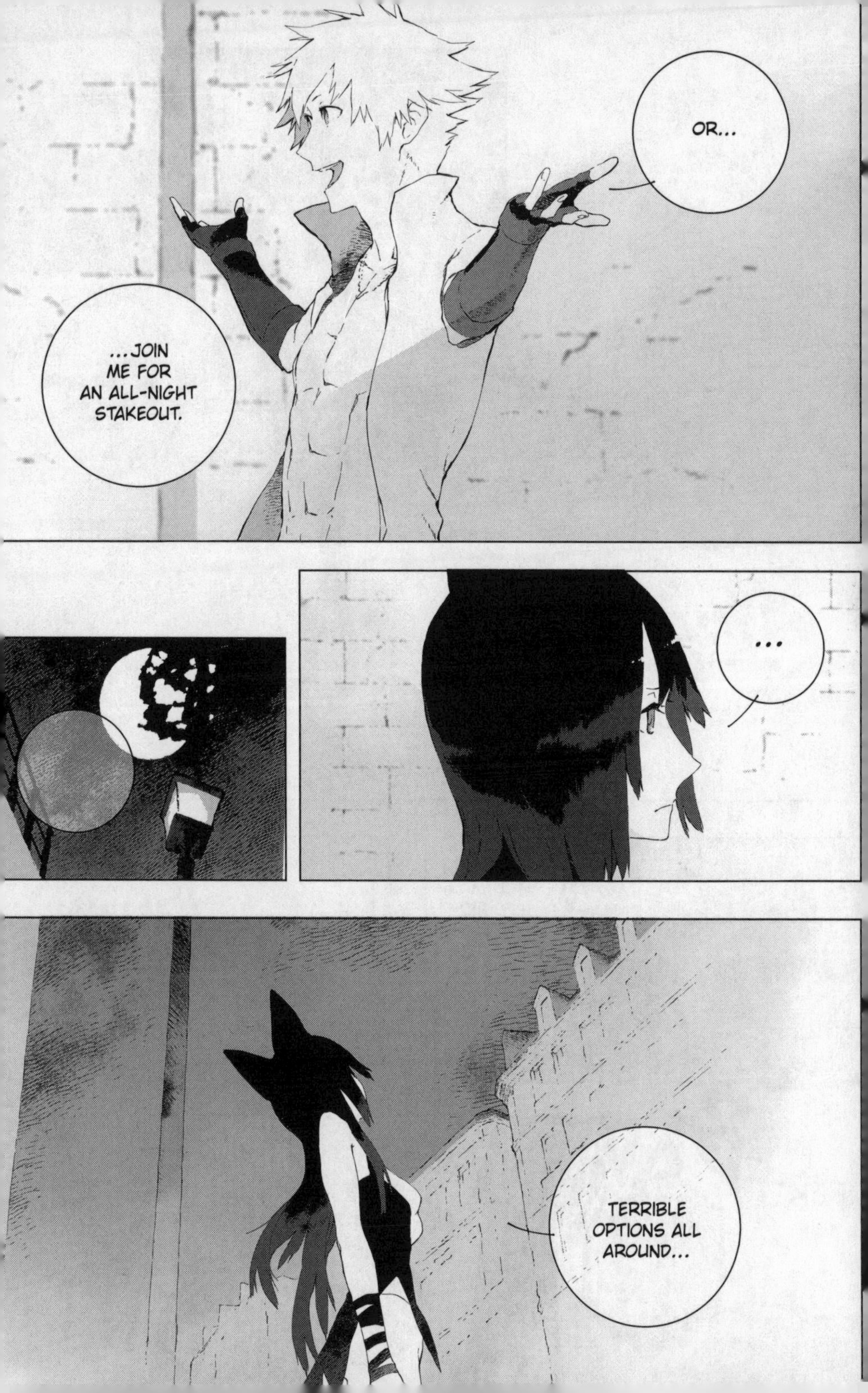
OR...
...JOIN ME FOR AN ALL-NIGHT STAKEOUT.
...
TERRIBLE OPTIONS ALL AROUND...

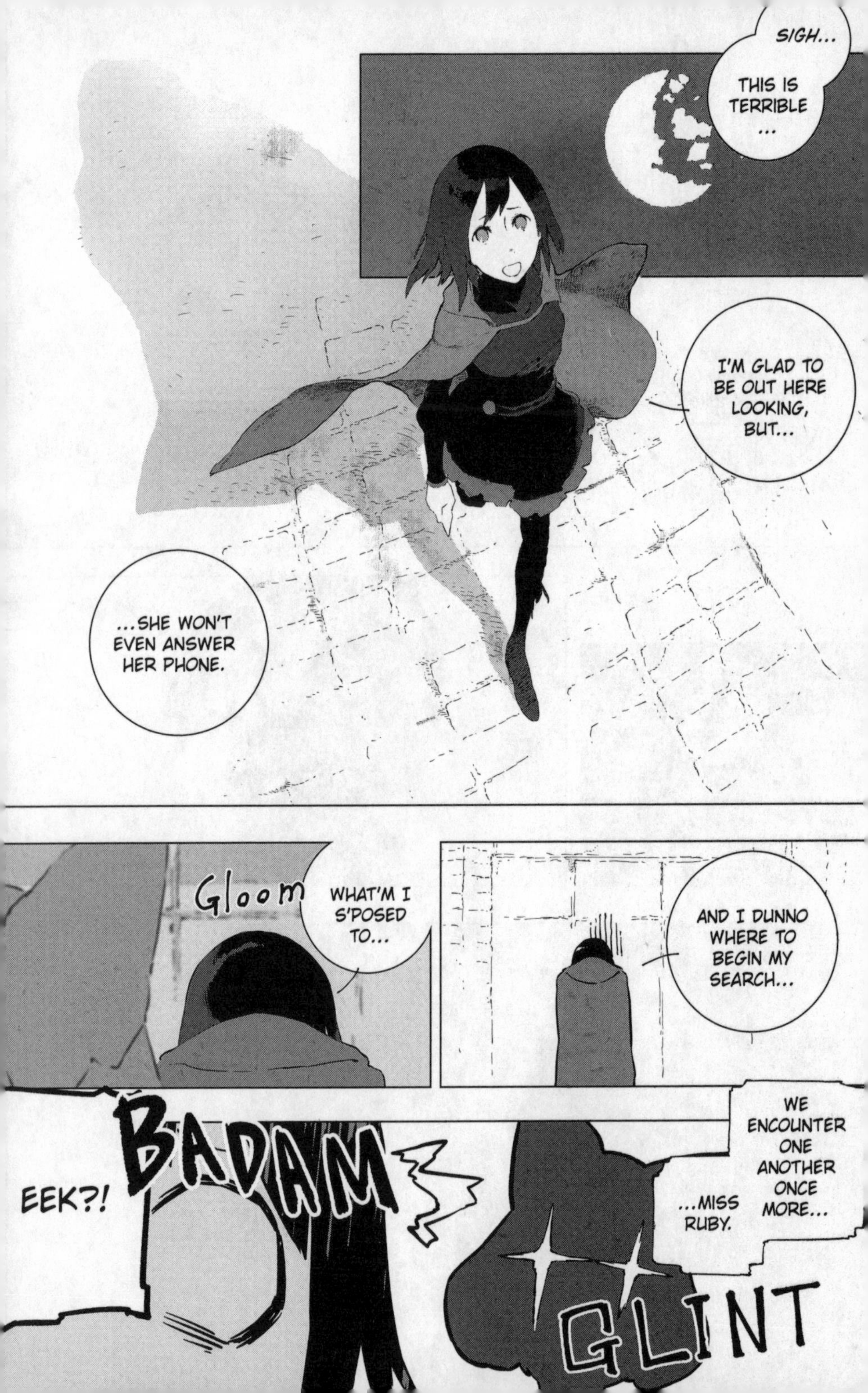
SIGH...
THIS IS TERRIBLE...
I'M GLAD TO BE OUT HERE LOOKING, BUT...
...SHE WON'T EVEN ANSWER HER PHONE.
AND I DUNNO WHERE TO BEGIN MY SEARCH...
Gloom
WHAT'M I S'POSED TO...
WE ENCOUNTER ONE ANOTHER ONCE MORE...
...MISS RUBY.
GLINT
BADAM
EEK?!

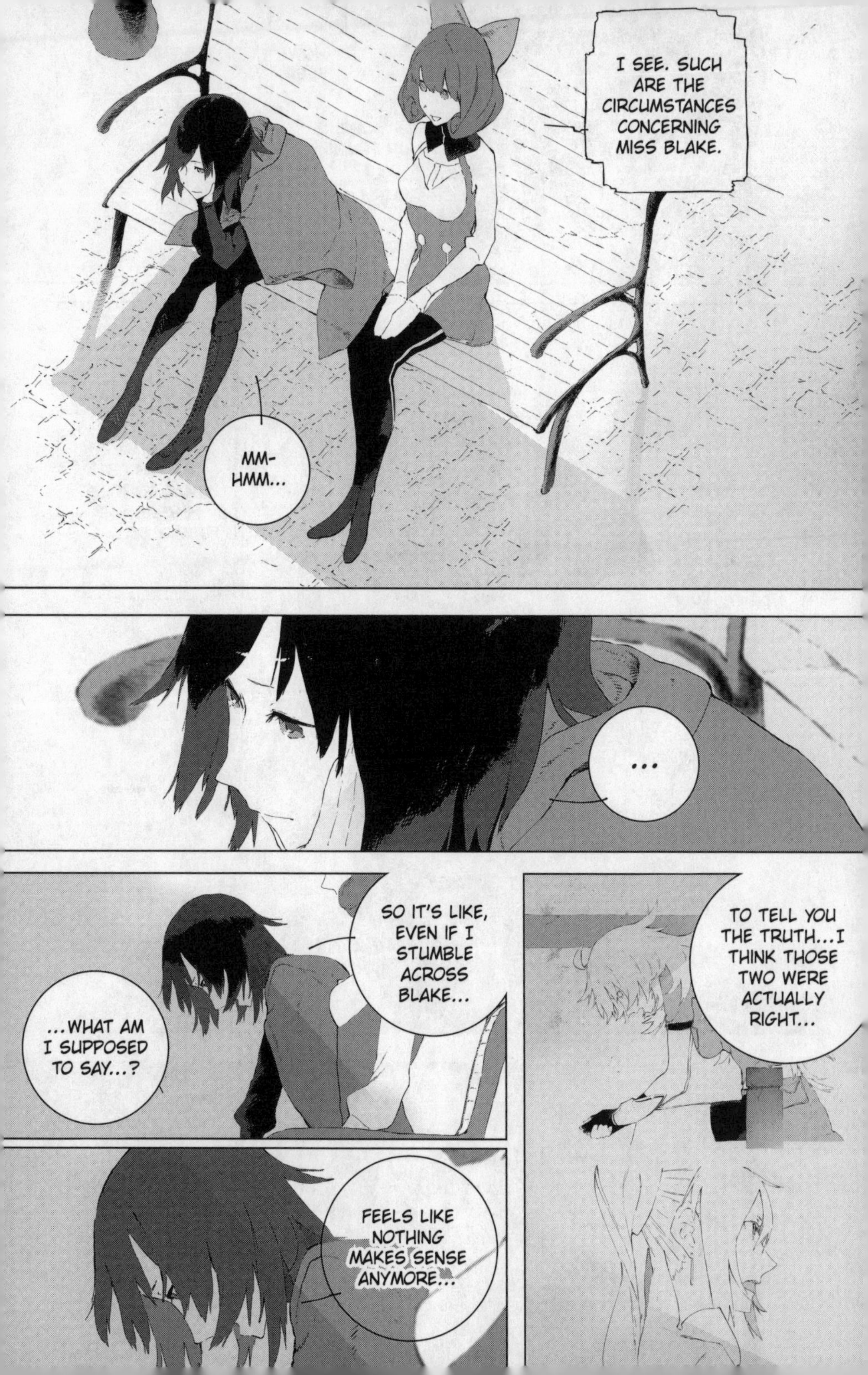
I SEE. SUCH ARE THE CIRCUMSTANCES CONCERNING MISS BLAKE.
MM-HMM...
...
TO TELL YOU THE TRUTH...I THINK THOSE TWO WERE ACTUALLY RIGHT...
SO IT'S LIKE, EVEN IF I STUMBLE ACROSS BLAKE...
...WHAT AM I SUPPOSED TO SAY...?
FEELS LIKE NOTHING MAKES SENSE ANYMORE...

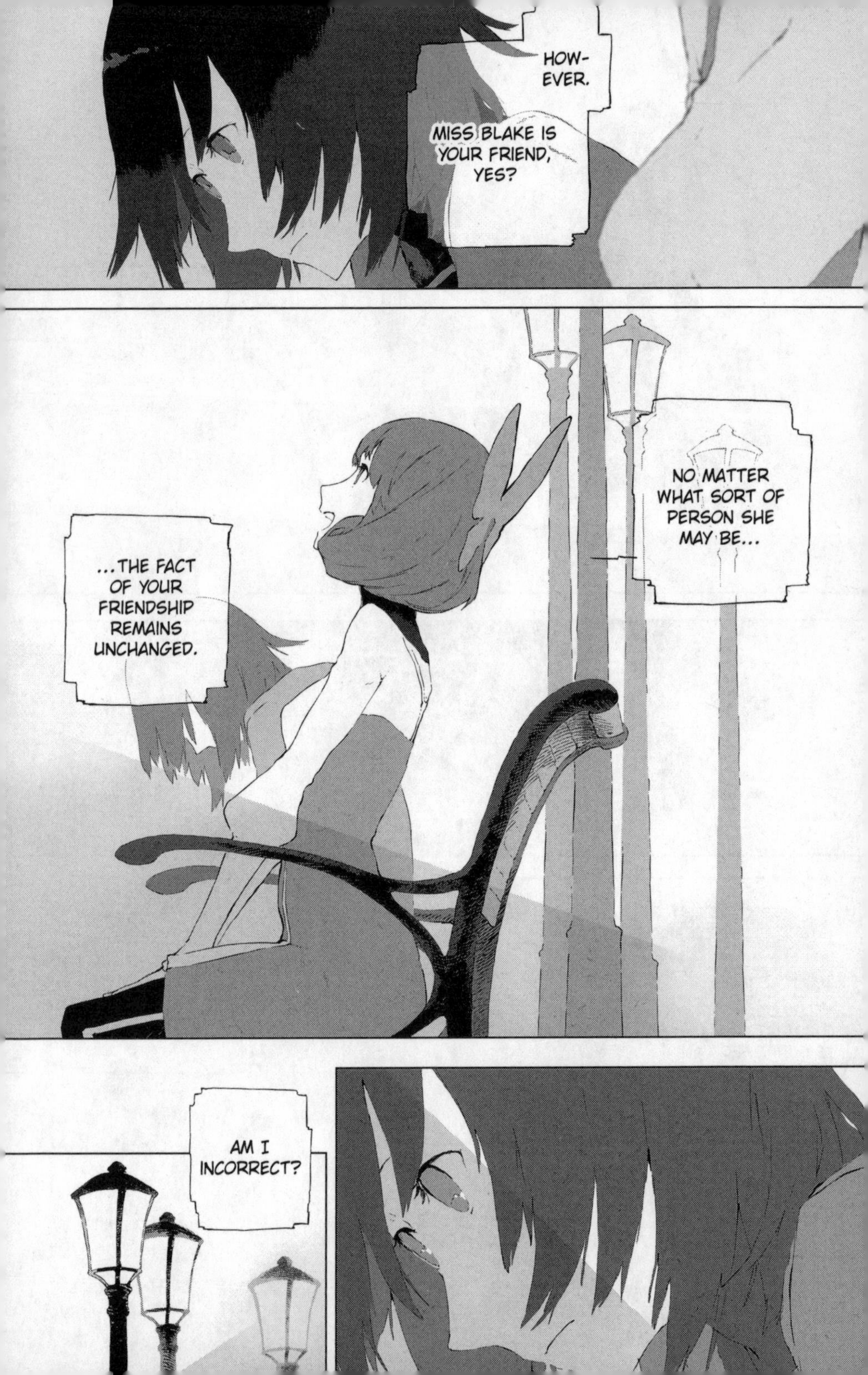
HOW-EVER.
MISS BLAKE IS YOUR FRIEND, YES?
NO MATTER WHAT SORT OF PERSON SHE MAY BE...
...THE FACT OF YOUR FRIENDSHIP REMAINS UNCHANGED.
AM I INCORRECT?

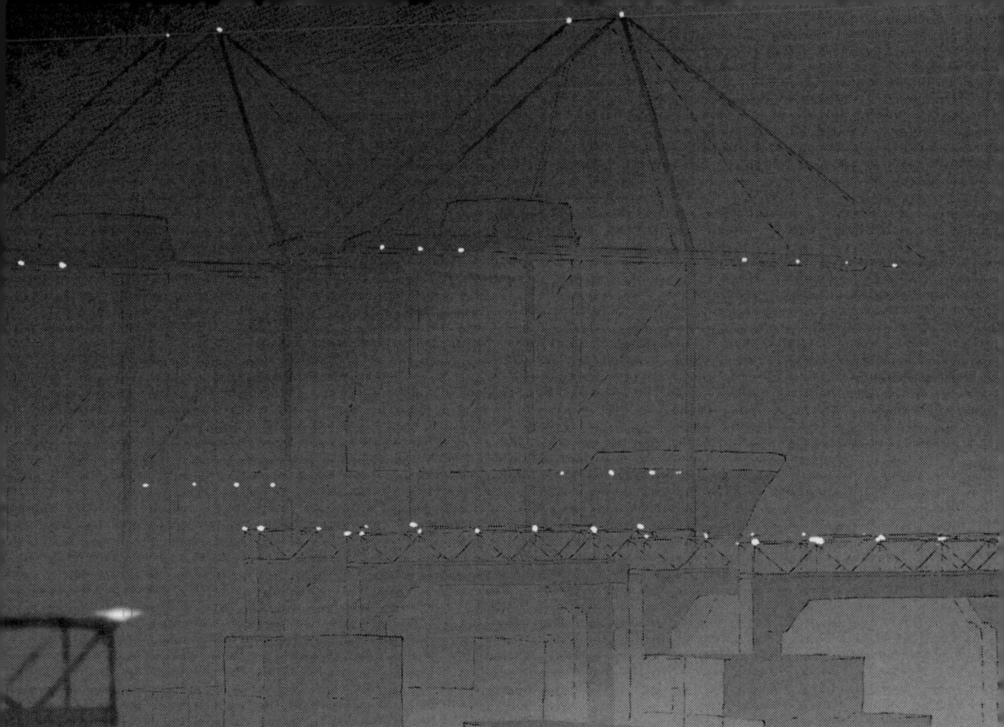

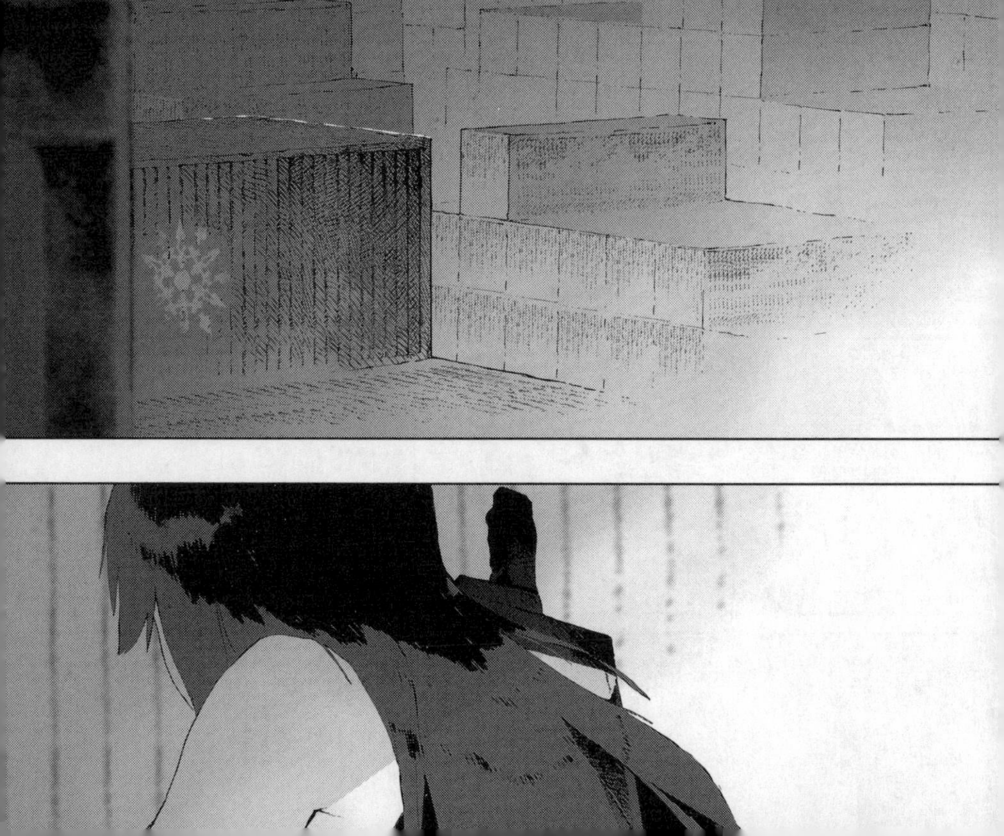

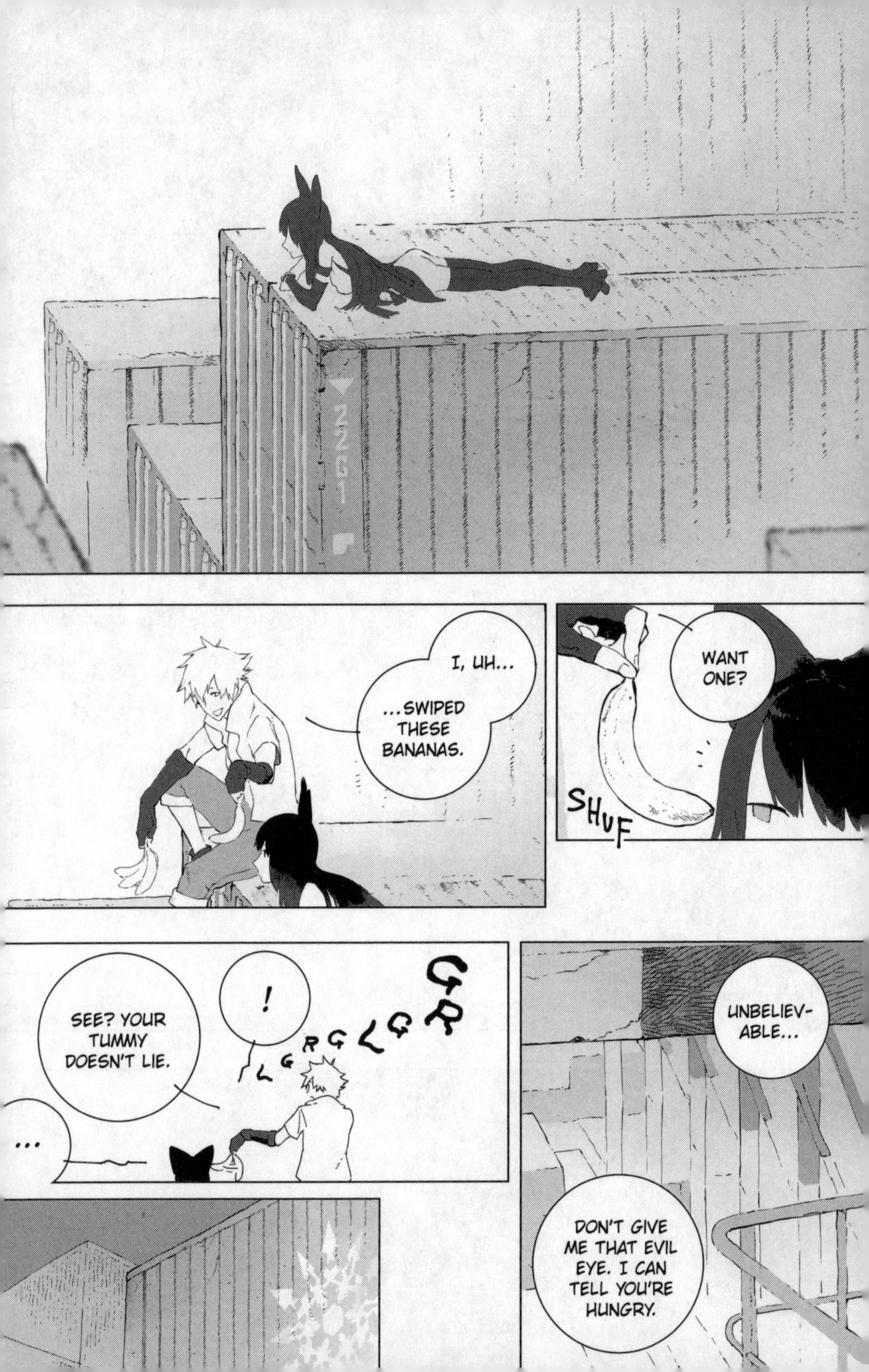
WANT ONE?
SHUF
I, UH...
...SWIPED THESE BANANAS.
UNBELIEV-ABLE...
DON'T GIVE ME THAT EVIL EYE. I CAN TELL YOU'RE HUNGRY.
GRGLGRGL
!
SEE? YOUR TUMMY DOESN'T LIE.
...

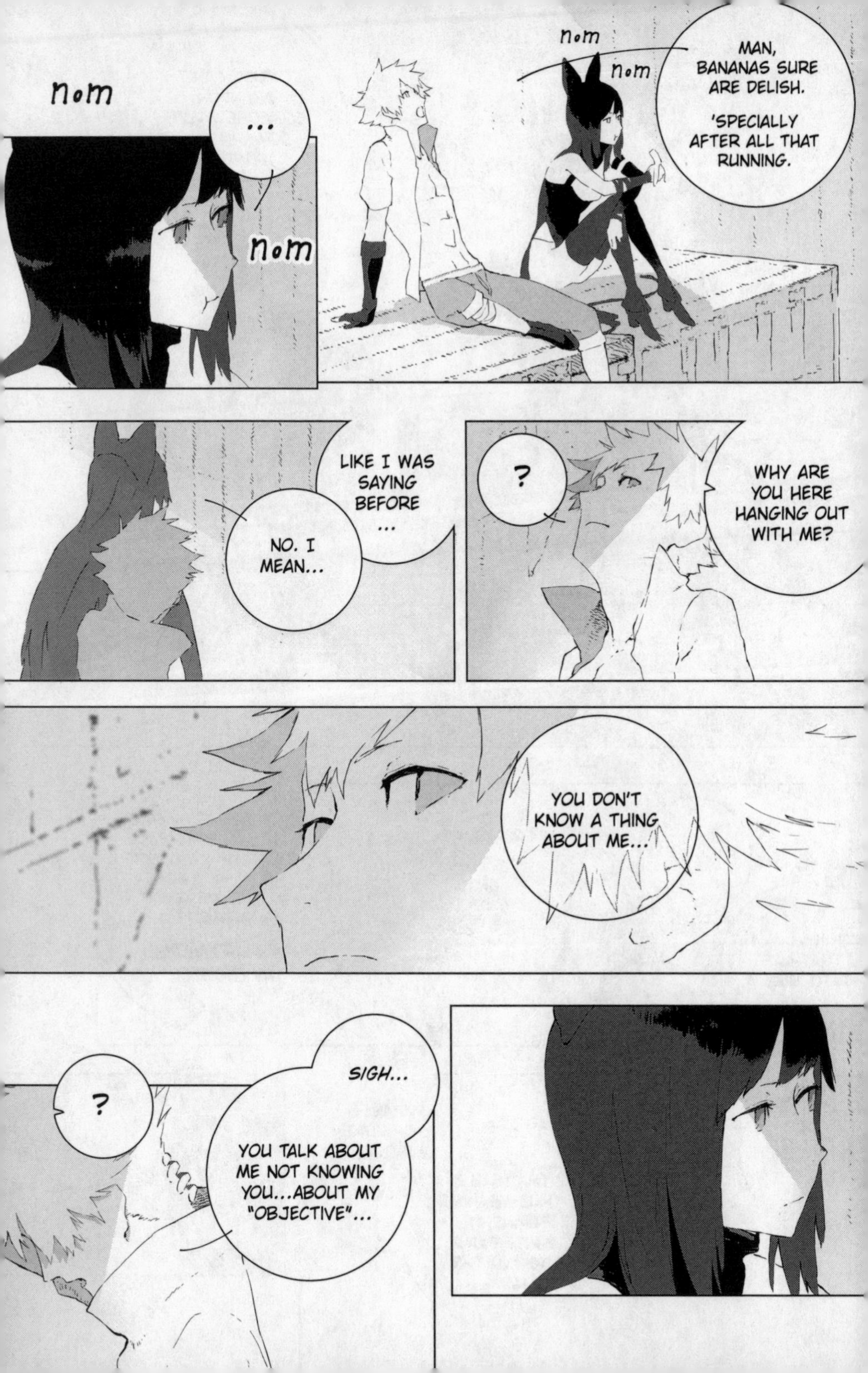
nom
nom
MAN, BANANAS SURE ARE DELISH.
'SPECIALLY AFTER ALL THAT RUNNING.
nom
...
nom
WHY ARE YOU HERE HANGING OUT WITH ME?
?
LIKE I WAS SAYING BEFORE ...
NO. I MEAN...
YOU DON'T KNOW A THING ABOUT ME...
SIGH...
YOU TALK ABOUT ME NOT KNOWING YOU...ABOUT MY "OBJECTIVE"...
?

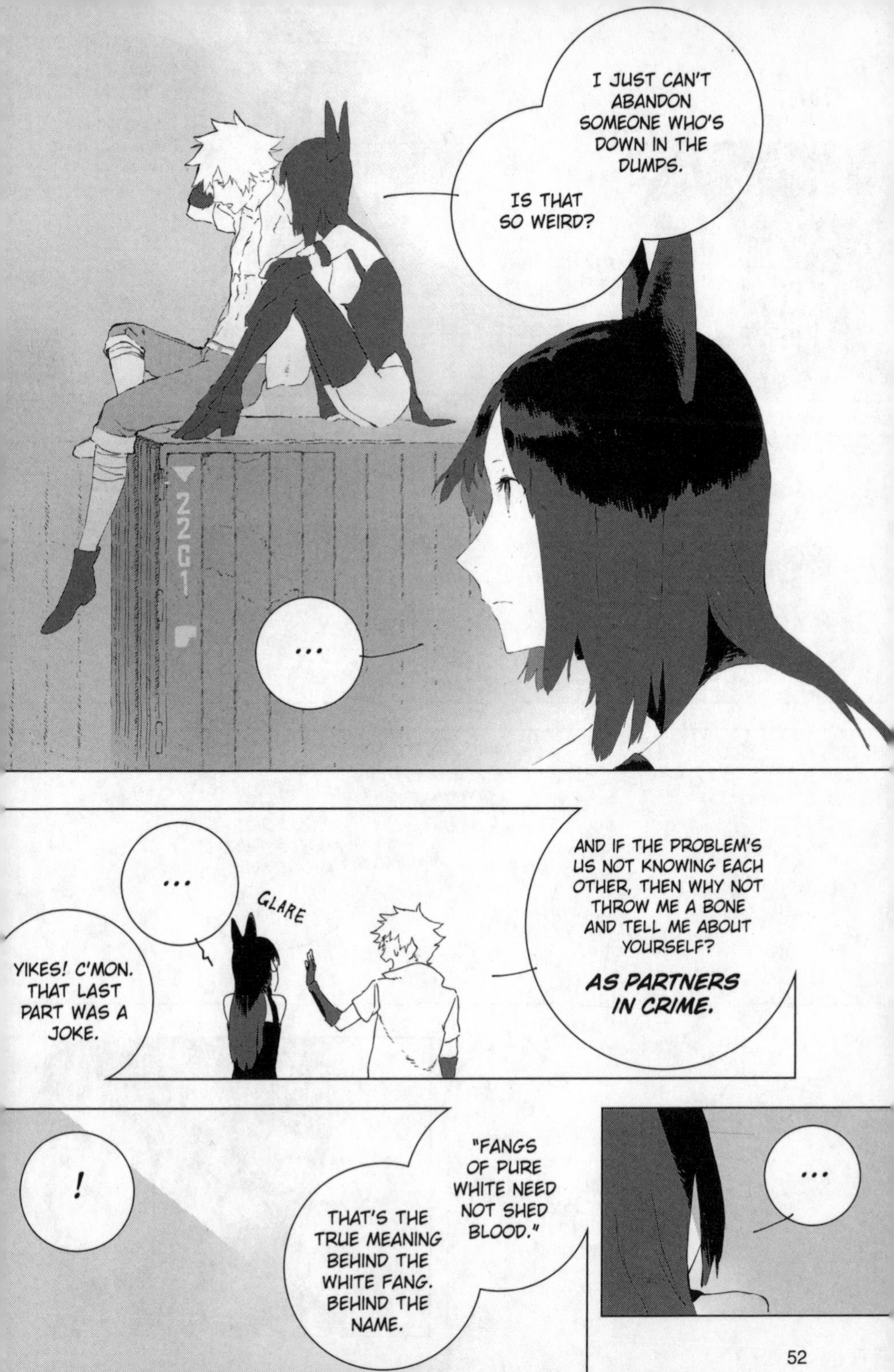
I JUST CAN'T ABANDON SOMEONE WHO'S DOWN IN THE DUMPS.
IS THAT SO WEIRD?
...
AND IF THE PROBLEM'S US NOT KNOWING EACH OTHER, THEN WHY NOT THROW ME A BONE AND TELL ME ABOUT YOURSELF?
AS PARTNERS IN CRIME.
...
GLARE
YIKES! C'MON. THAT LAST PART WAS A JOKE.
...
"FANGS OF PURE WHITE NEED NOT SHED BLOOD."
THAT'S THE TRUE MEANING BEHIND THE WHITE FANG. BEHIND THE NAME.
!

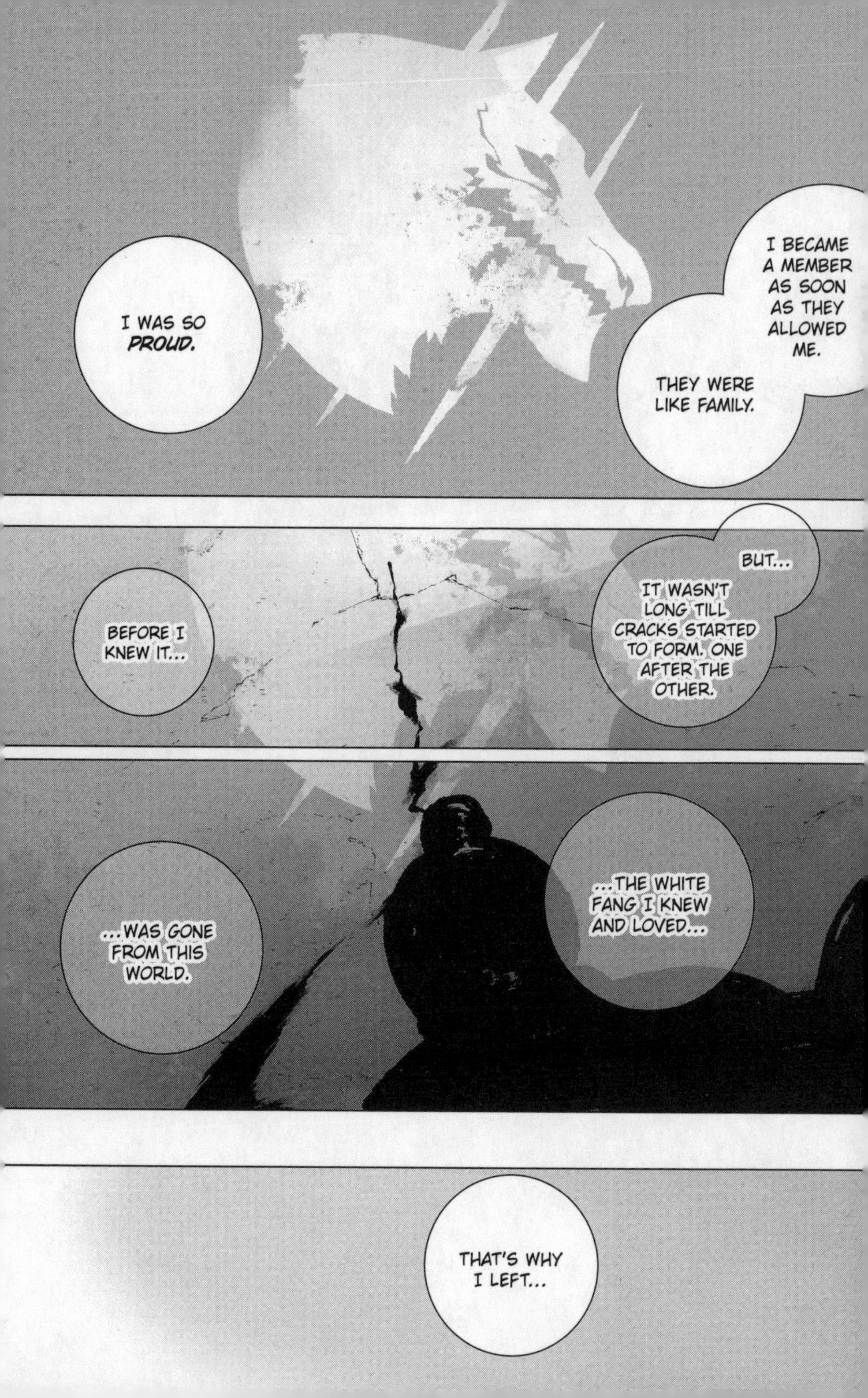

I BECAME A MEMBER AS SOON AS THEY ALLOWED ME.
THEY WERE LIKE FAMILY.
I WAS SO *PROUD.*
BUT...
IT WASN'T LONG TILL CRACKS STARTED TO FORM. ONE AFTER THE OTHER.
BEFORE I KNEW IT...
...THE WHITE FANG I KNEW AND LOVED...
...WAS GONE FROM THIS WORLD.
THAT'S WHY I LEFT...

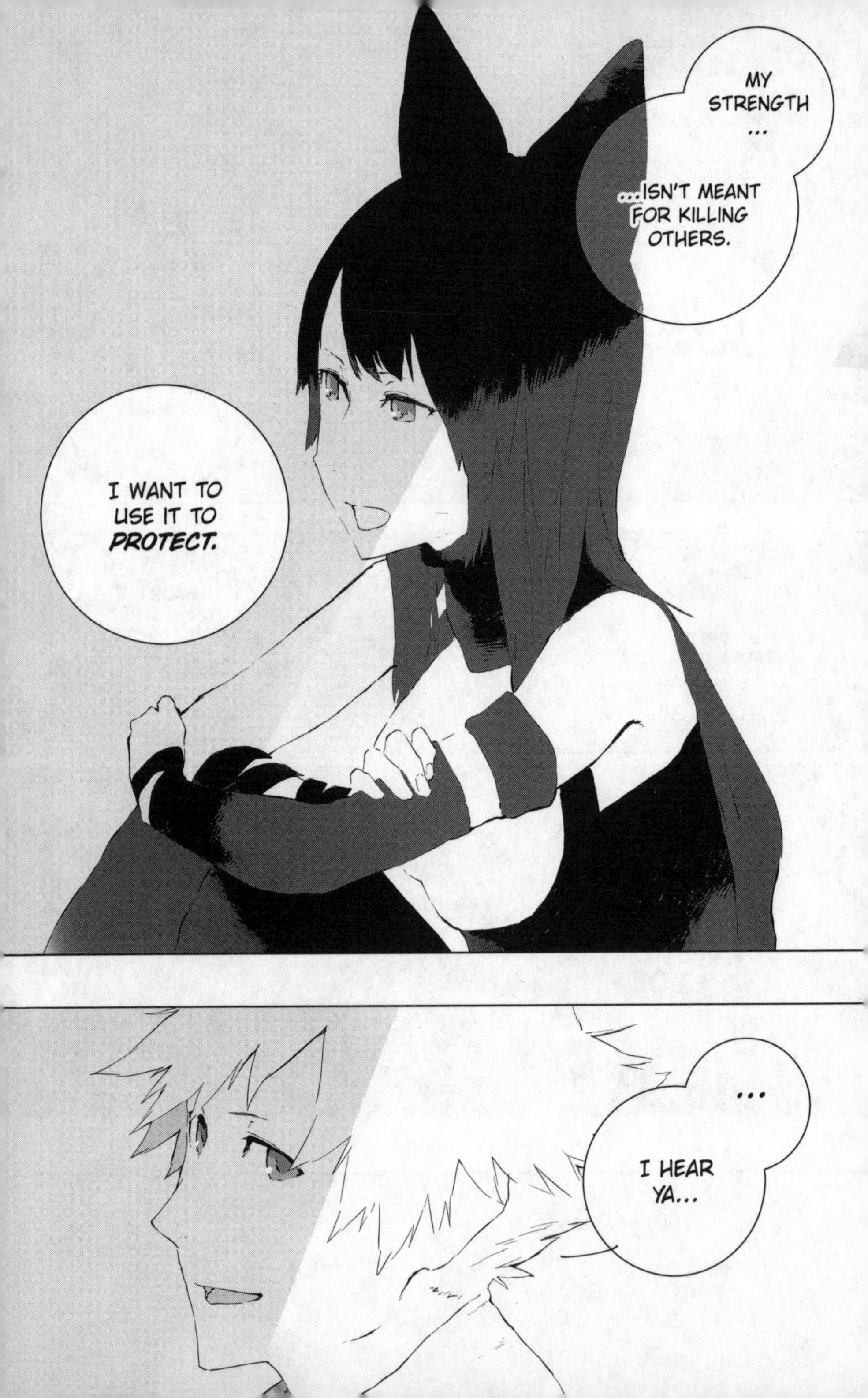
MY STRENGTH ...
...ISN'T MEANT FOR KILLING OTHERS.
I WANT TO USE IT TO *PROTECT.*
...
I HEAR YA...

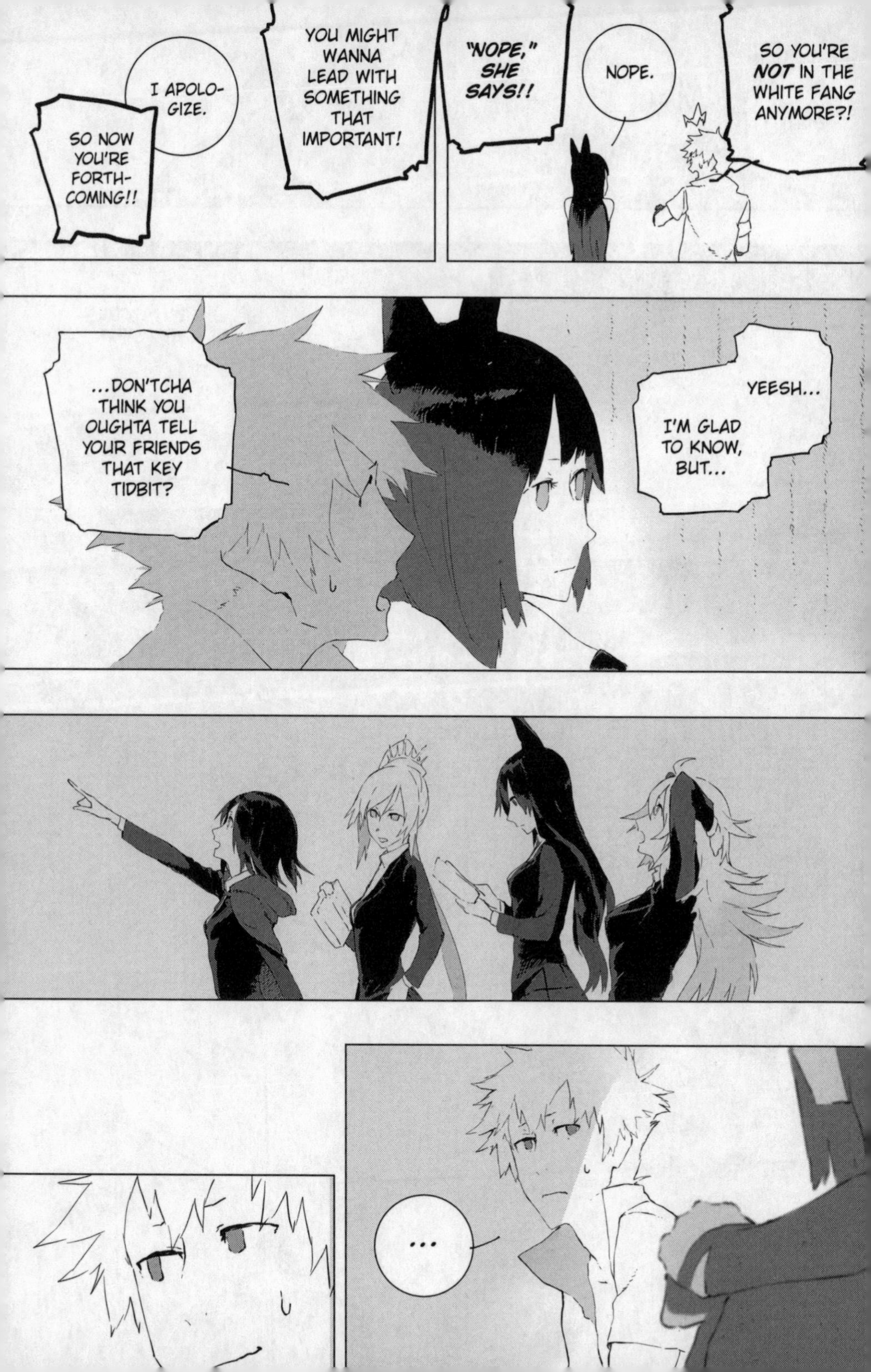
SO YOU'RE ***NOT*** IN THE WHITE FANG ANYMORE?!
NOPE.
"NOPE," SHE SAYS!!
YOU MIGHT WANNA LEAD WITH SOMETHING THAT IMPORTANT!
I APOLO-GIZE.
SO NOW YOU'RE FORTH-COMING!!
YEESH... I'M GLAD TO KNOW, BUT...
...DON'TCHA THINK YOU OUGHTA TELL YOUR FRIENDS THAT KEY TIDBIT?
...

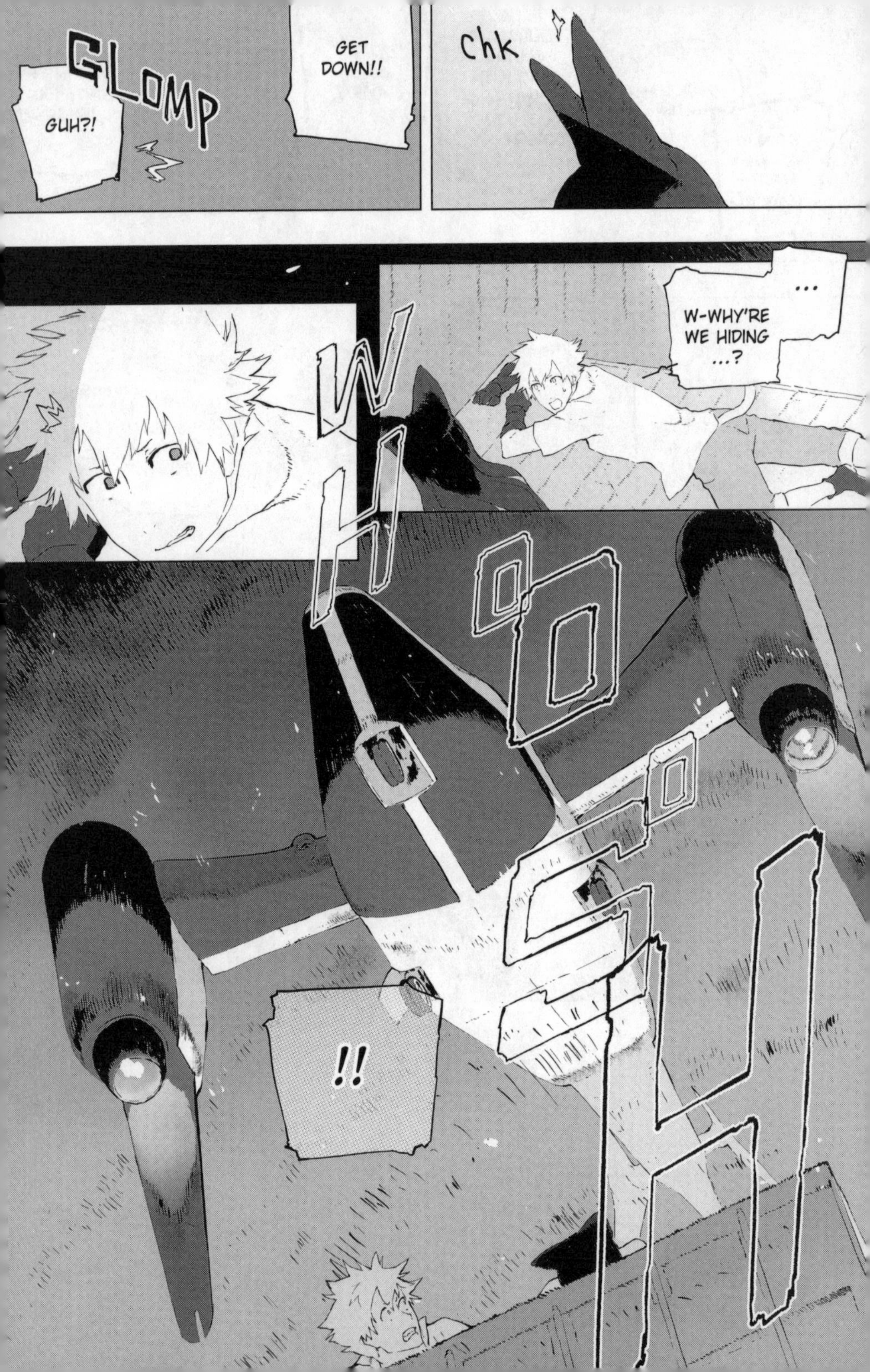
Chk
GET DOWN!!
GLOMP
GUH?!
...
W-WHY'RE WE HIDING ...?
WHOOOSH
!!

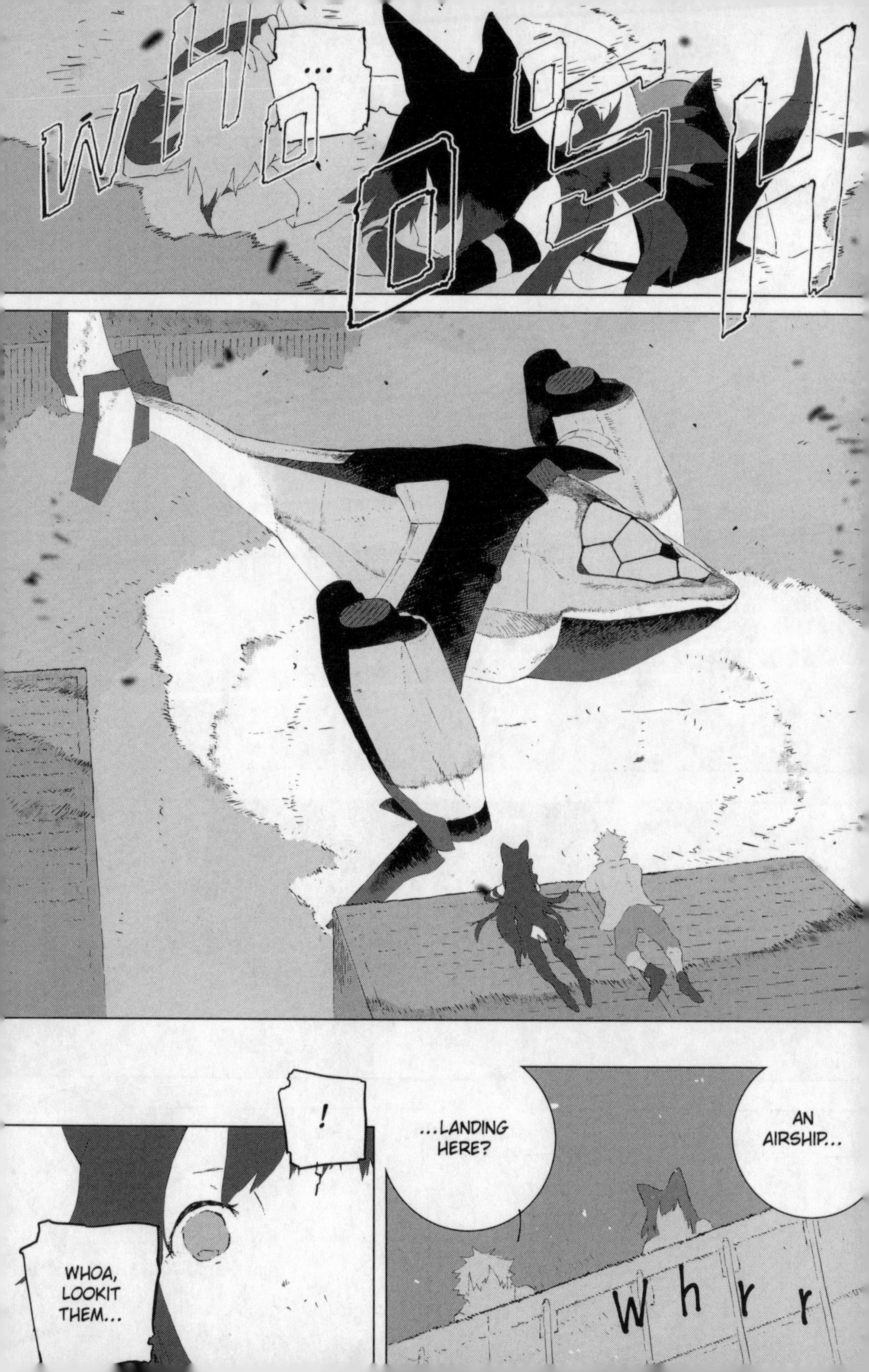
whoosh
...
AN AIRSHIP...
...LANDING HERE?
Whrr
!
WHOA, LOOKIT THEM...

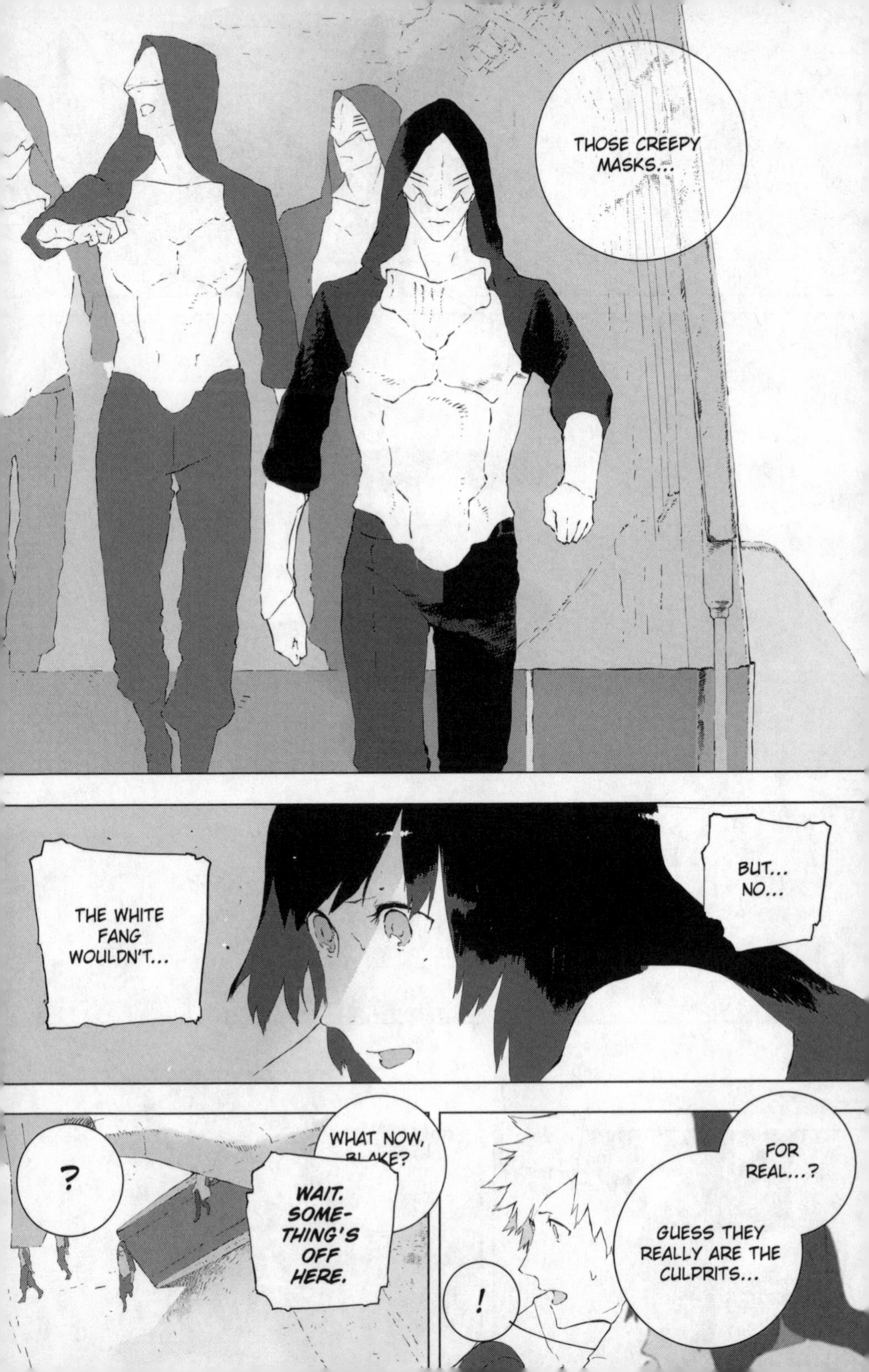
THOSE CREEPY MASKS...
BUT... NO...
THE WHITE FANG WOULDN'T...
FOR REAL...?
GUESS THEY REALLY ARE THE CULPRITS...
!
WHAT NOW, BLAKE?
WAIT. SOME-THING'S OFF HERE.
?

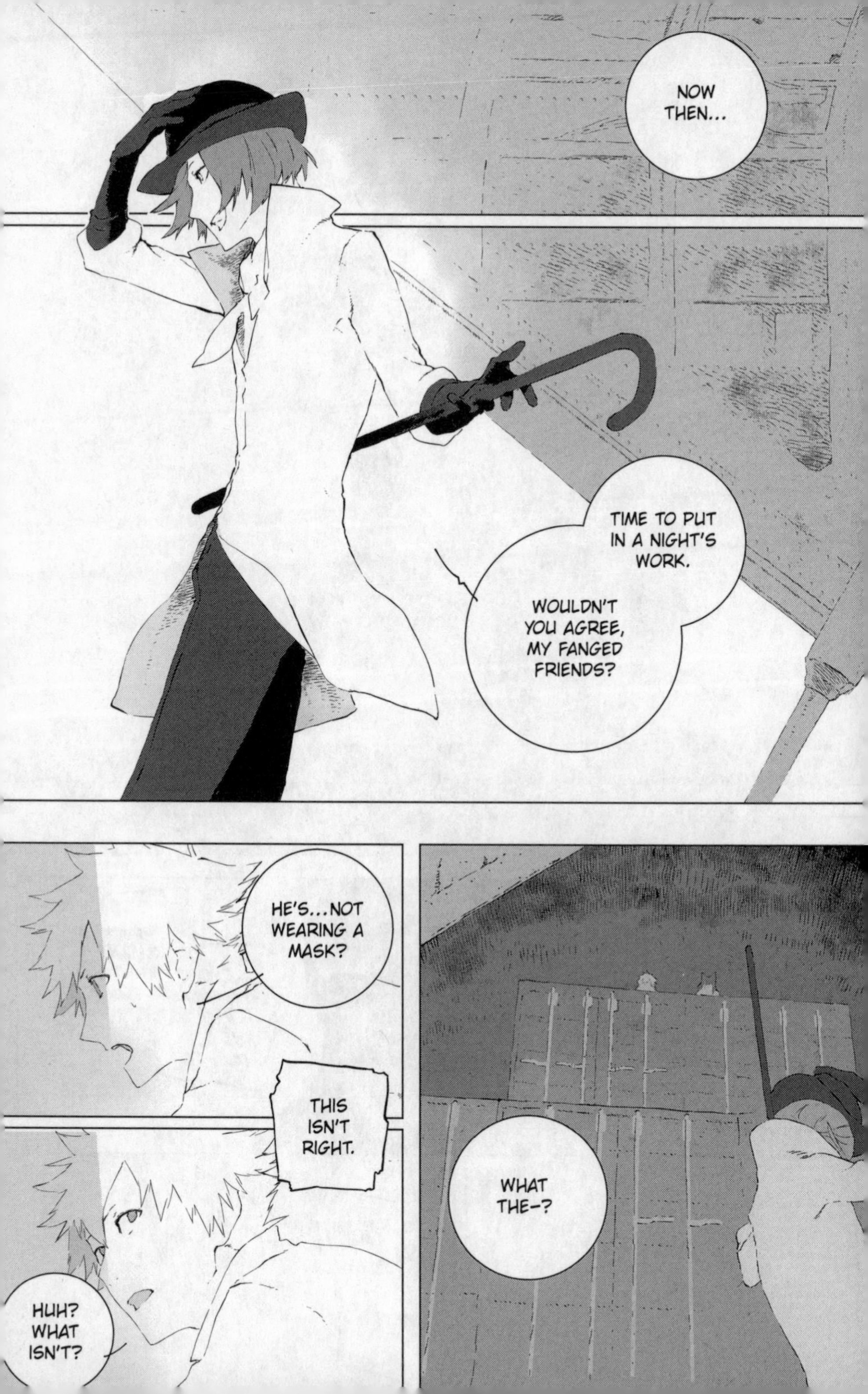
NOW THEN...
TIME TO PUT IN A NIGHT'S WORK.
WOULDN'T YOU AGREE, MY FANGED FRIENDS?
WHAT THE-?
HE'S...NOT WEARING A MASK?
THIS ISN'T RIGHT.
HUH? WHAT ISN'T?

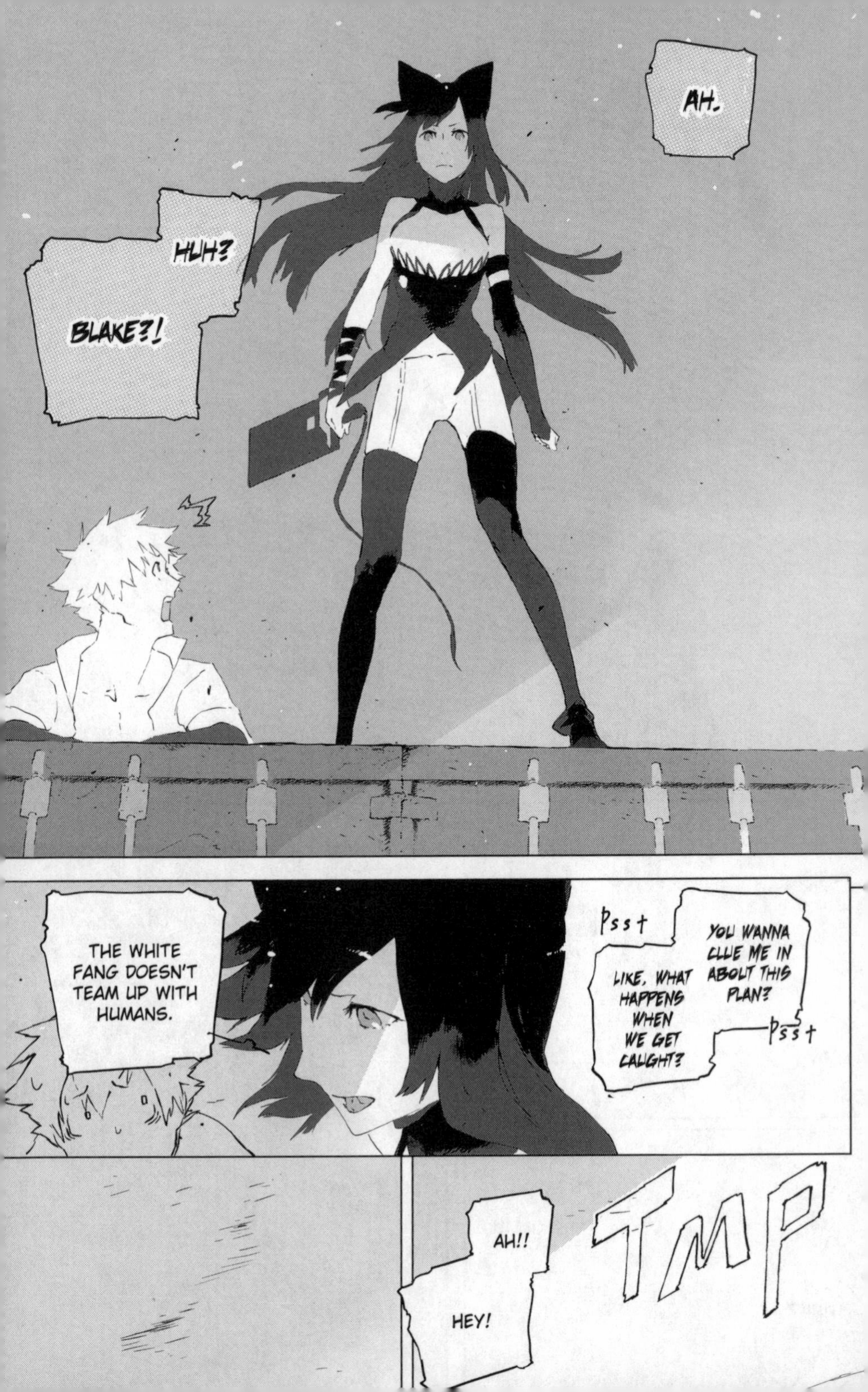
AH.
HUH?
BLAKE?!
Psst
YOU WANNA CLUE ME IN ABOUT THIS PLAN?
LIKE, WHAT HAPPENS WHEN WE GET CAUGHT?
Psst
THE WHITE FANG DOESN'T TEAM UP WITH HUMANS.
TMP
AH!!
HEY!

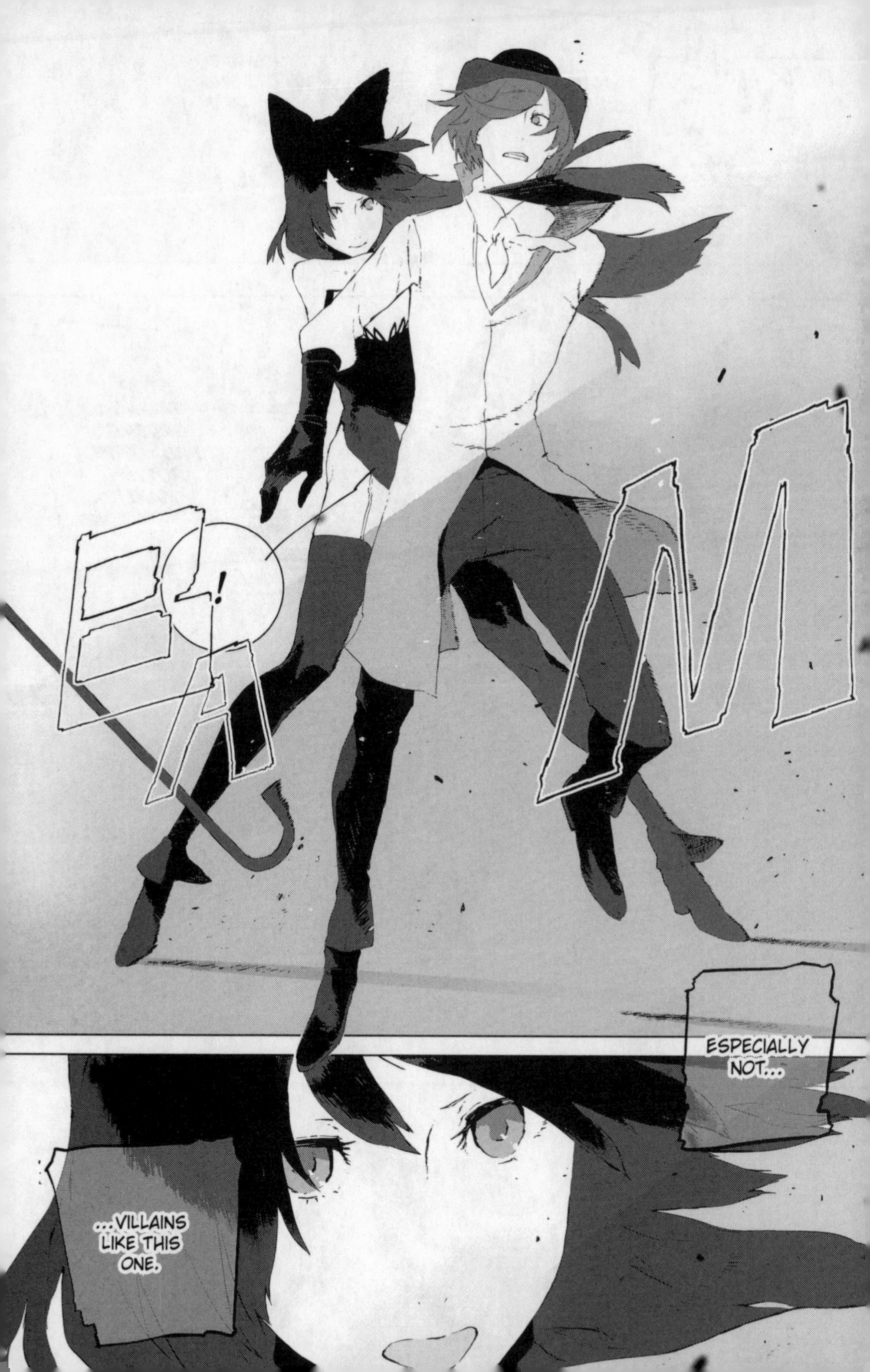
BAM
ESPECIALLY NOT...
...VILLAINS LIKE THIS ONE.

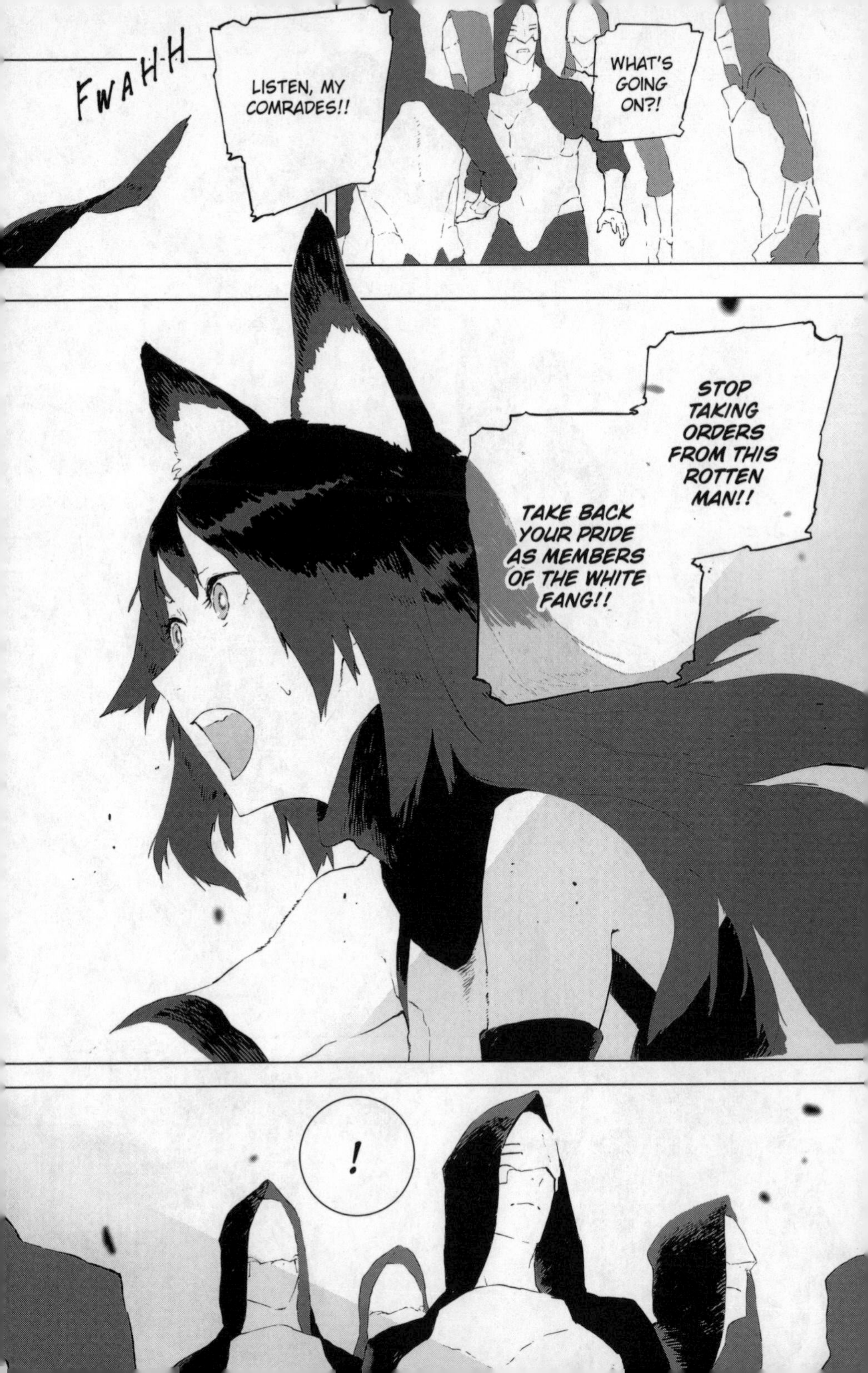
WHAT'S GOING ON?!
LISTEN, MY COMRADES!!
FWAHH
STOP TAKING ORDERS FROM THIS ROTTEN MAN!!
TAKE BACK YOUR PRIDE AS MEMBERS OF THE WHITE FANG!!
!

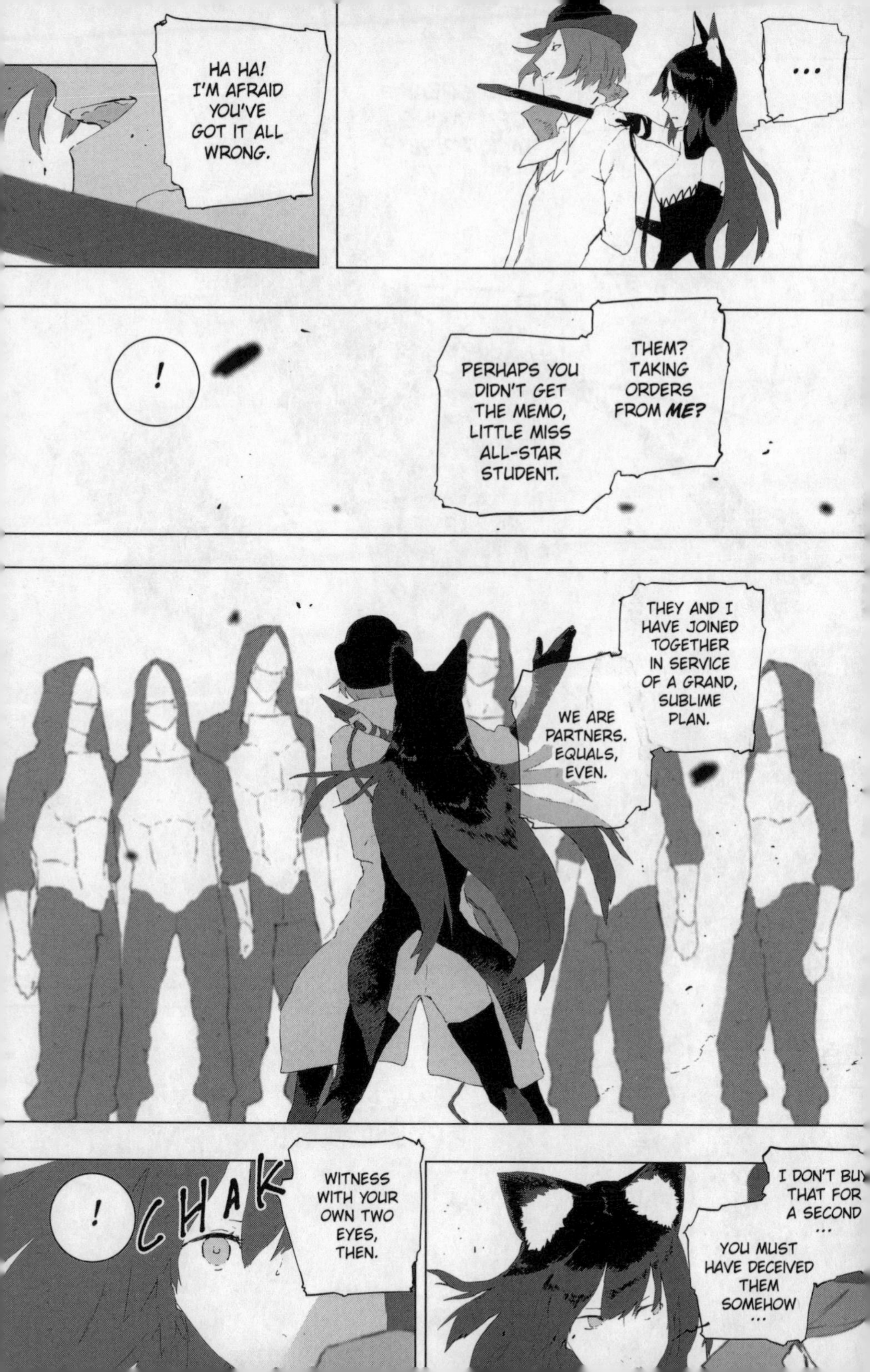
...
HA HA! I'M AFRAID YOU'VE GOT IT ALL WRONG.
THEM? TAKING ORDERS FROM *ME?*
PERHAPS YOU DIDN'T GET THE MEMO, LITTLE MISS ALL-STAR STUDENT.
!
THEY AND I HAVE JOINED TOGETHER IN SERVICE OF A GRAND, SUBLIME PLAN.
WE ARE PARTNERS. EQUALS, EVEN.
I DON'T BU
THAT FOR A SECOND...
YOU MUST HAVE DECEIVED THEM SOMEHOW...
WITNESS WITH YOUR OWN TWO EYES, THEN.
CHAK
!

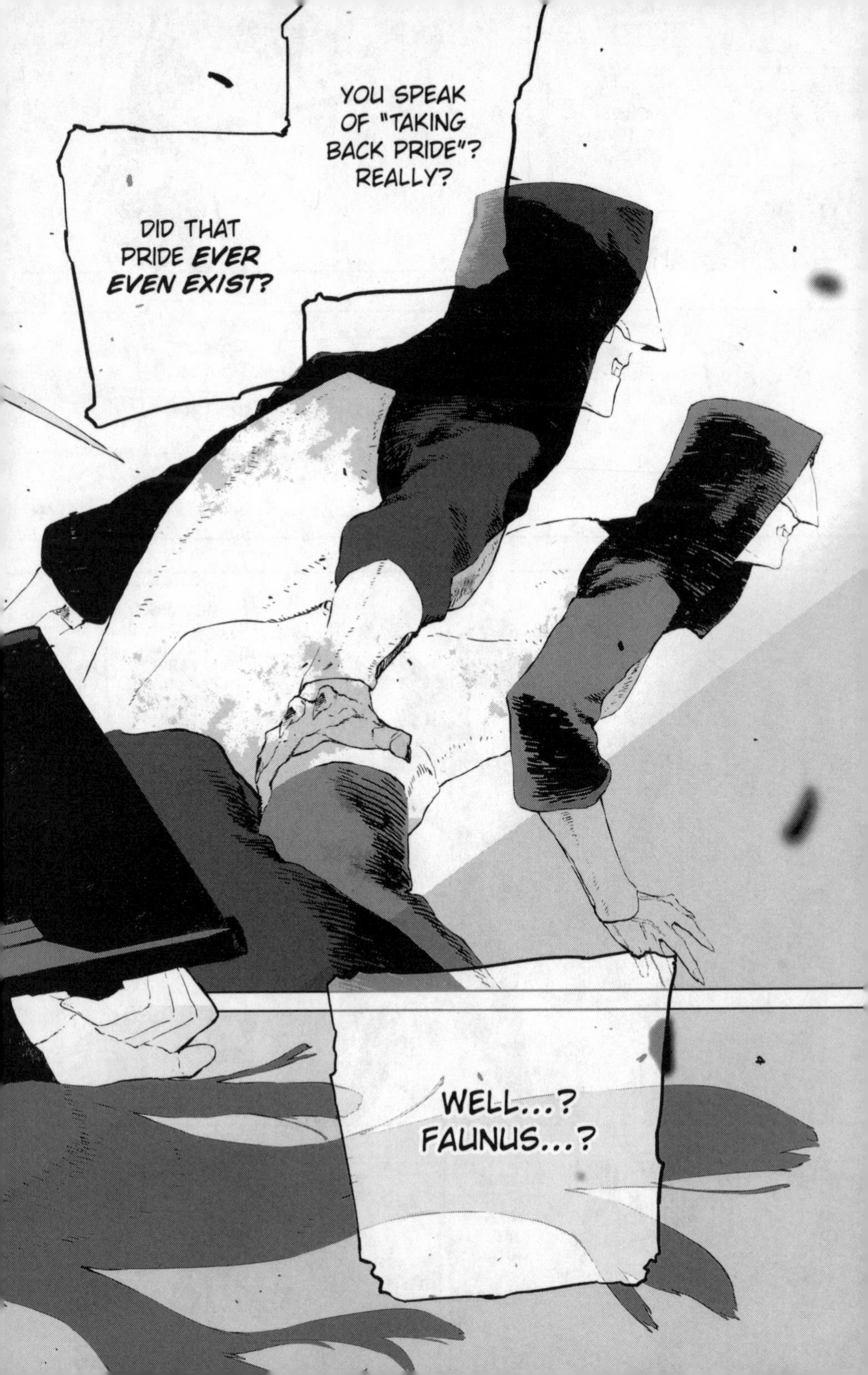
YOU SPEAK OF "TAKING BACK PRIDE"? REALLY?
DID THAT PRIDE *EVER EVEN EXIST?*
WELL...? FAUNUS...?

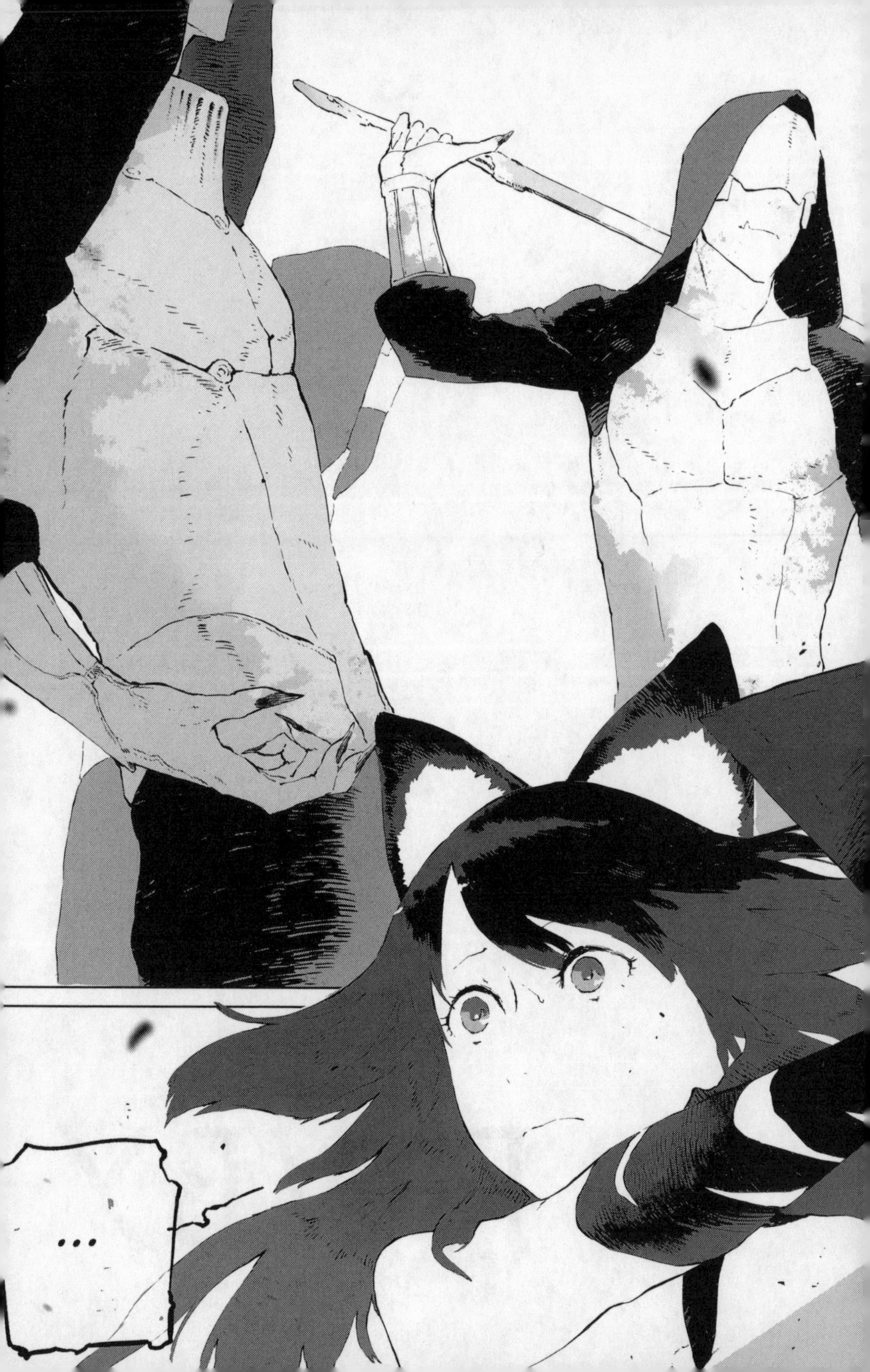
...

RWBY

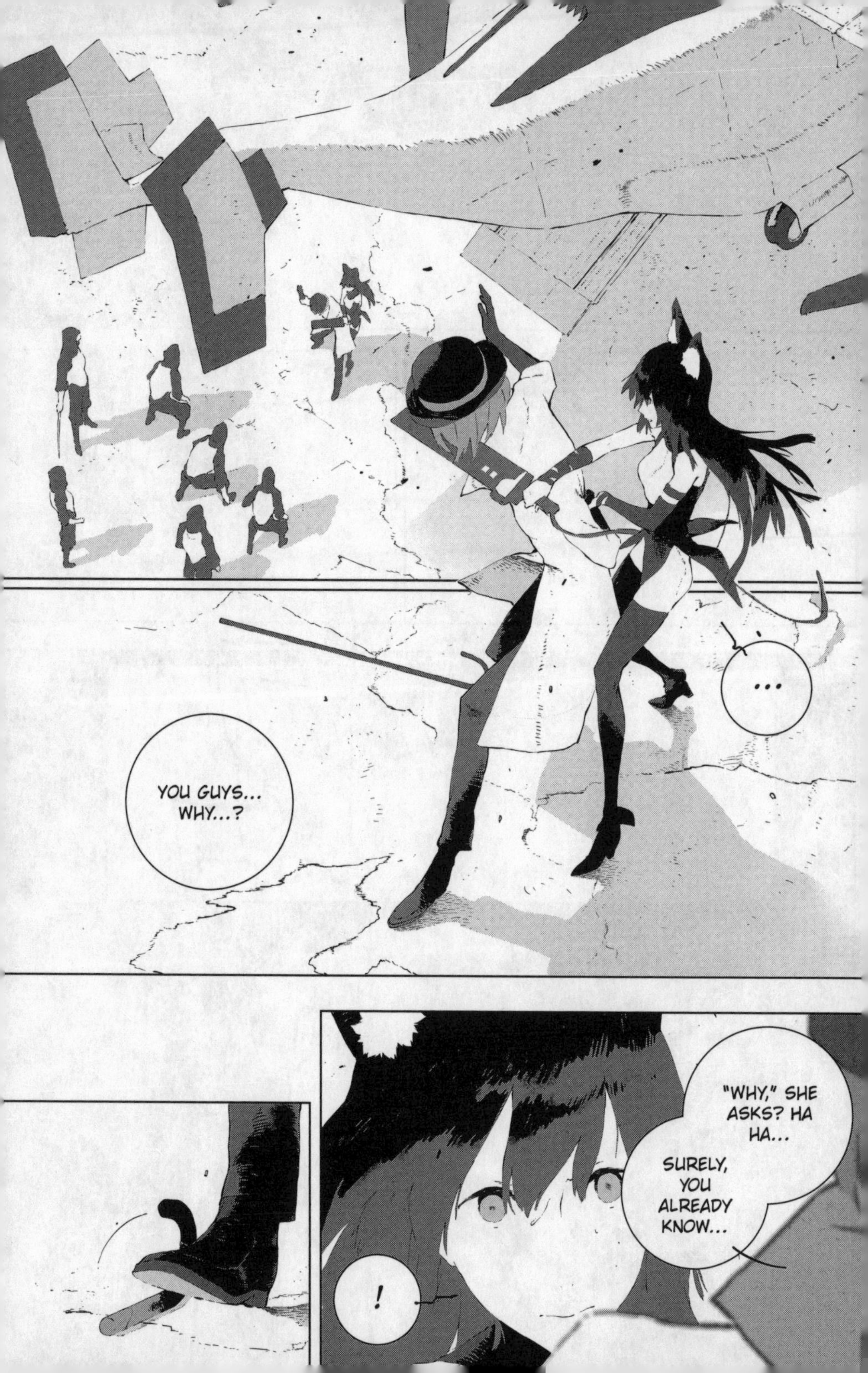
...
YOU GUYS... WHY...?
"WHY," SHE ASKS? HA HA...
SURELY, YOU ALREADY KNOW...
!

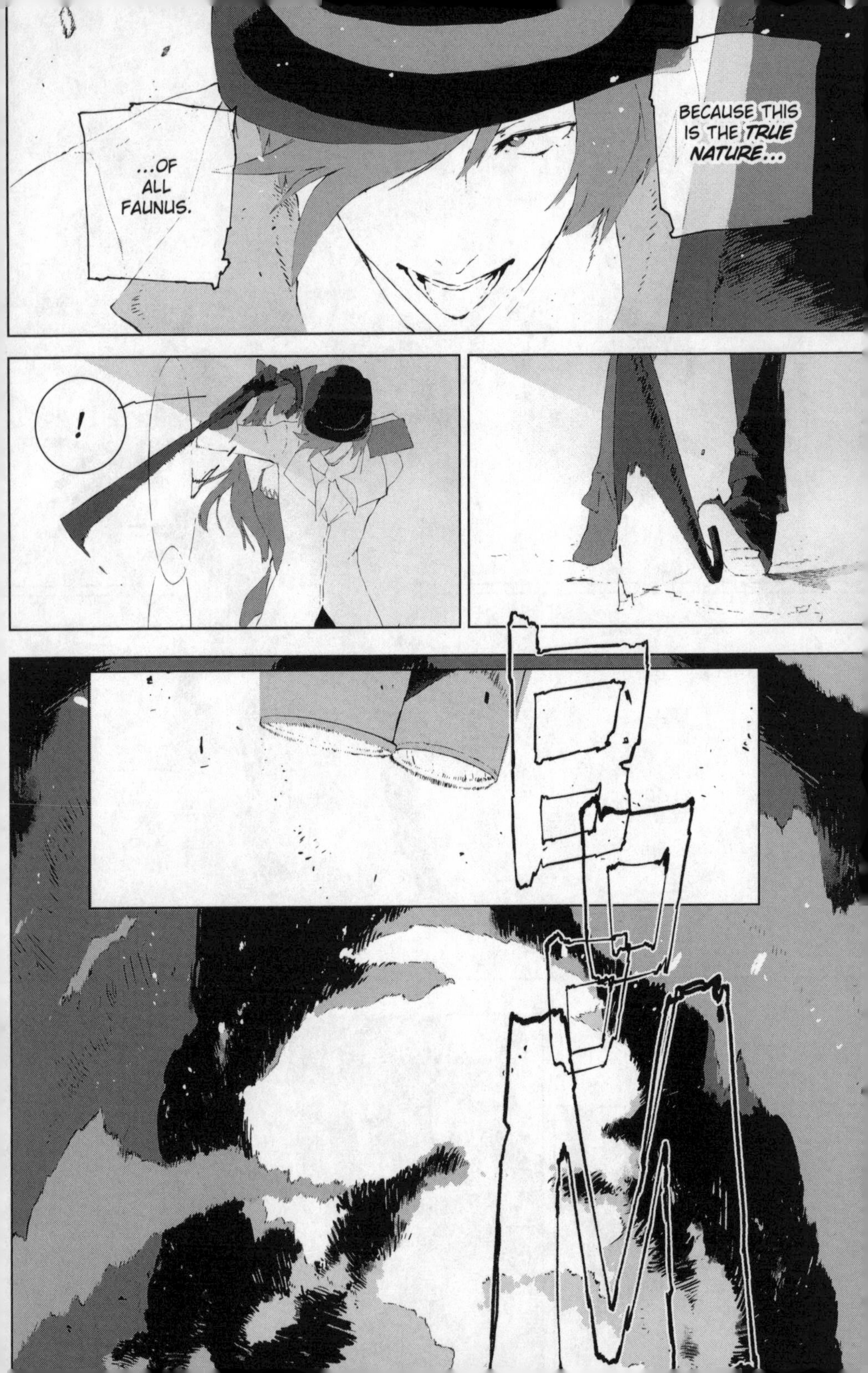
BECAUSE THIS IS THE *TRUE NATURE*...
...OF ALL FAUNUS.
!
BOOM

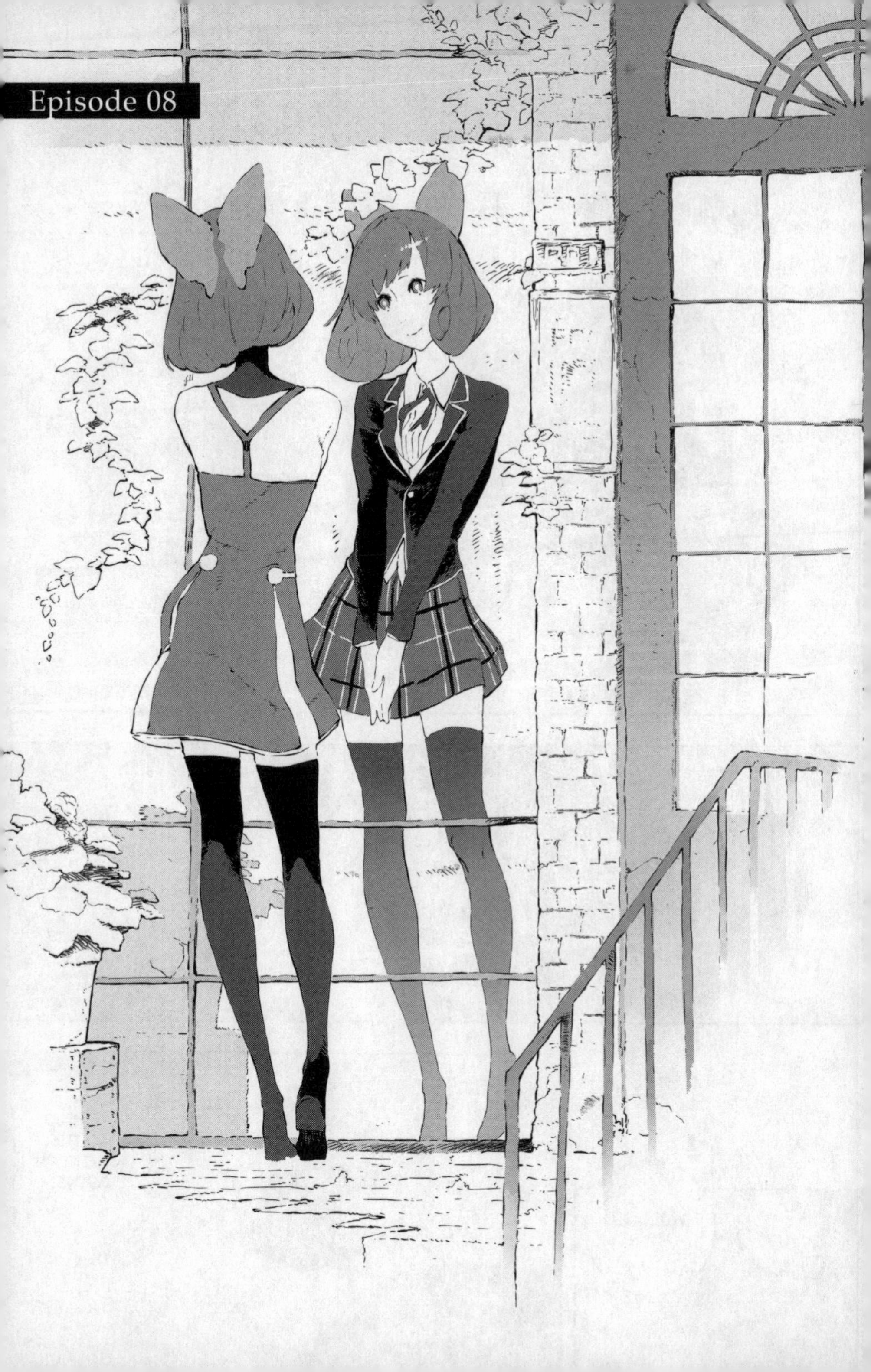
Episode 08

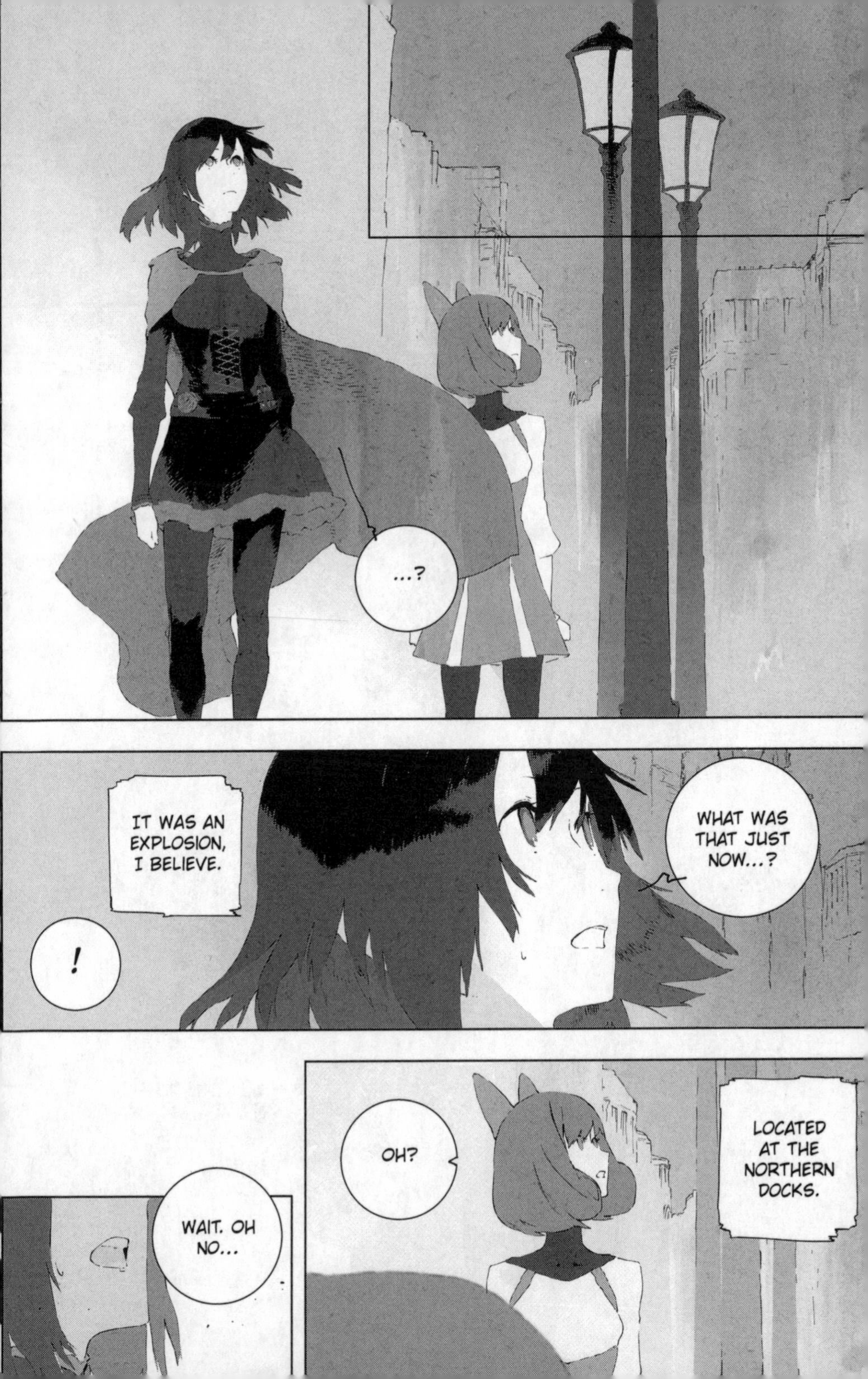
...?
WHAT WAS THAT JUST NOW...?
IT WAS AN EXPLOSION, I BELIEVE.
!
LOCATED AT THE NORTHERN DOCKS.
OH?
WAIT. OH NO...

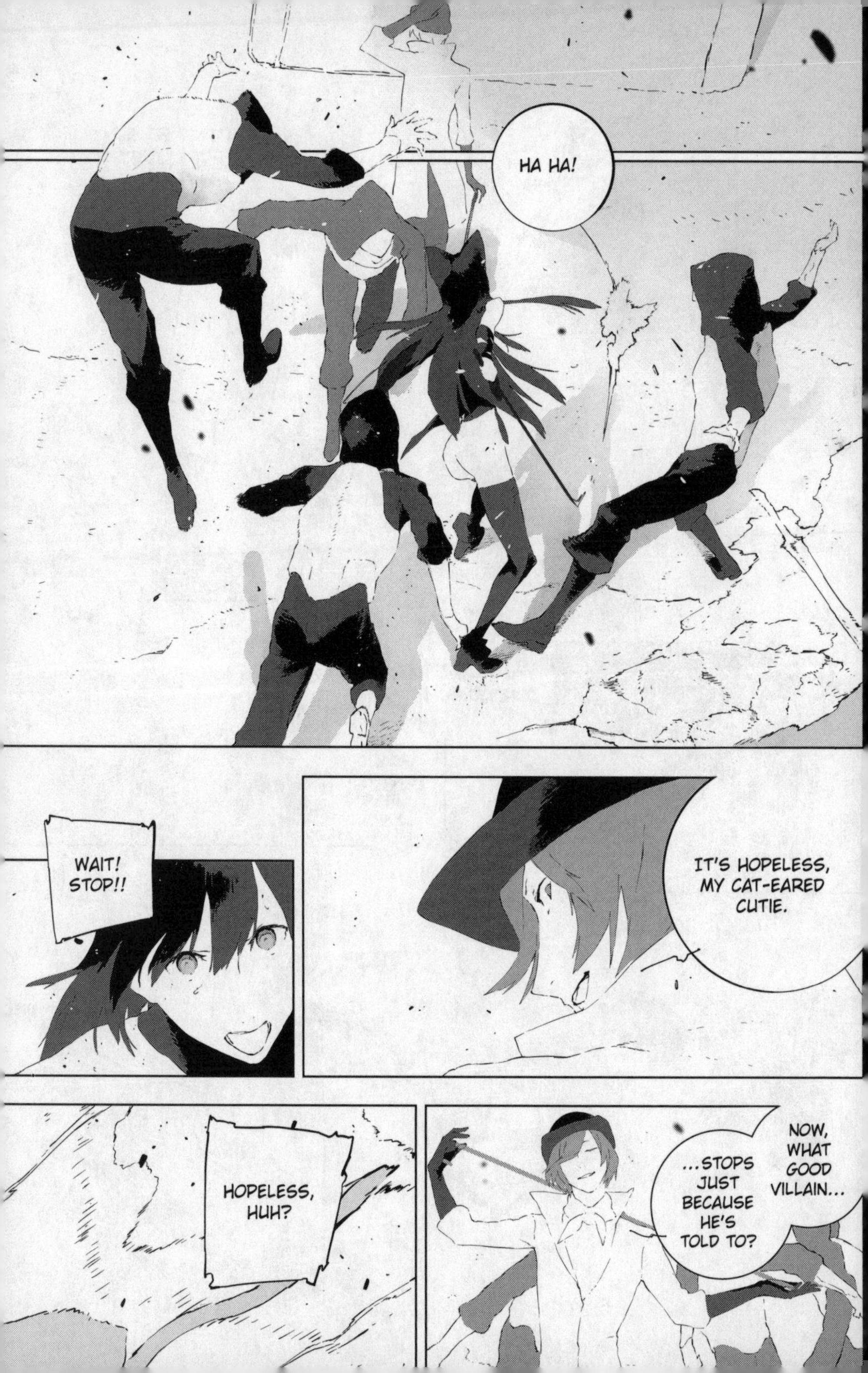
HA HA!
IT'S HOPELESS, MY CAT-EARED CUTIE.
WAIT! STOP!!
NOW, WHAT GOOD VILLAIN...
...STOPS JUST BECAUSE HE'S TOLD TO?
HOPELESS, HUH?

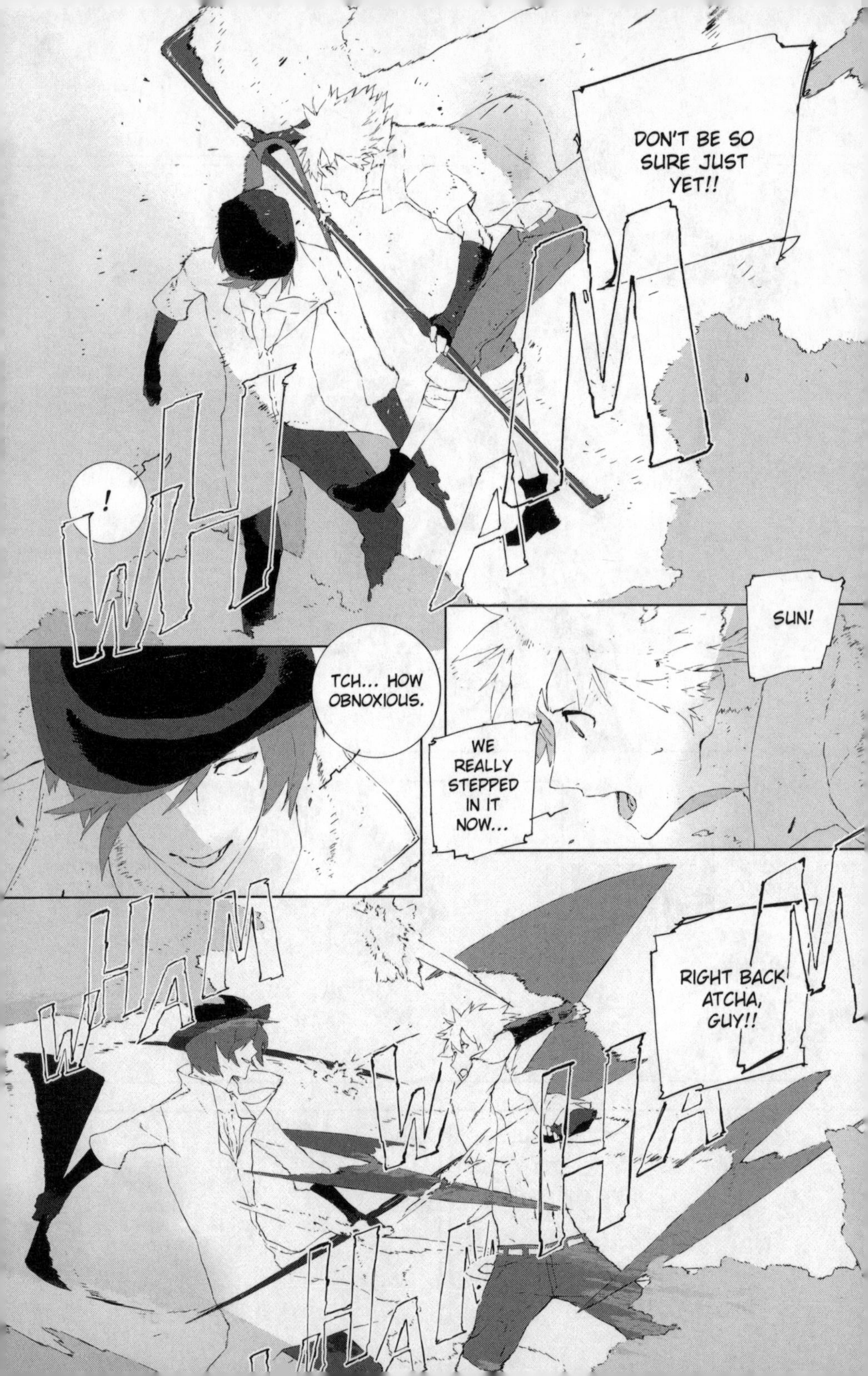
DON'T BE SO SURE JUST YET!!
WHAM
!
SUN!
WE REALLY STEPPED IN IT NOW...
TCH... HOW OBNOXIOUS.
RIGHT BACK ATCHA, GUY!!
WHAM
WHAM
WHAM

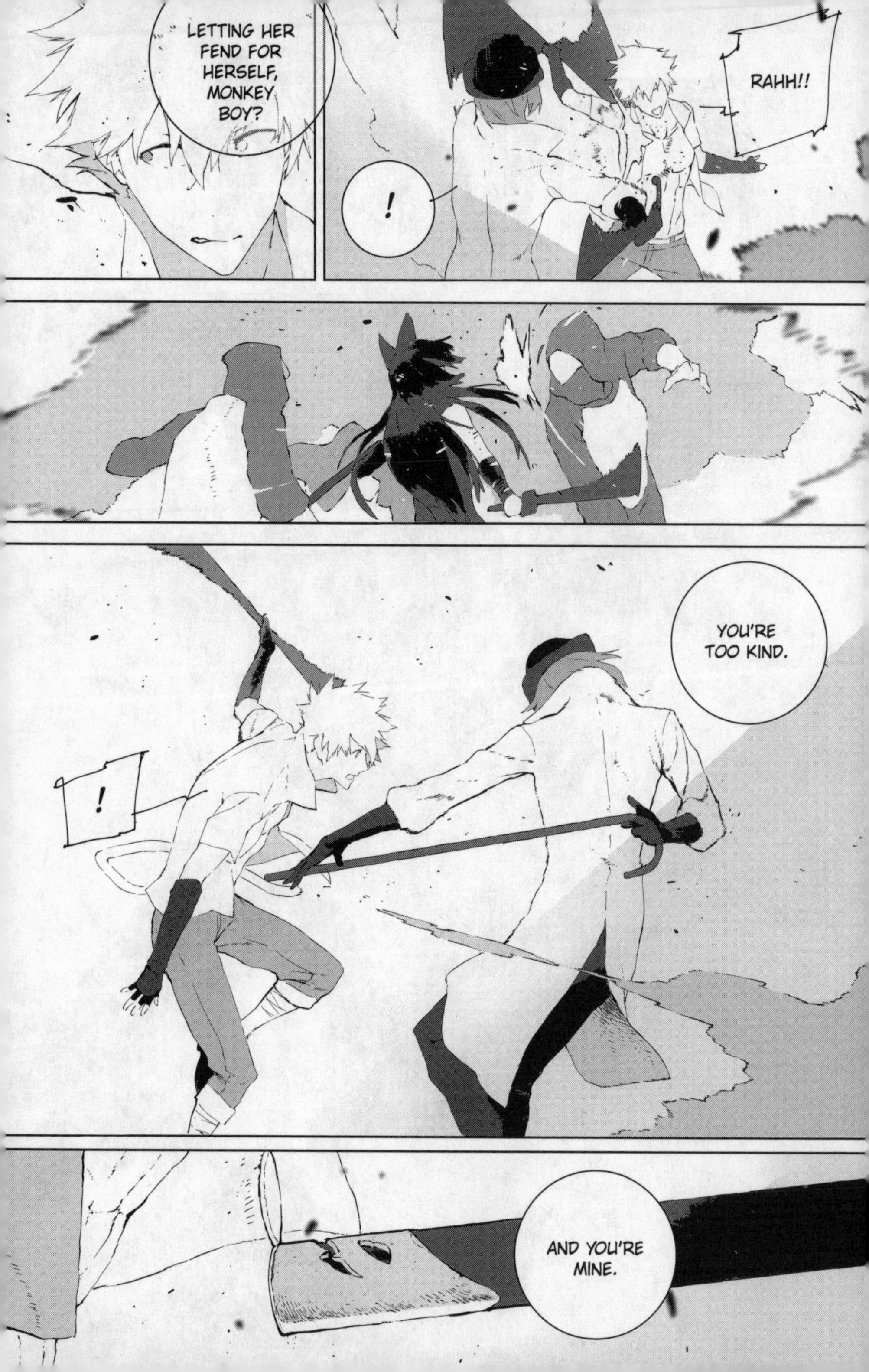
RAHH!!
!
LETTING HER FEND FOR HERSELF, MONKEY BOY?
YOU'RE TOO KIND.
!
AND YOU'RE MINE.

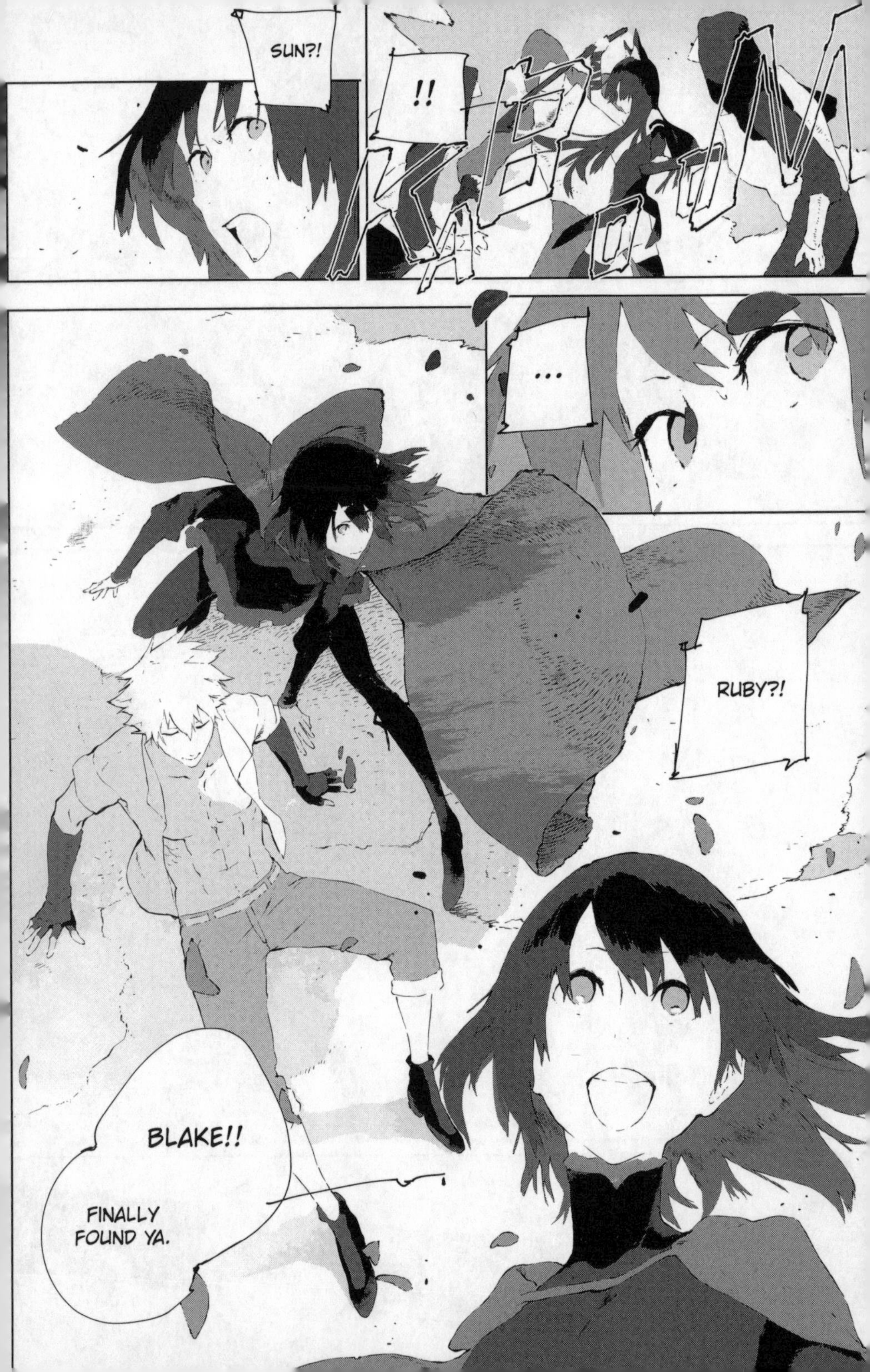
!!
KABOOM
SUN?!
...
RUBY?!
BLAKE!!
FINALLY FOUND YA.

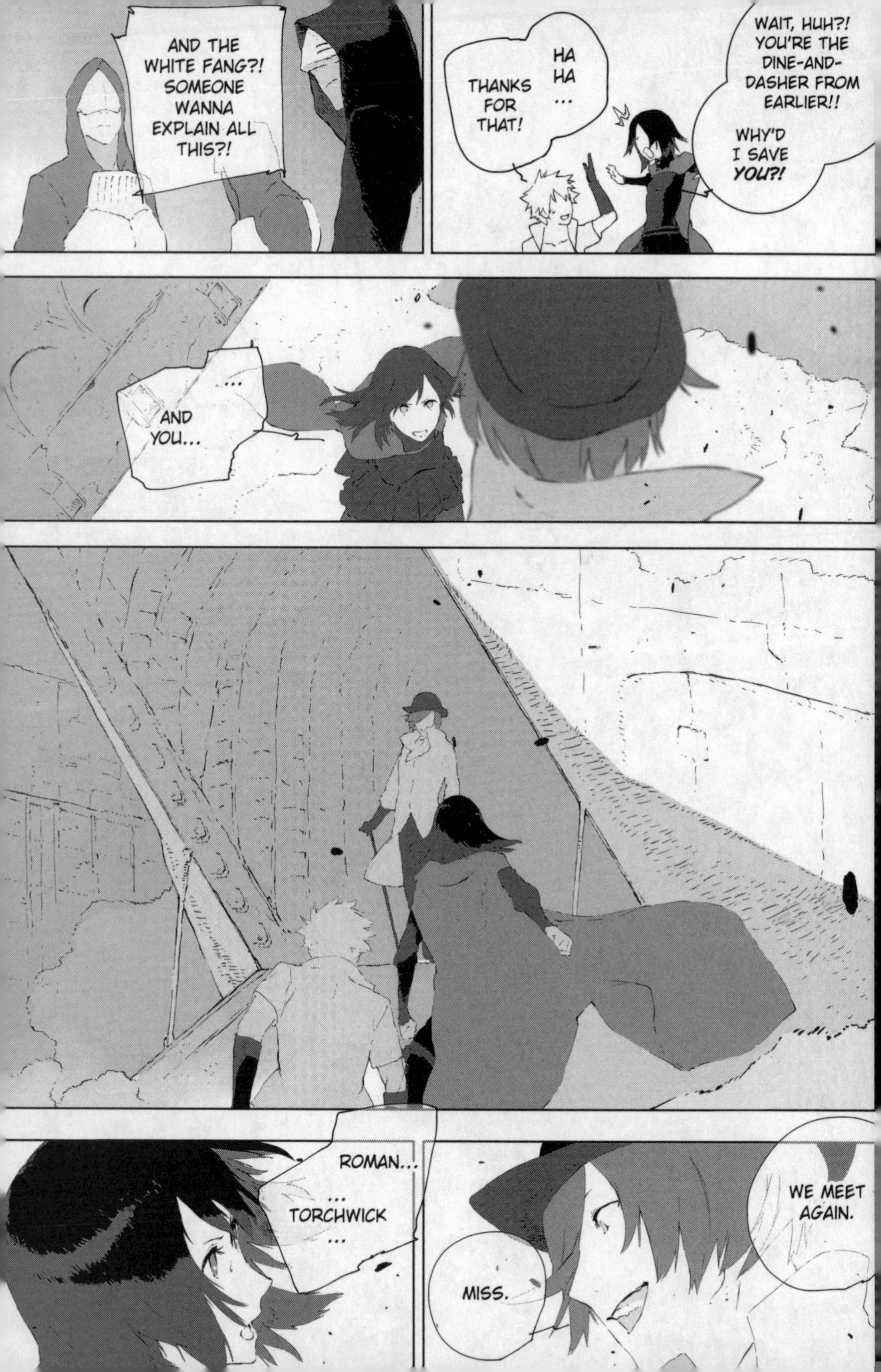
WAIT, HUH?! YOU'RE THE DINE-AND-DASHER FROM EARLIER!!
WHY'D I SAVE *YOU?!*
HA HA ...
THANKS FOR THAT!
AND THE WHITE FANG?! SOMEONE WANNA EXPLAIN ALL THIS?!
... AND YOU...
WE MEET AGAIN.
MISS.
ROMAN... ... TORCHWICK ...

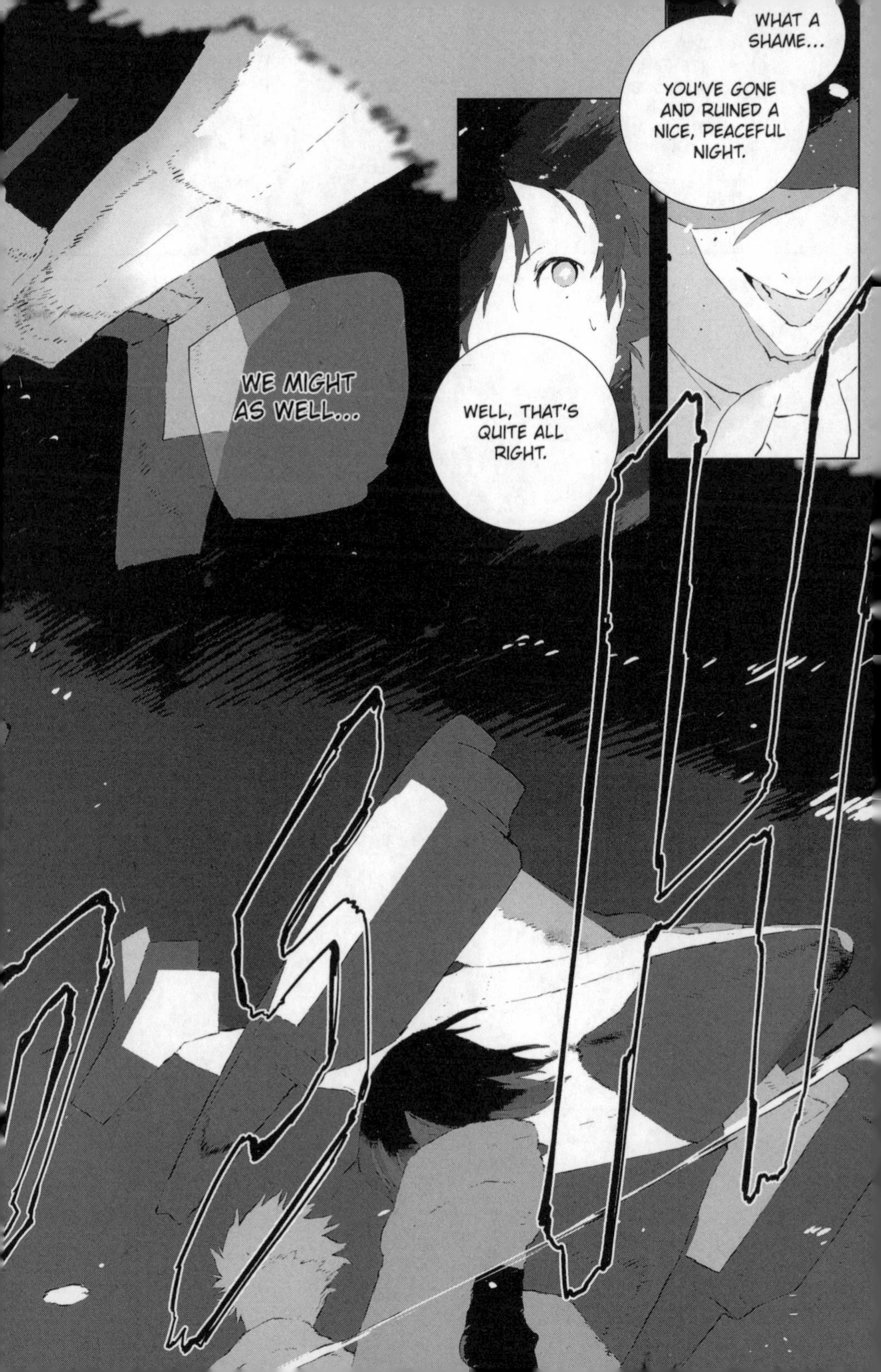
WHAT A SHAME...
YOU'VE GONE AND RUINED A NICE, PEACEFUL NIGHT.
WELL, THAT'S QUITE ALL RIGHT.
WE MIGHT AS WELL...

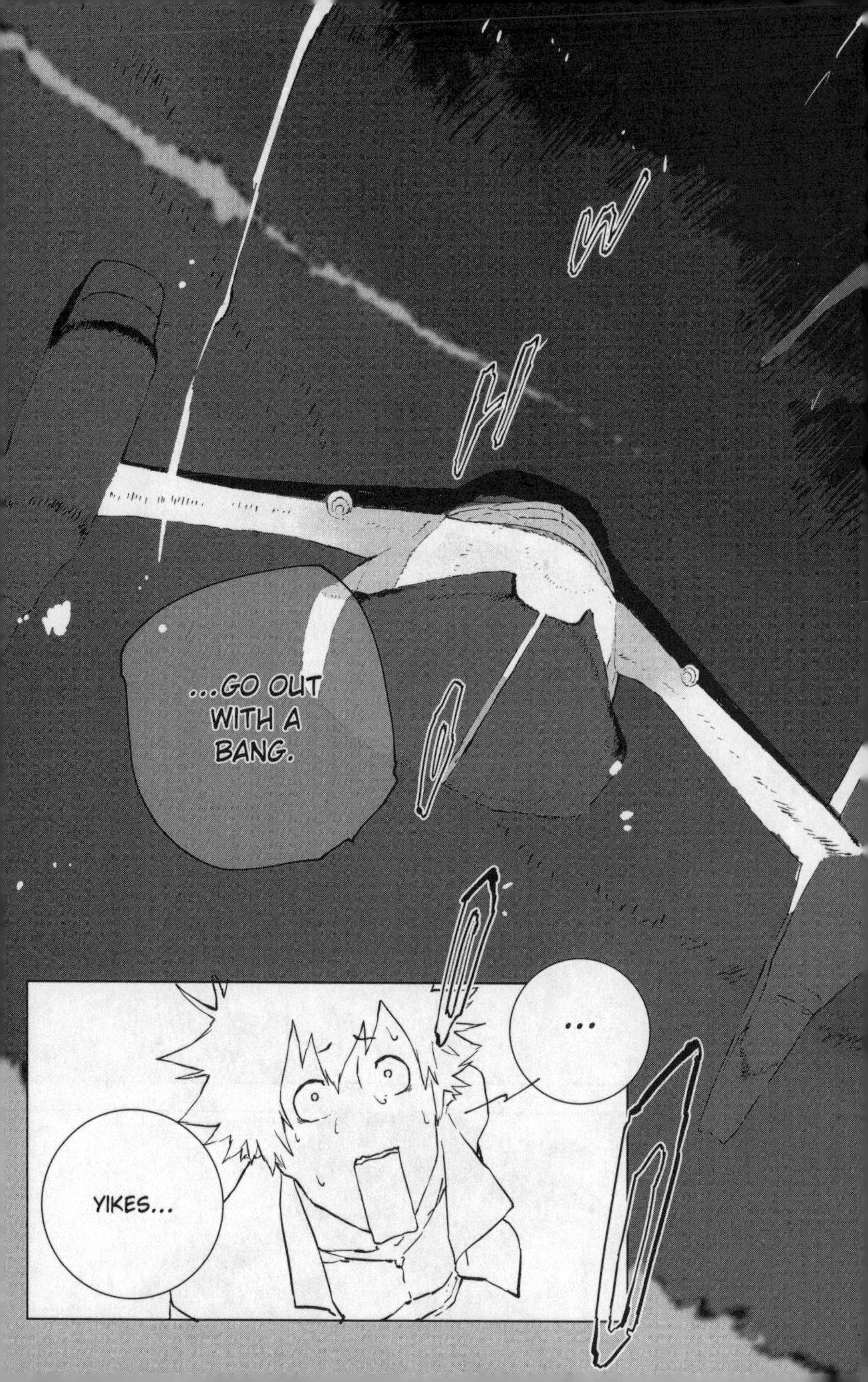
...GO OUT WITH A BANG.
...
YIKES...

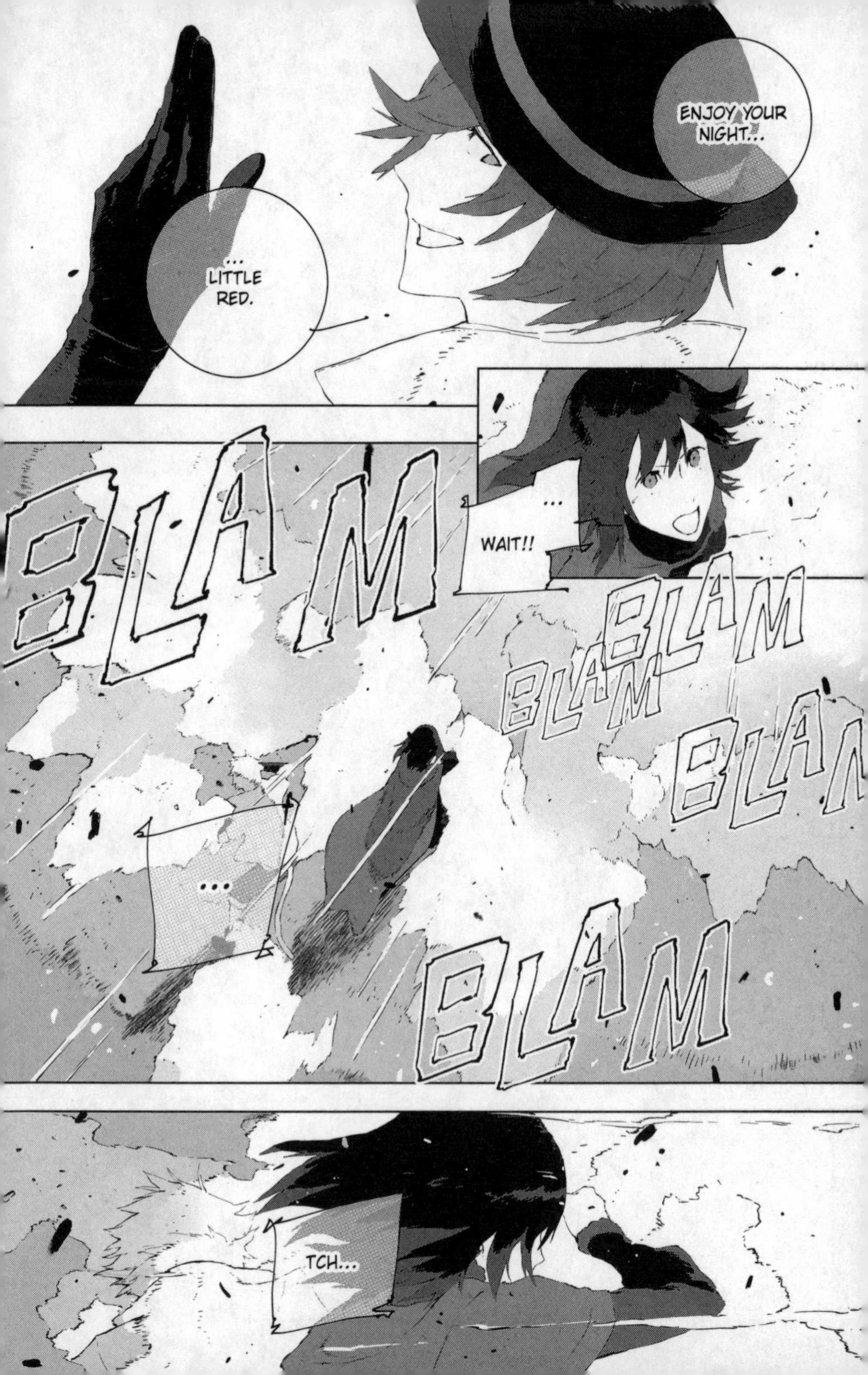
ENJOY YOUR NIGHT...
...LITTLE RED.
...
WAIT!!
BLAM
BLAM
BLAM
BLAM
BLAM
...
BLAM
TCH...

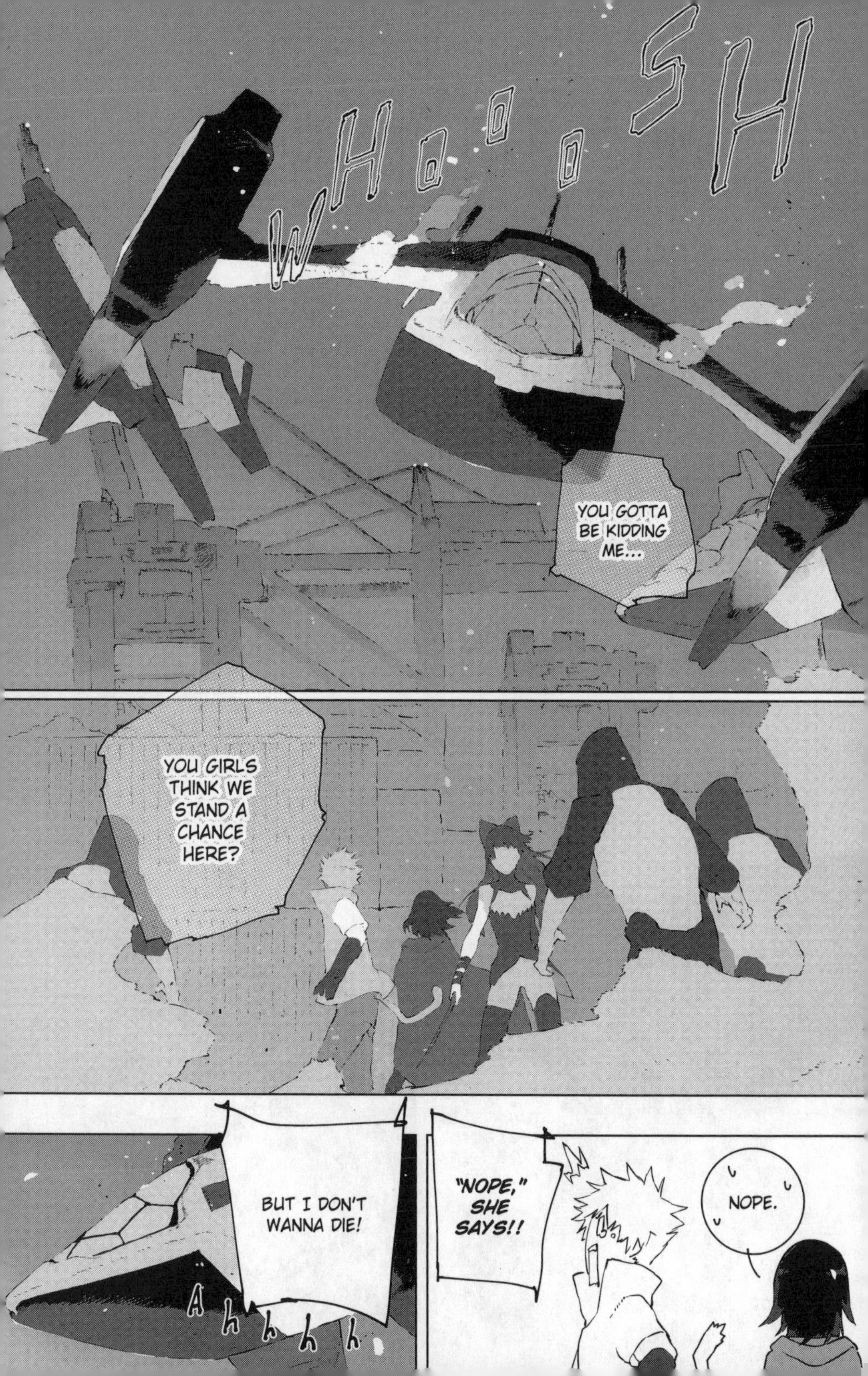
WHoooSH
YOU GOTTA BE KIDDING ME...
YOU GIRLS THINK WE STAND A CHANCE HERE?
NOPE.
"NOPE," SHE SAYS!!
BUT I DON'T WANNA DIE!
Ahhhhh

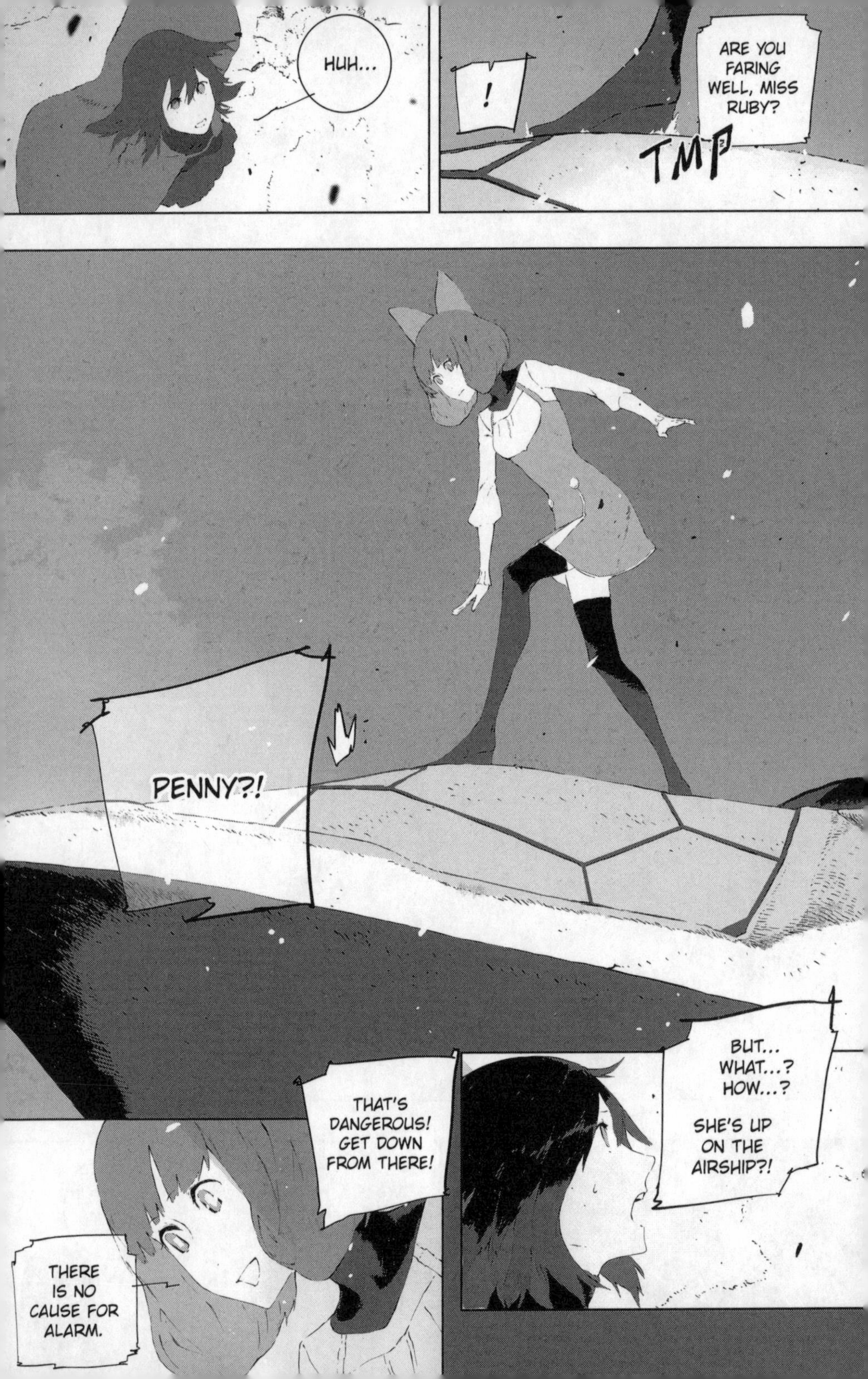
ARE YOU FARING WELL, MISS RUBY?
!
TMP
HUH...
PENNY?!
BUT... WHAT...? HOW...?
SHE'S UP ON THE AIRSHIP?!
THAT'S DANGEROUS! GET DOWN FROM THERE!
THERE IS NO CAUSE FOR ALARM.

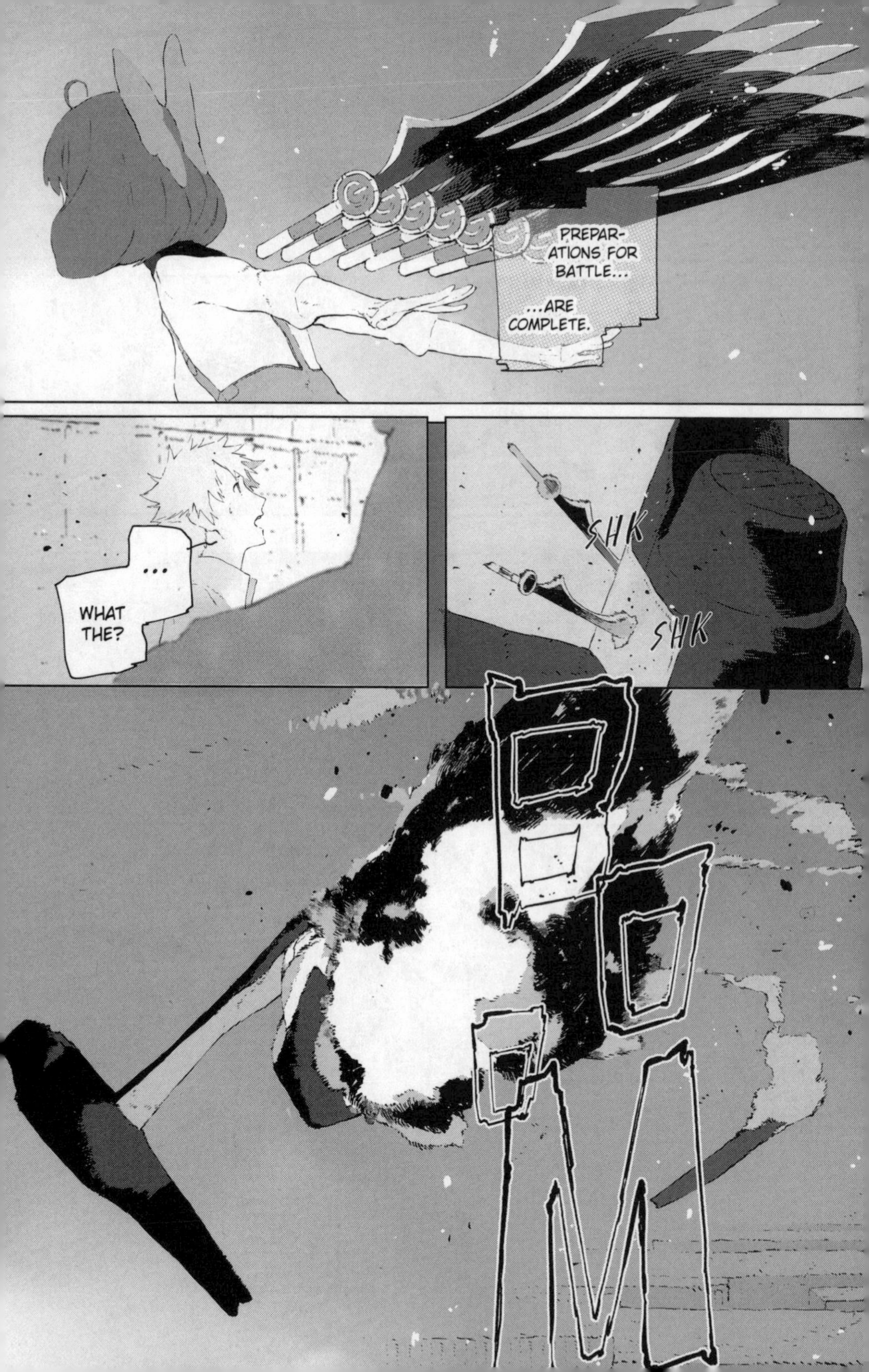
PREPARATIONS FOR BATTLE...
...ARE COMPLETE.
SHK
SHK
...
WHAT THE?
BOOM

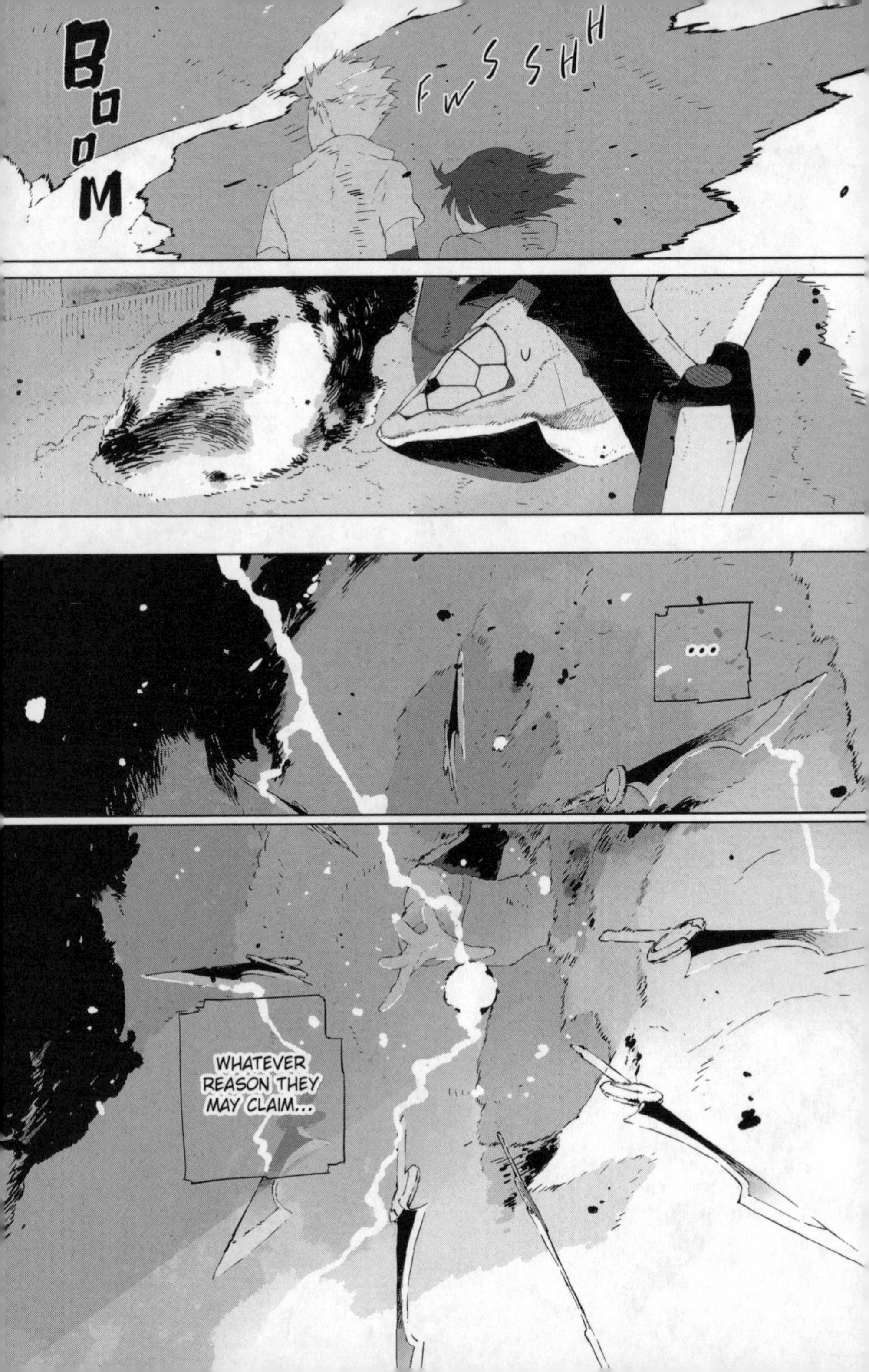
BOOM
FWSSHH
...
WHATEVER REASON THEY MAY CLAIM...

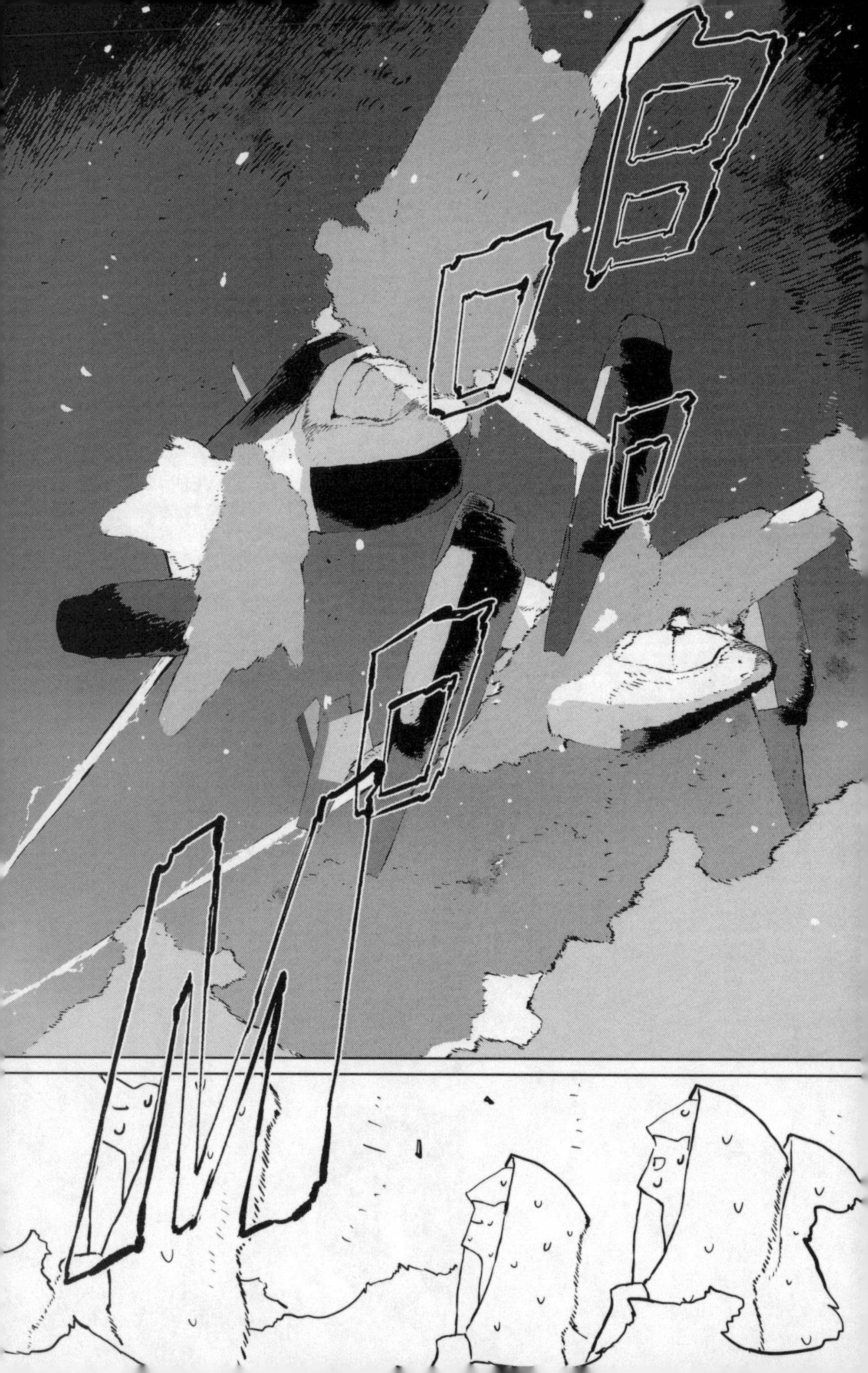
BOOOM

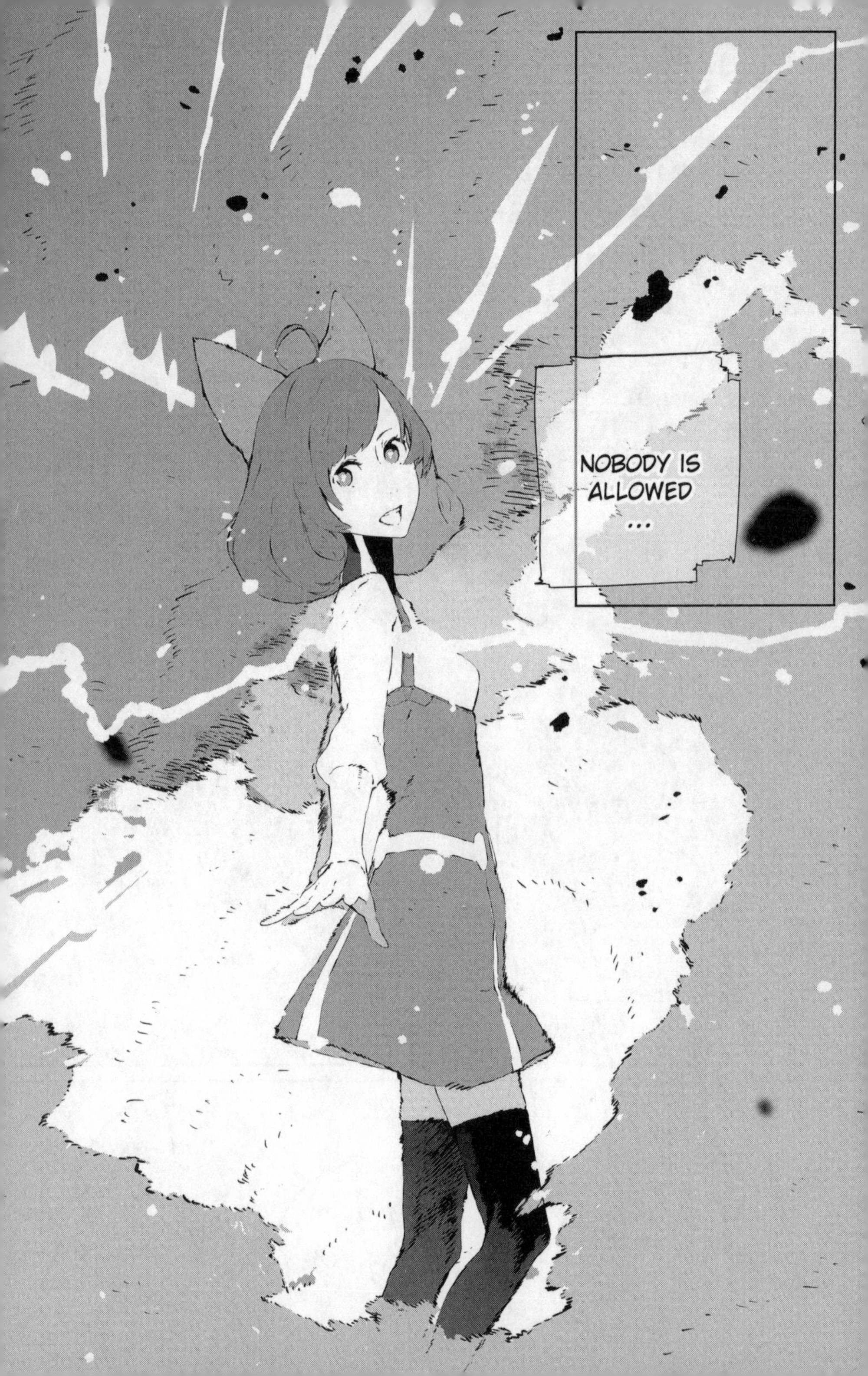
NOBODY IS ALLOWED ...

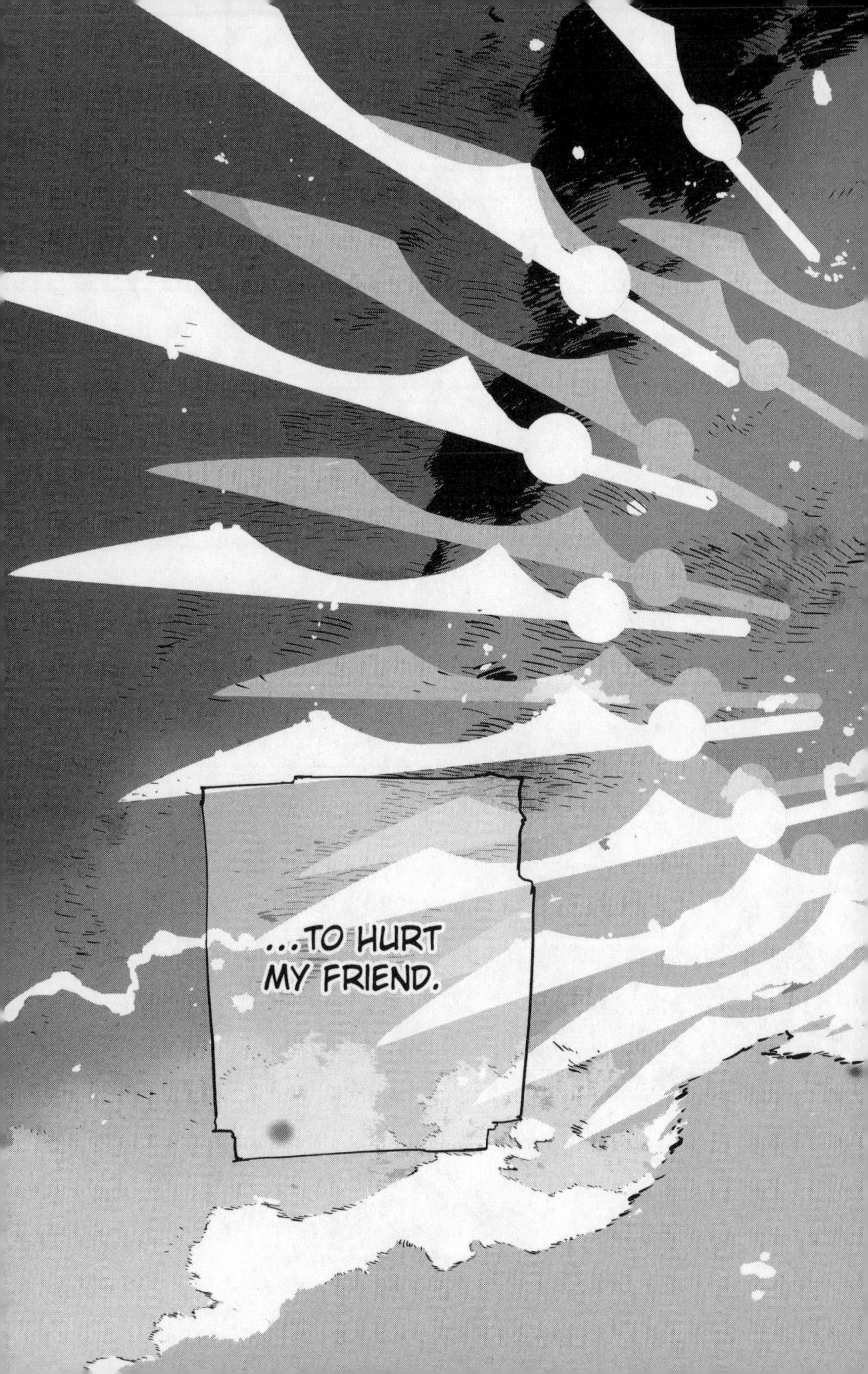
...TO HURT MY FRIEND.

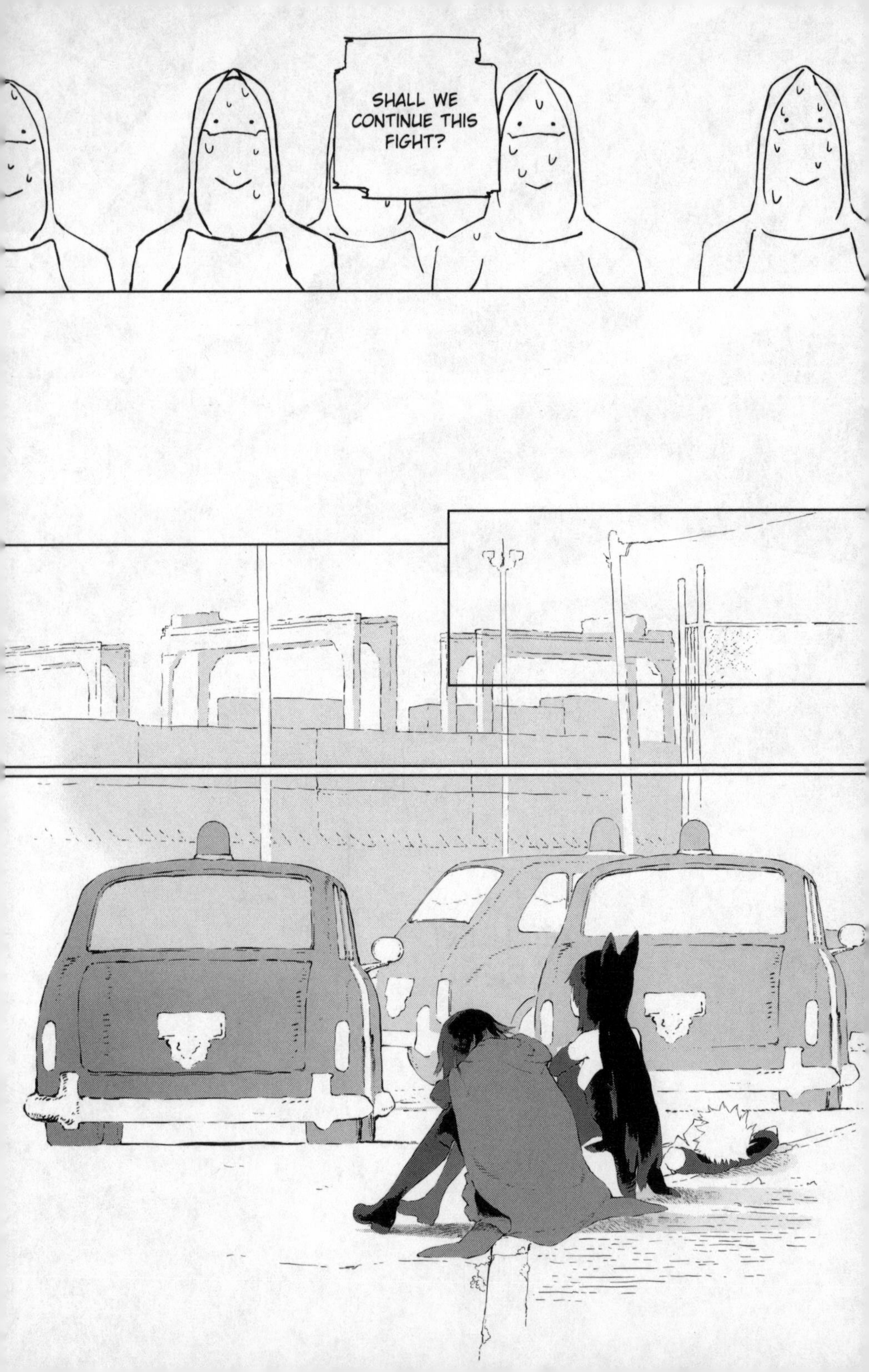
SHALL WE CONTINUE THIS FIGHT?

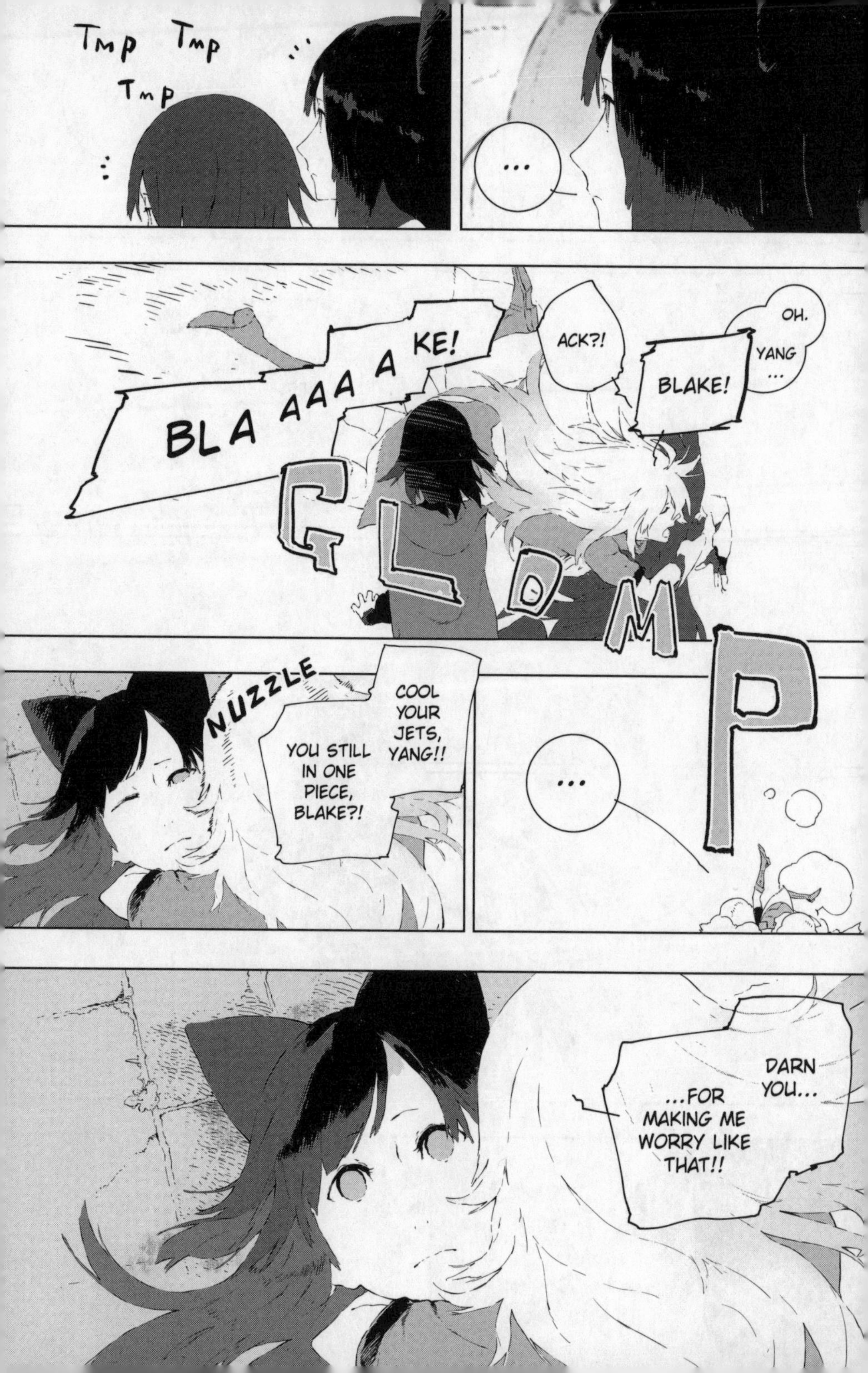
...
TMP TMP TMP
OH. YANG ...
BLAKE!
ACK?!
BLAAAAKE!
GLOMP
...
COOL YOUR JETS, YANG!!
YOU STILL IN ONE PIECE, BLAKE?!
NUZZLE
DARN YOU...
...FOR MAKING ME WORRY LIKE THAT!!

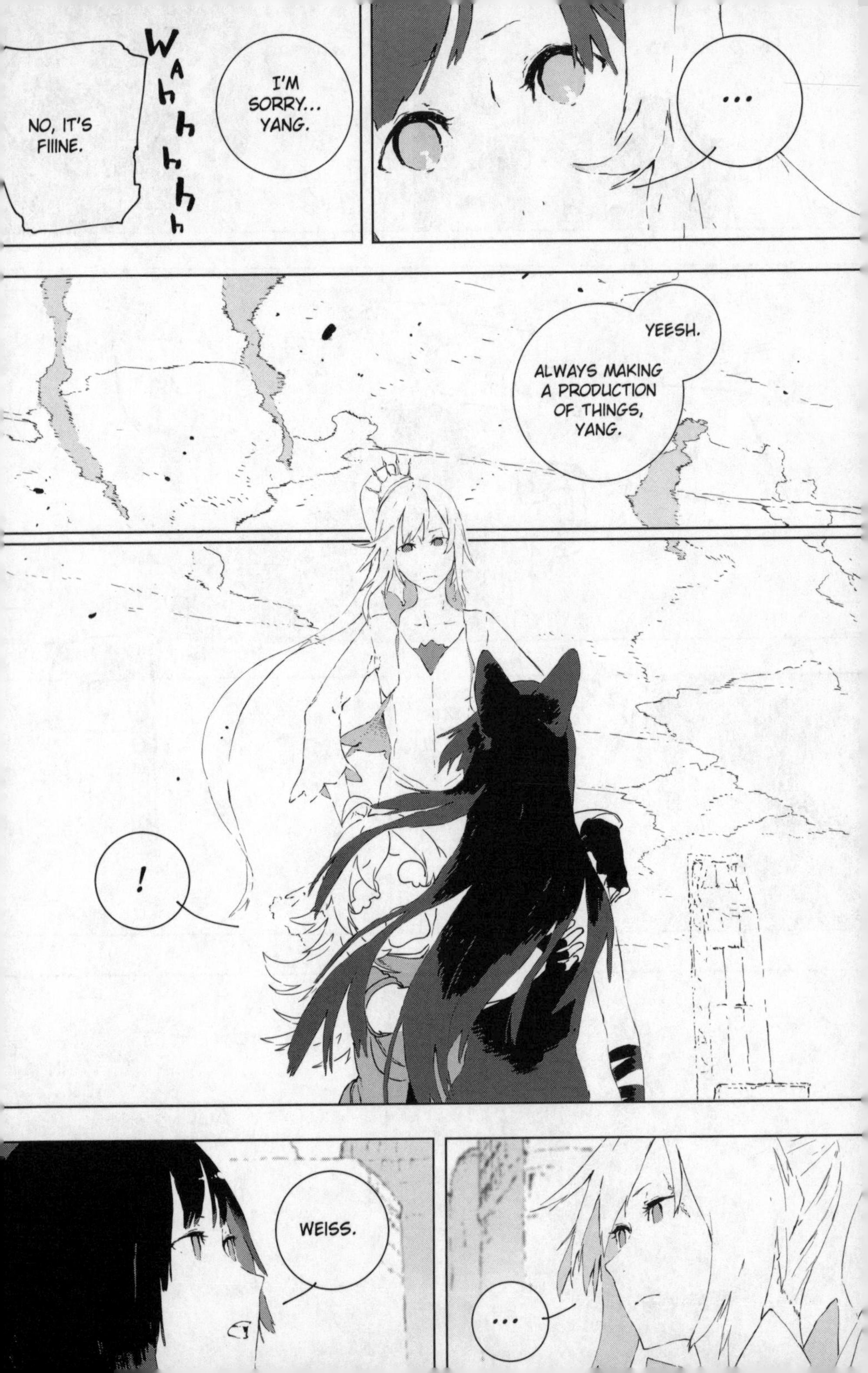
...
I'M SORRY... YANG.
WAhhhhh
NO, IT'S FIIINE.
YEESH.
ALWAYS MAKING A PRODUCTION OF THINGS, YANG.
!
...
WEISS.

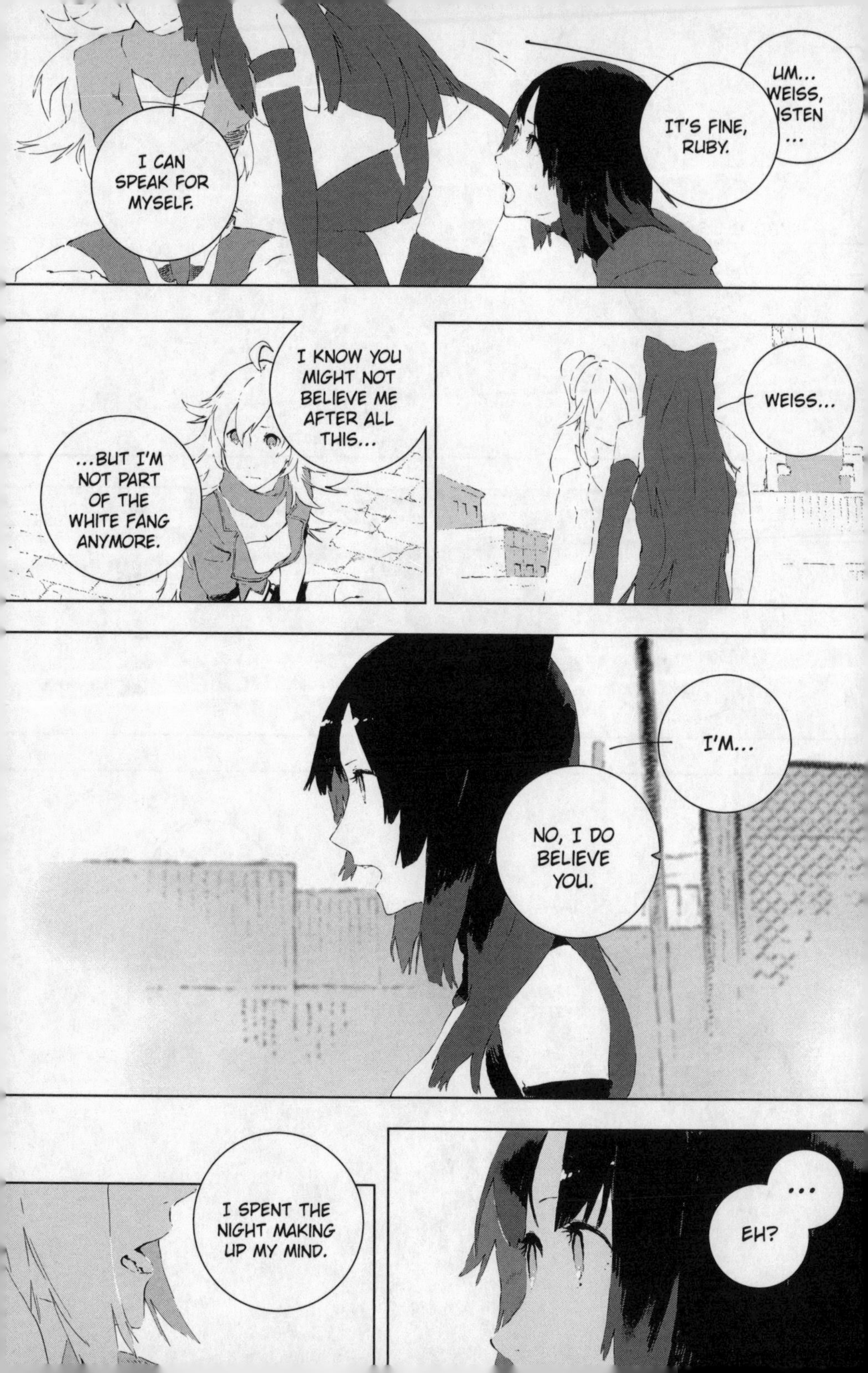
UM... WEISS, ISTEN...
IT'S FINE, RUBY.
I CAN SPEAK FOR MYSELF.
WEISS...
I KNOW YOU MIGHT NOT BELIEVE ME AFTER ALL THIS...
...BUT I'M NOT PART OF THE WHITE FANG ANYMORE.
I'M...
NO, I DO BELIEVE YOU.
...
EH?
I SPENT THE NIGHT MAKING UP MY MIND.

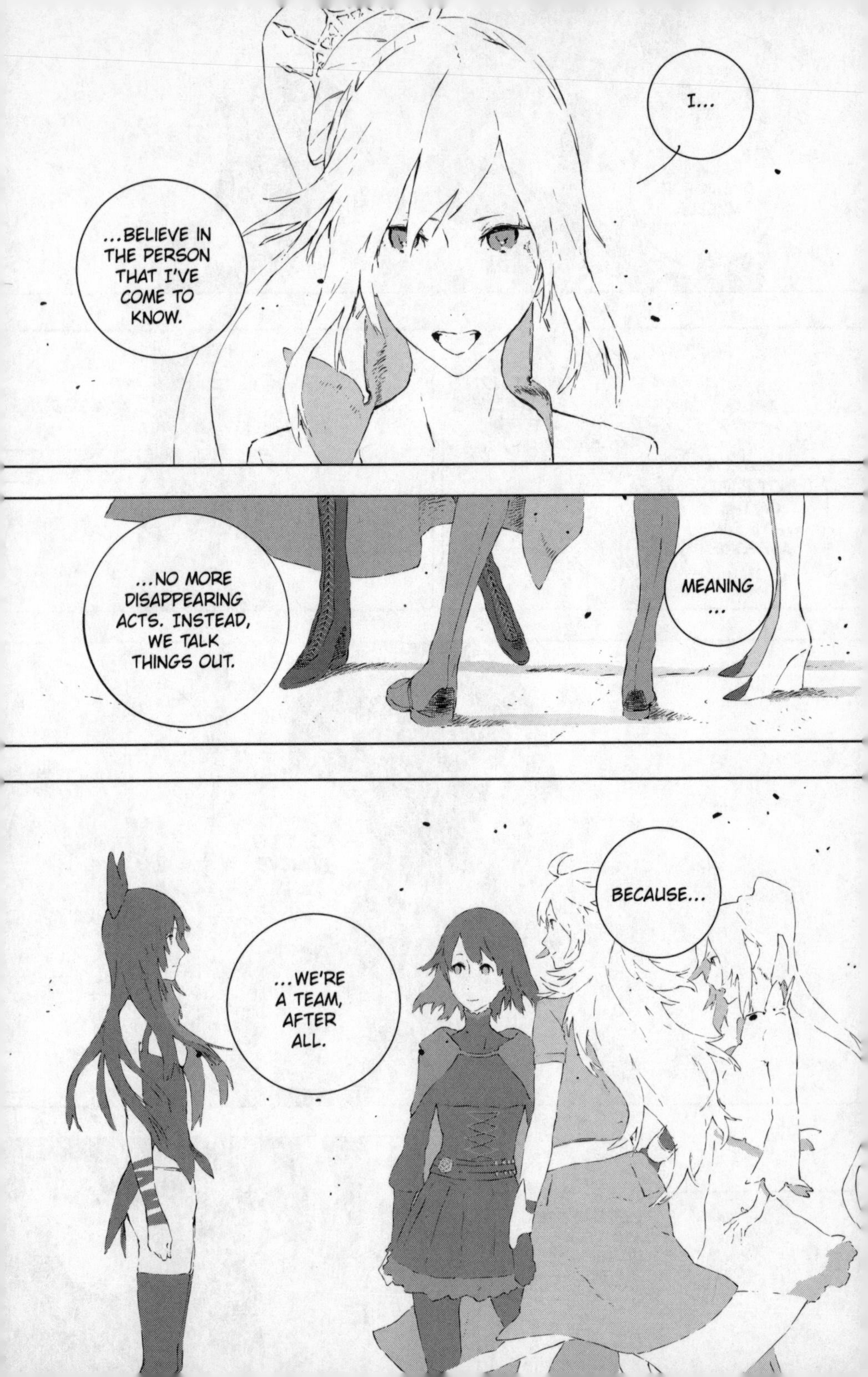
I...
...BELIEVE IN THE PERSON THAT I'VE COME TO KNOW.
MEANING...
...NO MORE DISAPPEARING ACTS. INSTEAD, WE TALK THINGS OUT.
BECAUSE...
...WE'RE A TEAM, AFTER ALL.

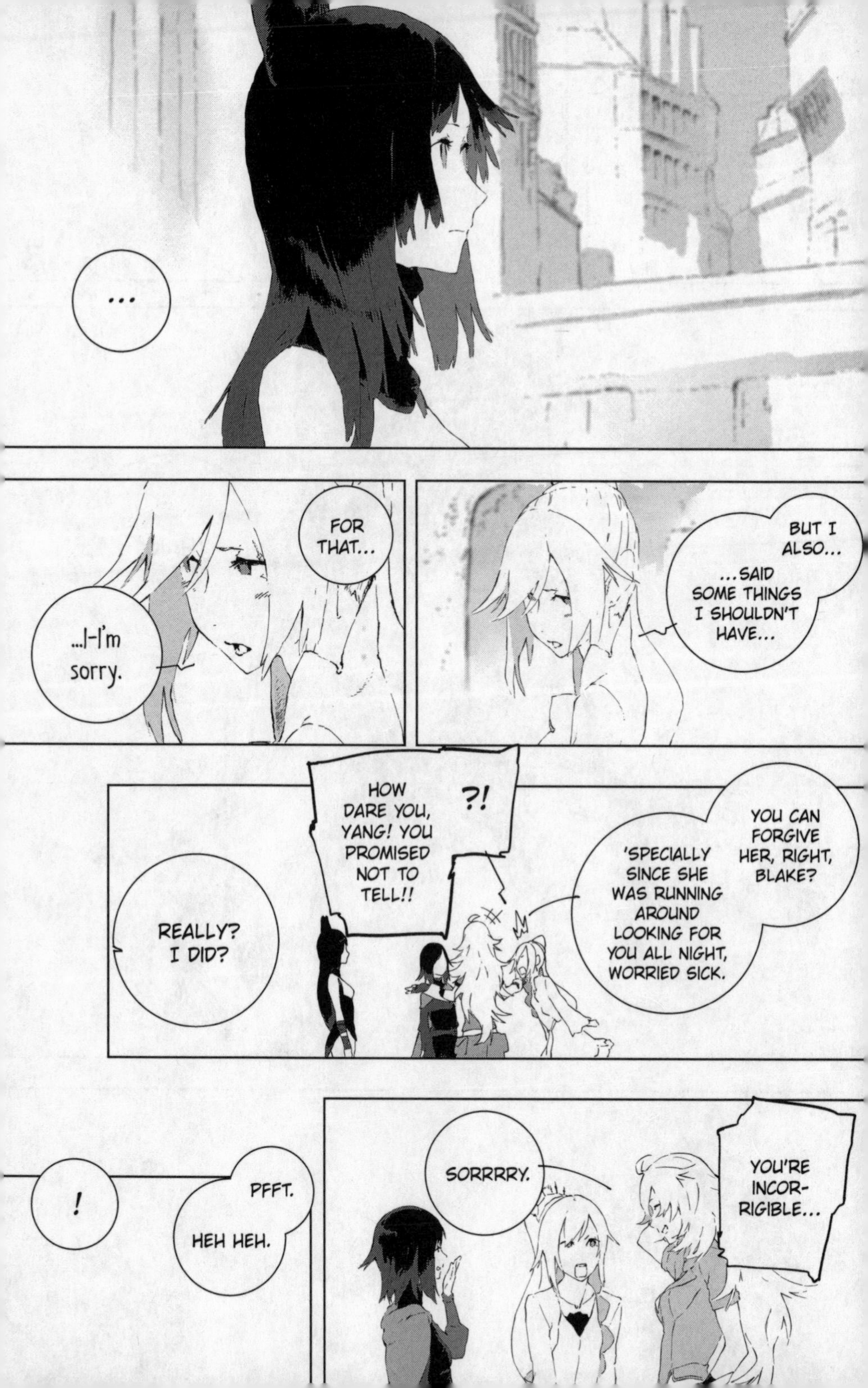
...
BUT I ALSO...
...SAID SOME THINGS I SHOULDN'T HAVE...
FOR THAT...
...I-I'm sorry.
YOU CAN FORGIVE HER, RIGHT, BLAKE?
'SPECIALLY SINCE SHE WAS RUNNING AROUND LOOKING FOR YOU ALL NIGHT, WORRIED SICK.
?!
HOW DARE YOU, YANG! YOU PROMISED NOT TO TELL!!
REALLY? I DID?
YOU'RE INCOR-RIGIBLE...
SORRRRY.
PFFT.
HEH HEH.
!

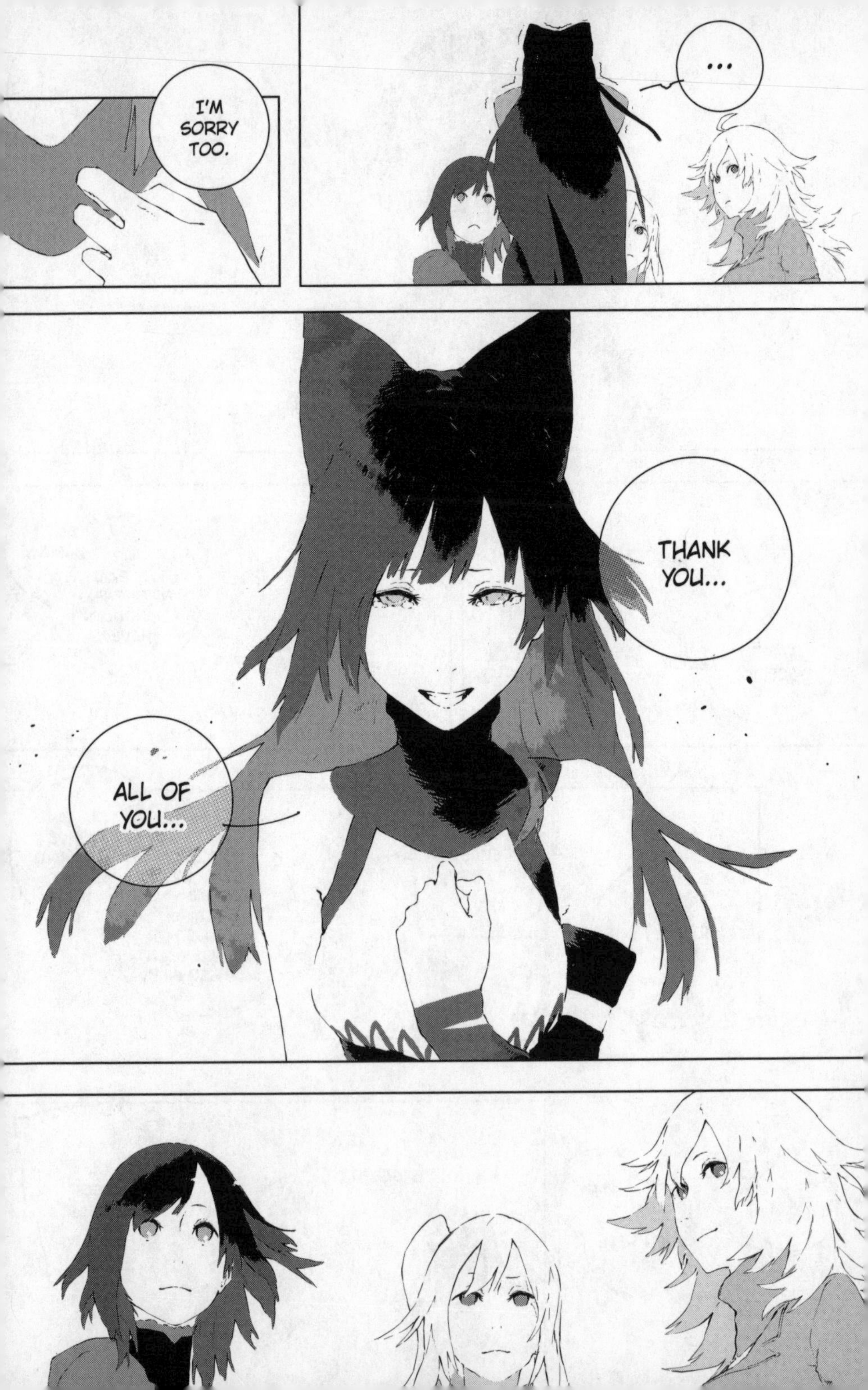
...
I'M SORRY TOO.
THANK YOU...
ALL OF YOU...

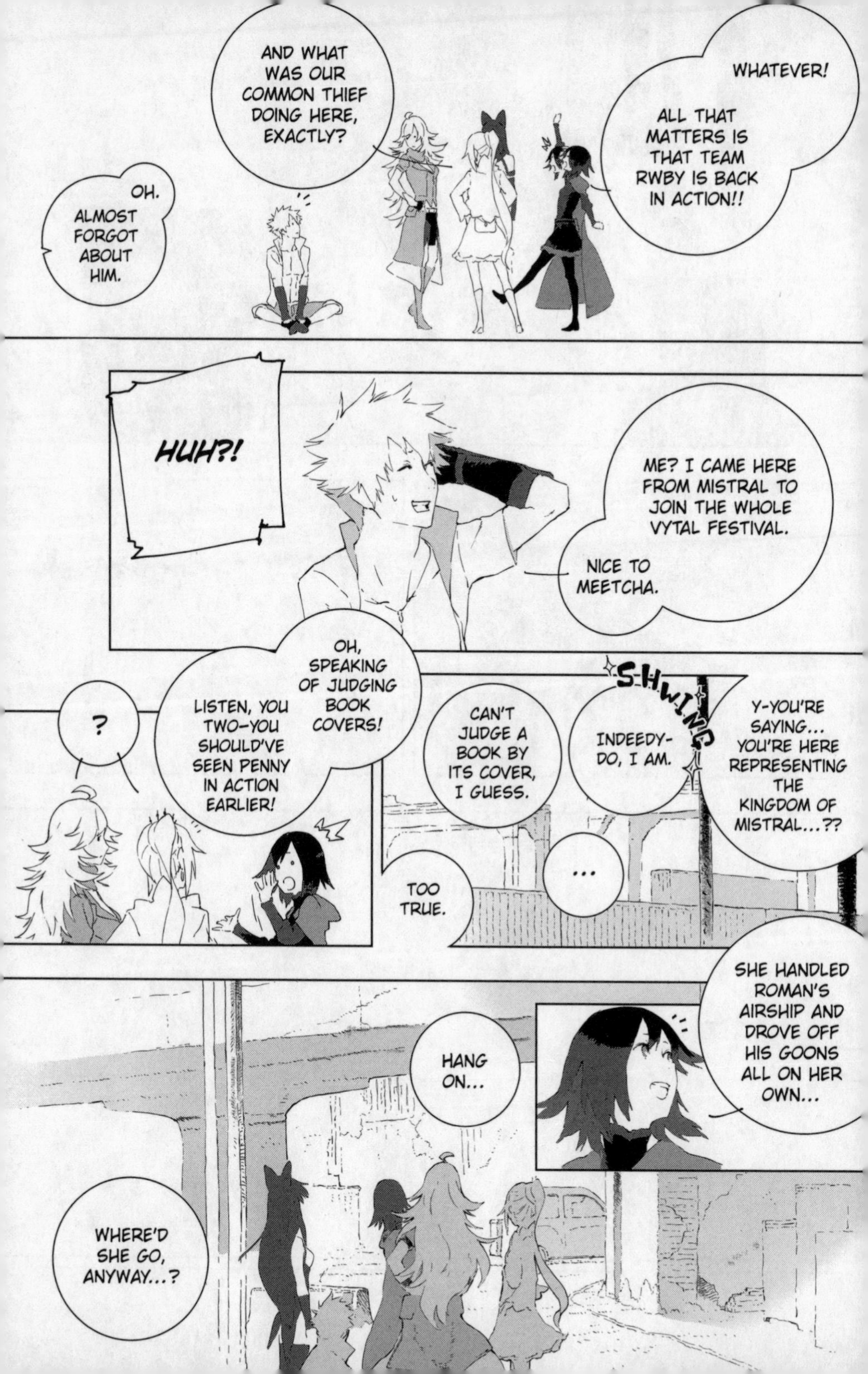
WHATEVER!
ALL THAT MATTERS IS THAT TEAM RWBY IS BACK IN ACTION!!
AND WHAT WAS OUR COMMON THIEF DOING HERE, EXACTLY?
OH. ALMOST FORGOT ABOUT HIM.
ME? I CAME HERE FROM MISTRAL TO JOIN THE WHOLE VYTAL FESTIVAL.
NICE TO MEETCHA.
HUH?!
Y-YOU'RE SAYING... YOU'RE HERE REPRESENTING THE KINGDOM OF MISTRAL...??
SHWING
INDEEDY-DO, I AM.
CAN'T JUDGE A BOOK BY ITS COVER, I GUESS.
...
TOO TRUE.
OH, SPEAKING OF JUDGING BOOK COVERS!
LISTEN, YOU TWO—YOU SHOULD'VE SEEN PENNY IN ACTION EARLIER!
?
SHE HANDLED ROMAN'S AIRSHIP AND DROVE OFF HIS GOONS ALL ON HER OWN...
HANG ON...
WHERE'D SHE GO, ANYWAY...?

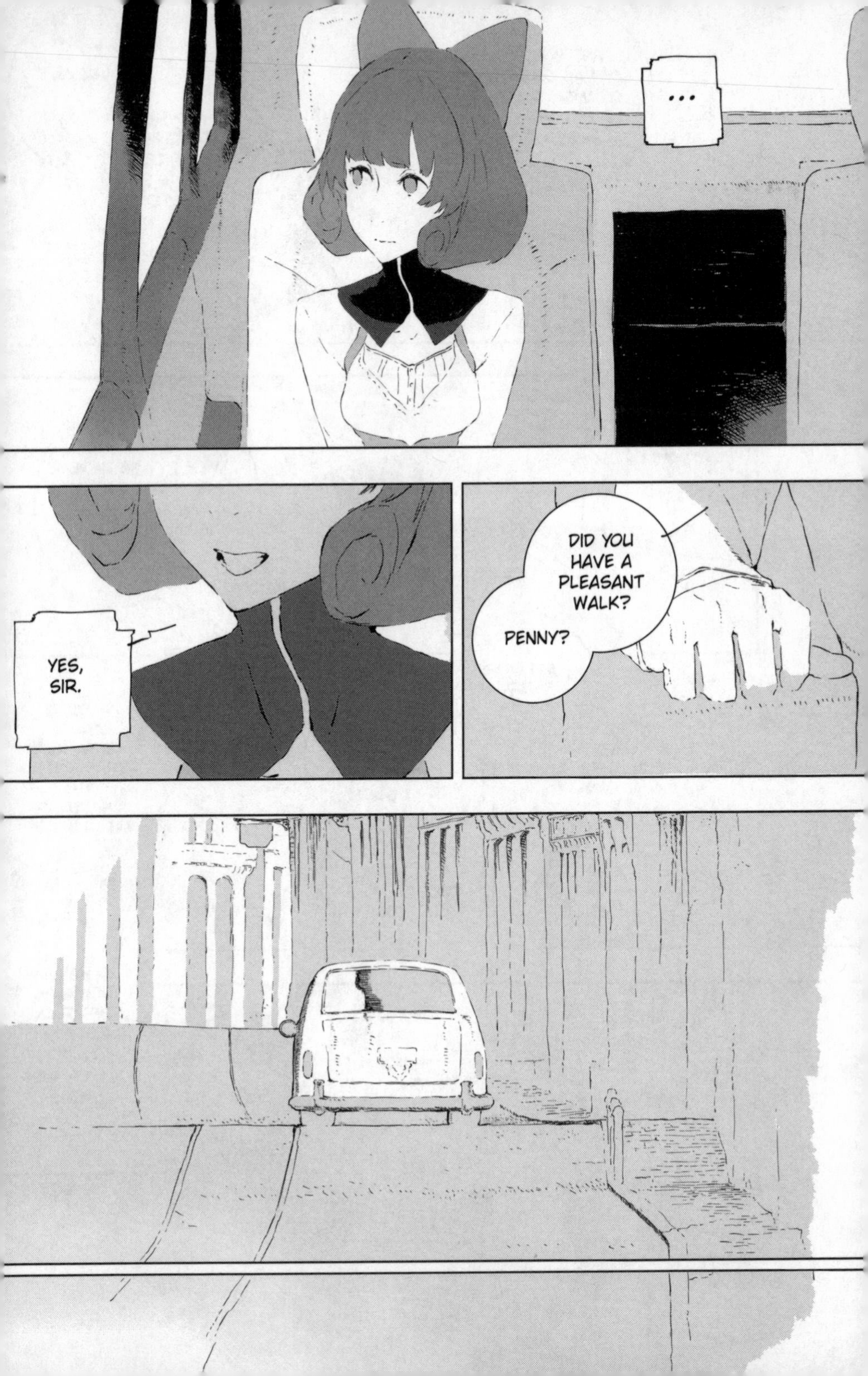
...
DID YOU HAVE A PLEASANT WALK?
PENNY?
YES, SIR.

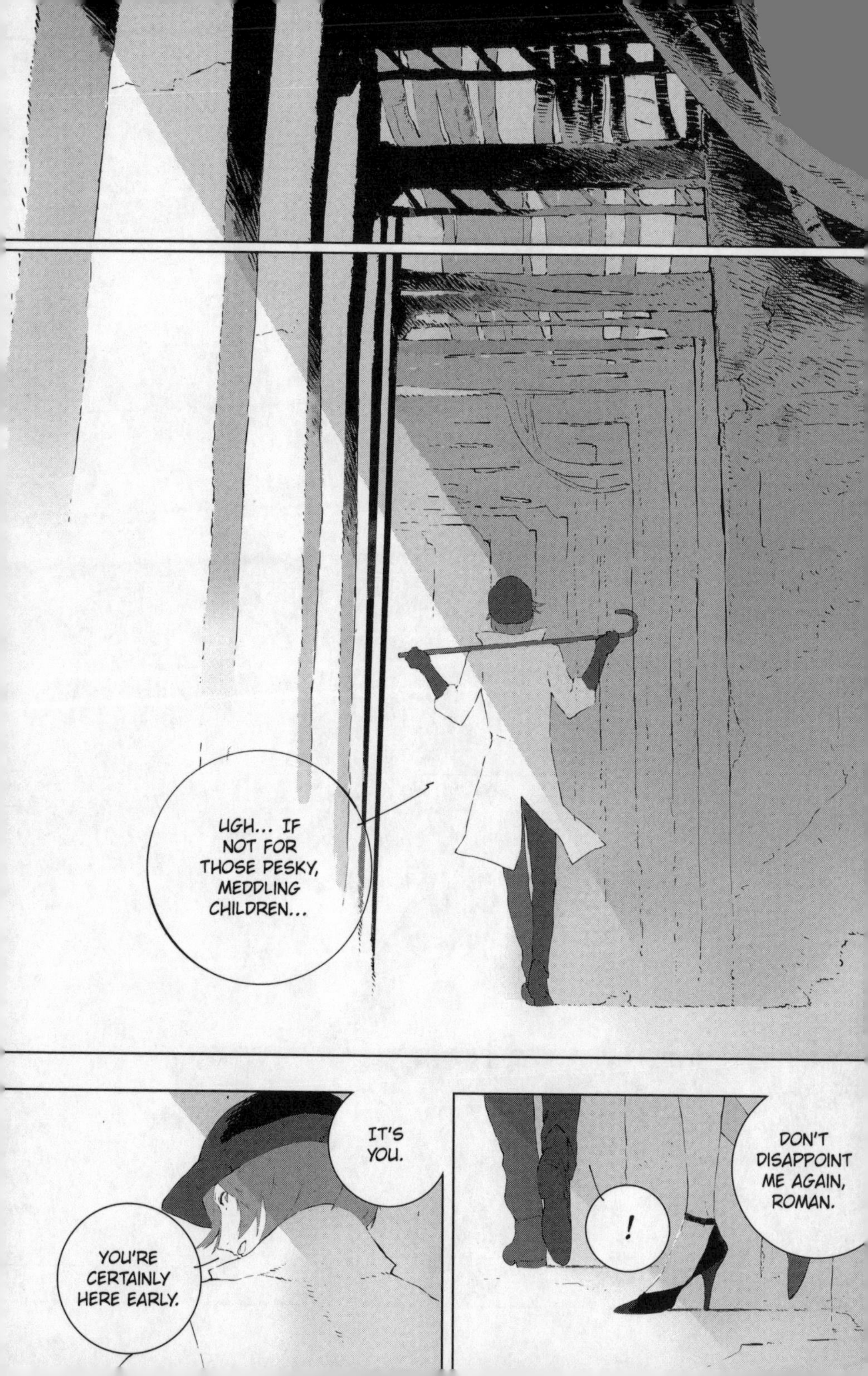
UGH... IF NOT FOR THOSE PESKY, MEDDLING CHILDREN...
DON'T DISAPPOINT ME AGAIN, ROMAN.
!
IT'S YOU.
YOU'RE CERTAINLY HERE EARLY.

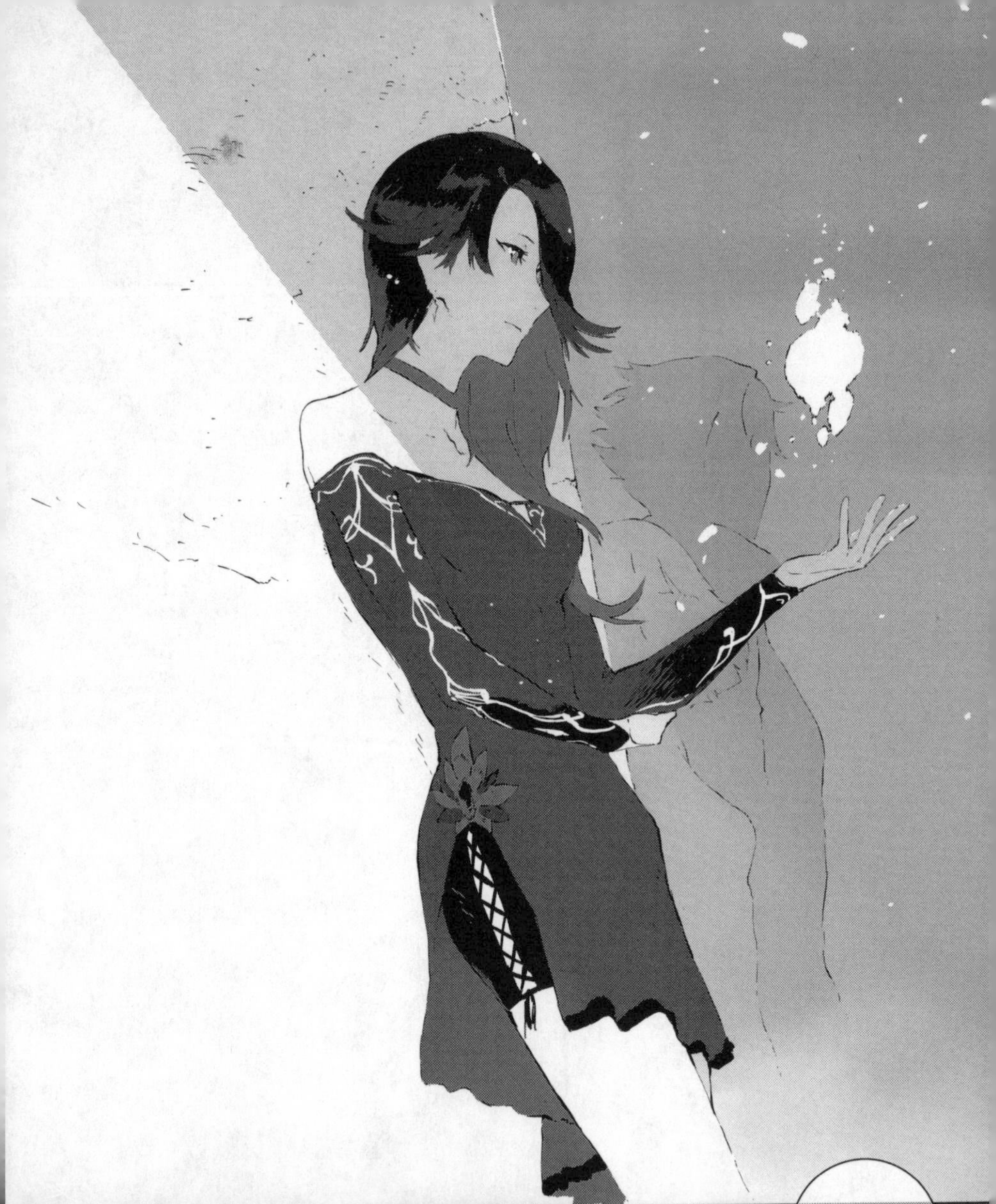
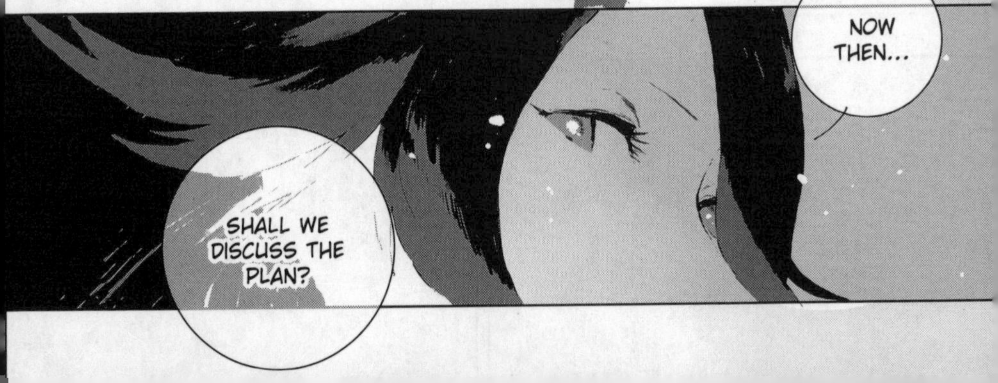
NOW THEN...
SHALL WE DISCUSS THE PLAN?

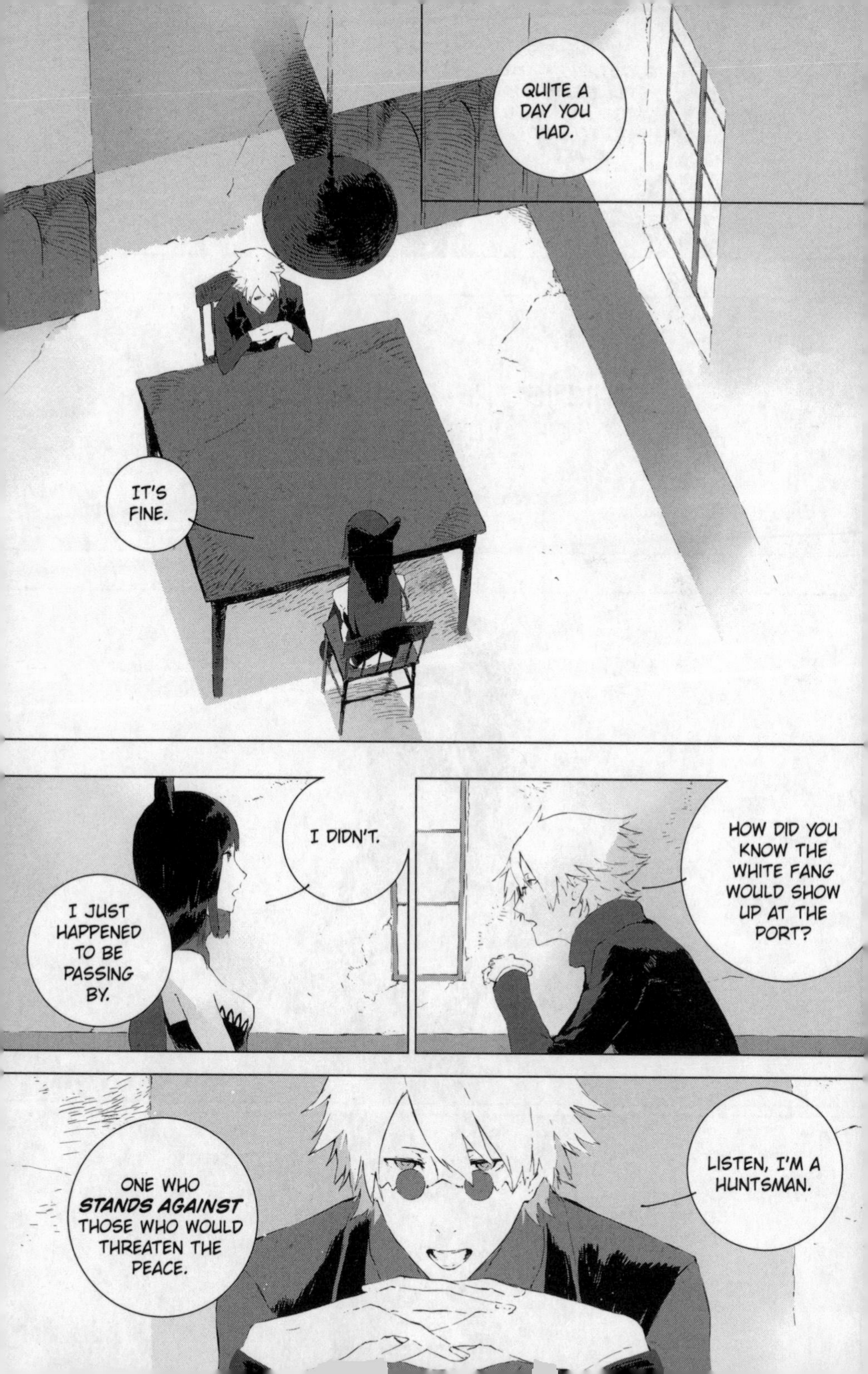
QUITE A DAY YOU HAD.
IT'S FINE.
HOW DID YOU KNOW THE WHITE FANG WOULD SHOW UP AT THE PORT?
I DIDN'T.
I JUST HAPPENED TO BE PASSING BY.
LISTEN, I'M A HUNTSMAN.
ONE WHO **STANDS AGAINST** THOSE WHO WOULD THREATEN THE PEACE.

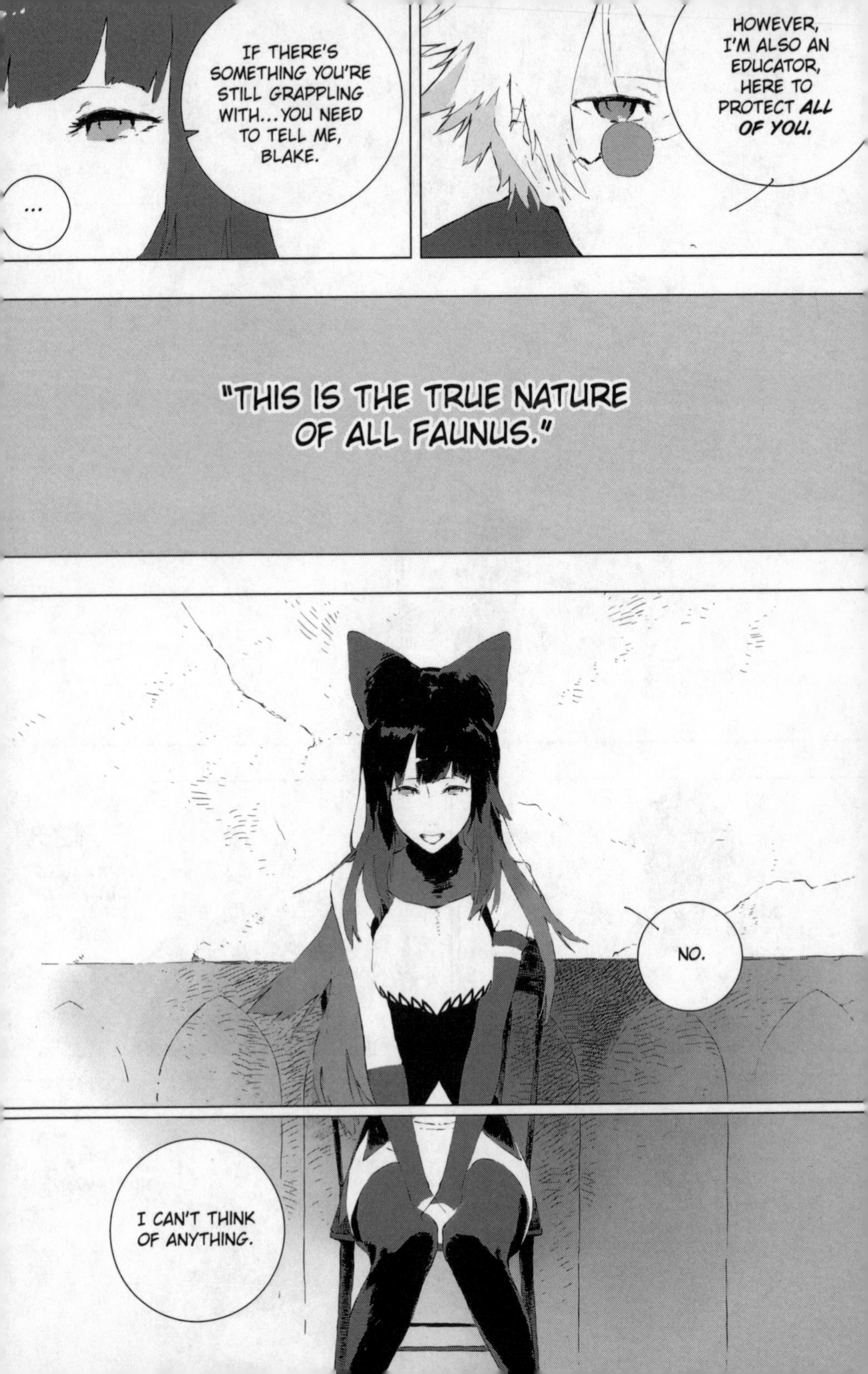
HOWEVER, I'M ALSO AN EDUCATOR, HERE TO PROTECT ALL OF YOU.
IF THERE'S SOMETHING YOU'RE STILL GRAPPLING WITH...YOU NEED TO TELL ME, BLAKE.
...
"THIS IS THE TRUE NATURE OF ALL FAUNUS."
NO.
I CAN'T THINK OF ANYTHING.

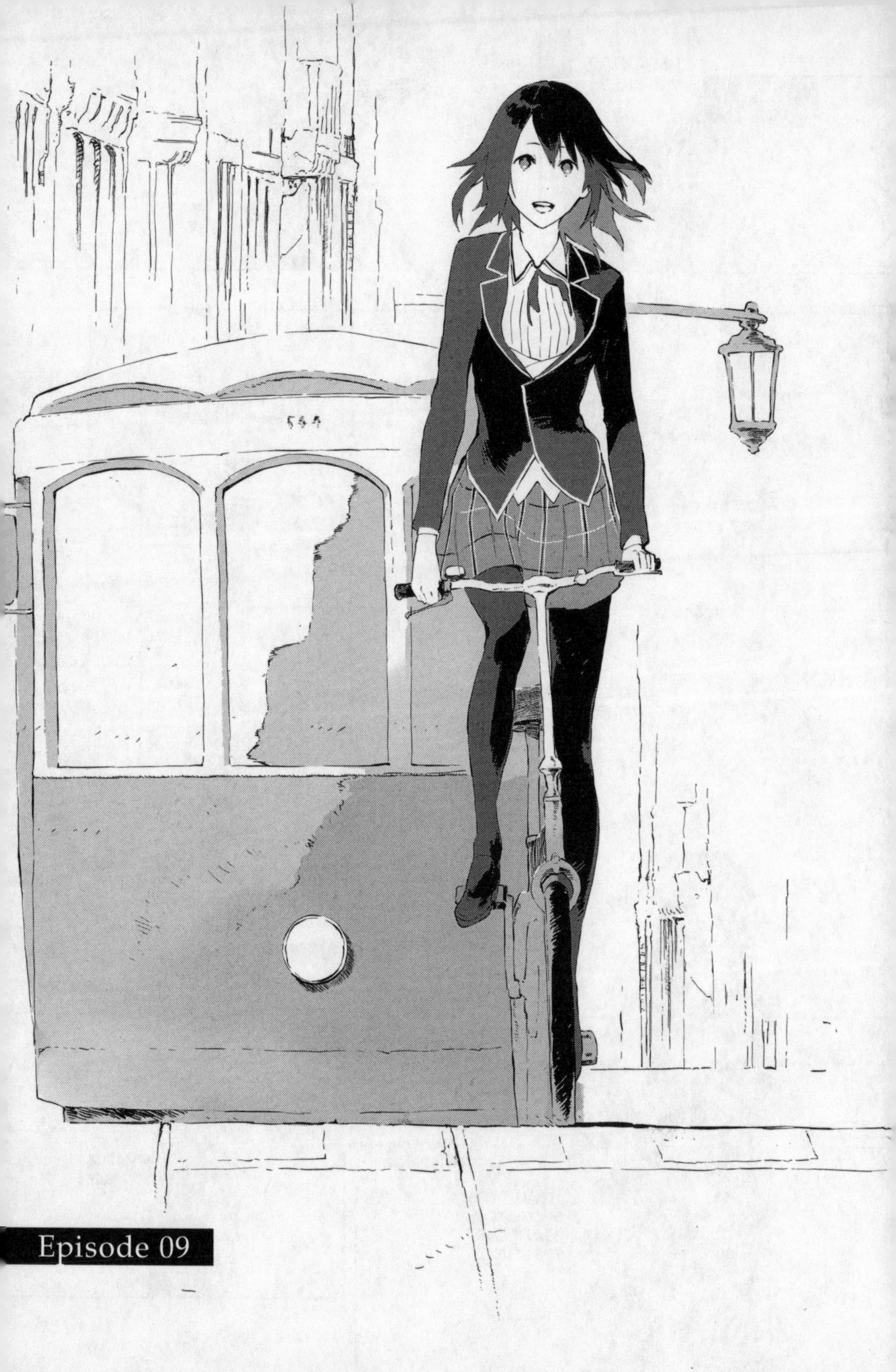

Episode 09

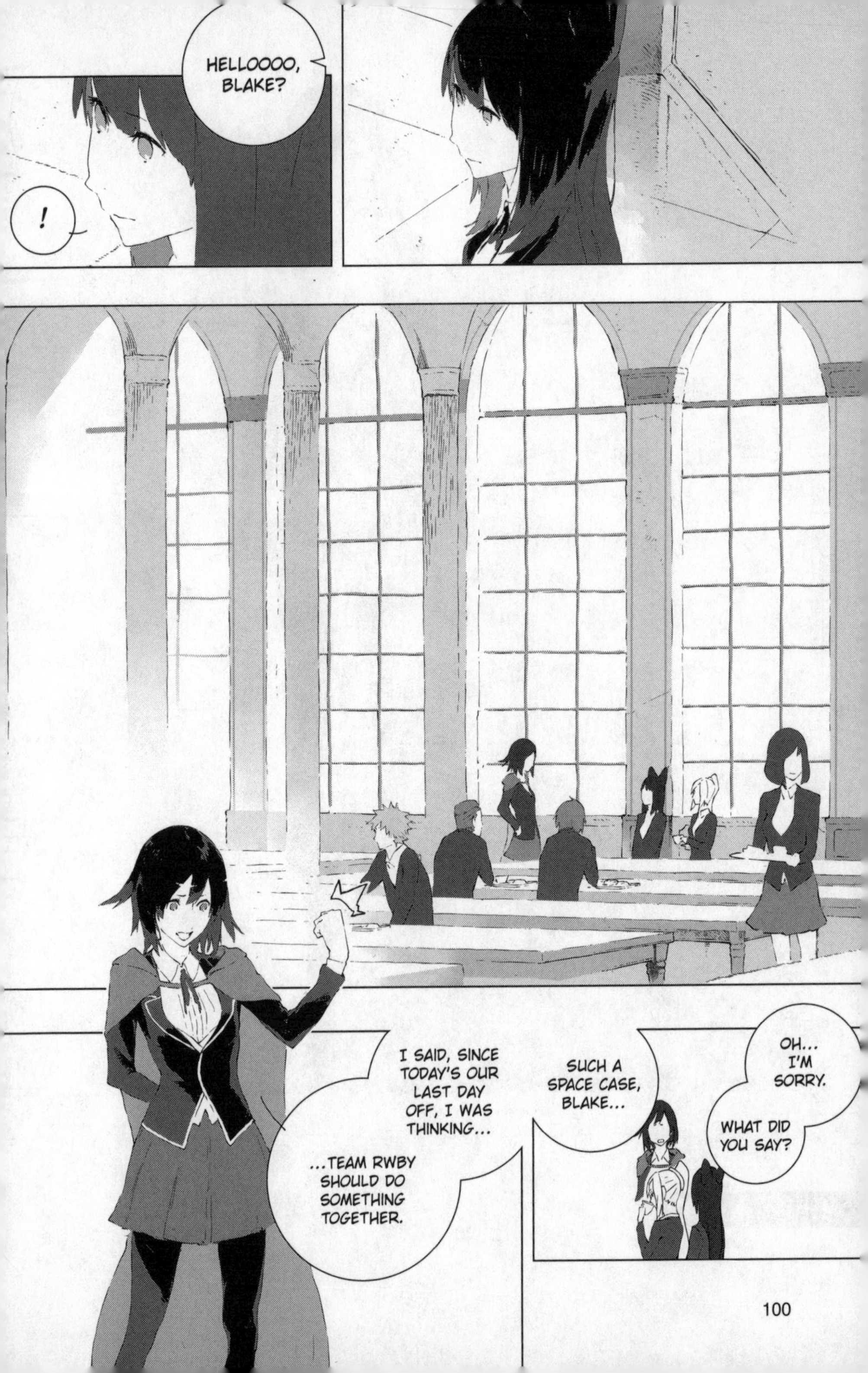
HELLOOOO, BLAKE?
!
OH... I'M SORRY.
WHAT DID YOU SAY?
SUCH A SPACE CASE, BLAKE...
I SAID, SINCE TODAY'S OUR LAST DAY OFF, I WAS THINKING...
...TEAM RWBY SHOULD DO SOMETHING TOGETHER.

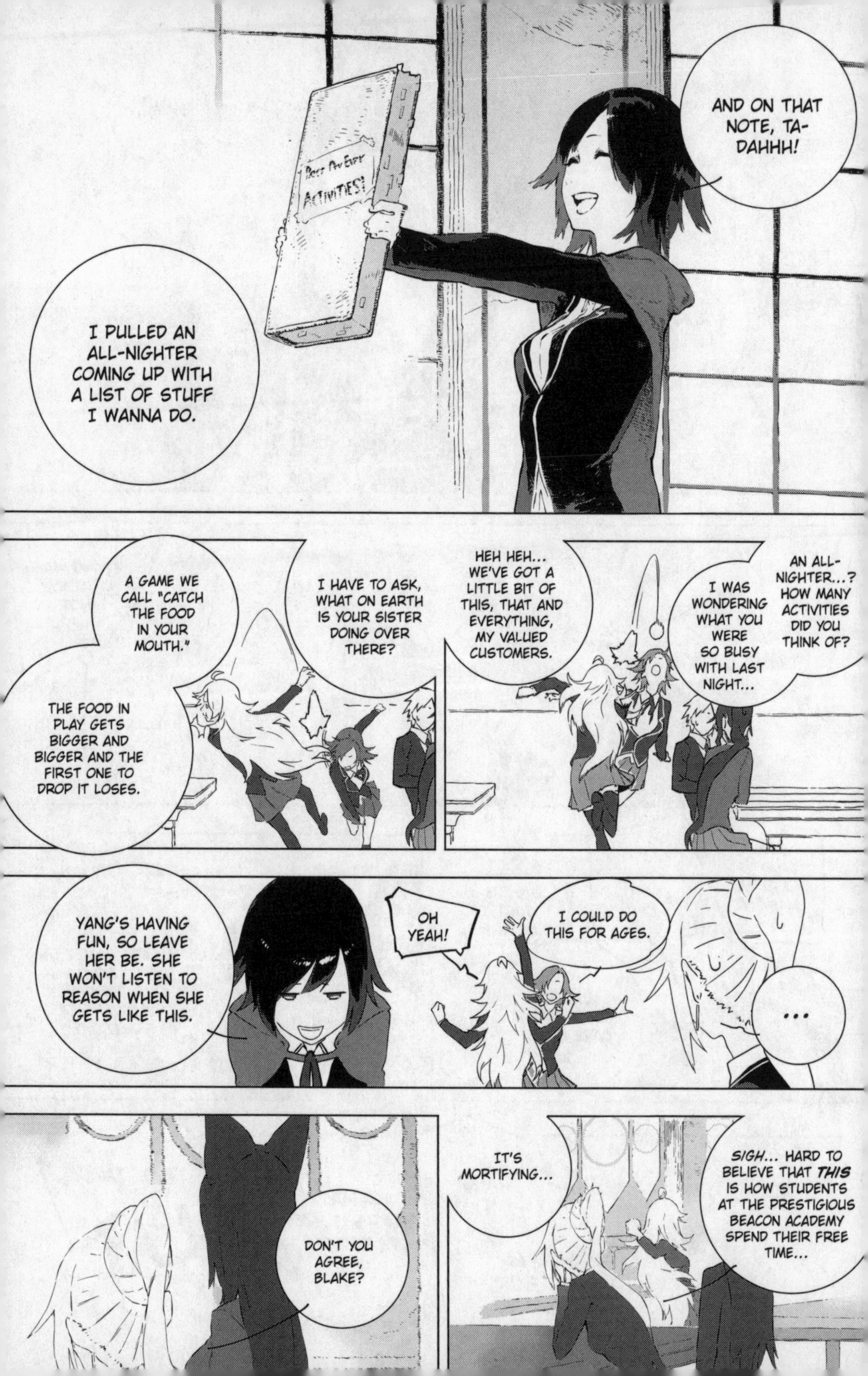
AND ON THAT NOTE, TA-DAHHH!
ACTIVITIES!
I PULLED AN ALL-NIGHTER COMING UP WITH A LIST OF STUFF I WANNA DO.
AN ALL-NIGHTER...? HOW MANY ACTIVITIES DID YOU THINK OF?
I WAS WONDERING WHAT YOU WERE SO BUSY WITH LAST NIGHT...
HEH HEH... WE'VE GOT A LITTLE BIT OF THIS, THAT AND EVERYTHING, MY VALUED CUSTOMERS.
I HAVE TO ASK, WHAT ON EARTH IS YOUR SISTER DOING OVER THERE?
A GAME WE CALL "CATCH THE FOOD IN YOUR MOUTH."
THE FOOD IN PLAY GETS BIGGER AND BIGGER AND THE FIRST ONE TO DROP IT LOSES.
...
I COULD DO THIS FOR AGES.
OH YEAH!
YANG'S HAVING FUN, SO LEAVE HER BE. SHE WON'T LISTEN TO REASON WHEN SHE GETS LIKE THIS.
SIGH... HARD TO BELIEVE THAT ***THIS*** IS HOW STUDENTS AT THE PRESTIGIOUS BEACON ACADEMY SPEND THEIR FREE TIME...
IT'S MORTIFYING...
DON'T YOU AGREE, BLAKE?

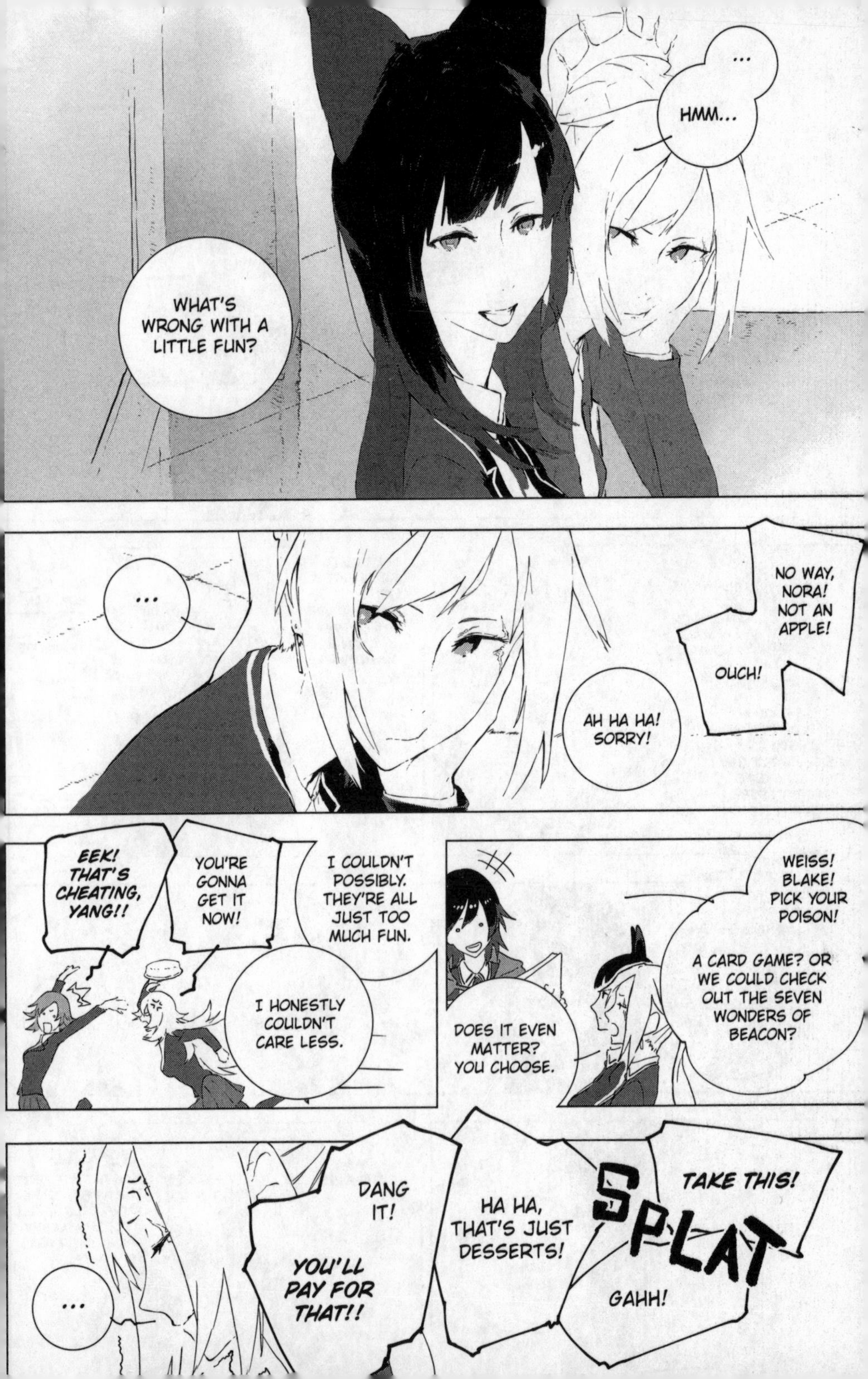
...
HMM...
WHAT'S WRONG WITH A LITTLE FUN?
NO WAY, NORA! NOT AN APPLE!
OUCH!
AH HA HA! SORRY!
...
WEISS! BLAKE! PICK YOUR POISON!
A CARD GAME? OR WE COULD CHECK OUT THE SEVEN WONDERS OF BEACON?
DOES IT EVEN MATTER? YOU CHOOSE.
I COULDN'T POSSIBLY. THEY'RE ALL JUST TOO MUCH FUN.
YOU'RE GONNA GET IT NOW!
EEK! THAT'S CHEATING, YANG!!
I HONESTLY COULDN'T CARE LESS.
TAKE THIS!
SPLAT
GAHH!
HA HA, THAT'S JUST DESSERTS!
DANG IT!
YOU'LL PAY FOR THAT!!
...

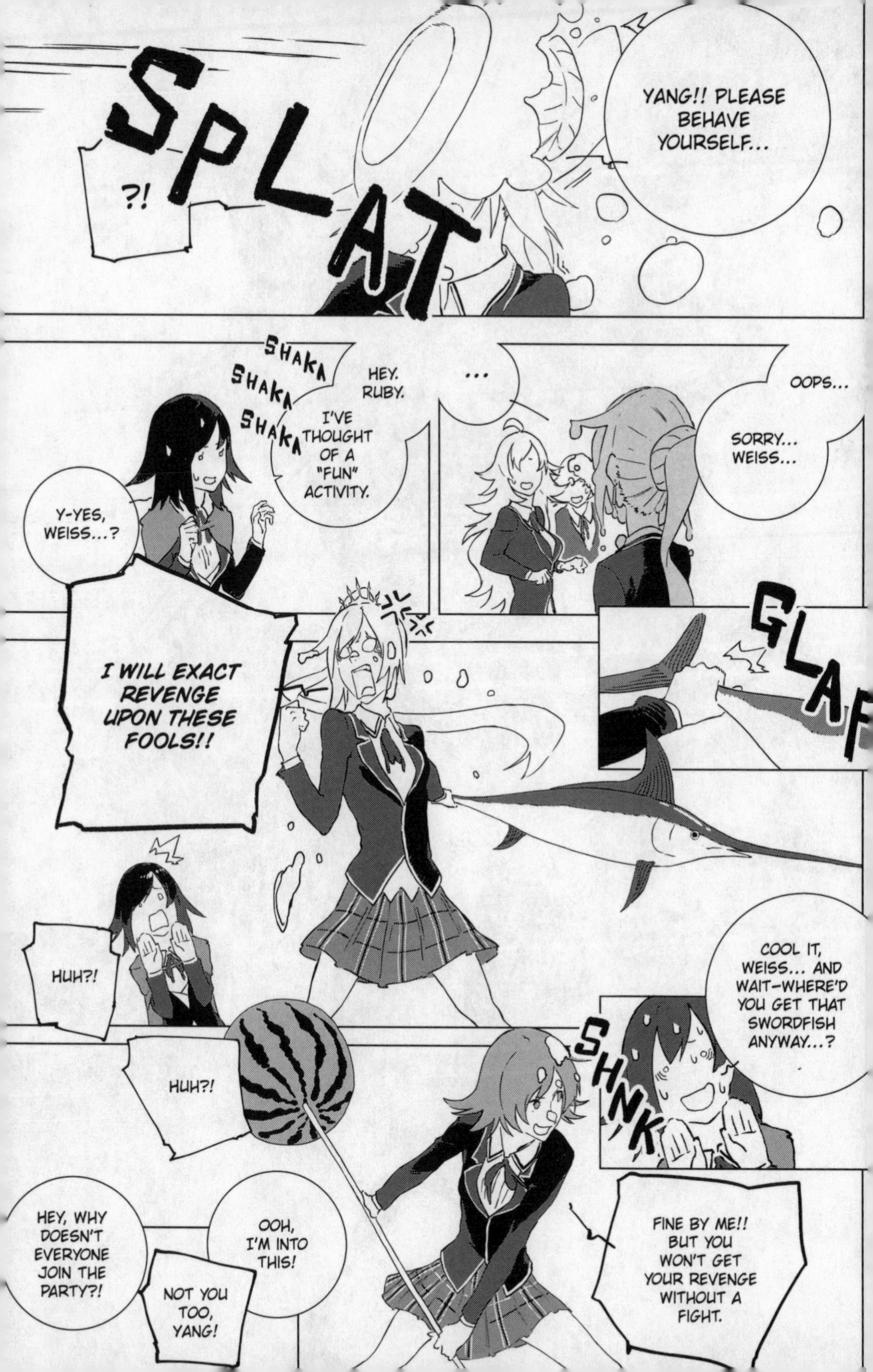
YANG!! PLEASE BEHAVE YOURSELF...
SPLAT
?!
OOPS...
SORRY... WEISS...
...
HEY. RUBY.
I'VE THOUGHT OF A "FUN" ACTIVITY.
SHAKA SHAKA SHAKA
Y-YES, WEISS...?
GLAF
I WILL EXACT REVENGE UPON THESE FOOLS!!
HUH?!
COOL IT, WEISS... AND WAIT—WHERE'D YOU GET THAT SWORDFISH ANYWAY...?
SHNK
HUH?!
FINE BY ME!! BUT YOU WON'T GET YOUR REVENGE WITHOUT A FIGHT.
OOH, I'M INTO THIS!
HEY, WHY DOESN'T EVERYONE JOIN THE PARTY?!
NOT YOU TOO, YANG!

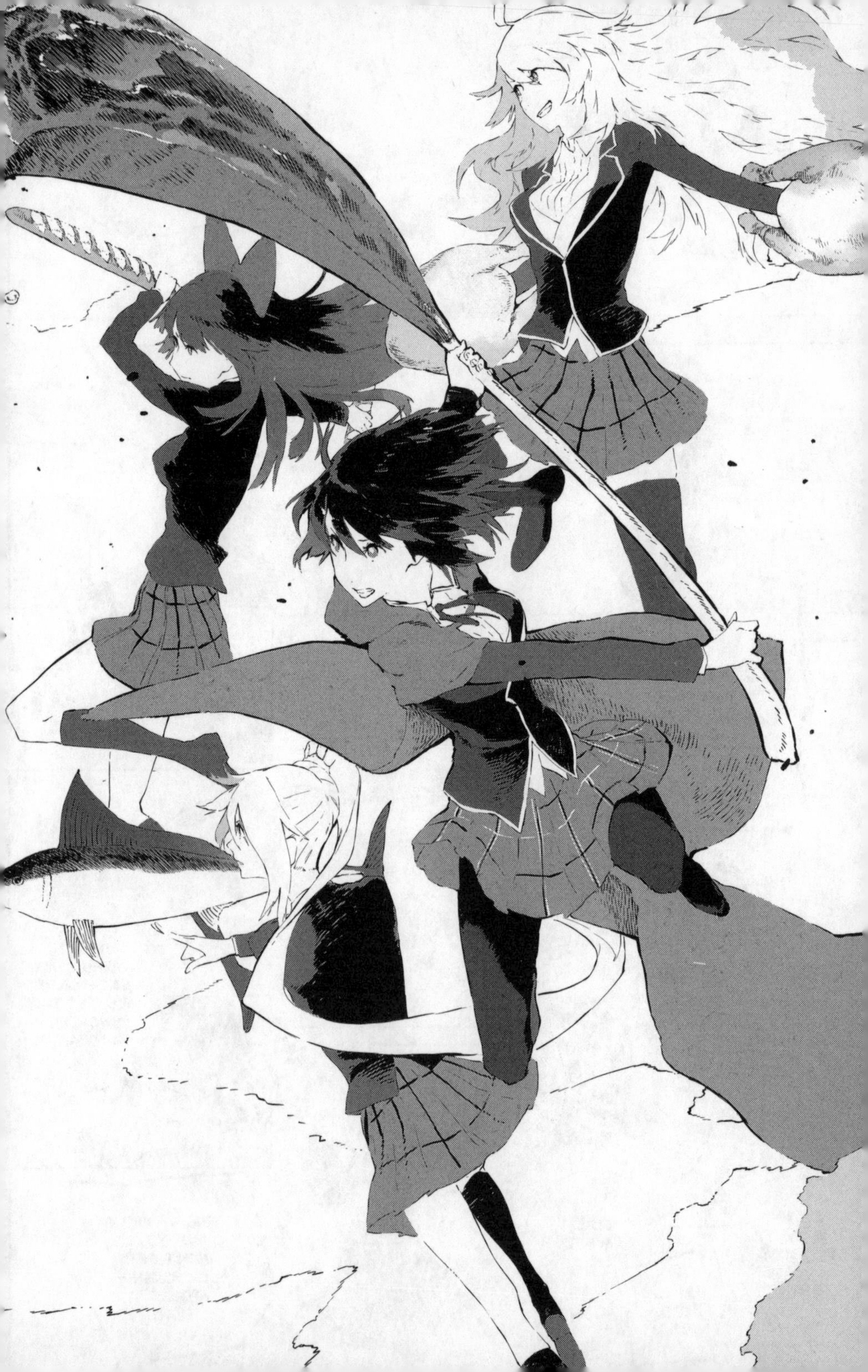

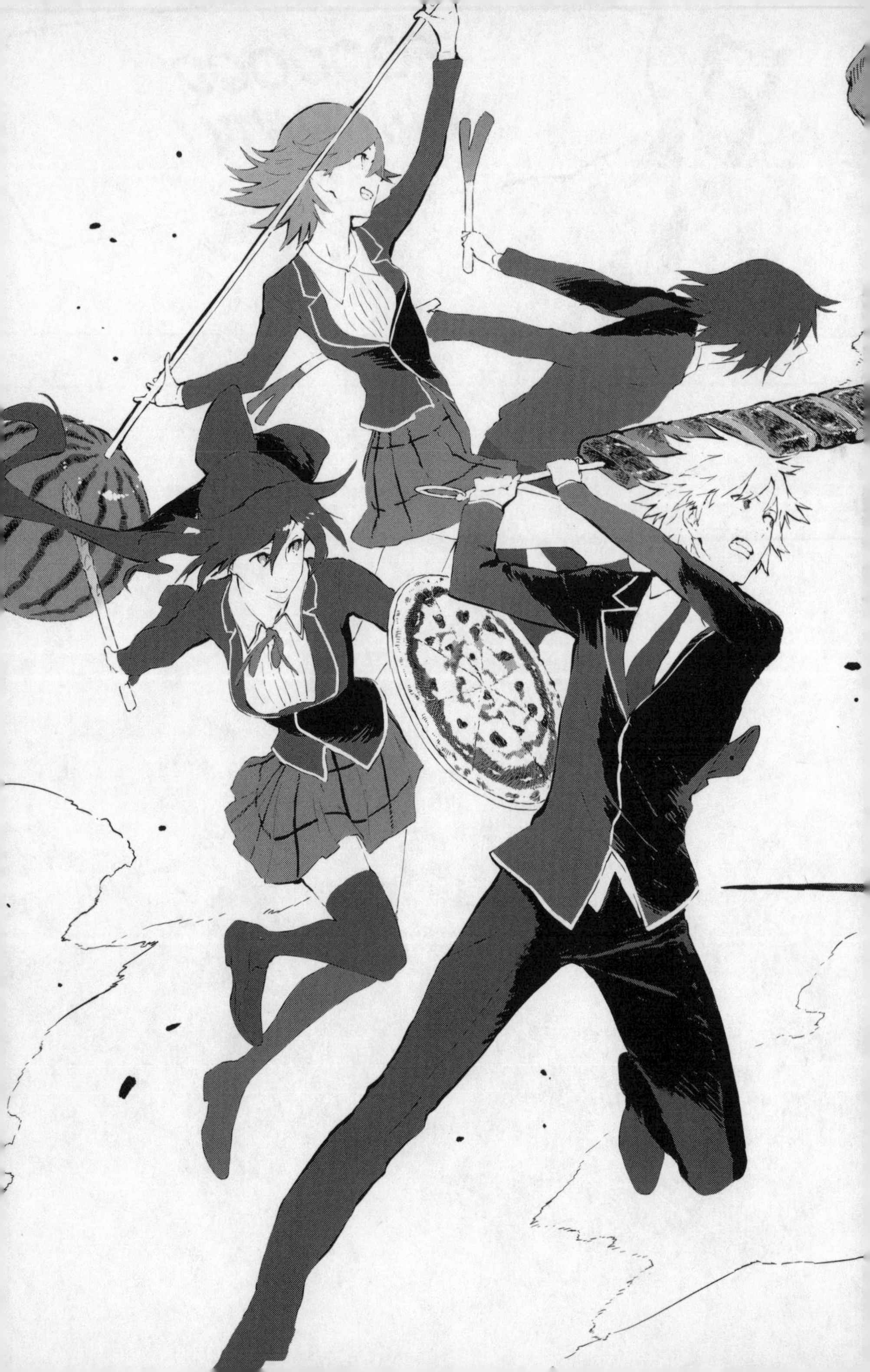

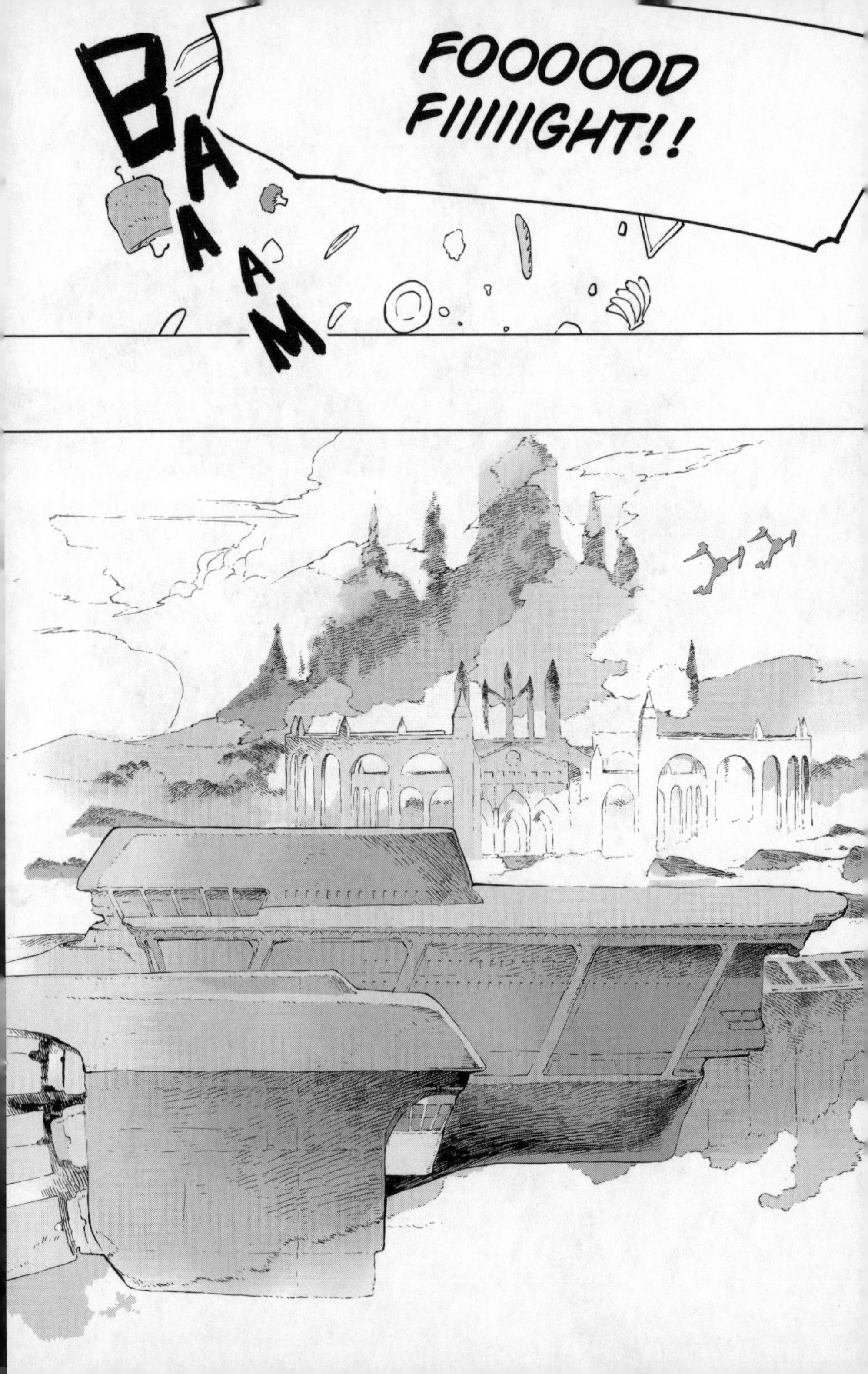
FOOOOOD FIIIIIGHT!!
BAAAM

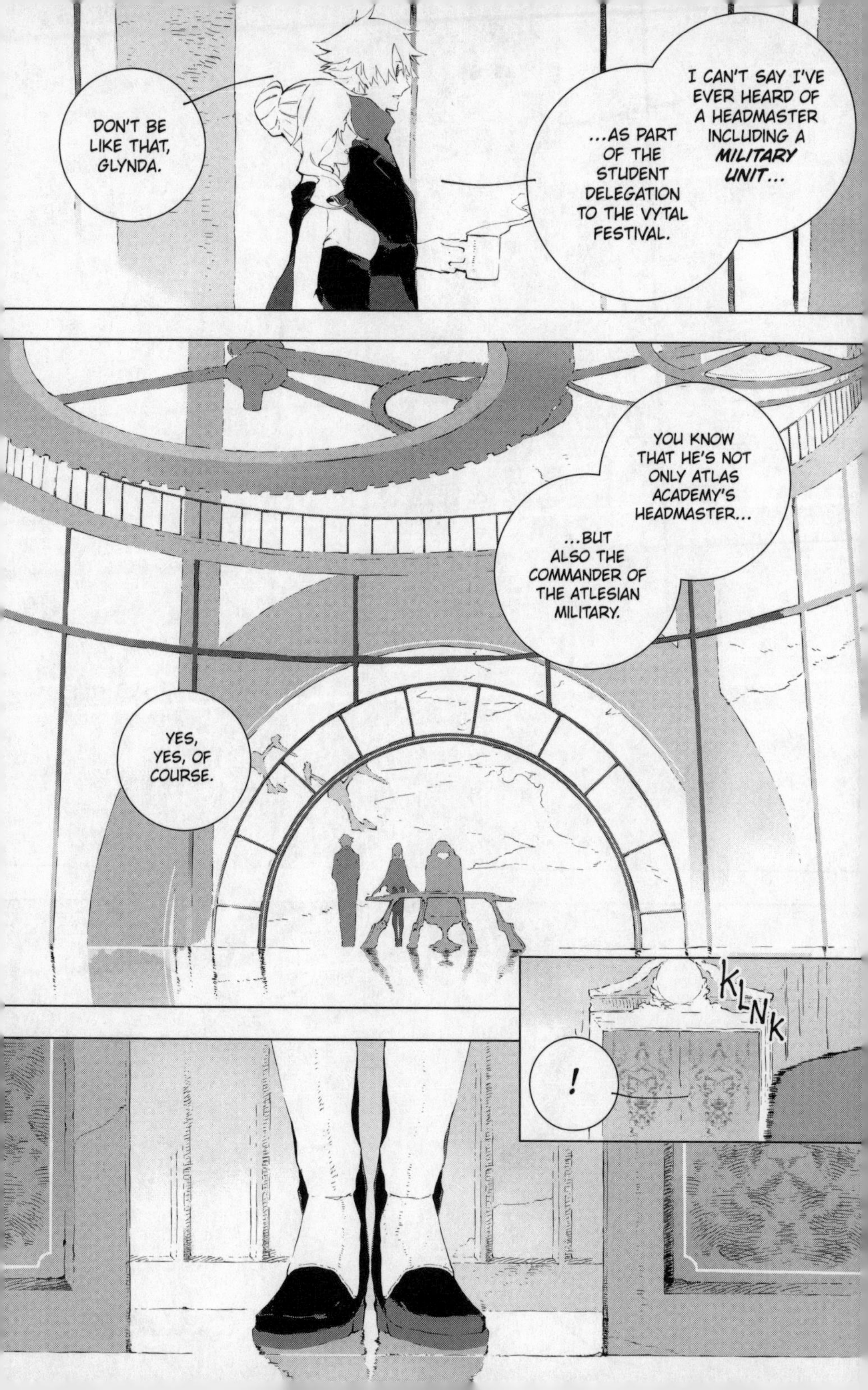
I CAN'T SAY I'VE EVER HEARD OF A HEADMASTER INCLUDING A *MILITARY UNIT*...
...AS PART OF THE STUDENT DELEGATION TO THE VYTAL FESTIVAL.
DON'T BE LIKE THAT, GLYNDA.
YOU KNOW THAT HE'S NOT ONLY ATLAS ACADEMY'S HEADMASTER...
...BUT ALSO THE COMMANDER OF THE ATLESIAN MILITARY.
YES, YES, OF COURSE.
KLNK
!

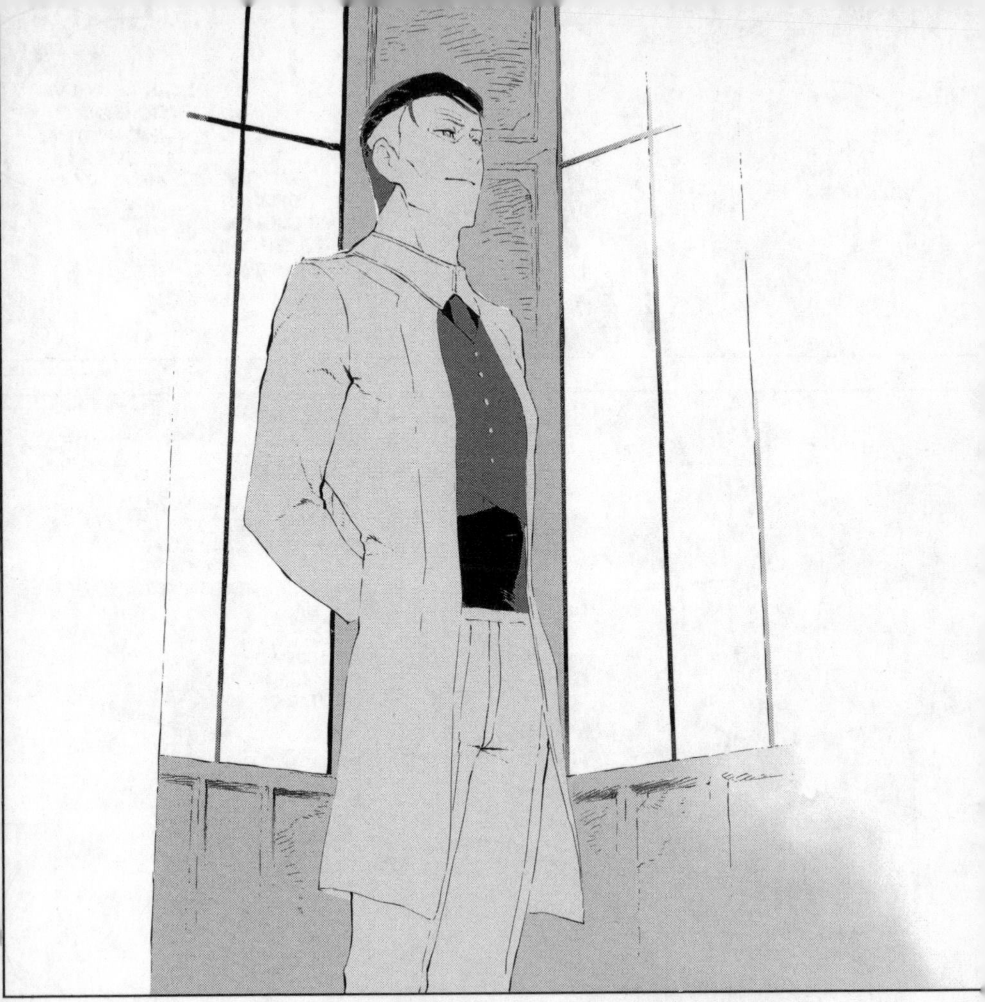

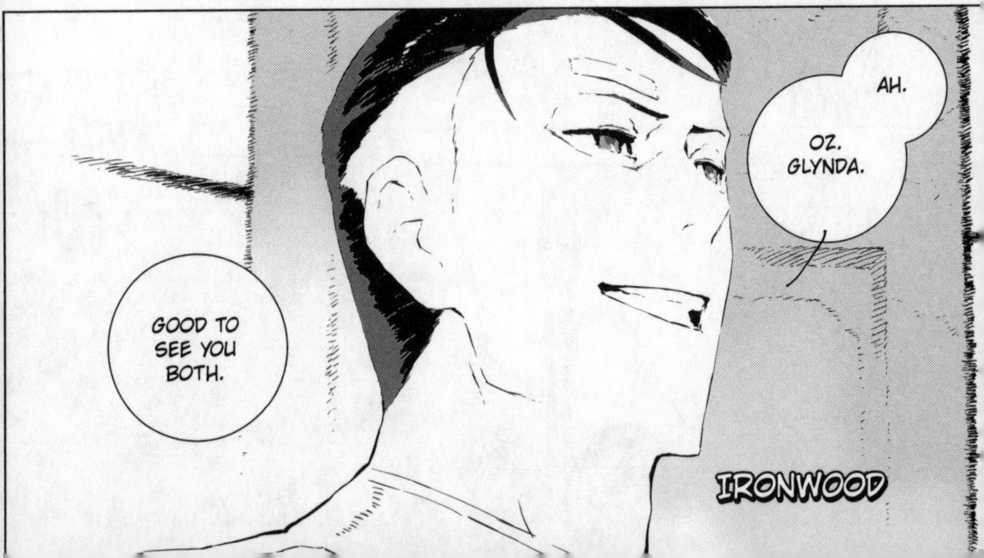
AH.
OZ. GLYNDA.
IRONWOOD
GOOD TO SEE YOU BOTH.

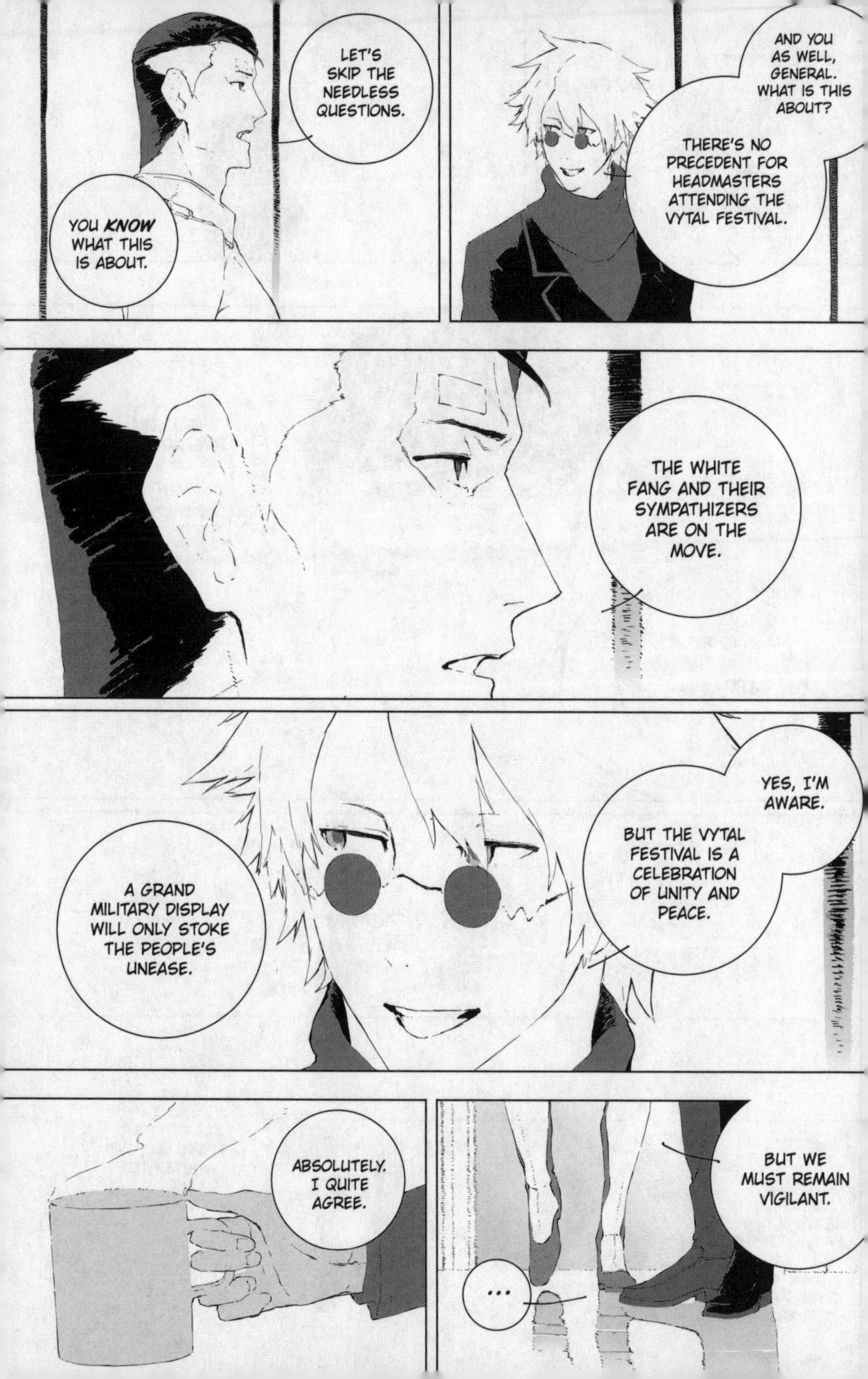
AND YOU AS WELL, GENERAL. WHAT IS THIS ABOUT?
THERE'S NO PRECEDENT FOR HEADMASTERS ATTENDING THE VYTAL FESTIVAL.
LET'S SKIP THE NEEDLESS QUESTIONS.
YOU *KNOW* WHAT THIS IS ABOUT.
THE WHITE FANG AND THEIR SYMPATHIZERS ARE ON THE MOVE.
YES, I'M AWARE.
BUT THE VYTAL FESTIVAL IS A CELEBRATION OF UNITY AND PEACE.
A GRAND MILITARY DISPLAY WILL ONLY STOKE THE PEOPLE'S UNEASE.
BUT WE MUST REMAIN VIGILANT.
...
ABSOLUTELY. I QUITE AGREE.

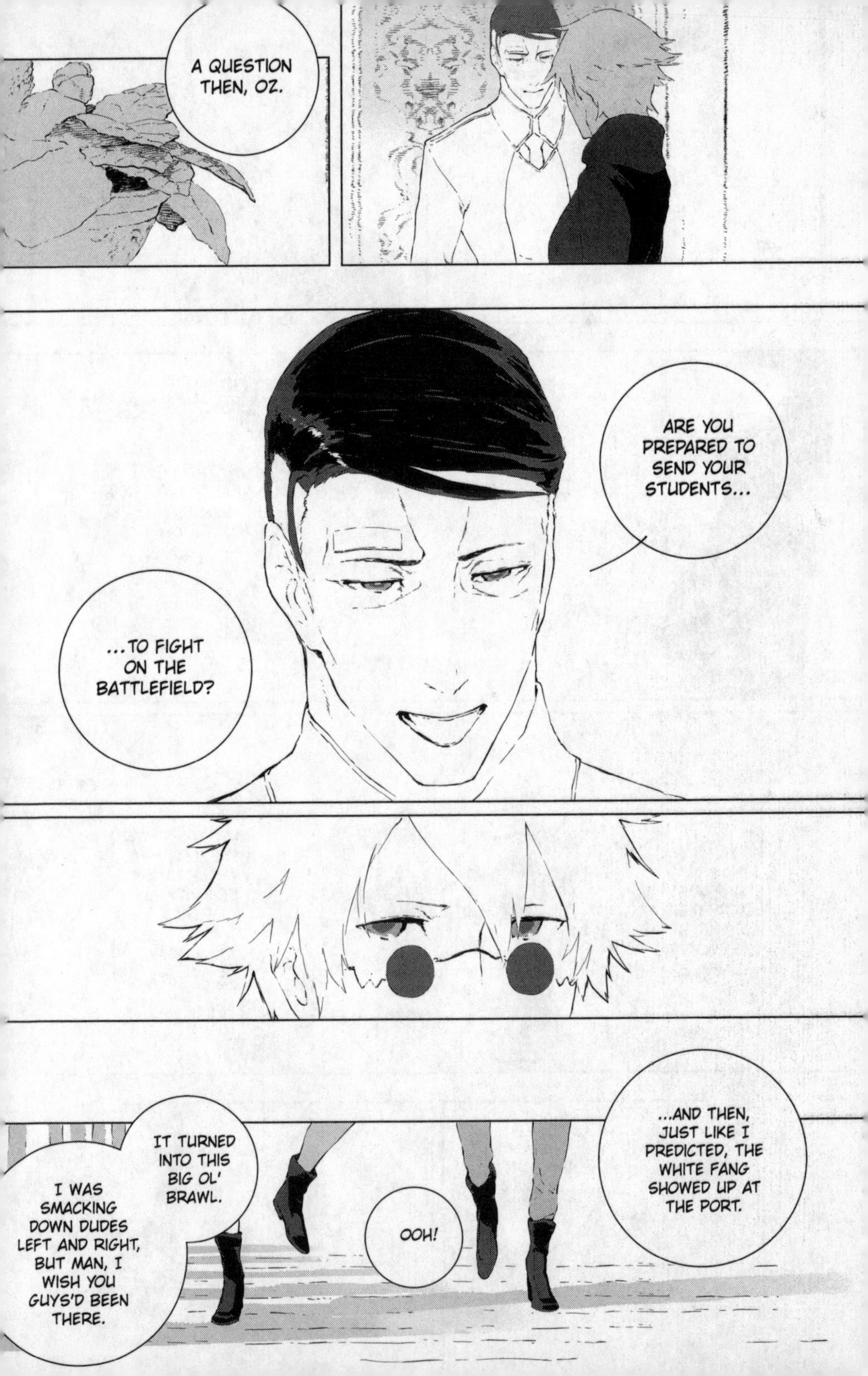
A QUESTION THEN, OZ.
ARE YOU PREPARED TO SEND YOUR STUDENTS...
...TO FIGHT ON THE BATTLEFIELD?
...AND THEN, JUST LIKE I PREDICTED, THE WHITE FANG SHOWED UP AT THE PORT.
OOH!
IT TURNED INTO THIS BIG OL' BRAWL.
I WAS SMACKING DOWN DUDES LEFT AND RIGHT, BUT MAN, I WISH YOU GUYS'D BEEN THERE.

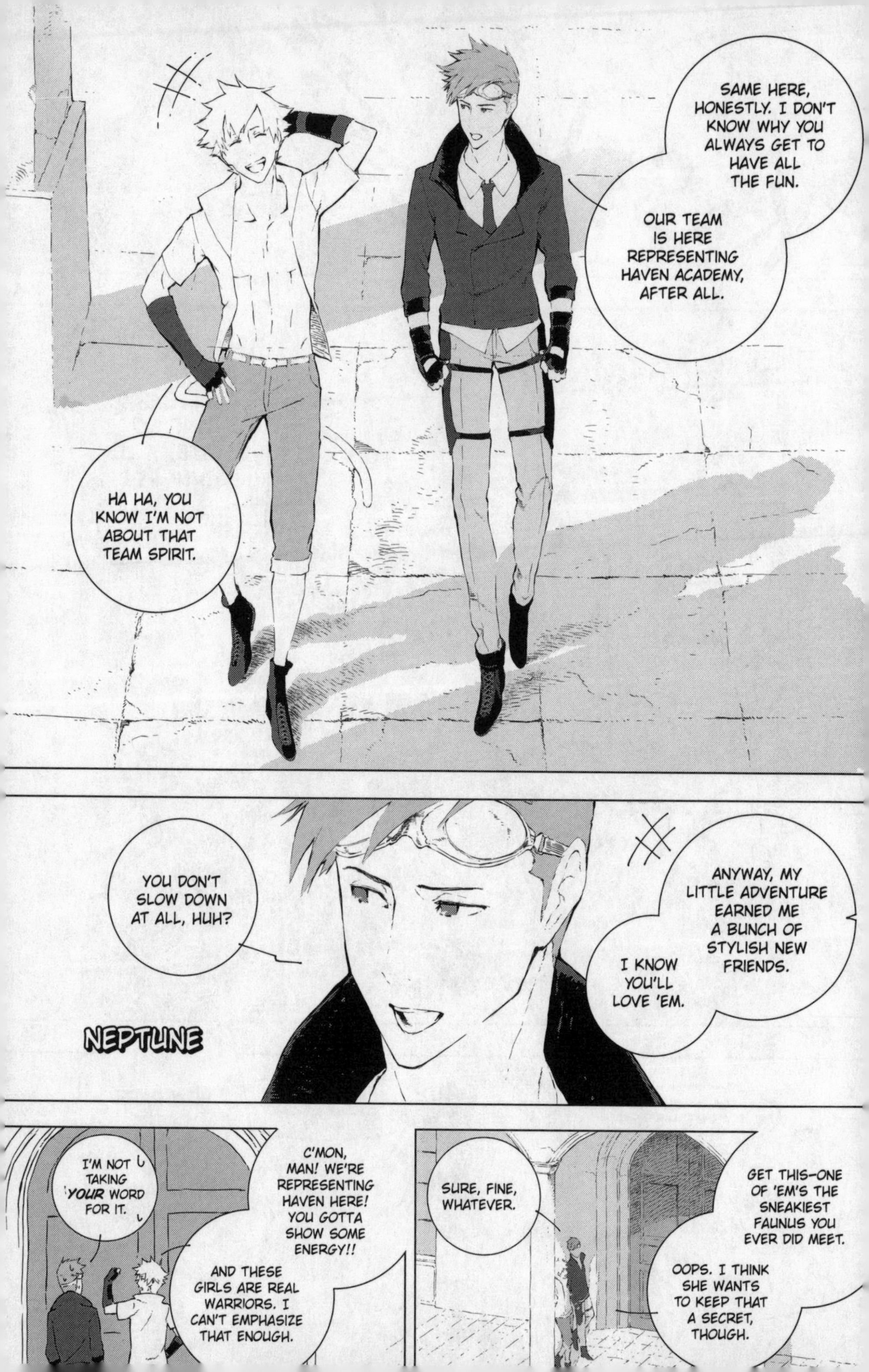
SAME HERE, HONESTLY. I DON'T KNOW WHY YOU ALWAYS GET TO HAVE ALL THE FUN.
OUR TEAM IS HERE REPRESENTING HAVEN ACADEMY, AFTER ALL.
HA HA, YOU KNOW I'M NOT ABOUT THAT TEAM SPIRIT.
ANYWAY, MY LITTLE ADVENTURE EARNED ME A BUNCH OF STYLISH NEW FRIENDS.
I KNOW YOU'LL LOVE 'EM.
YOU DON'T SLOW DOWN AT ALL, HUH?
NEPTUNE
GET THIS—ONE OF 'EM'S THE SNEAKIEST FAUNUS YOU EVER DID MEET.
SURE, FINE, WHATEVER.
OOPS. I THINK SHE WANTS TO KEEP THAT A SECRET, THOUGH.
C'MON, MAN! WE'RE REPRESENTING HAVEN HERE! YOU GOTTA SHOW SOME ENERGY!!
I'M NOT TAKING *YOUR* WORD FOR IT.
AND THESE GIRLS ARE REAL WARRIORS. I CAN'T EMPHASIZE THAT ENOUGH.

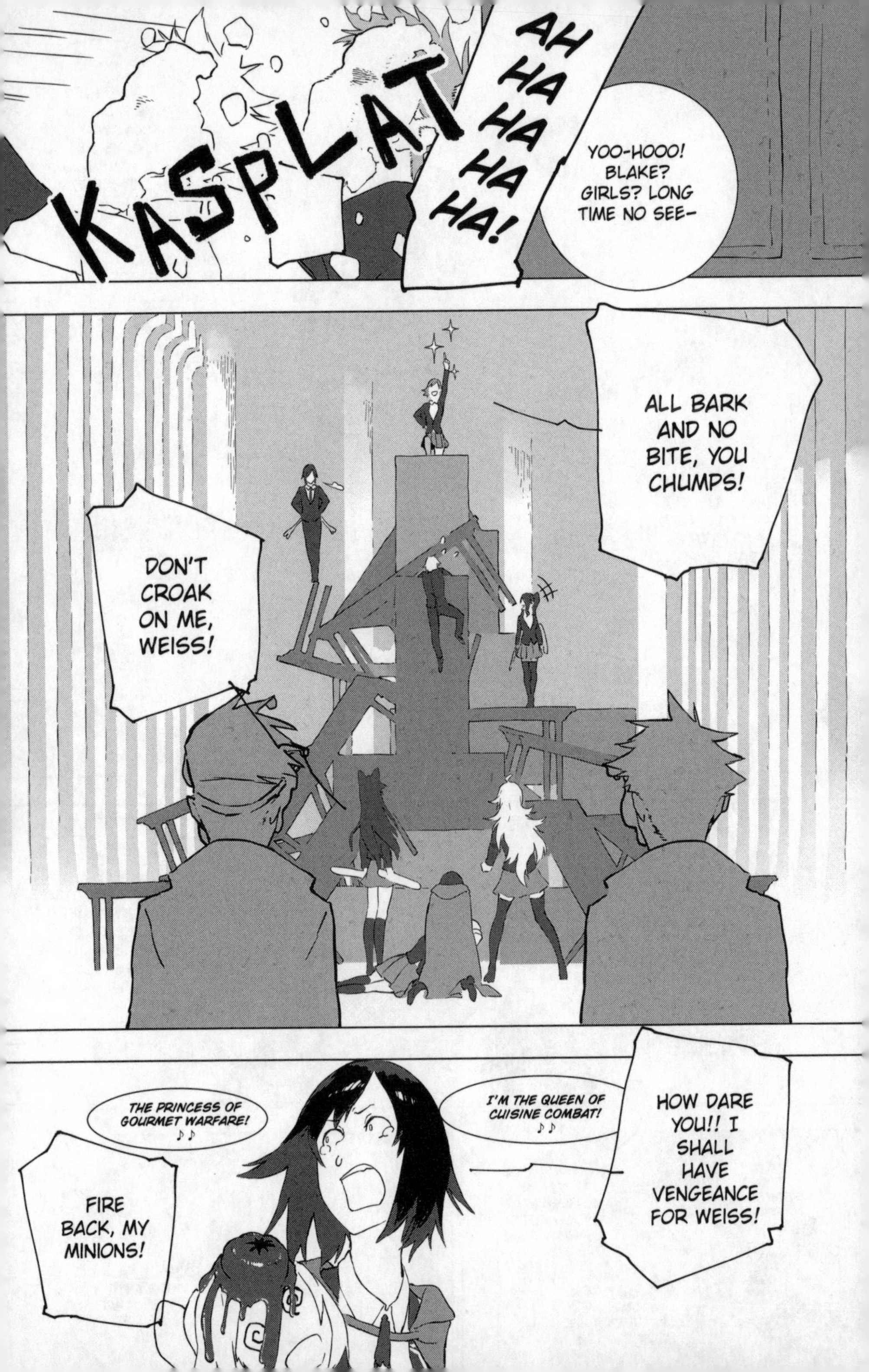
YOO-HOOO! BLAKE? GIRLS? LONG TIME NO SEE-
AH HA HA HA HA!
KASPLAT
ALL BARK AND NO BITE, YOU CHUMPS!
DON'T CROAK ON ME, WEISS!
HOW DARE YOU!! I SHALL HAVE VENGEANCE FOR WEISS!
I'M THE QUEEN OF CUISINE COMBAT! ♪♪
THE PRINCESS OF GOURMET WARFARE! ♪♪
FIRE BACK, MY MINIONS!

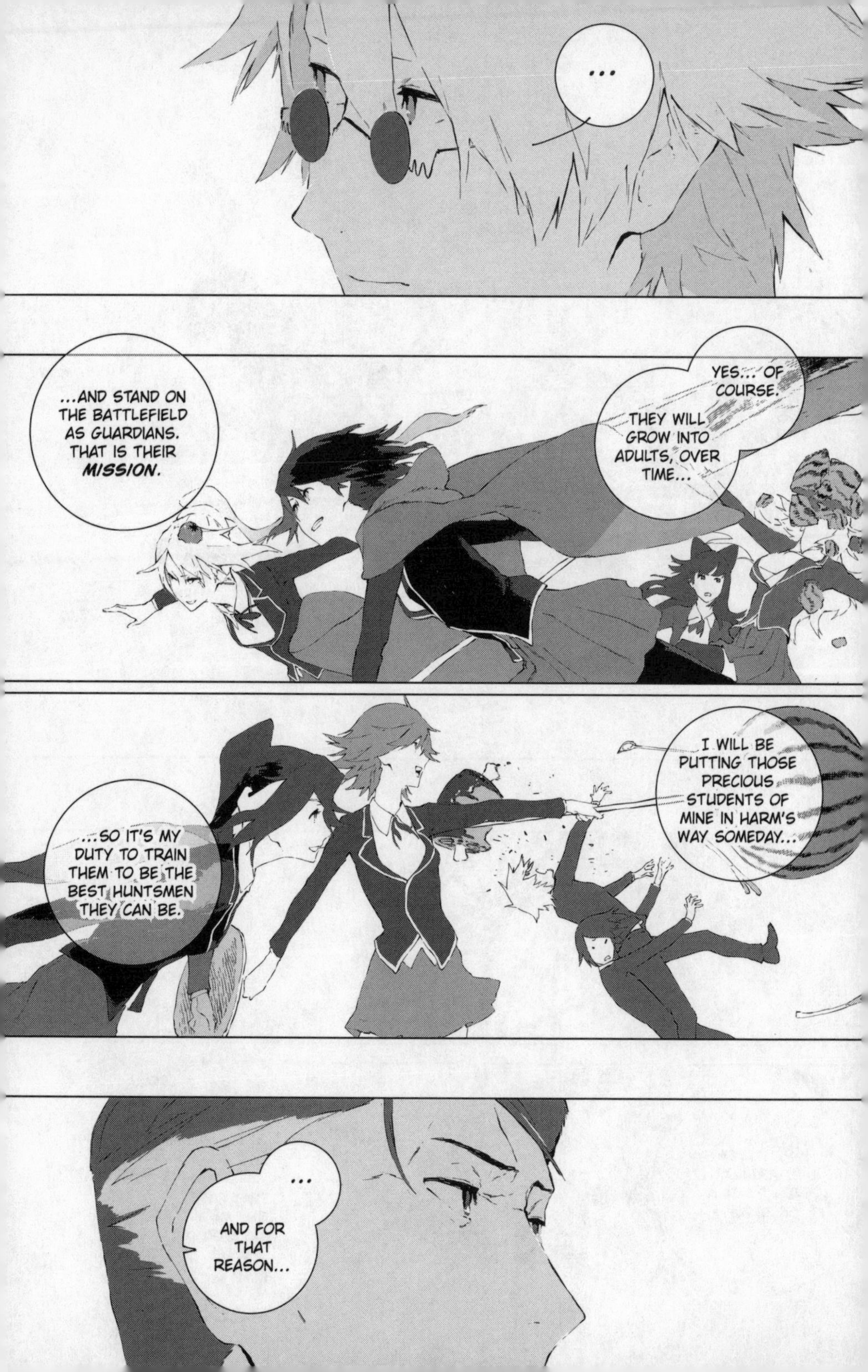
...
YES... OF COURSE. THEY WILL GROW INTO ADULTS, OVER TIME...
...AND STAND ON THE BATTLEFIELD AS GUARDIANS. THAT IS THEIR *MISSION*.
I WILL BE PUTTING THOSE PRECIOUS STUDENTS OF MINE IN HARM'S WAY SOMEDAY...
...SO IT'S MY DUTY TO TRAIN THEM TO BE THE BEST HUNTSMEN THEY CAN BE.
... AND FOR THAT REASON...

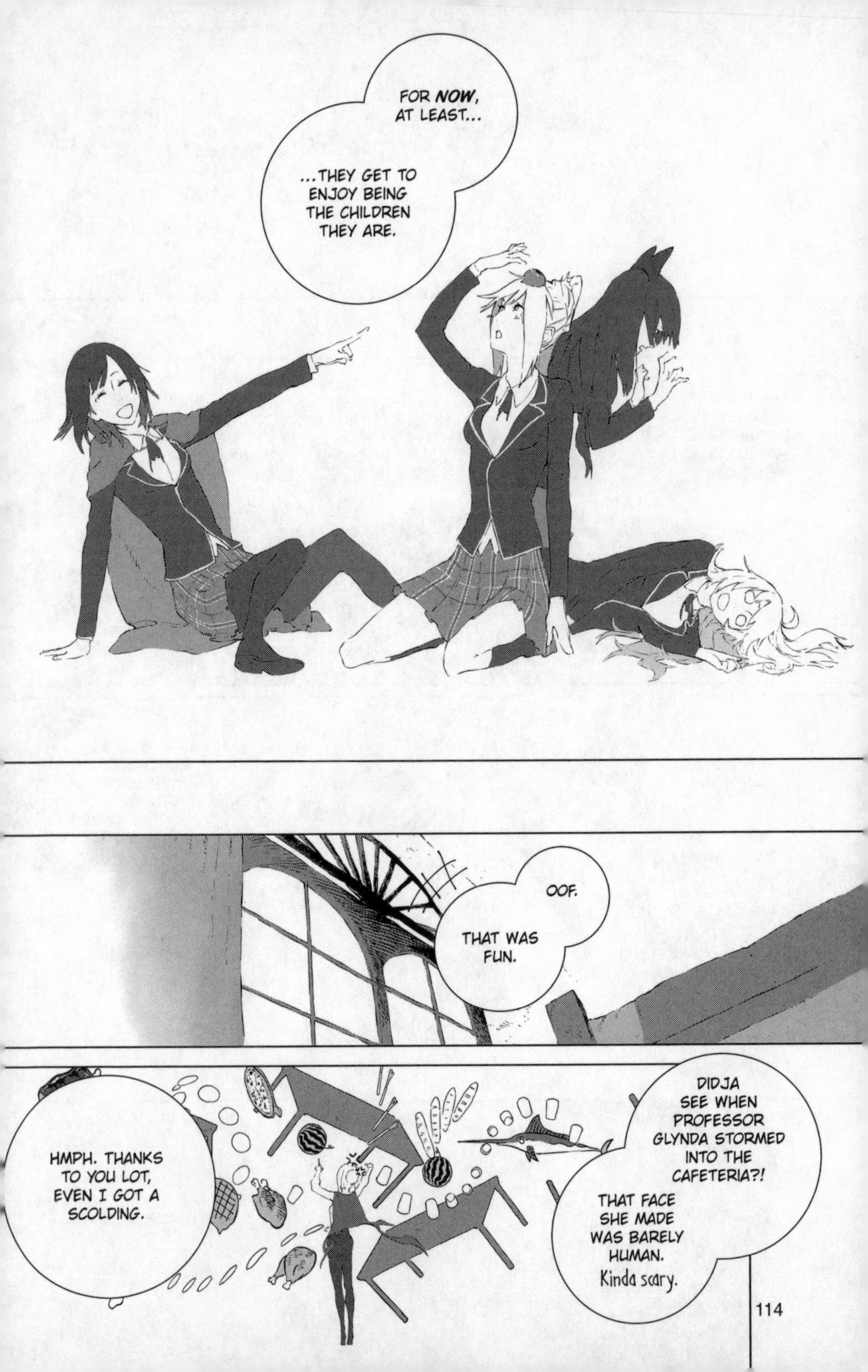
FOR NOW, AT LEAST...
...THEY GET TO ENJOY BEING THE CHILDREN THEY ARE.
OOF.
THAT WAS FUN.
DIDJA SEE WHEN PROFESSOR GLYNDA STORMED INTO THE CAFETERIA?!
THAT FACE SHE MADE WAS BARELY HUMAN.
Kinda scary.
HMPH. THANKS TO YOU LOT, EVEN I GOT A SCOLDING.

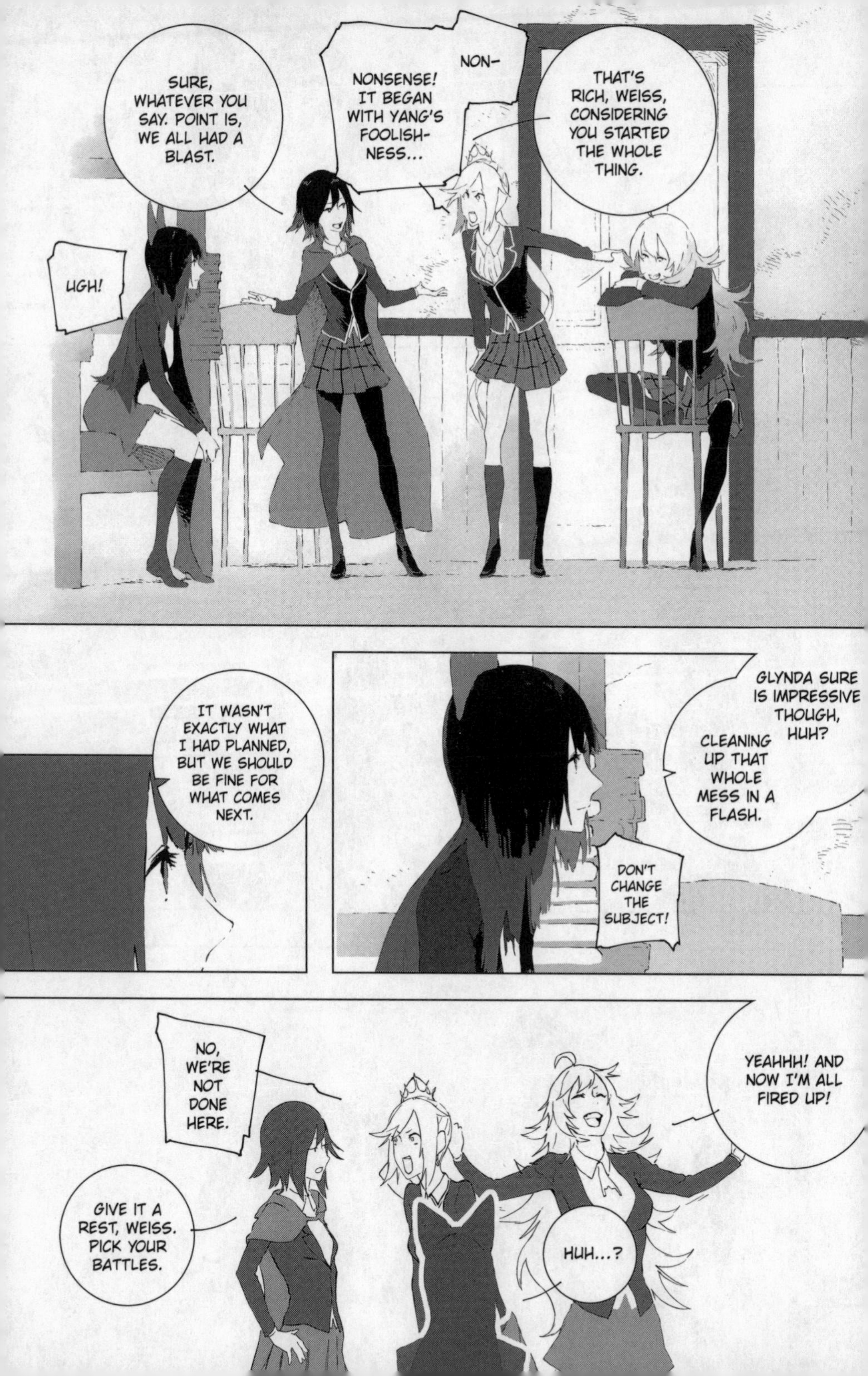
THAT'S RICH, WEISS, CONSIDERING YOU STARTED THE WHOLE THING.
NON-
NONSENSE! IT BEGAN WITH YANG'S FOOLISH-NESS...
SURE, WHATEVER YOU SAY. POINT IS, WE ALL HAD A BLAST.
UGH!
GLYNDA SURE IS IMPRESSIVE THOUGH, HUH?
CLEANING UP THAT WHOLE MESS IN A FLASH.
DON'T CHANGE THE SUBJECT!
IT WASN'T EXACTLY WHAT I HAD PLANNED, BUT WE SHOULD BE FINE FOR WHAT COMES NEXT.
YEAHHH! AND NOW I'M ALL FIRED UP!
NO, WE'RE NOT DONE HERE.
HUH...?
GIVE IT A REST, WEISS. PICK YOUR BATTLES.

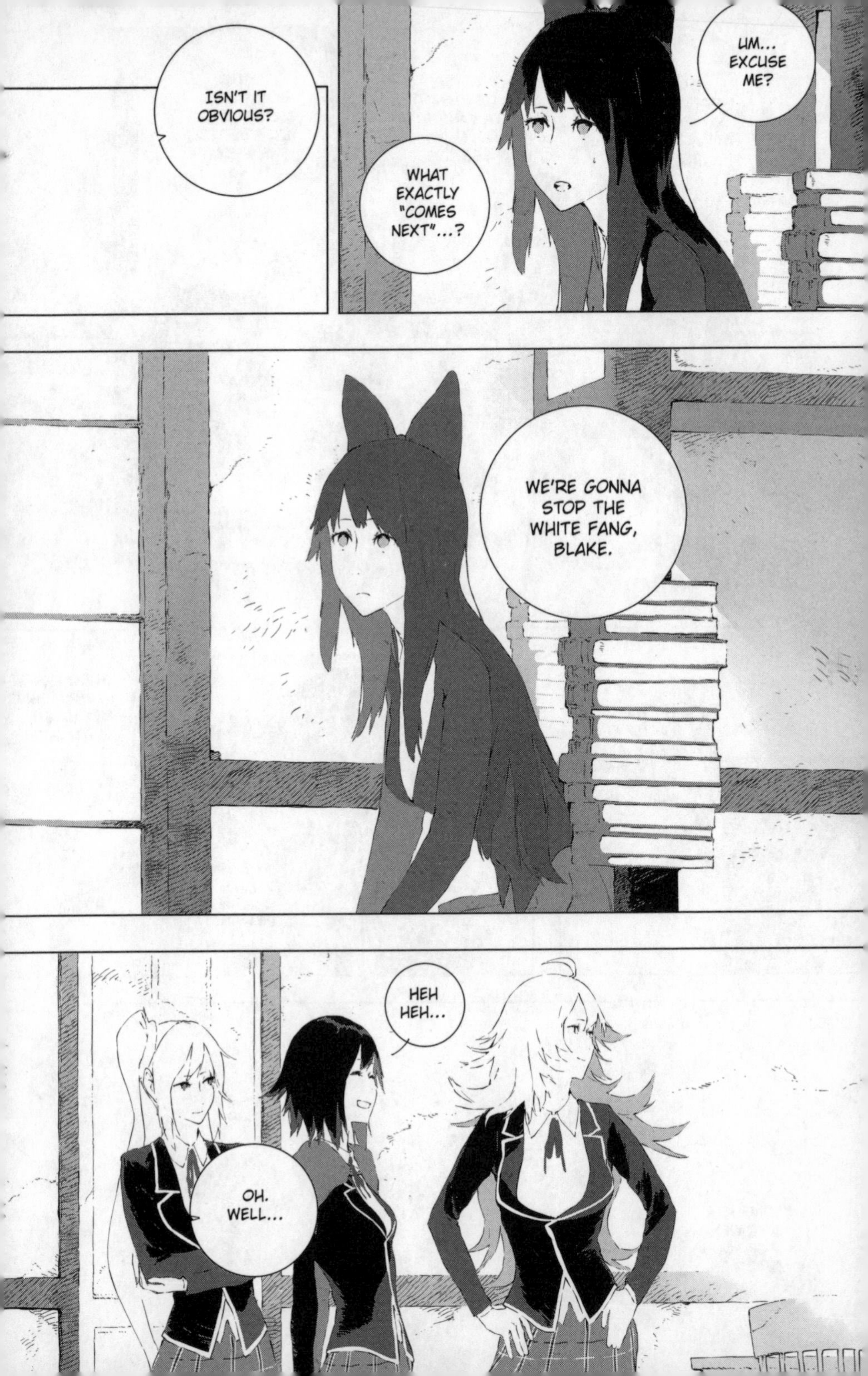
UM... EXCUSE ME?
WHAT EXACTLY "COMES NEXT"...?
ISN'T IT OBVIOUS?
WE'RE GONNA STOP THE WHITE FANG, BLAKE.
HEH HEH...
OH. WELL...

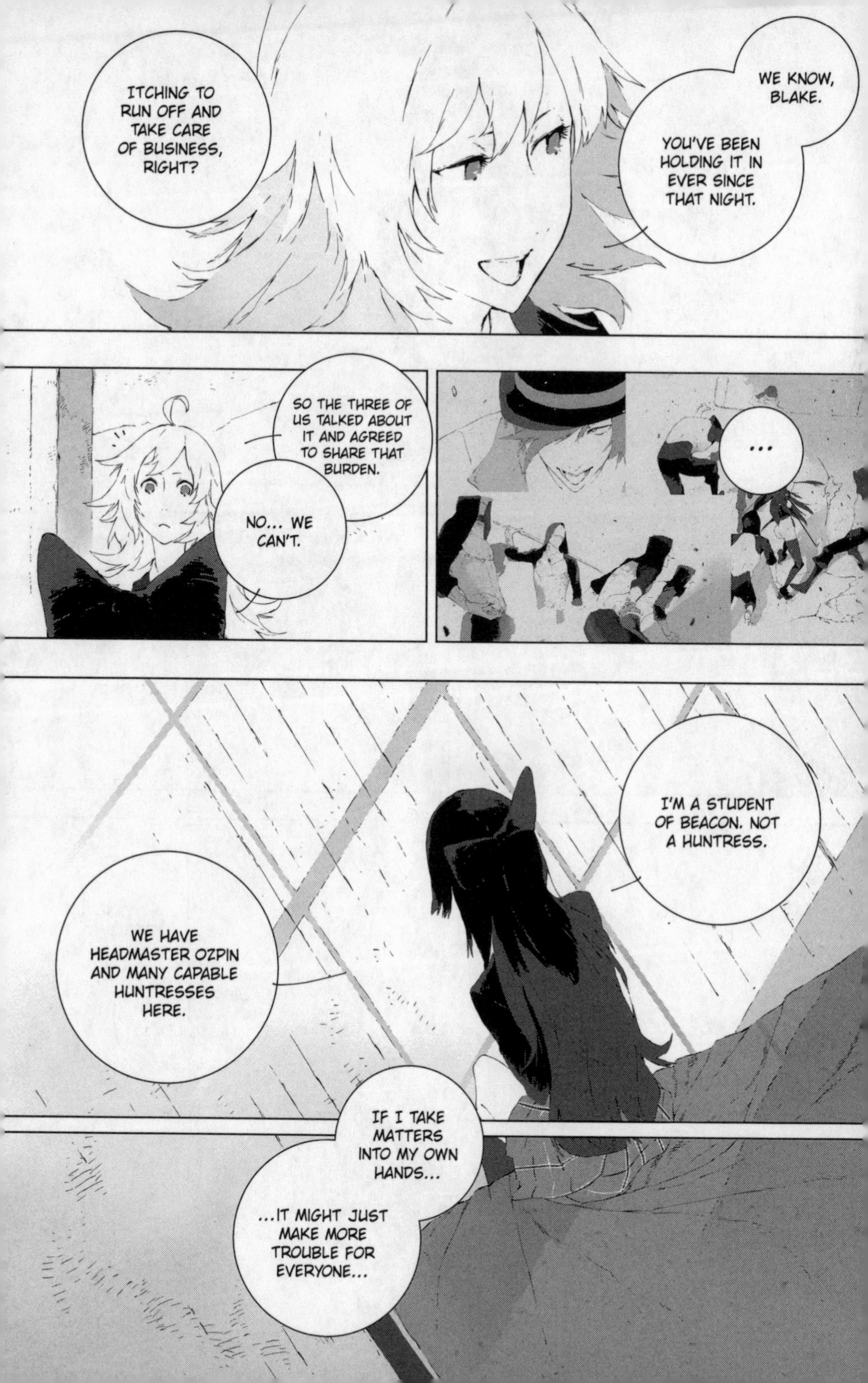
WE KNOW, BLAKE.
YOU'VE BEEN HOLDING IT IN EVER SINCE THAT NIGHT.
ITCHING TO RUN OFF AND TAKE CARE OF BUSINESS, RIGHT?
...
SO THE THREE OF US TALKED ABOUT IT AND AGREED TO SHARE THAT BURDEN.
NO... WE CAN'T.
I'M A STUDENT OF BEACON. NOT A HUNTRESS.
WE HAVE HEADMASTER OZPIN AND MANY CAPABLE HUNTRESSES HERE.
IF I TAKE MATTERS INTO MY OWN HANDS...
...IT MIGHT JUST MAKE MORE TROUBLE FOR EVERYONE...

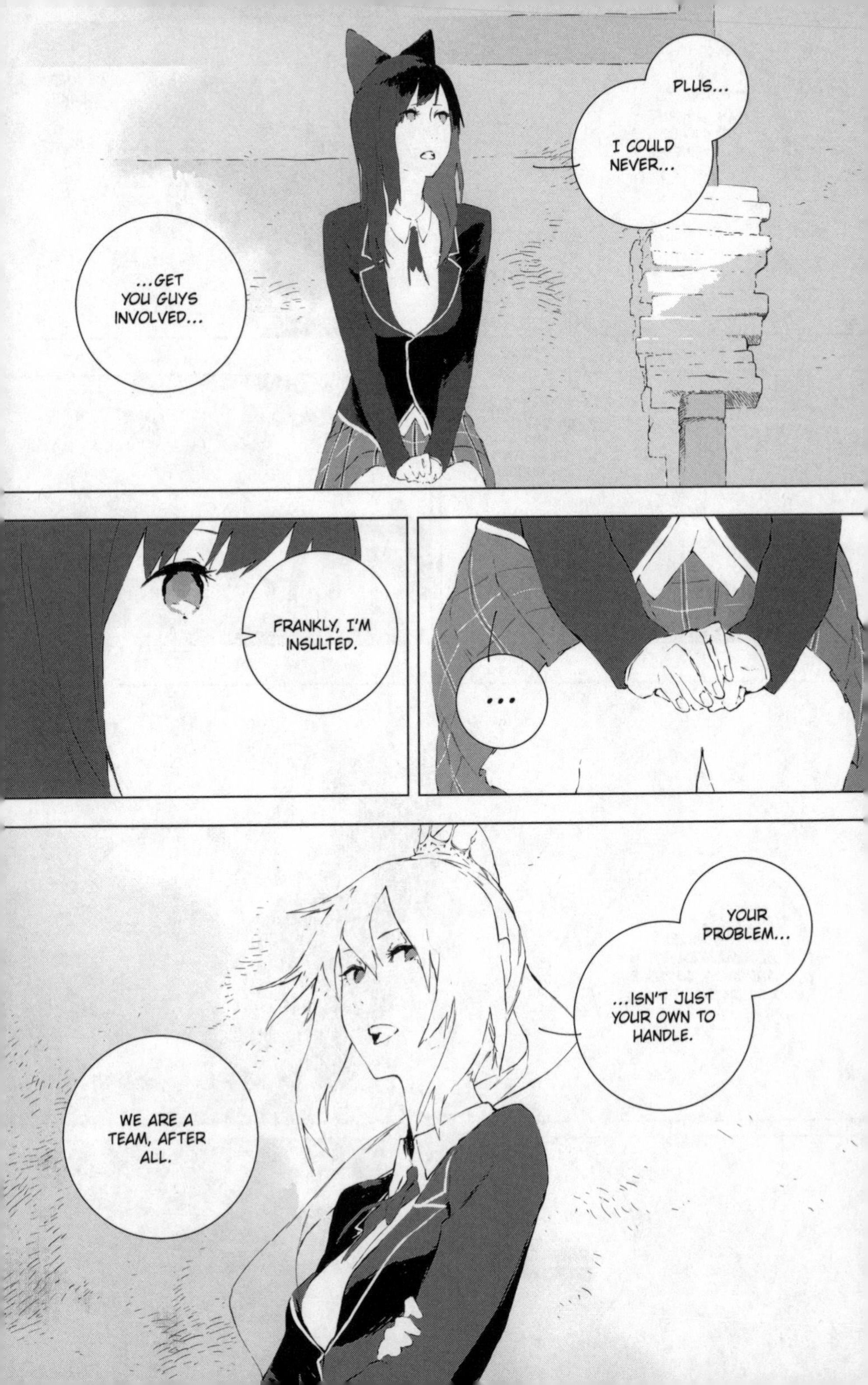
PLUS... I COULD NEVER...
...GET YOU GUYS INVOLVED...
...
FRANKLY, I'M INSULTED.
YOUR PROBLEM... ...ISN'T JUST YOUR OWN TO HANDLE.
WE ARE A TEAM, AFTER ALL.

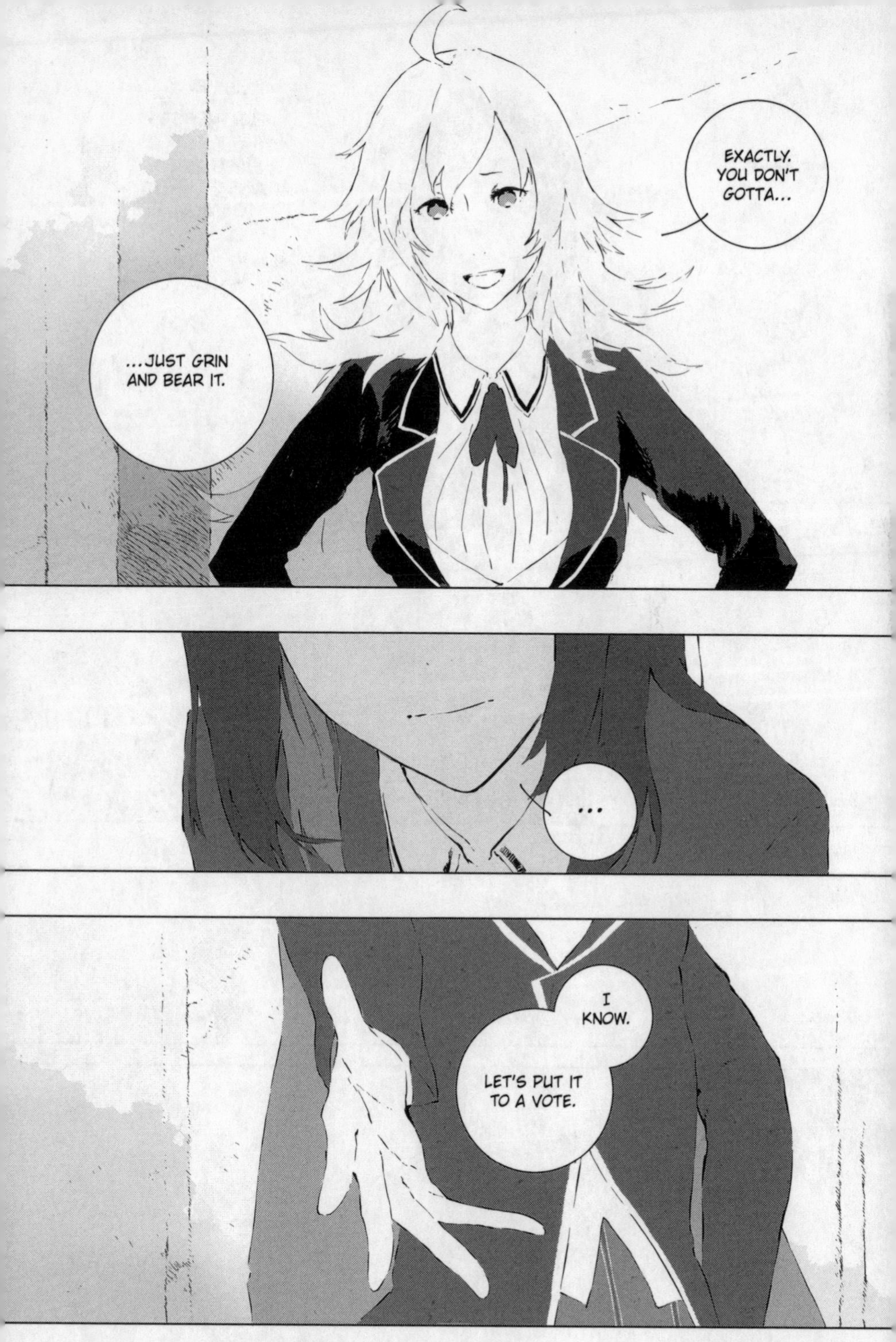
EXACTLY. YOU DON'T GOTTA...
...JUST GRIN AND BEAR IT.
...
I KNOW.
LET'S PUT IT TO A VOTE.

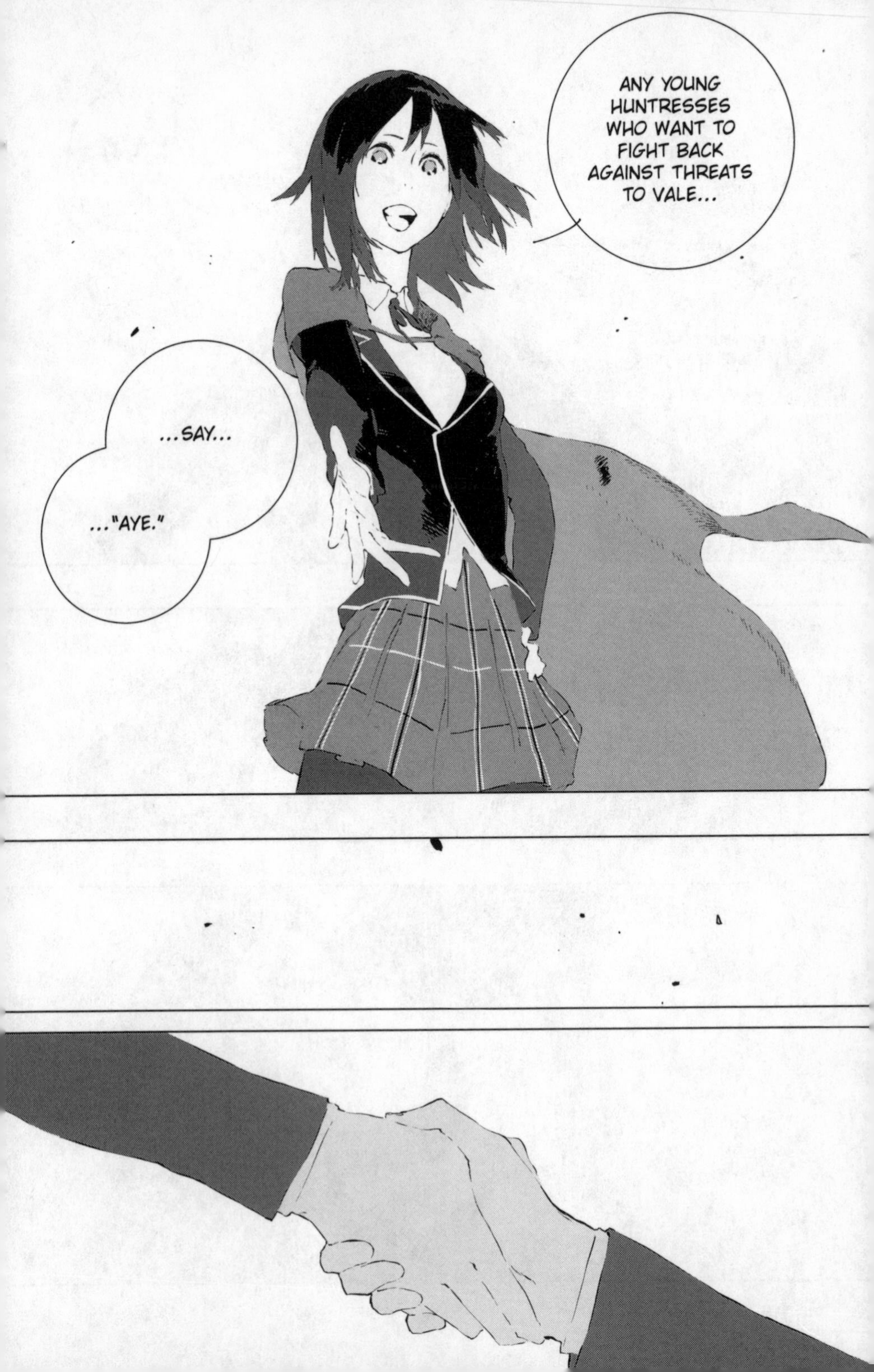
ANY YOUNG HUNTRESSES WHO WANT TO FIGHT BACK AGAINST THREATS TO VALE...
...SAY...
..."AYE."

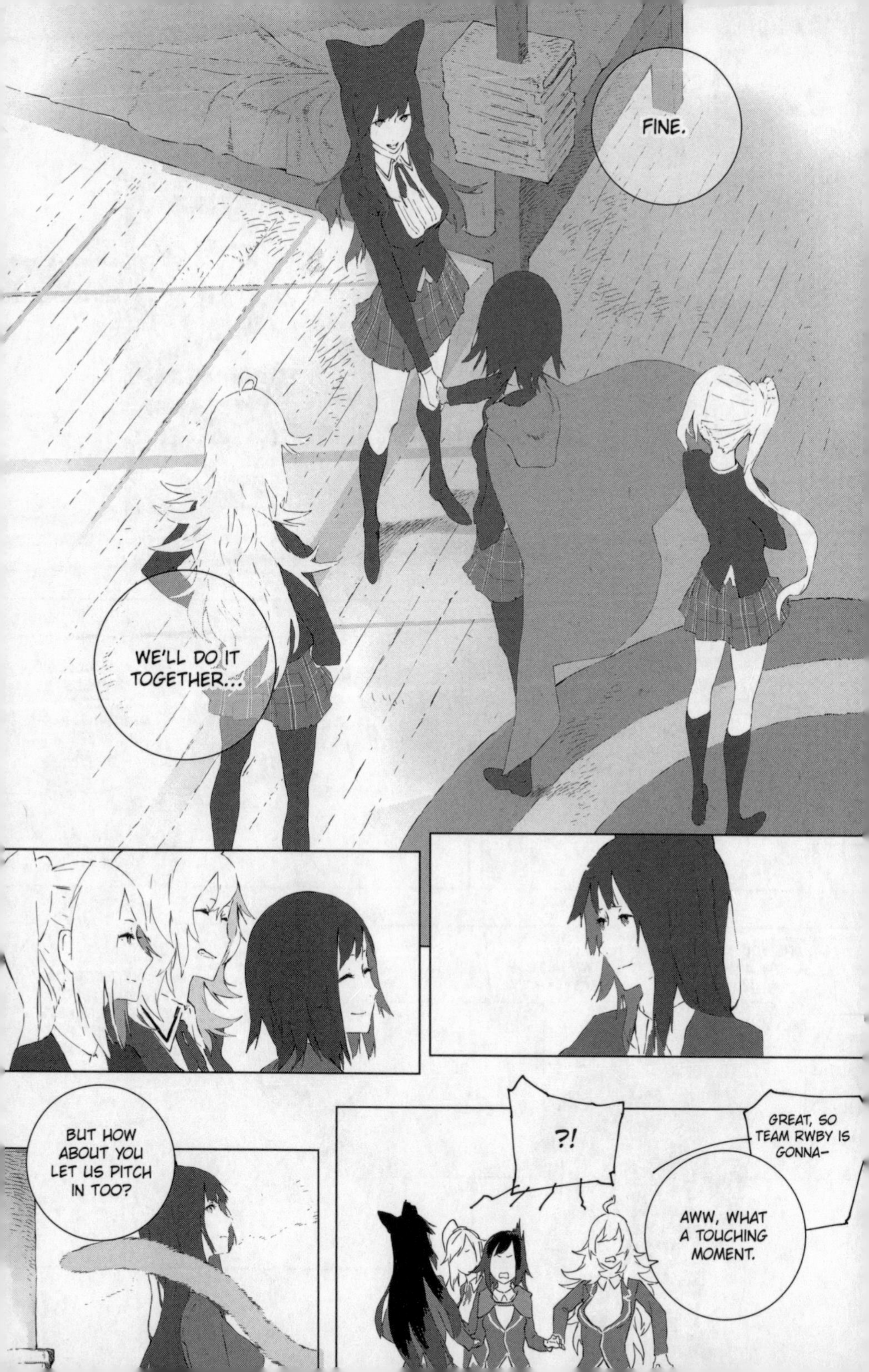
FINE.
WE'LL DO IT TOGETHER...
GREAT, SO TEAM RWBY IS GONNA-
?!
AWW, WHAT A TOUCHING MOMENT.
BUT HOW ABOUT YOU LET US PITCH IN TOO?

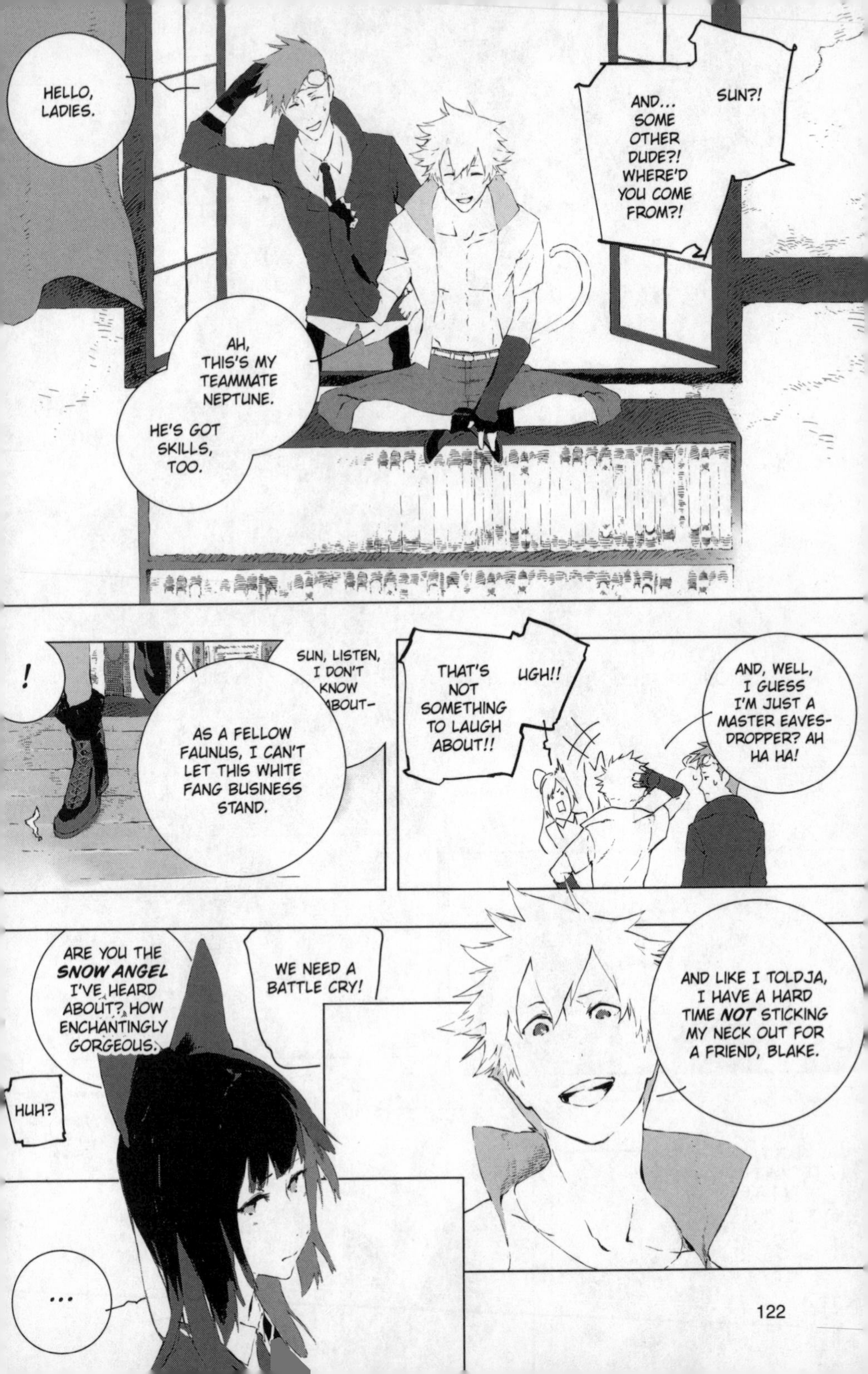
SUN?!
AND... SOME OTHER DUDE?! WHERE'D YOU COME FROM?!
HELLO, LADIES.
AH, THIS'S MY TEAMMATE NEPTUNE.
HE'S GOT SKILLS, TOO.
AND, WELL, I GUESS I'M JUST A MASTER EAVES-DROPPER? AH HA HA!
UGH!!
THAT'S NOT SOMETHING TO LAUGH ABOUT!!
SUN, LISTEN, I DON'T KNOW ABOUT-
AS A FELLOW FAUNUS, I CAN'T LET THIS WHITE FANG BUSINESS STAND.
!
AND LIKE I TOLDJA, I HAVE A HARD TIME NOT STICKING MY NECK OUT FOR A FRIEND, BLAKE.
WE NEED A BATTLE CRY!
ARE YOU THE SNOW ANGEL I'VE HEARD ABOUT? HOW ENCHANTINGLY GORGEOUS.
HUH?
...

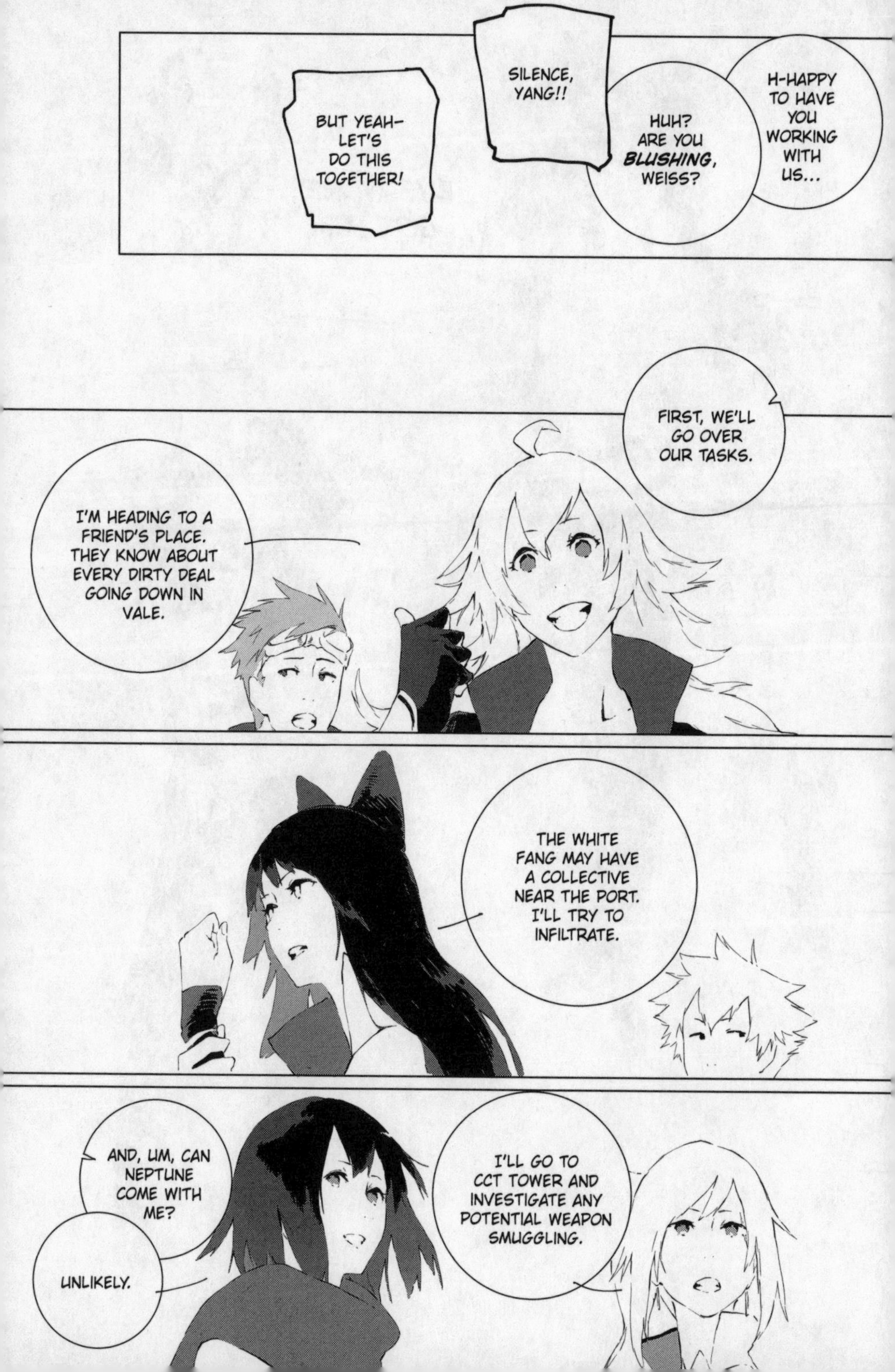
H-HAPPY TO HAVE YOU WORKING WITH US...
HUH? ARE YOU *BLUSHING*, WEISS?
SILENCE, YANG!!
BUT YEAH- LET'S DO THIS TOGETHER!
FIRST, WE'LL GO OVER OUR TASKS.
I'M HEADING TO A FRIEND'S PLACE. THEY KNOW ABOUT EVERY DIRTY DEAL GOING DOWN IN VALE.
THE WHITE FANG MAY HAVE A COLLECTIVE NEAR THE PORT. I'LL TRY TO INFILTRATE.
I'LL GO TO CCT TOWER AND INVESTIGATE ANY POTENTIAL WEAPON SMUGGLING.
AND, UM, CAN NEPTUNE COME WITH ME?
UNLIKELY.

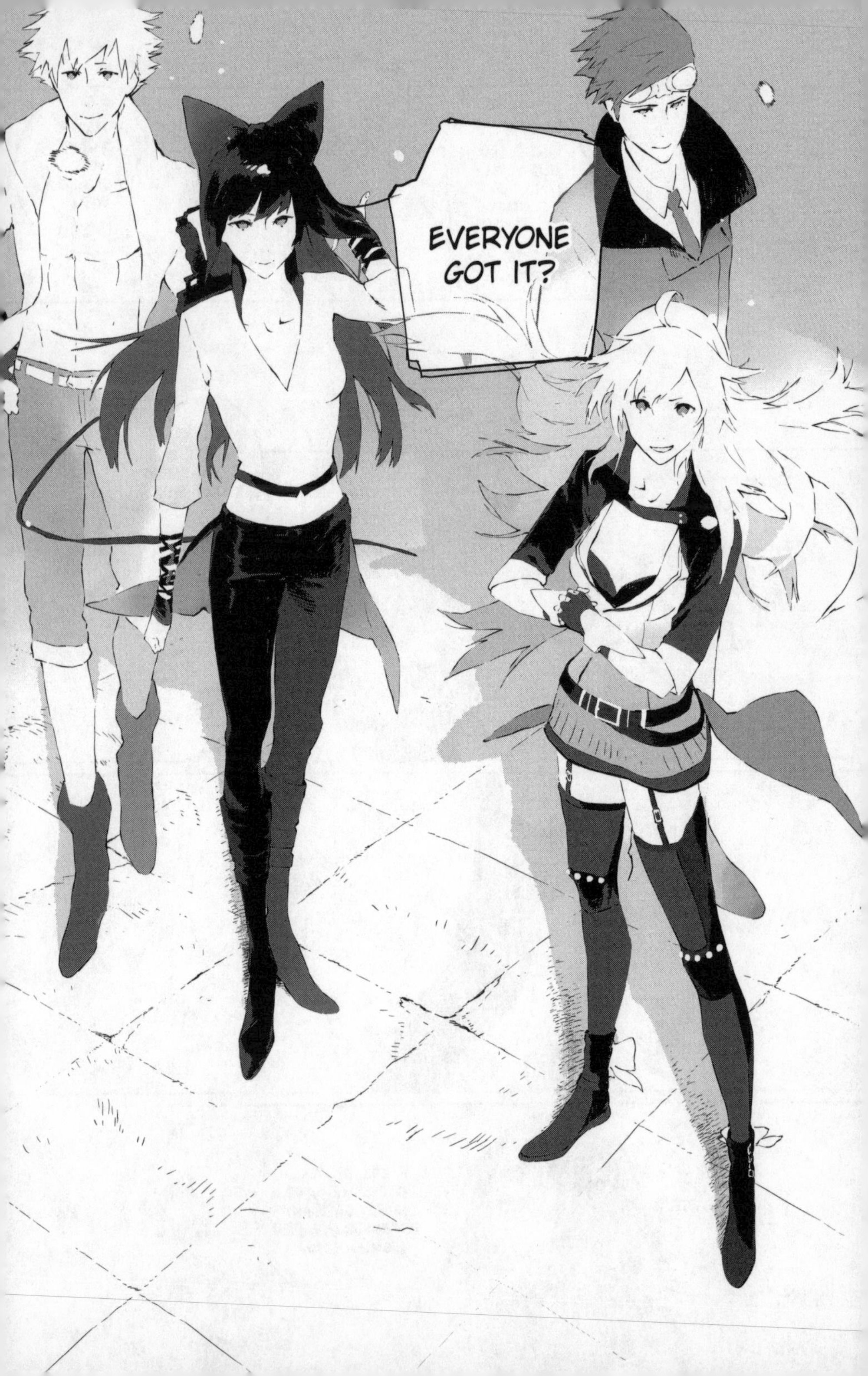
EVERYONE GOT IT?

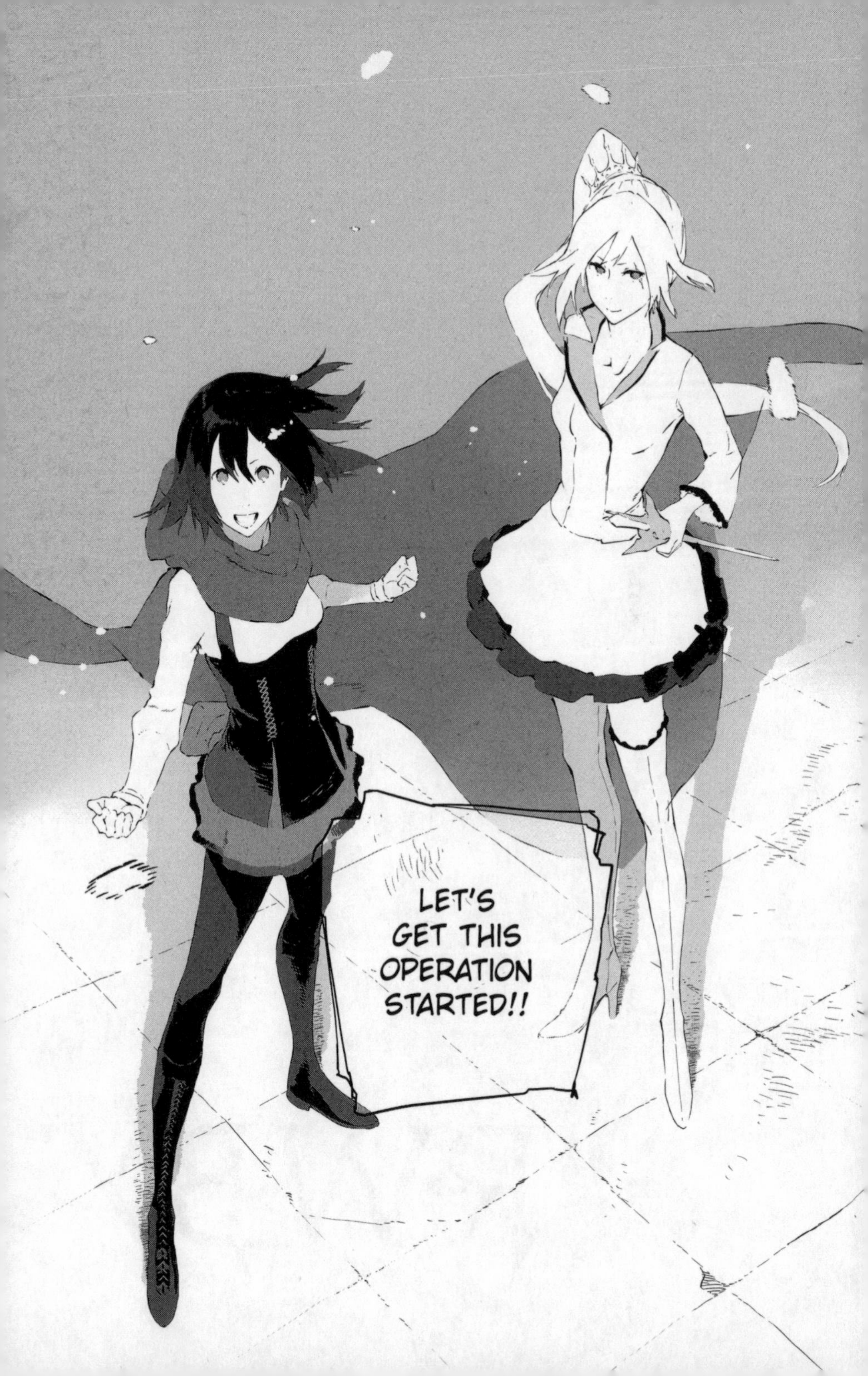
LET'S GET THIS OPERATION STARTED!!

RWBY

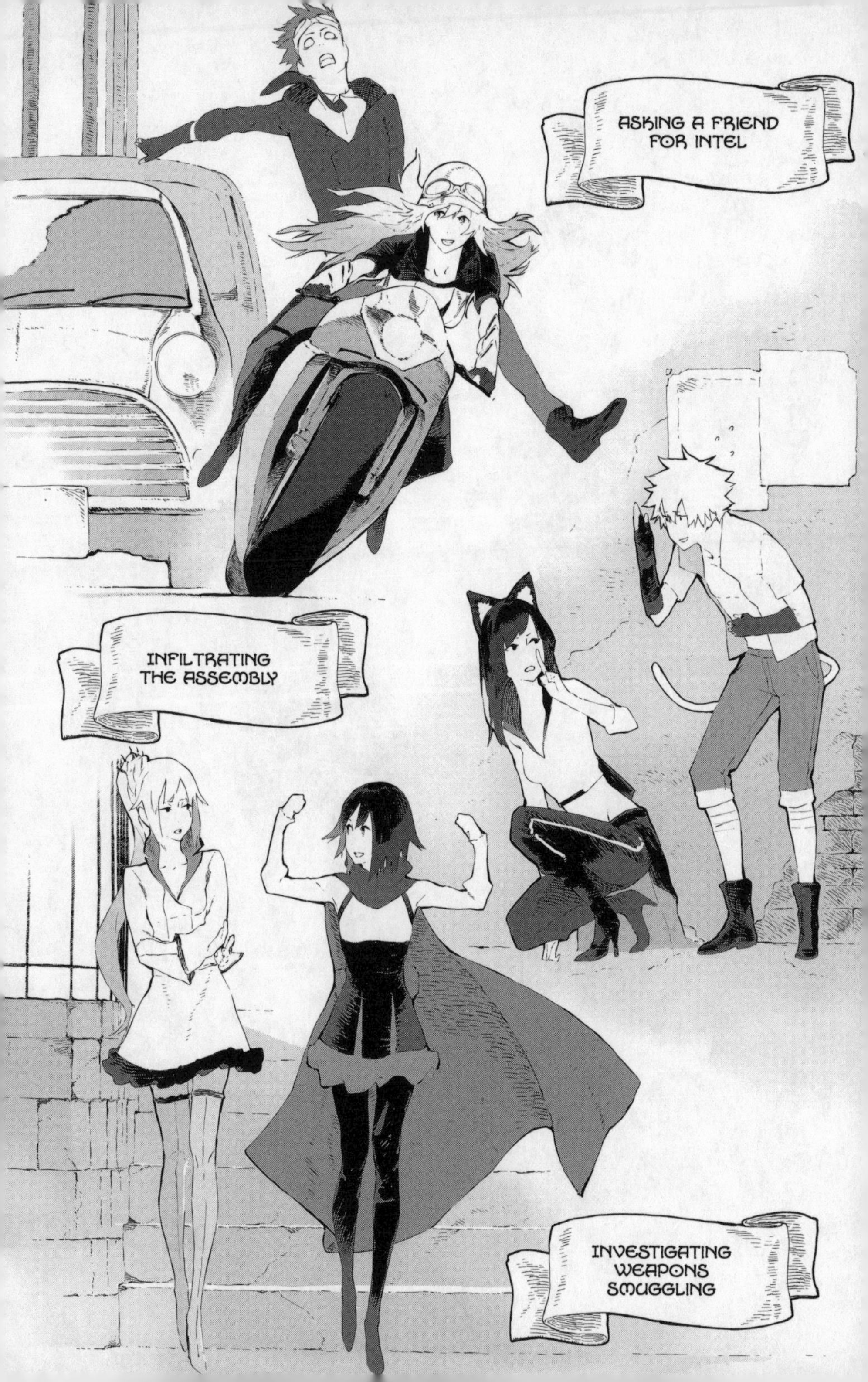
ASKING A FRIEND FOR INTEL
INFILTRATING THE ASSEMBLY
INVESTIGATING WEAPONS SMUGGLING

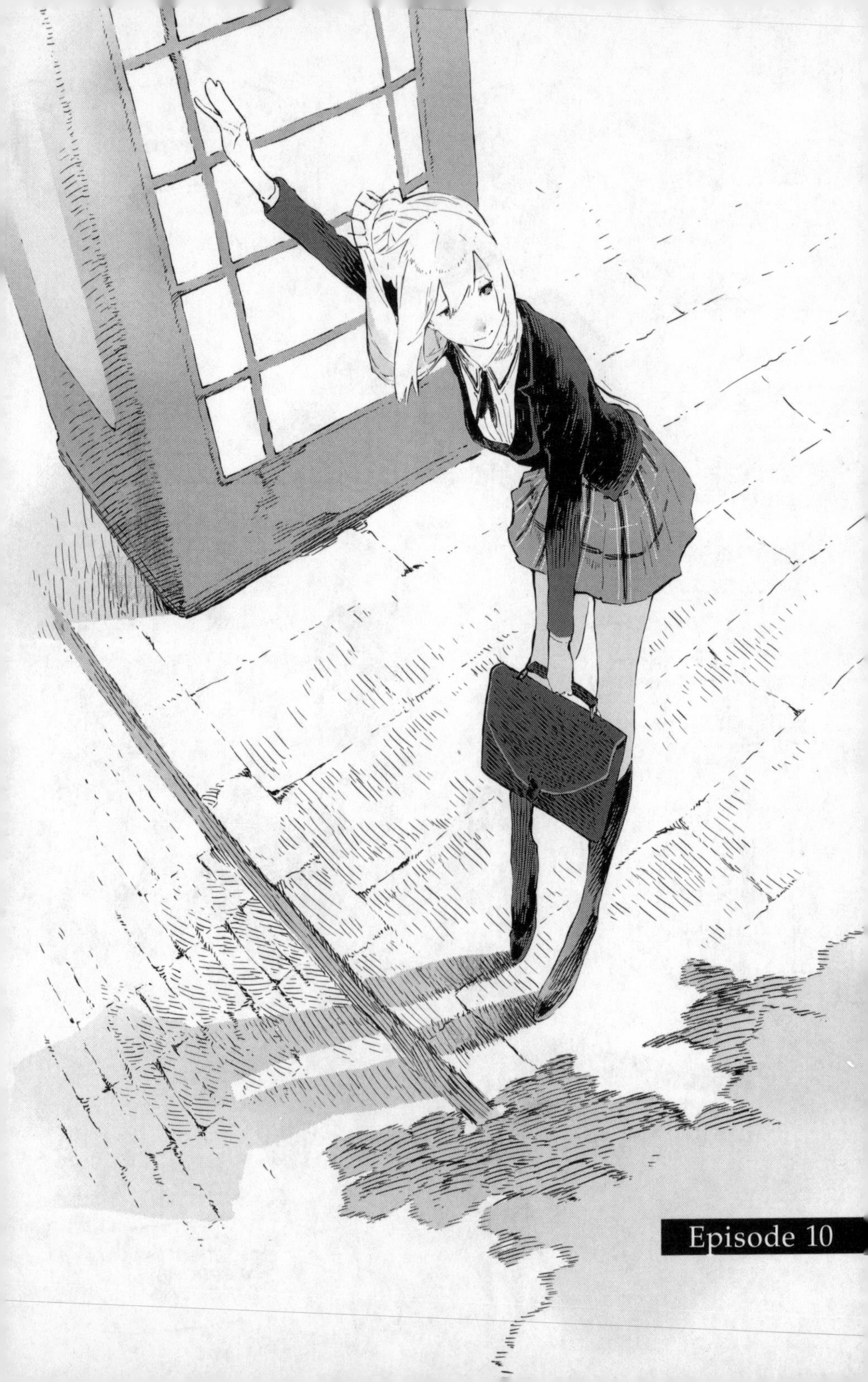
Episode 10

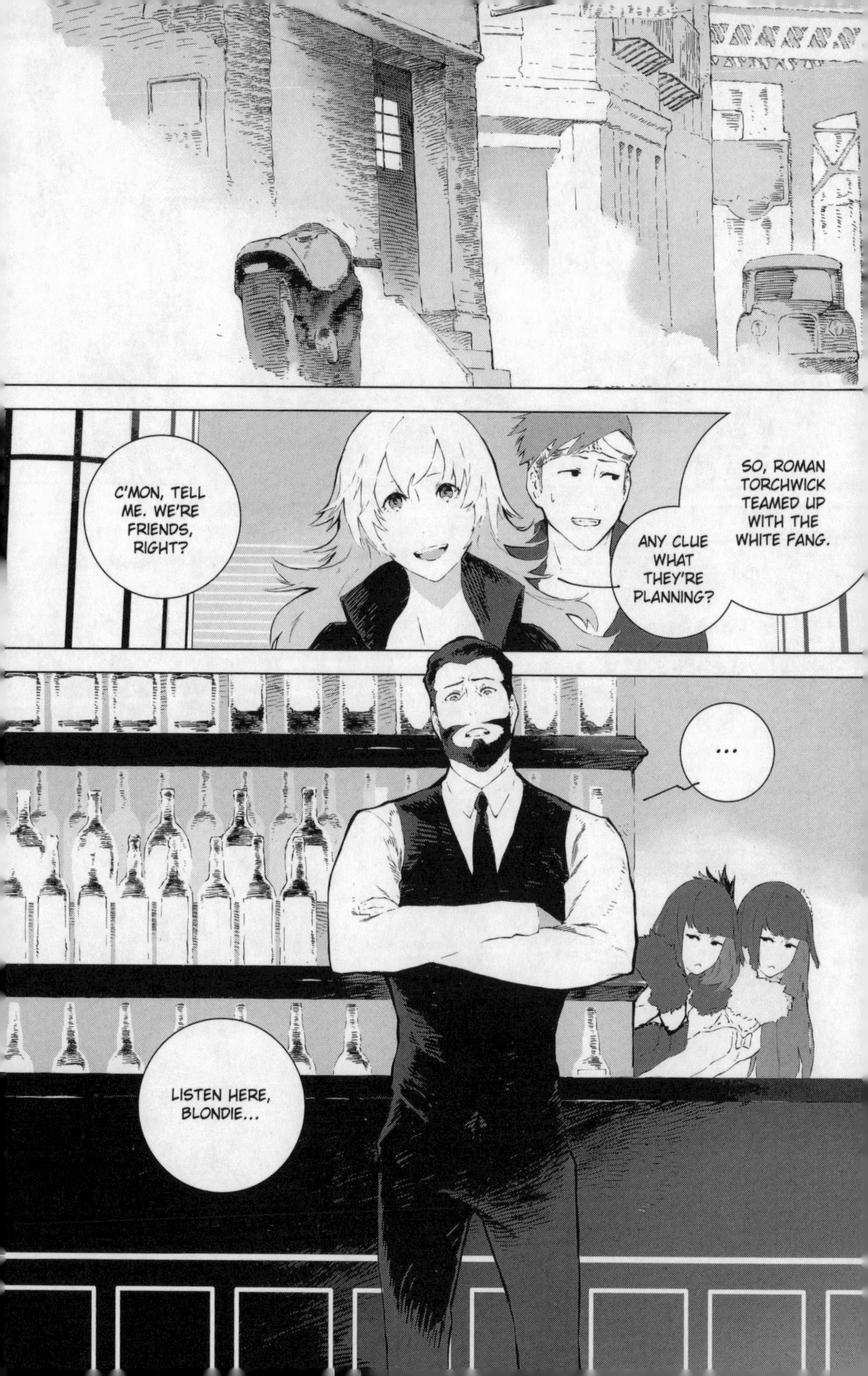
SO, ROMAN TORCHWICK TEAMED UP WITH THE WHITE FANG.
ANY CLUE WHAT THEY'RE PLANNING?
C'MON, TELL ME. WE'RE FRIENDS, RIGHT?
...
LISTEN HERE, BLONDIE...

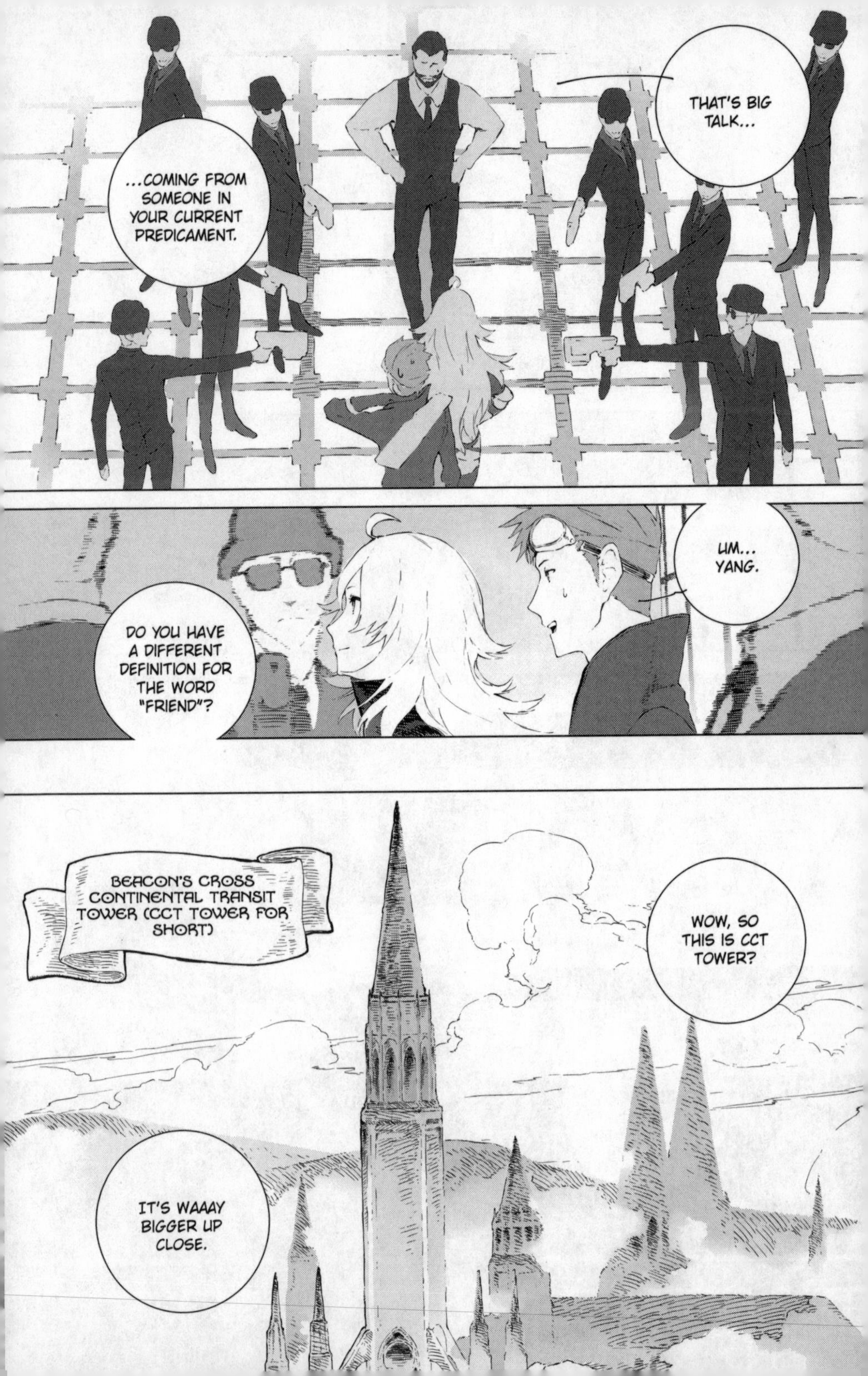
THAT'S BIG TALK...
...COMING FROM SOMEONE IN YOUR CURRENT PREDICAMENT.
UM... YANG.
DO YOU HAVE A DIFFERENT DEFINITION FOR THE WORD "FRIEND"?
BEACON'S CROSS CONTINENTAL TRANSIT TOWER (CCT TOWER FOR SHORT)
WOW, SO THIS IS CCT TOWER?
IT'S WAAAY BIGGER UP CLOSE.

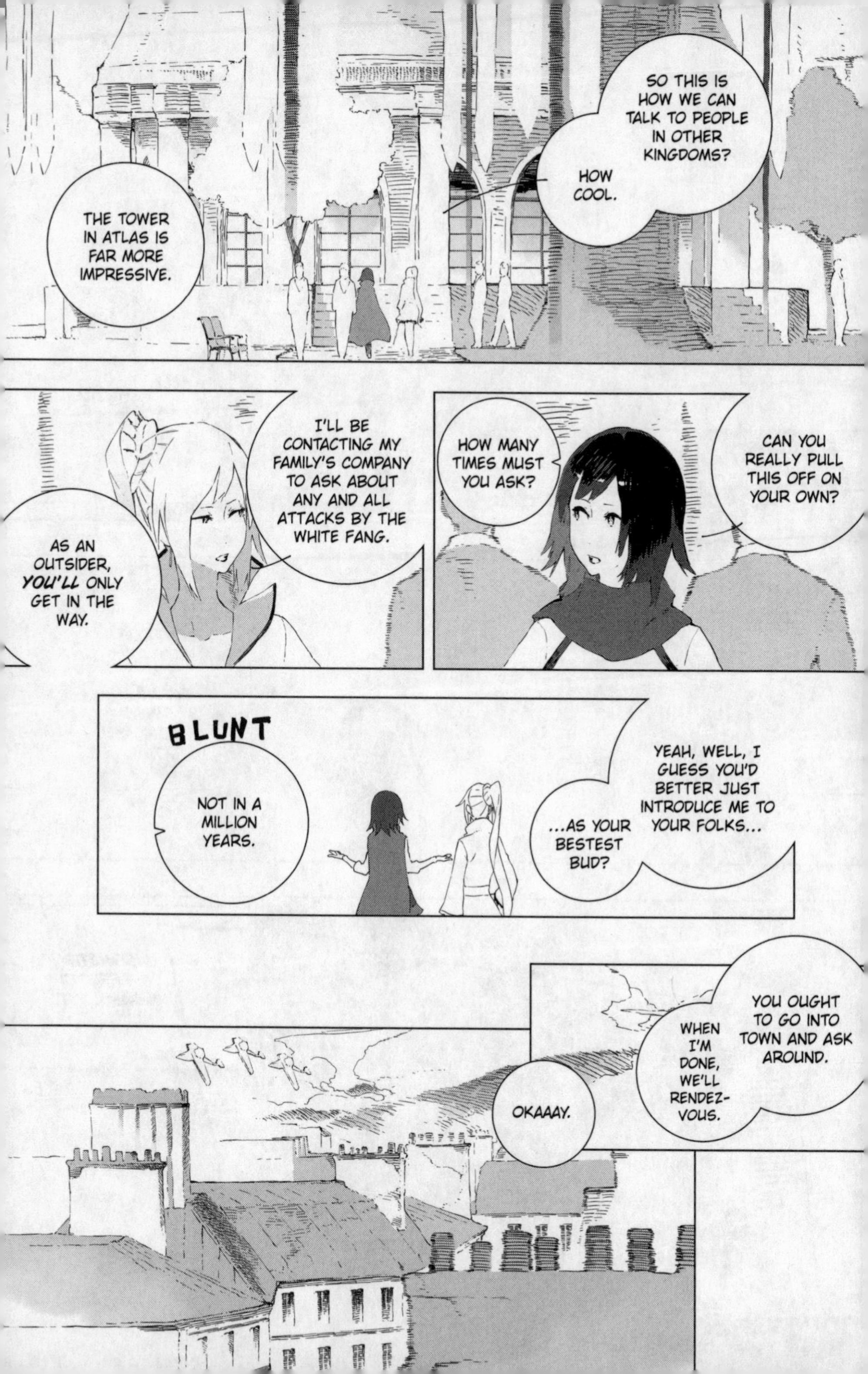

SO THIS IS HOW WE CAN TALK TO PEOPLE IN OTHER KINGDOMS?
HOW COOL.
THE TOWER IN ATLAS IS FAR MORE IMPRESSIVE.
CAN YOU REALLY PULL THIS OFF ON YOUR OWN?
HOW MANY TIMES MUST YOU ASK?
I'LL BE CONTACTING MY FAMILY'S COMPANY TO ASK ABOUT ANY AND ALL ATTACKS BY THE WHITE FANG.
AS AN OUTSIDER, *YOU'LL* ONLY GET IN THE WAY.
YEAH, WELL, I GUESS YOU'D BETTER JUST INTRODUCE ME TO YOUR FOLKS...
...AS YOUR BESTEST BUD?
BLUNT
NOT IN A MILLION YEARS.
YOU OUGHT TO GO INTO TOWN AND ASK AROUND.
WHEN I'M DONE, WE'LL RENDEZ-VOUS.
OKAAAY.

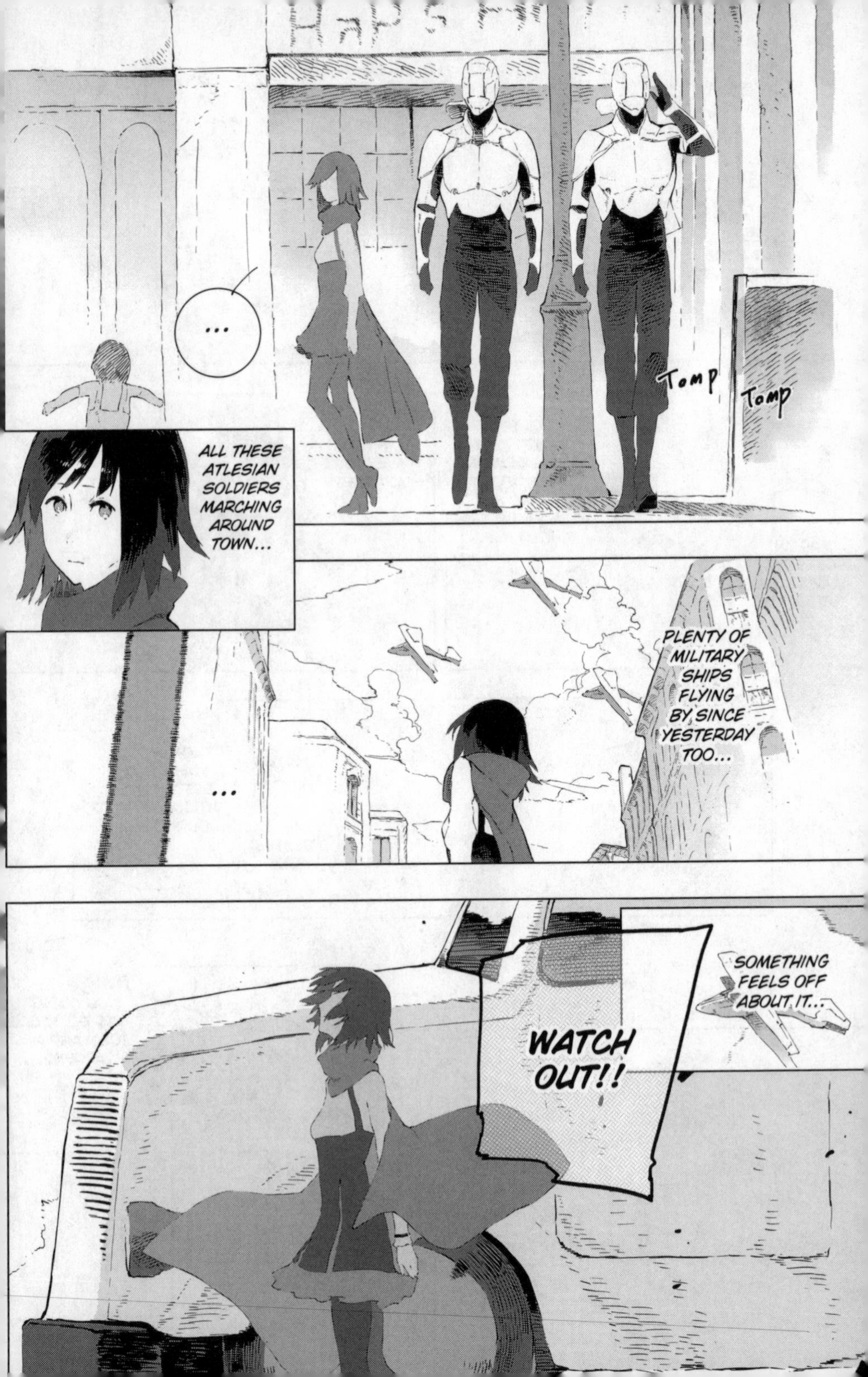
...
Tomp
Tomp
ALL THESE ATLESIAN SOLDIERS MARCHING AROUND TOWN...
PLENTY OF MILITARY SHIPS FLYING BY SINCE YESTERDAY TOO...
...
SOMETHING FEELS OFF ABOUT IT...
WATCH OUT!!

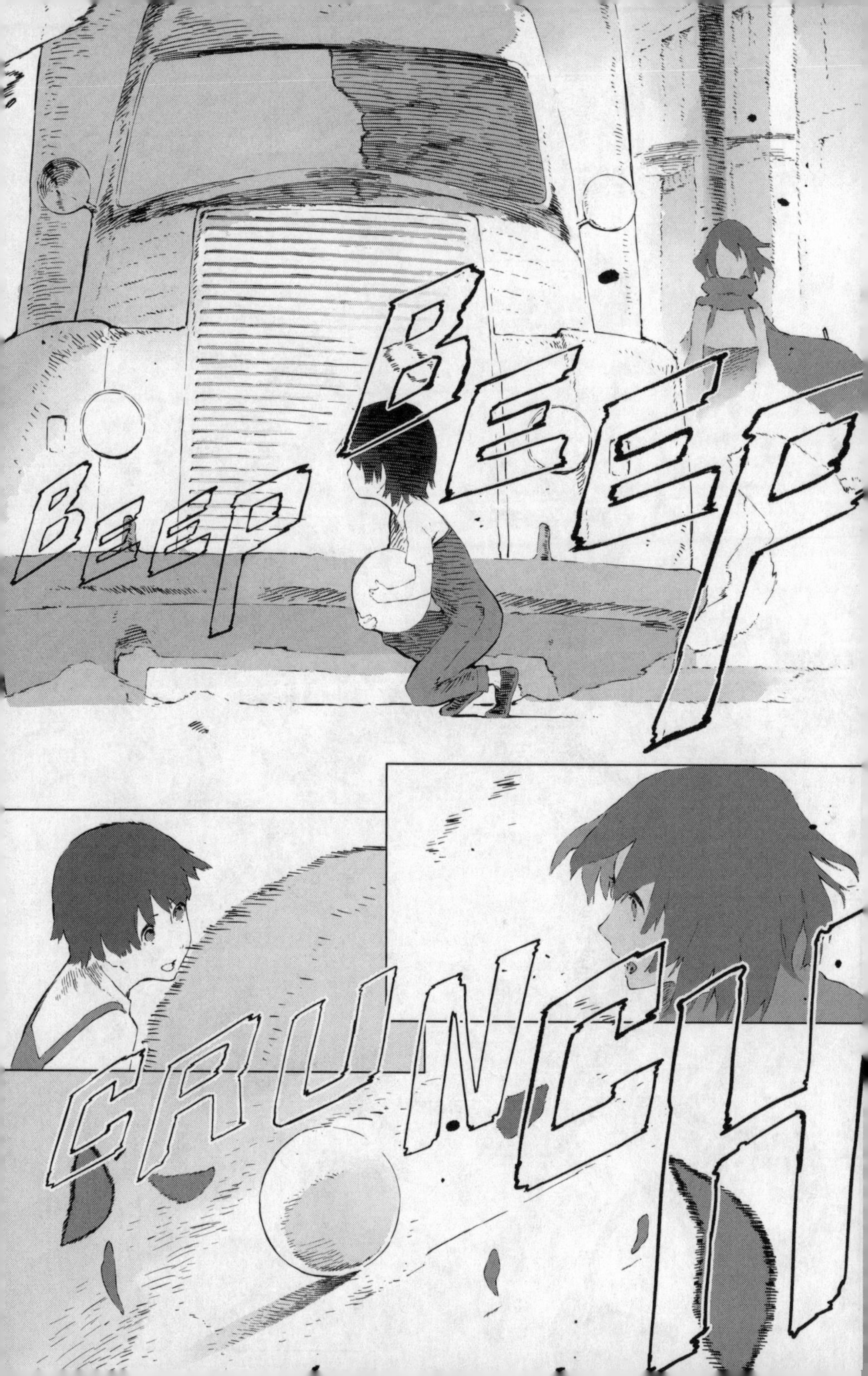
BEEP
BEEP
CRUNCH

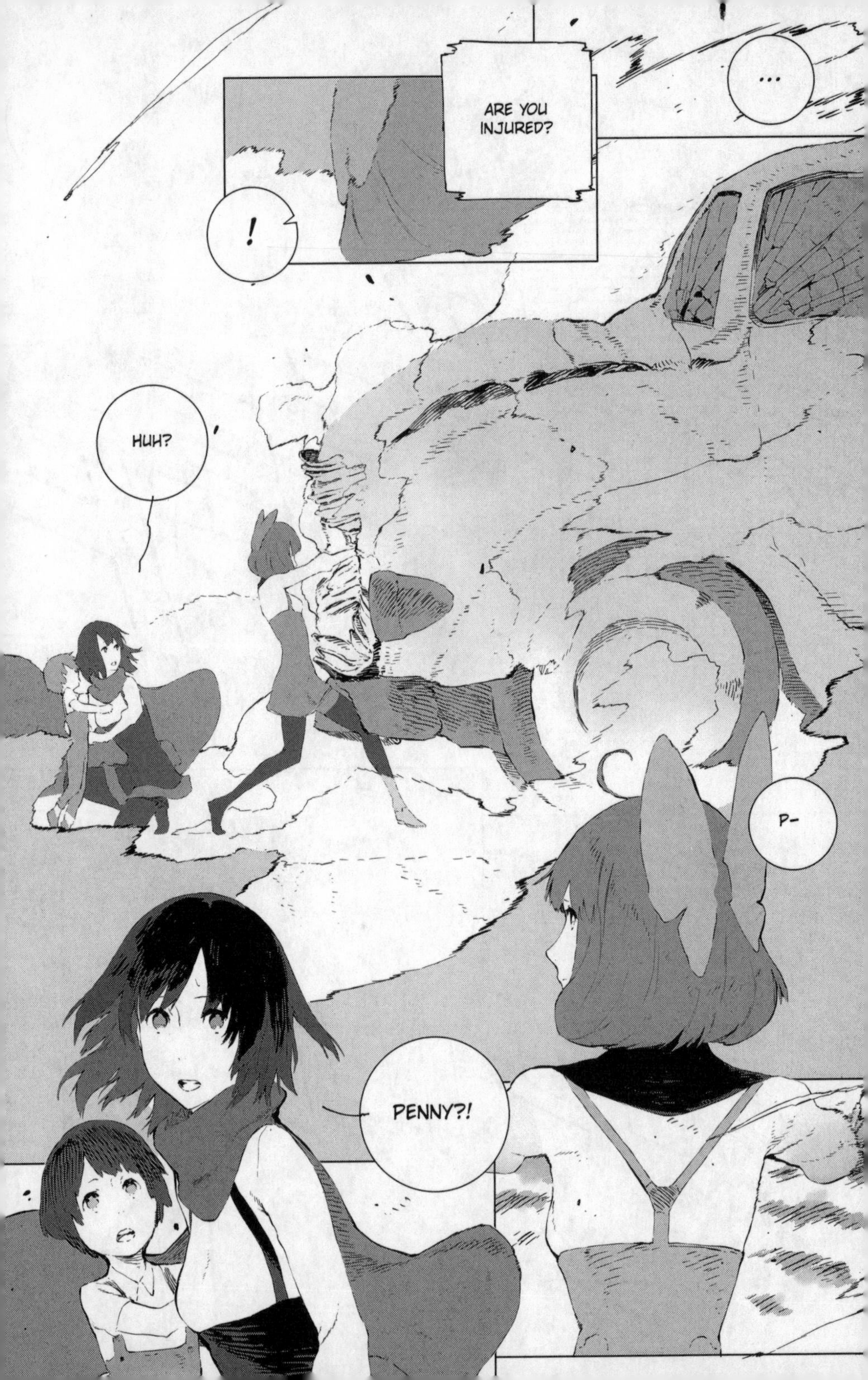
...
ARE YOU INJURED?
!
HUH?
P-
PENNY?!

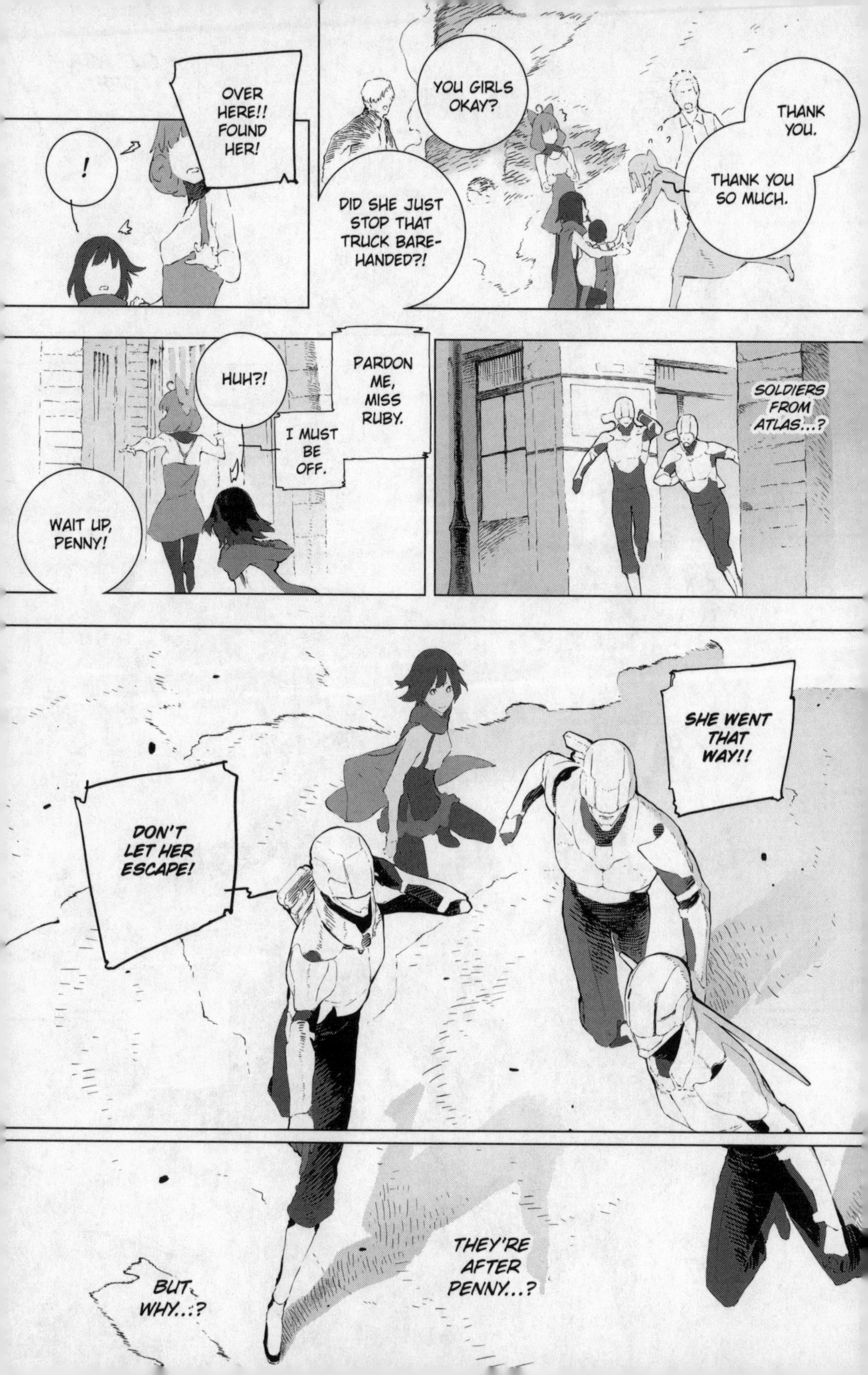
THANK YOU.
THANK YOU SO MUCH.
YOU GIRLS OKAY?
DID SHE JUST STOP THAT TRUCK BARE-HANDED?!
OVER HERE!! FOUND HER!
!
SOLDIERS FROM ATLAS...?
PARDON ME, MISS RUBY.
I MUST BE OFF.
HUH?!
WAIT UP, PENNY!
SHE WENT THAT WAY!!
DON'T LET HER ESCAPE!
THEY'RE AFTER PENNY...?
BUT WHY...?

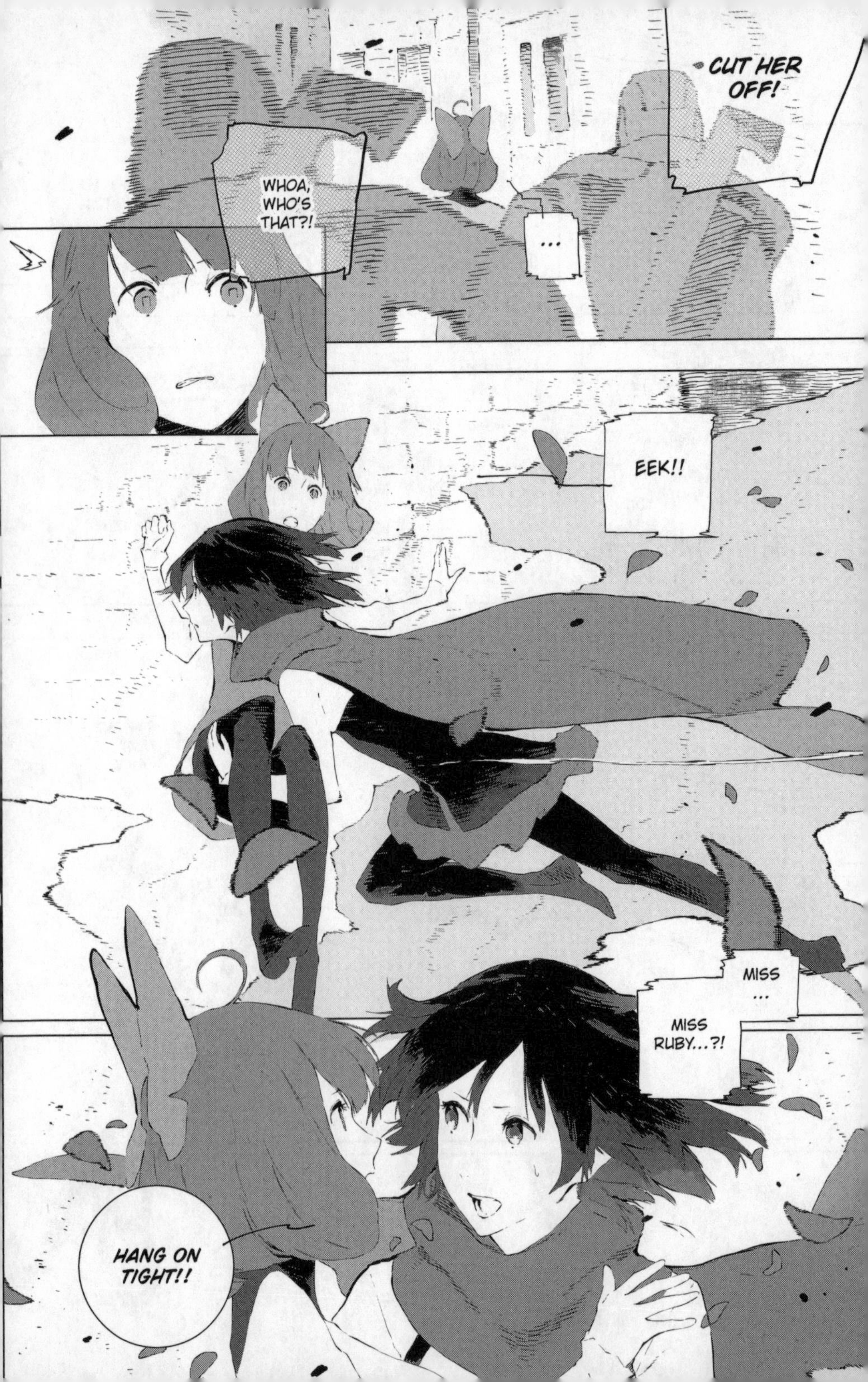
CUT HER OFF!
...
WHOA, WHO'S THAT?!
EEK!!
MISS ...
MISS RUBY...?!
HANG ON TIGHT!!

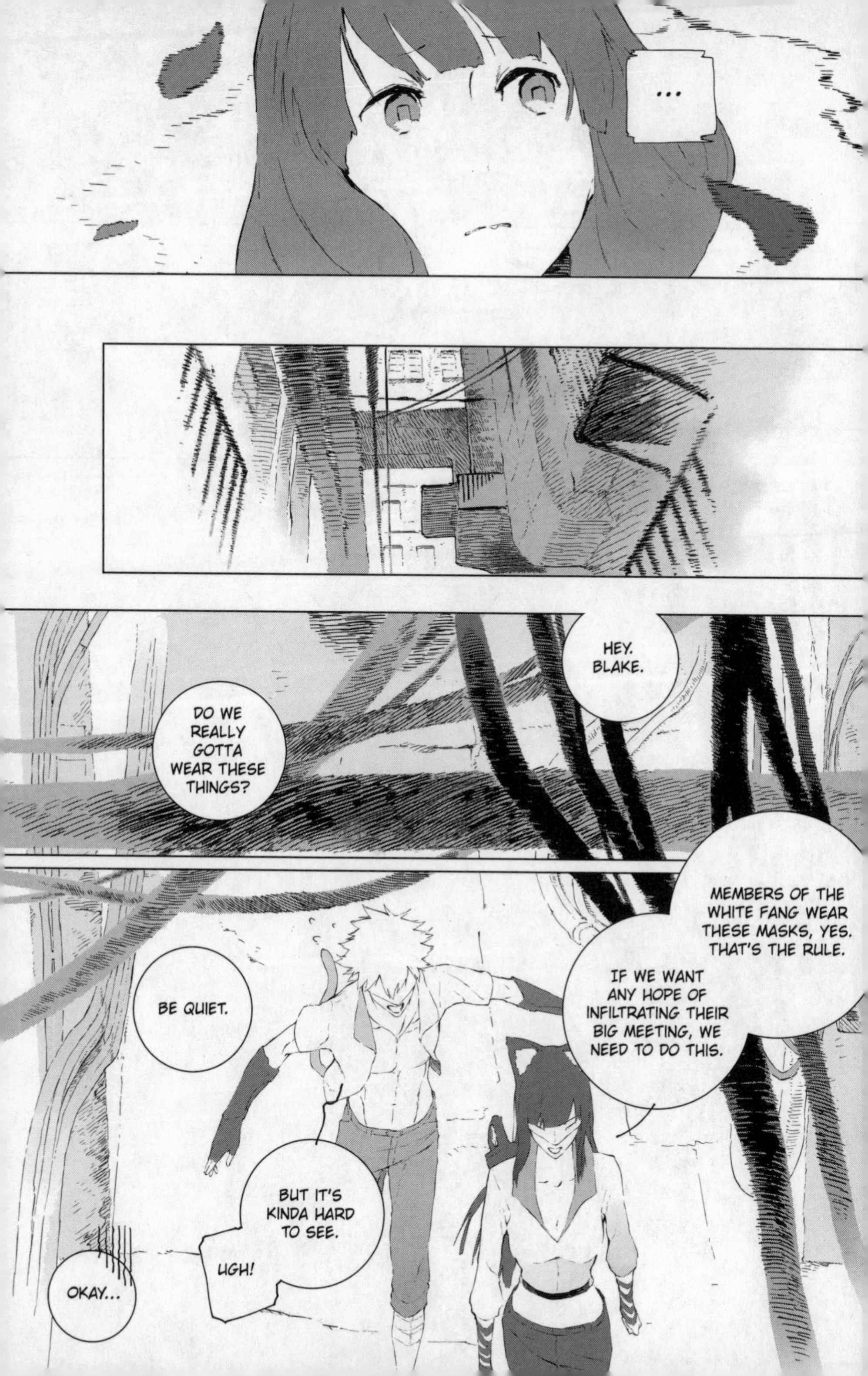
...
HEY. BLAKE.
DO WE REALLY GOTTA WEAR THESE THINGS?
MEMBERS OF THE WHITE FANG WEAR THESE MASKS, YES. THAT'S THE RULE.
IF WE WANT ANY HOPE OF INFILTRATING THEIR BIG MEETING, WE NEED TO DO THIS.
BUT IT'S KINDA HARD TO SEE.
BE QUIET.
UGH!
OKAY...

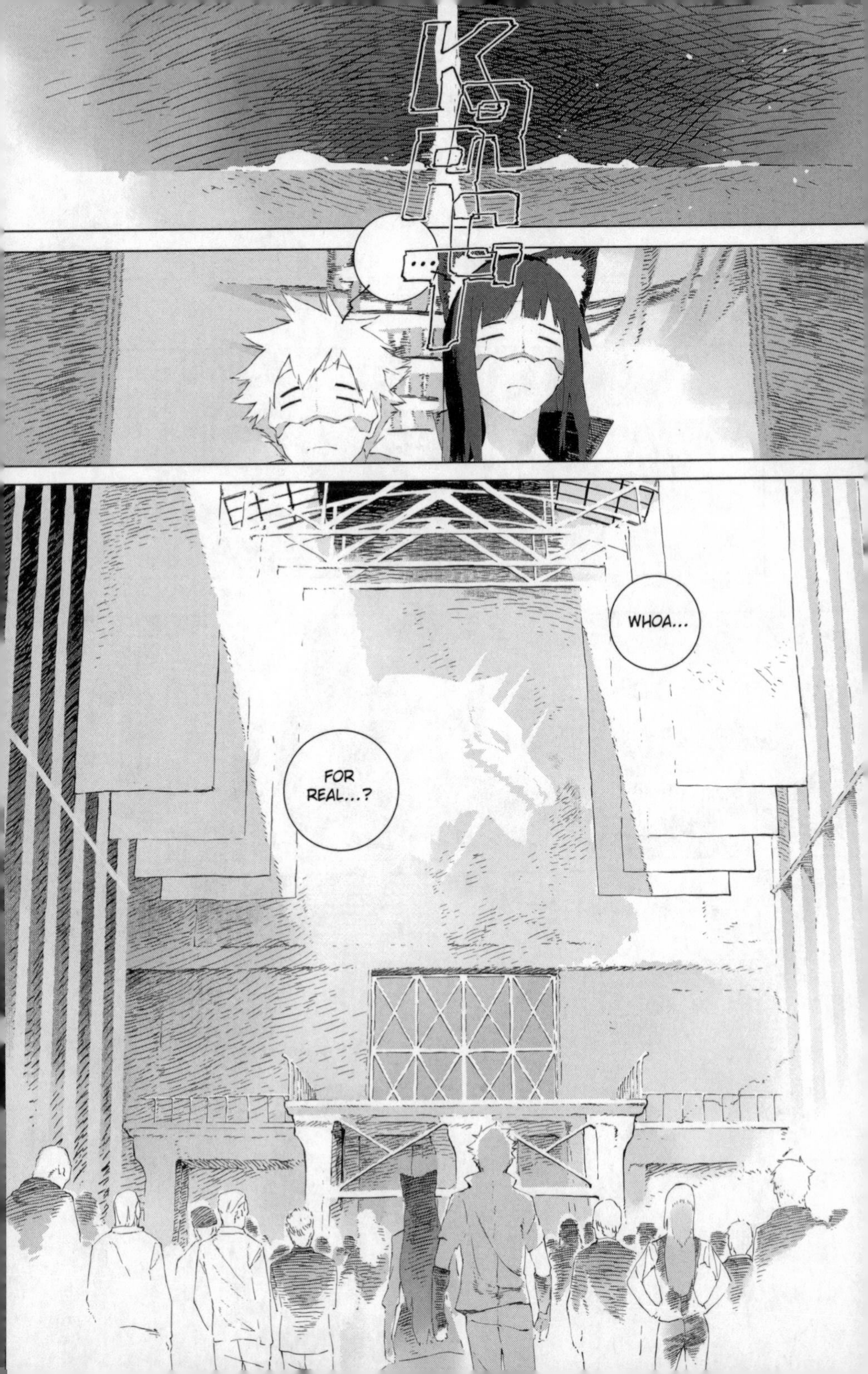
...
WHOA...
FOR REAL...?

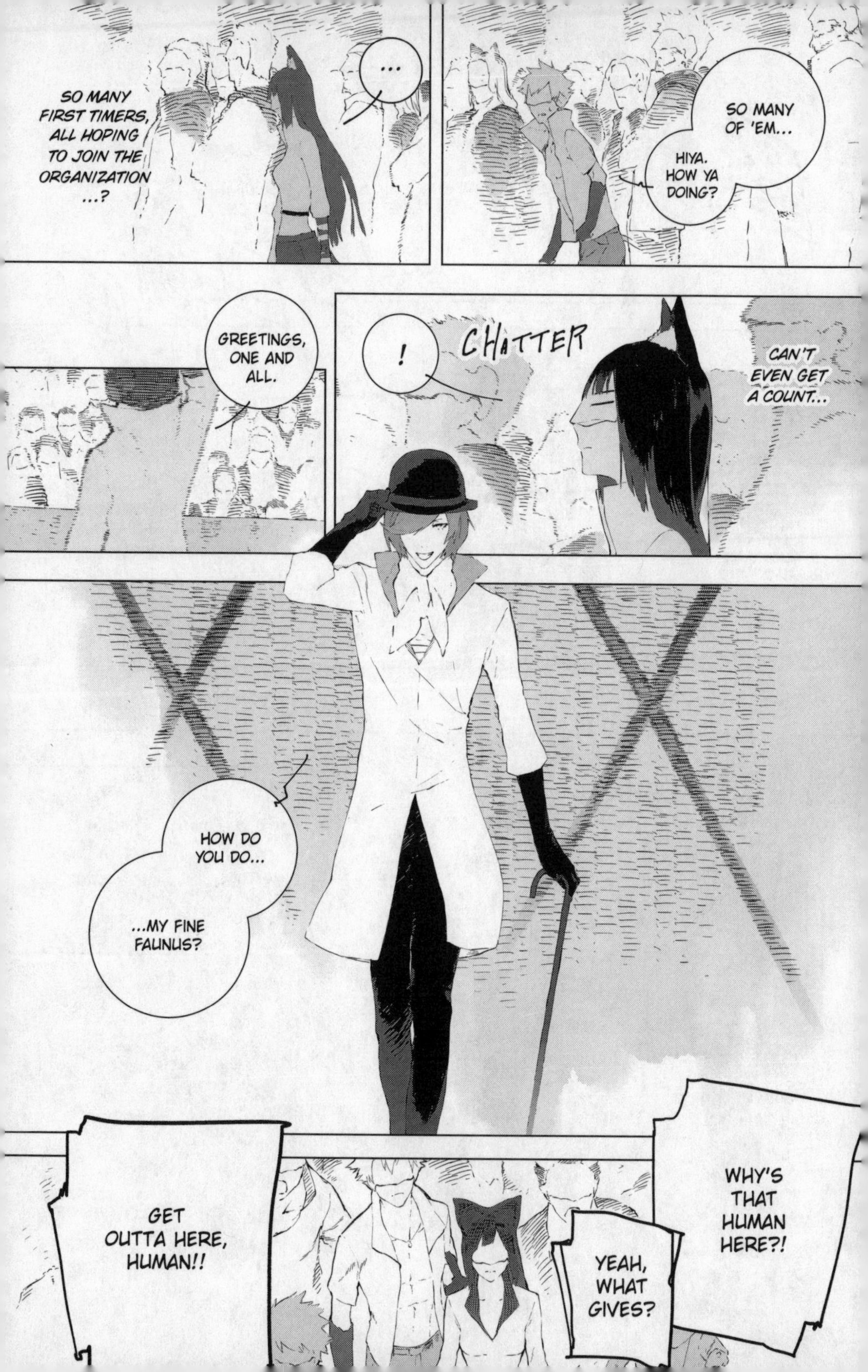
SO MANY OF 'EM...
HIYA. HOW YA DOING?
...
SO MANY FIRST TIMERS, ALL HOPING TO JOIN THE ORGANIZATION ...?
CAN'T EVEN GET A COUNT...
CHATTER
!
GREETINGS, ONE AND ALL.
HOW DO YOU DO...
...MY FINE FAUNUS?
WHY'S THAT HUMAN HERE?!
YEAH, WHAT GIVES?
GET OUTTA HERE, HUMAN!!

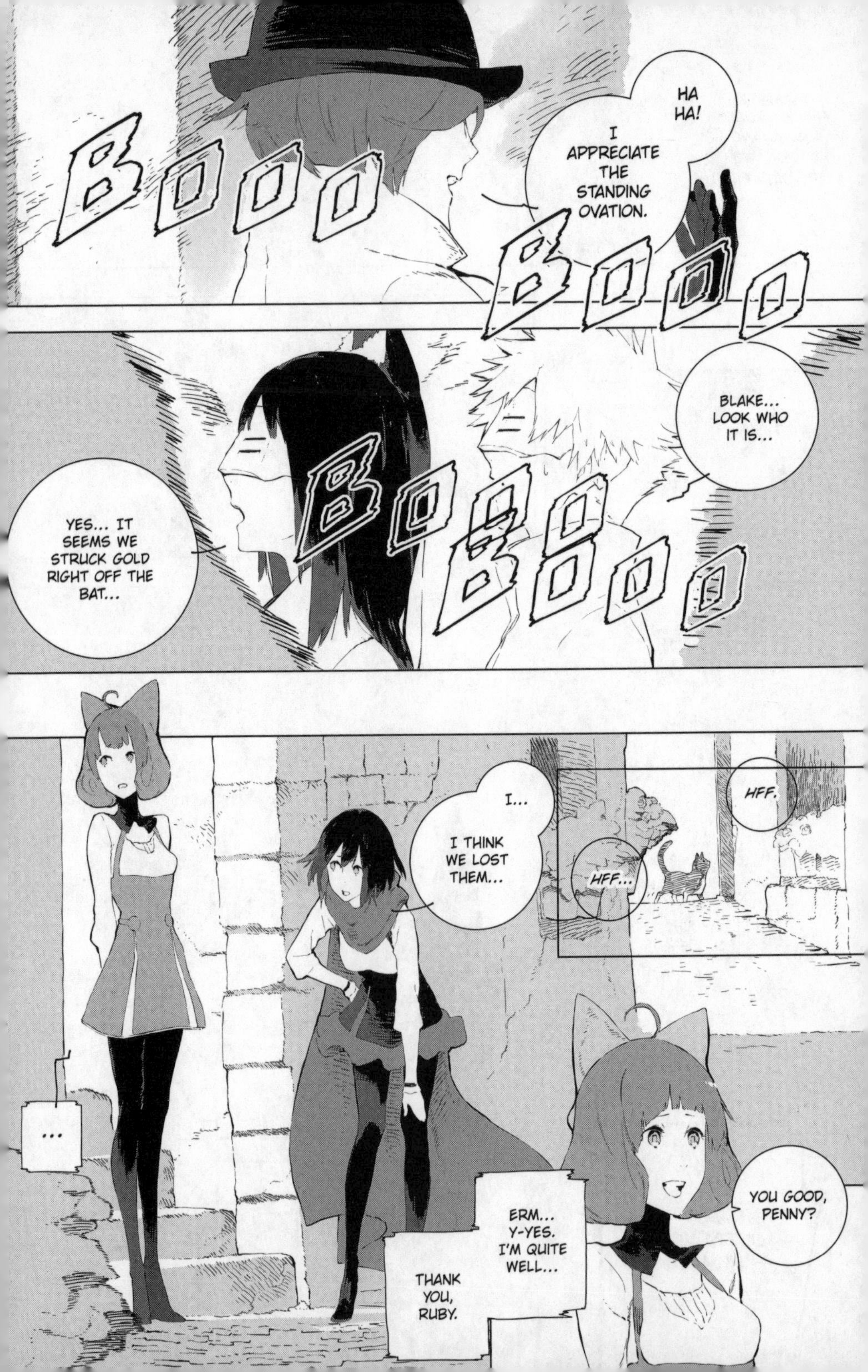
HA HA!
I APPRECIATE THE STANDING OVATION.
BOOOO
BOOOO
BLAKE... LOOK WHO IT IS...
BOOO
BOOOO
YES... IT SEEMS WE STRUCK GOLD RIGHT OFF THE BAT...
HFF.
HFF...
I...
I THINK WE LOST THEM...
...
YOU GOOD, PENNY?
ERM... Y-YES. I'M QUITE WELL...
THANK YOU, RUBY.

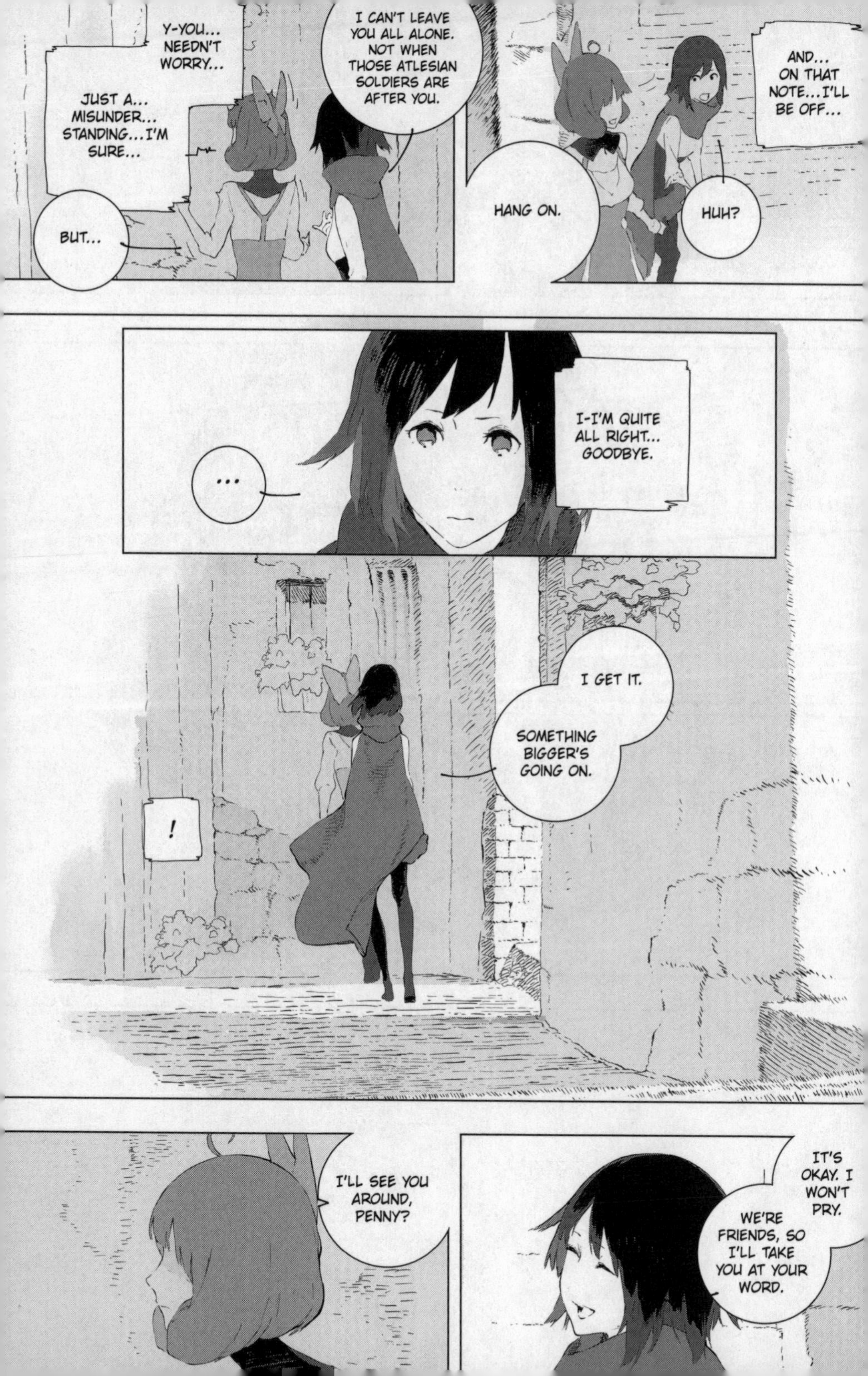
Y-YOU... NEEDN'T WORRY...
JUST A... MISUNDER... STANDING...I'M SURE...
BUT...
I CAN'T LEAVE YOU ALL ALONE. NOT WHEN THOSE ATLESIAN SOLDIERS ARE AFTER YOU.
AND... ON THAT NOTE...I'LL BE OFF...
HANG ON.
HUH?
...
I-I'M QUITE ALL RIGHT... GOODBYE.
!
I GET IT.
SOMETHING BIGGER'S GOING ON.
I'LL SEE YOU AROUND, PENNY?
IT'S OKAY. I WON'T PRY.
WE'RE FRIENDS, SO I'LL TAKE YOU AT YOUR WORD.

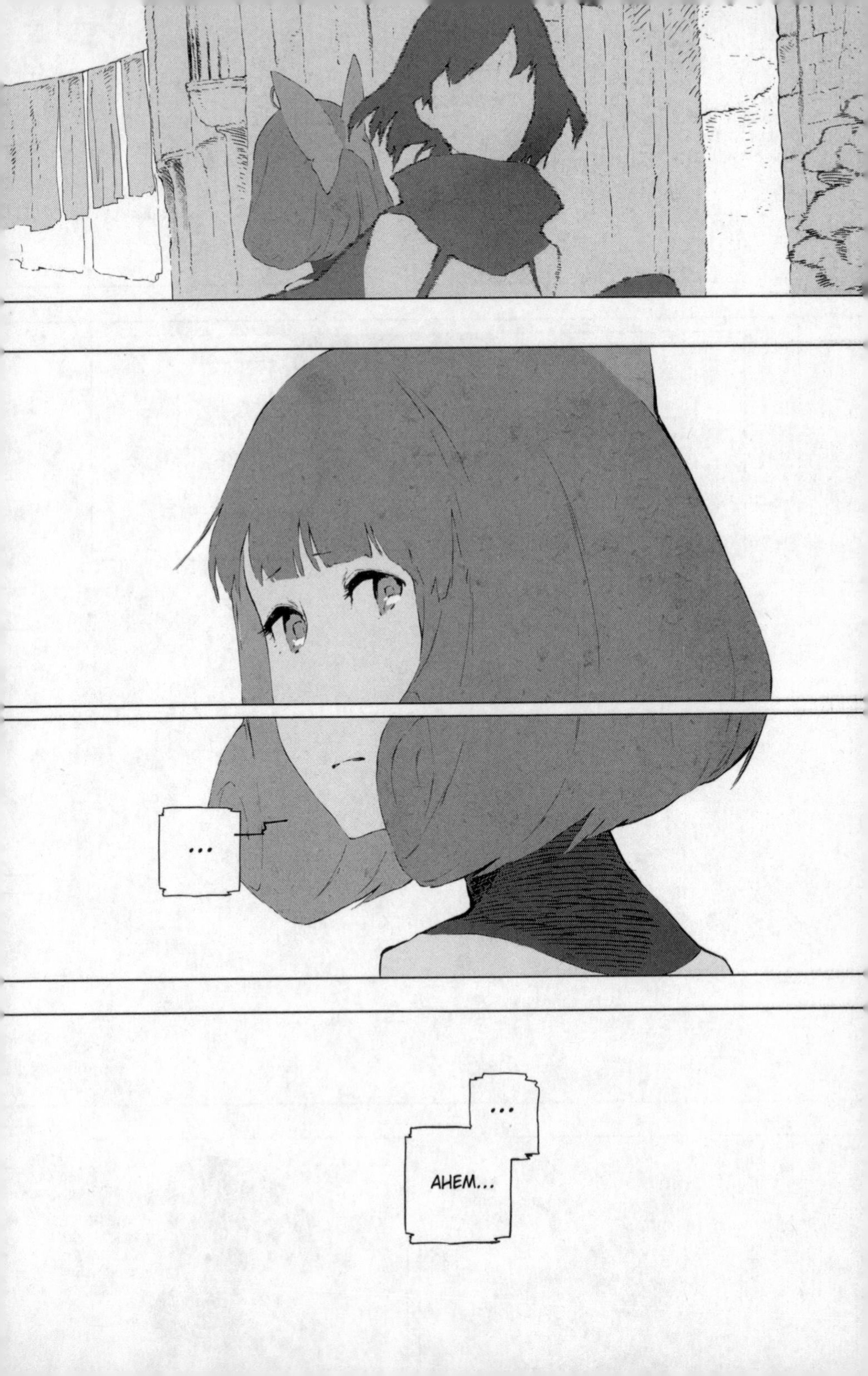
...
...
AHEM...

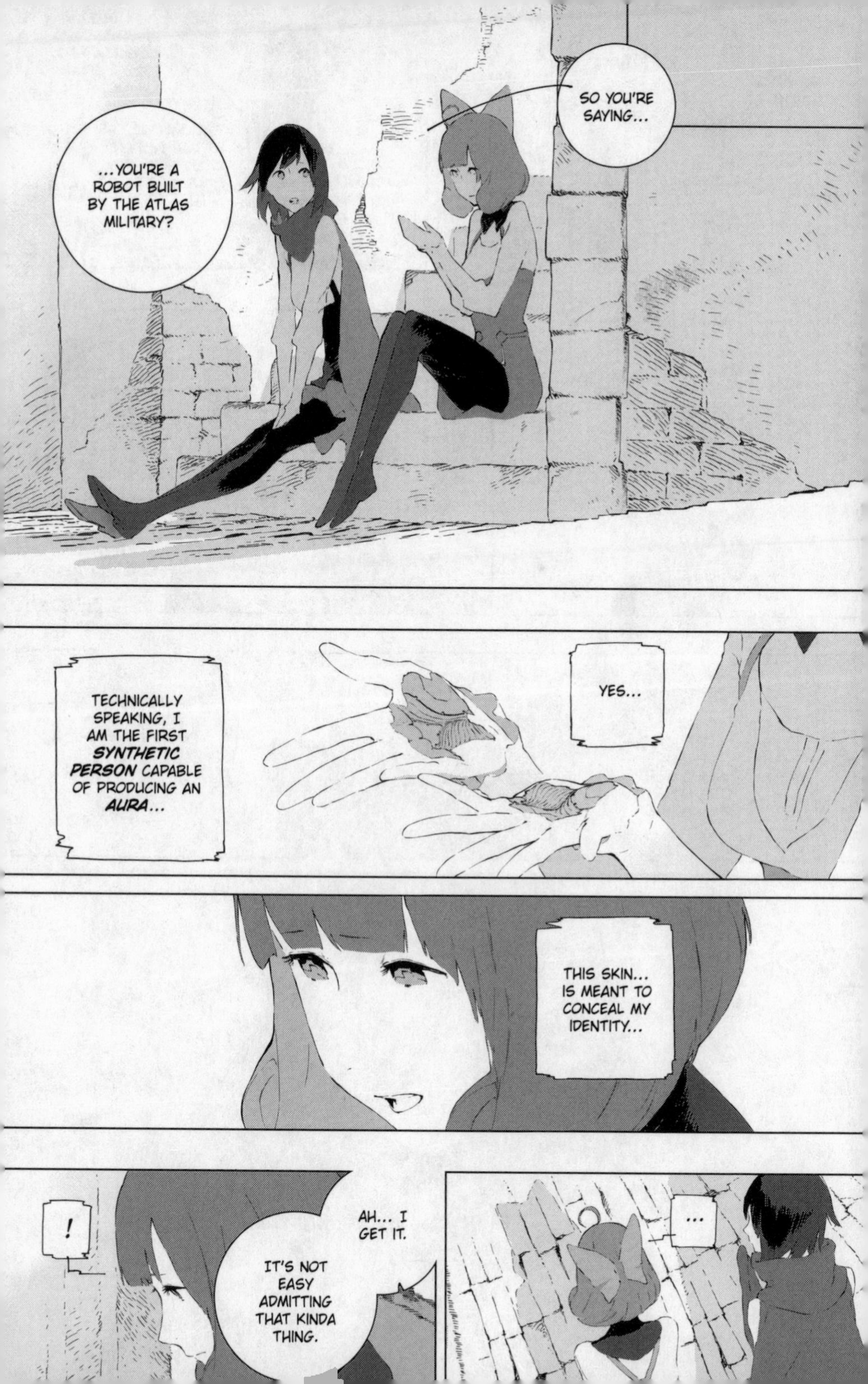
SO YOU'RE SAYING...
...YOU'RE A ROBOT BUILT BY THE ATLAS MILITARY?
YES...
TECHNICALLY SPEAKING, I AM THE FIRST *SYNTHETIC PERSON* CAPABLE OF PRODUCING AN *AURA*...
THIS SKIN... IS MEANT TO CONCEAL MY IDENTITY...
...
!
AH... I GET IT.
IT'S NOT EASY ADMITTING THAT KINDA THING.

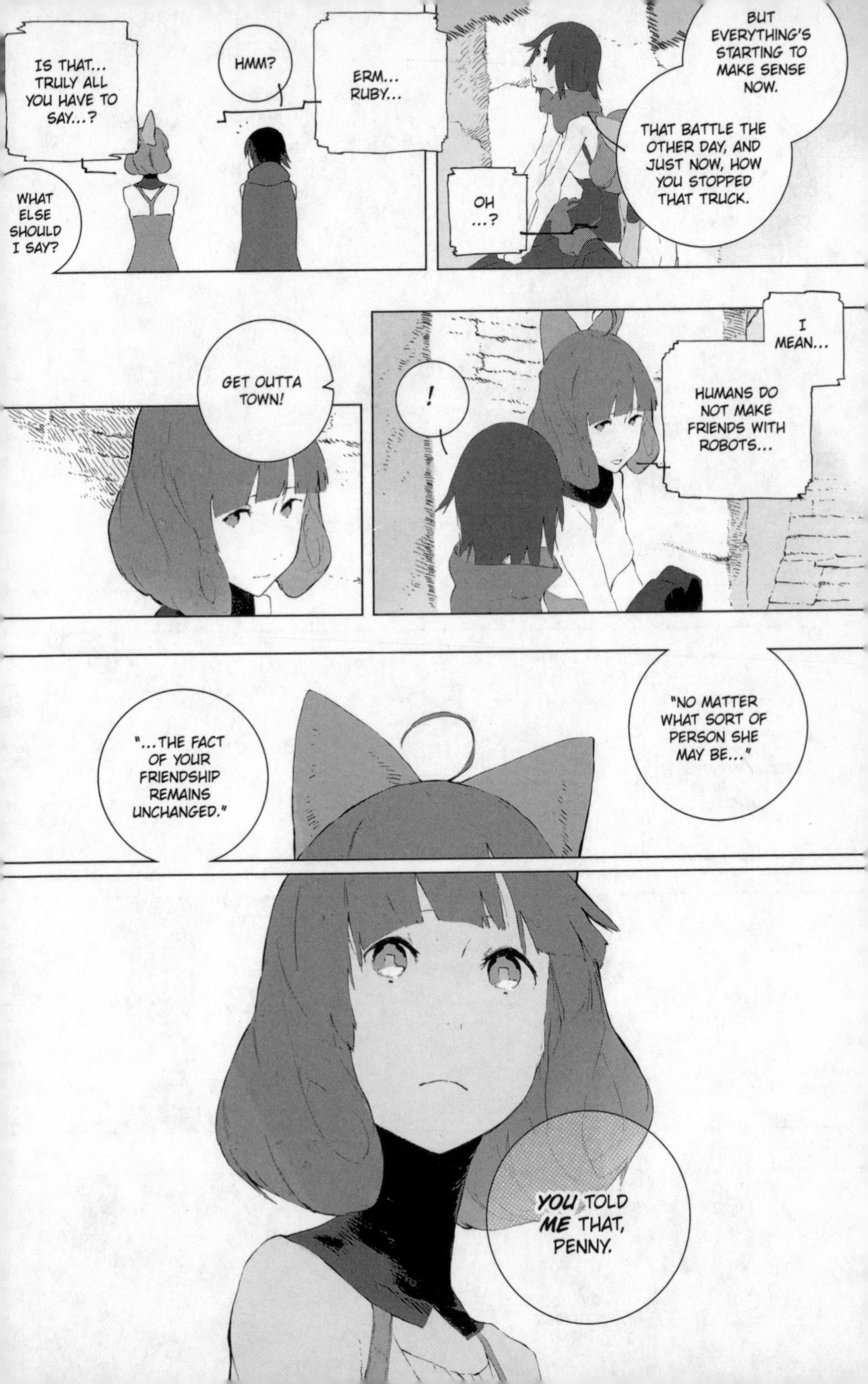
BUT EVERYTHING'S STARTING TO MAKE SENSE NOW.
THAT BATTLE THE OTHER DAY, AND JUST NOW, HOW YOU STOPPED THAT TRUCK.
OH ...?
ERM... RUBY...
HMM?
IS THAT... TRULY ALL YOU HAVE TO SAY...?
WHAT ELSE SHOULD I SAY?
I MEAN...
HUMANS DO NOT MAKE FRIENDS WITH ROBOTS...
!
GET OUTTA TOWN!
"NO MATTER WHAT SORT OF PERSON SHE MAY BE..."
"...THE FACT OF YOUR FRIENDSHIP REMAINS UNCHANGED."
YOU TOLD *ME* THAT, PENNY.

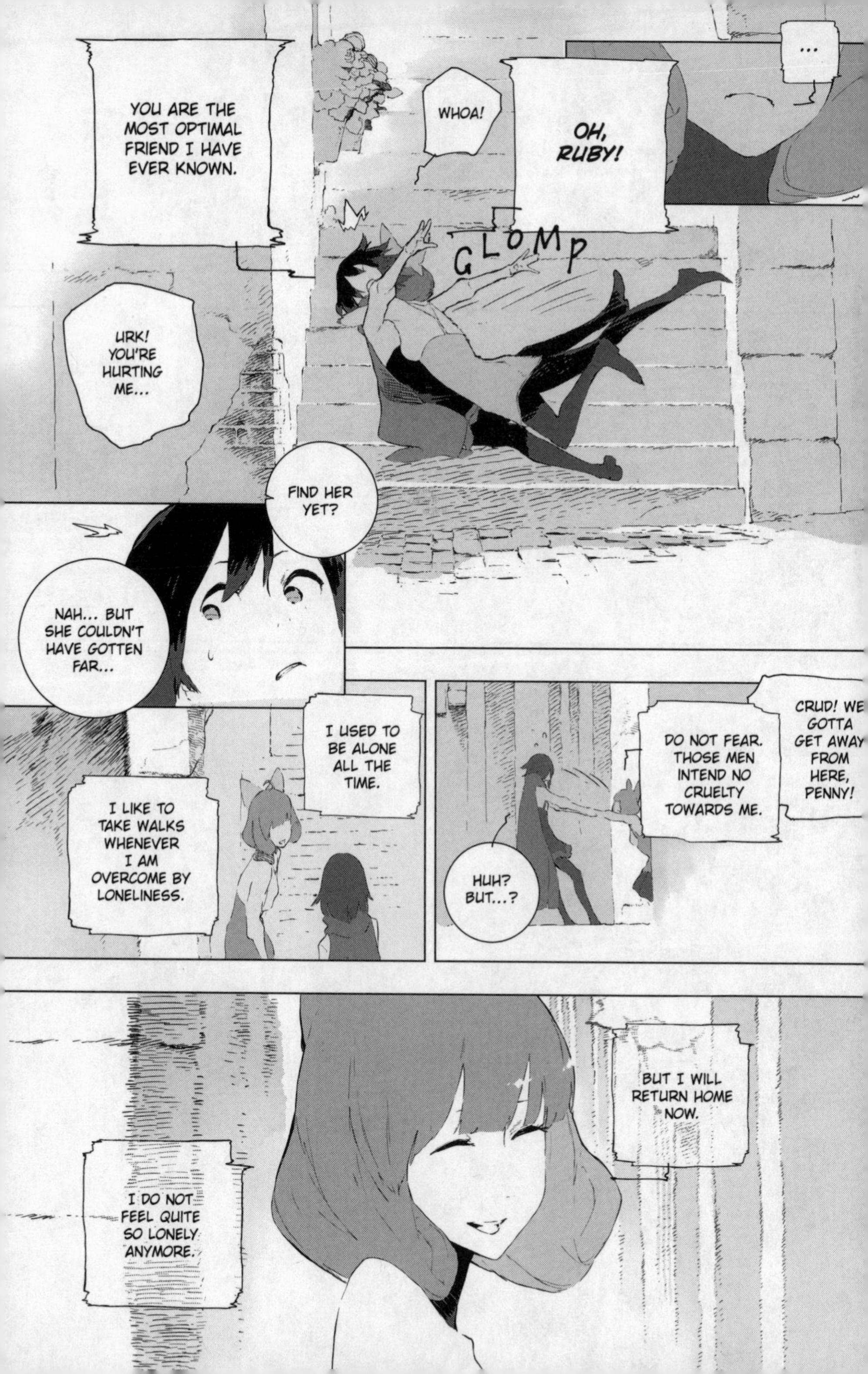
...
OH, RUBY!
WHOA!
YOU ARE THE MOST OPTIMAL FRIEND I HAVE EVER KNOWN.
GLOMP
URK! YOU'RE HURTING ME...
FIND HER YET?
NAH... BUT SHE COULDN'T HAVE GOTTEN FAR...
CRUD! WE GOTTA GET AWAY FROM HERE, PENNY!
DO NOT FEAR. THOSE MEN INTEND NO CRUELTY TOWARDS ME.
HUH? BUT...?
I USED TO BE ALONE ALL THE TIME.
I LIKE TO TAKE WALKS WHENEVER I AM OVERCOME BY LONELINESS.
BUT I WILL RETURN HOME NOW.
I DO NOT FEEL QUITE SO LONELY ANYMORE.

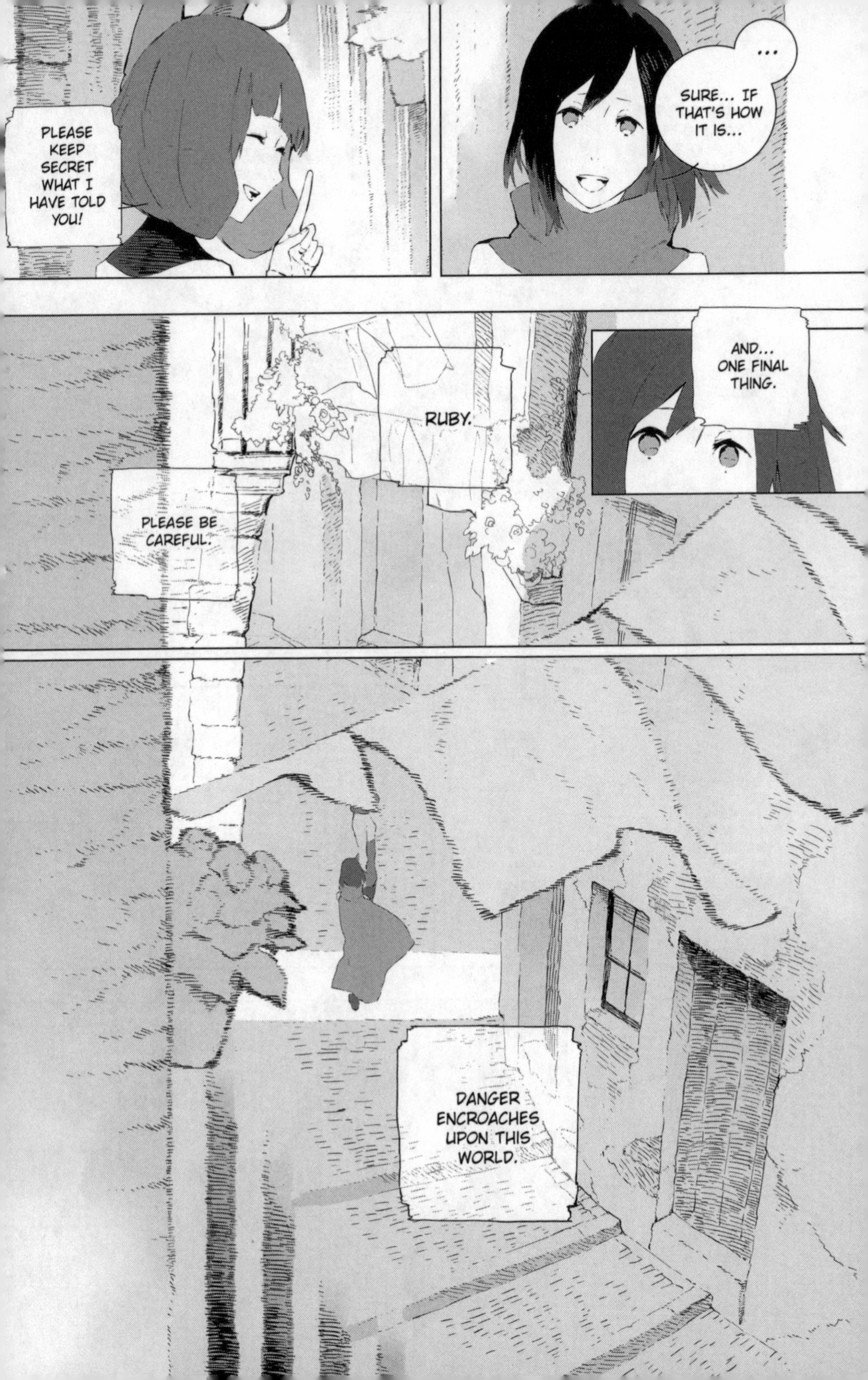
...
SURE... IF THAT'S HOW IT IS...
PLEASE KEEP SECRET WHAT I HAVE TOLD YOU!
AND... ONE FINAL THING.
RUBY.
PLEASE BE CAREFUL.
DANGER ENCROACHES UPON THIS WORLD.

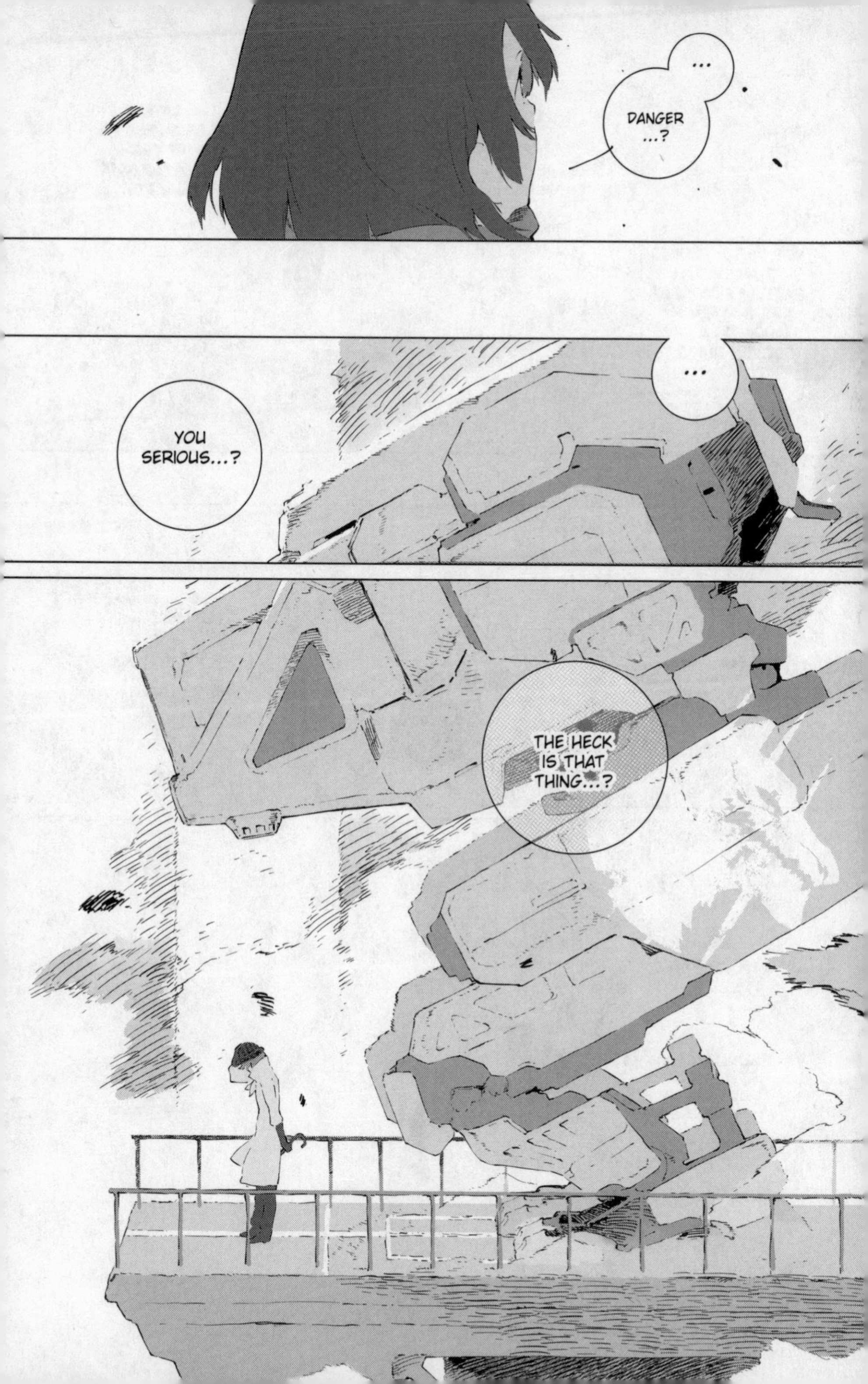
...
DANGER ...?
...
YOU SERIOUS...?
THE HECK IS THAT THING...?

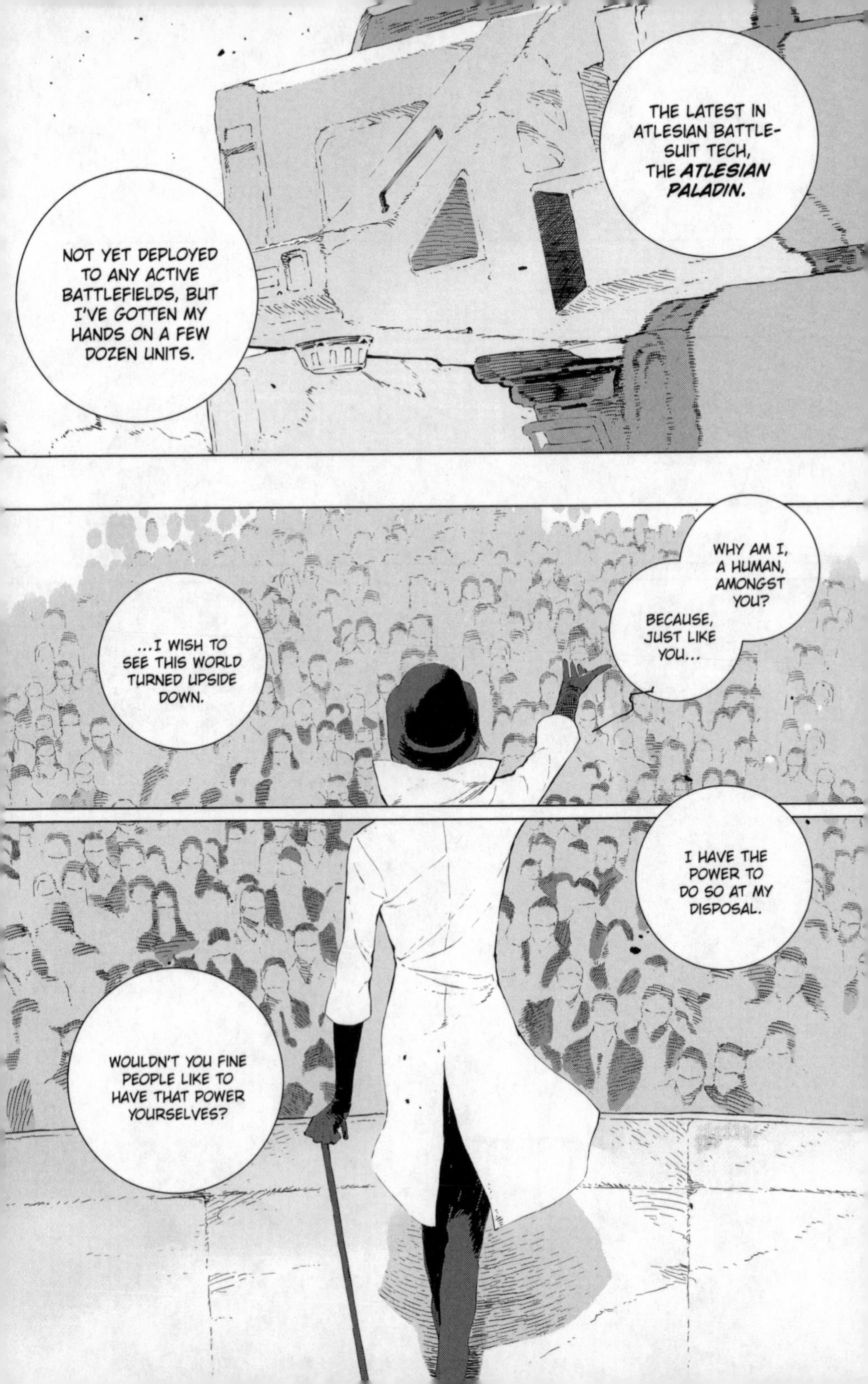
THE LATEST IN ATLESIAN BATTLE-SUIT TECH, THE ***ATLESIAN PALADIN.***
NOT YET DEPLOYED TO ANY ACTIVE BATTLEFIELDS, BUT I'VE GOTTEN MY HANDS ON A FEW DOZEN UNITS.
WHY AM I, A HUMAN, AMONGST YOU?
BECAUSE, JUST LIKE YOU...
...I WISH TO SEE THIS WORLD TURNED UPSIDE DOWN.
I HAVE THE POWER TO DO SO AT MY DISPOSAL.
WOULDN'T YOU FINE PEOPLE LIKE TO HAVE THAT POWER YOURSELVES?

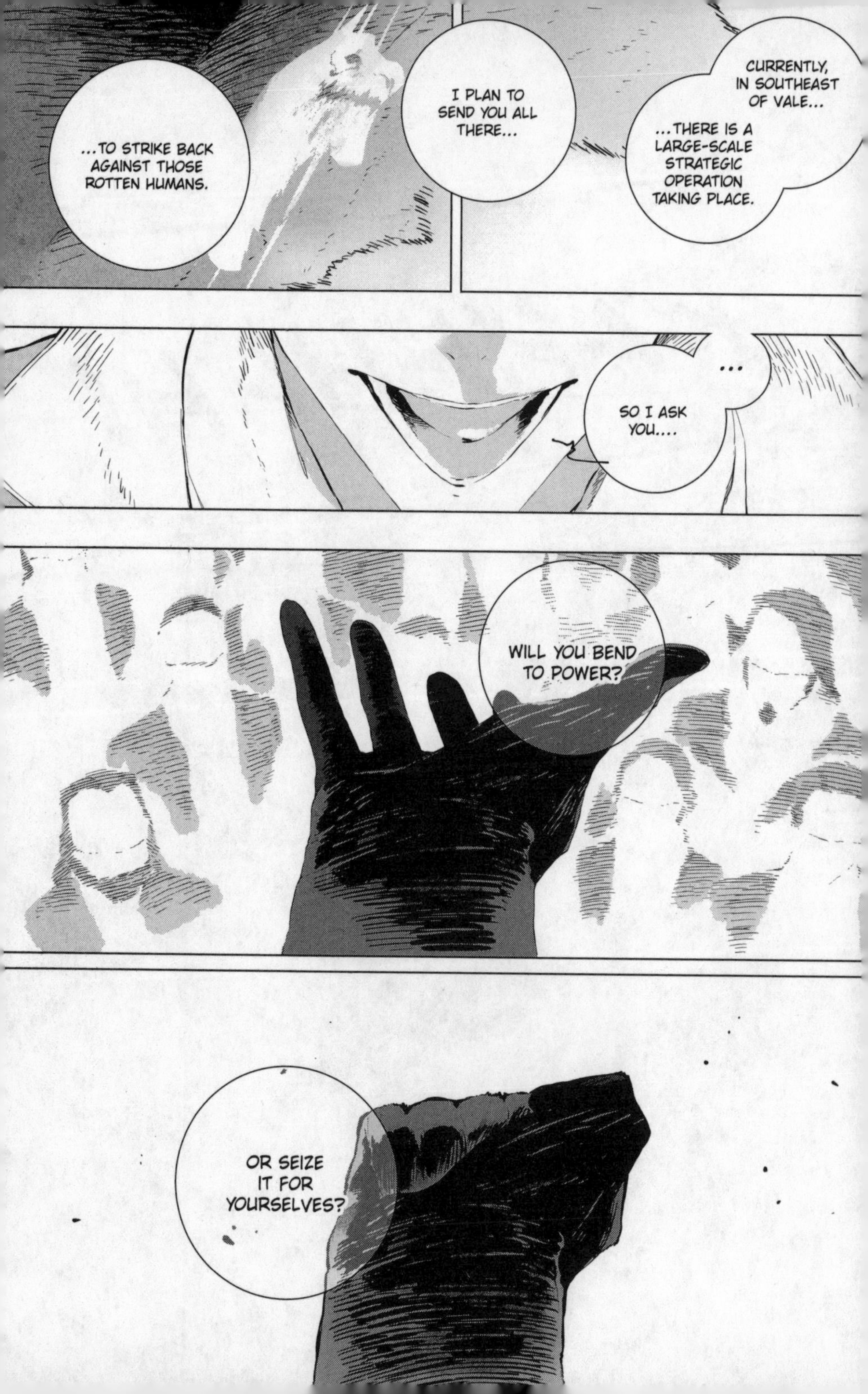
CURRENTLY, IN SOUTHEAST OF VALE...
...THERE IS A LARGE-SCALE STRATEGIC OPERATION TAKING PLACE.
I PLAN TO SEND YOU ALL THERE...
...TO STRIKE BACK AGAINST THOSE ROTTEN HUMANS.
...
SO I ASK YOU....
WILL YOU BEND TO POWER?
OR SEIZE IT FOR YOURSELVES?

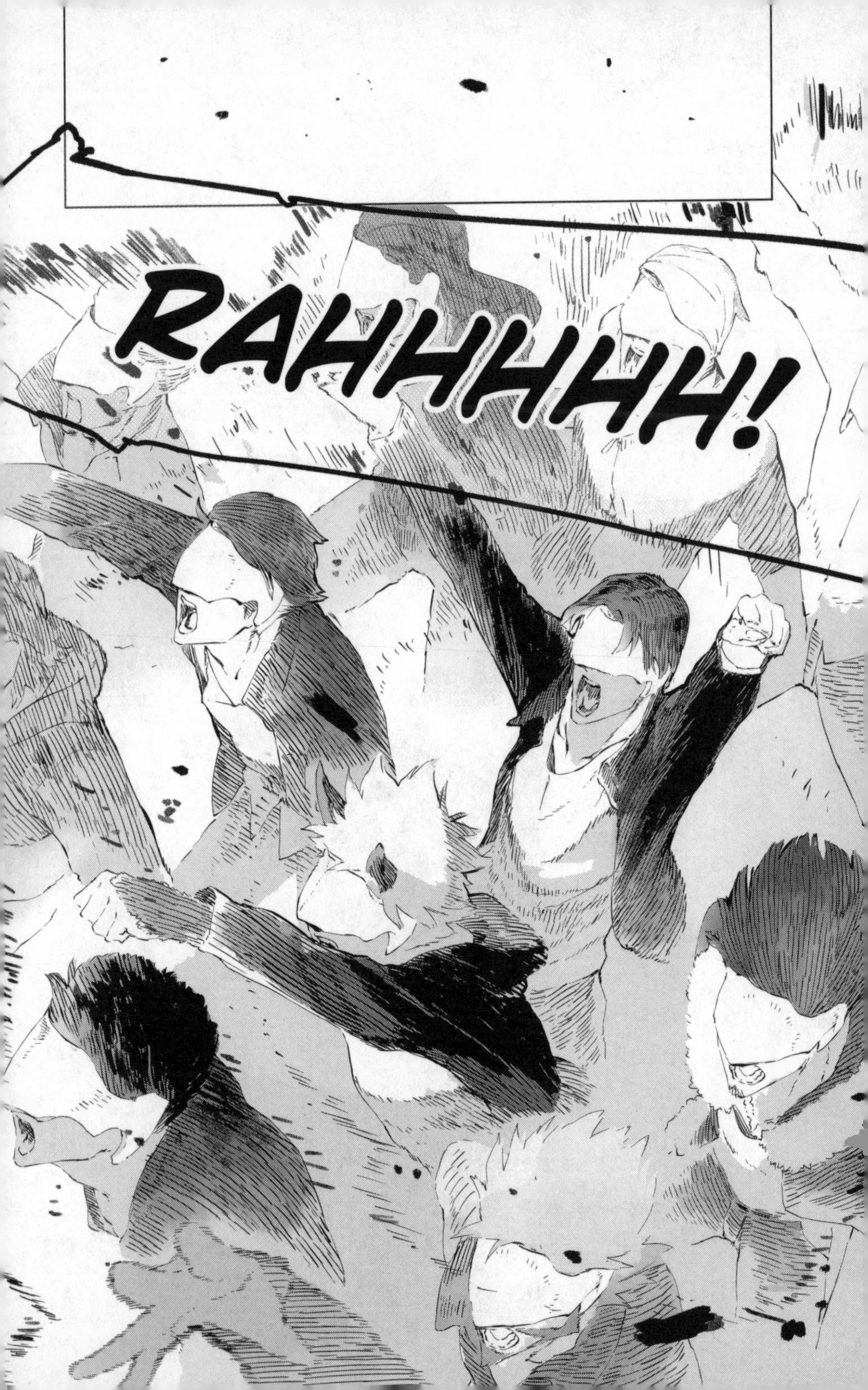
RAHHHHHH!

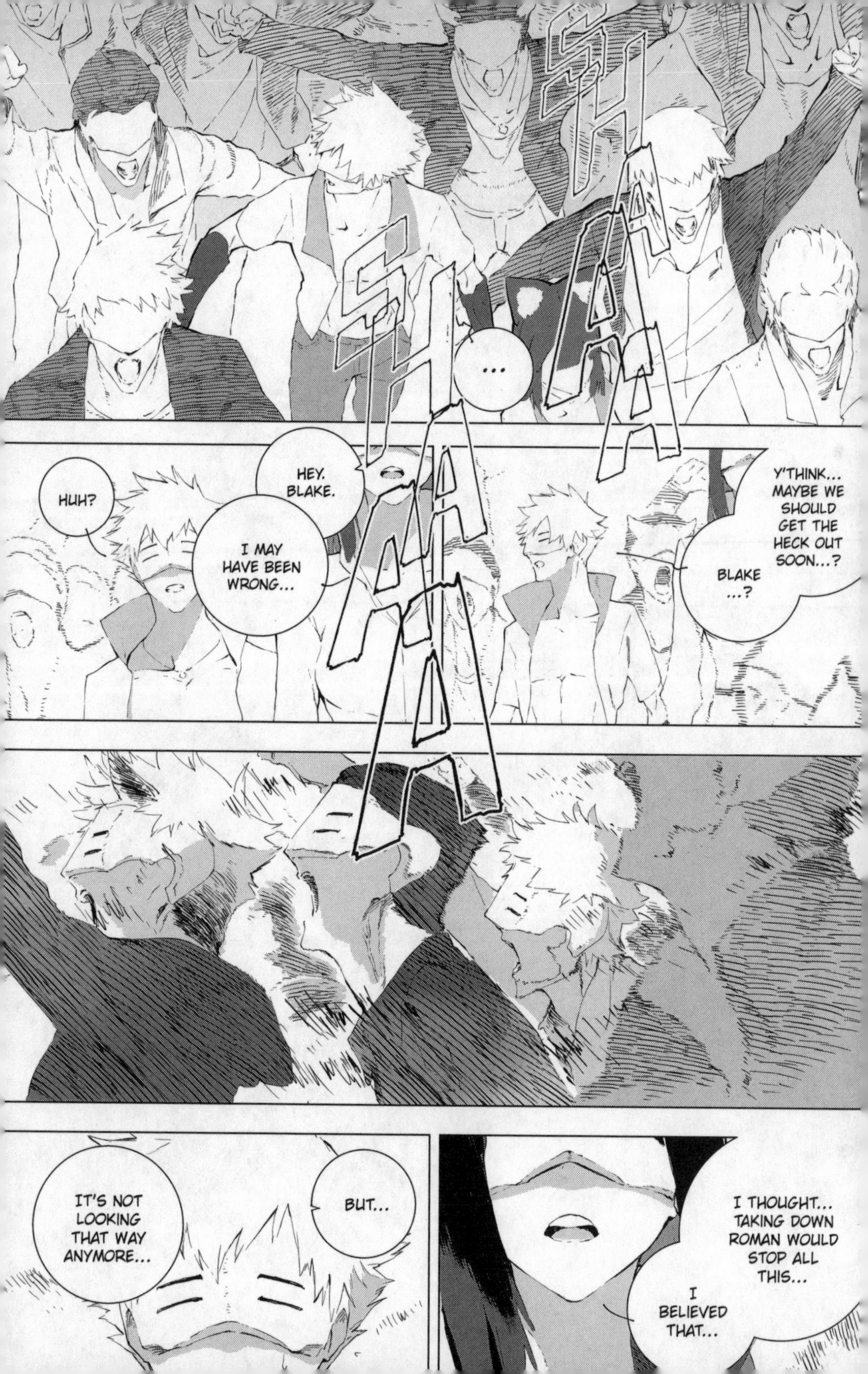
...
Y'THINK... MAYBE WE SHOULD GET THE HECK OUT SOON...?
BLAKE ...?
HEY. BLAKE.
HUH?
I MAY HAVE BEEN WRONG...
I THOUGHT... TAKING DOWN ROMAN WOULD STOP ALL THIS...
I BELIEVED THAT...
BUT...
IT'S NOT LOOKING THAT WAY ANYMORE...

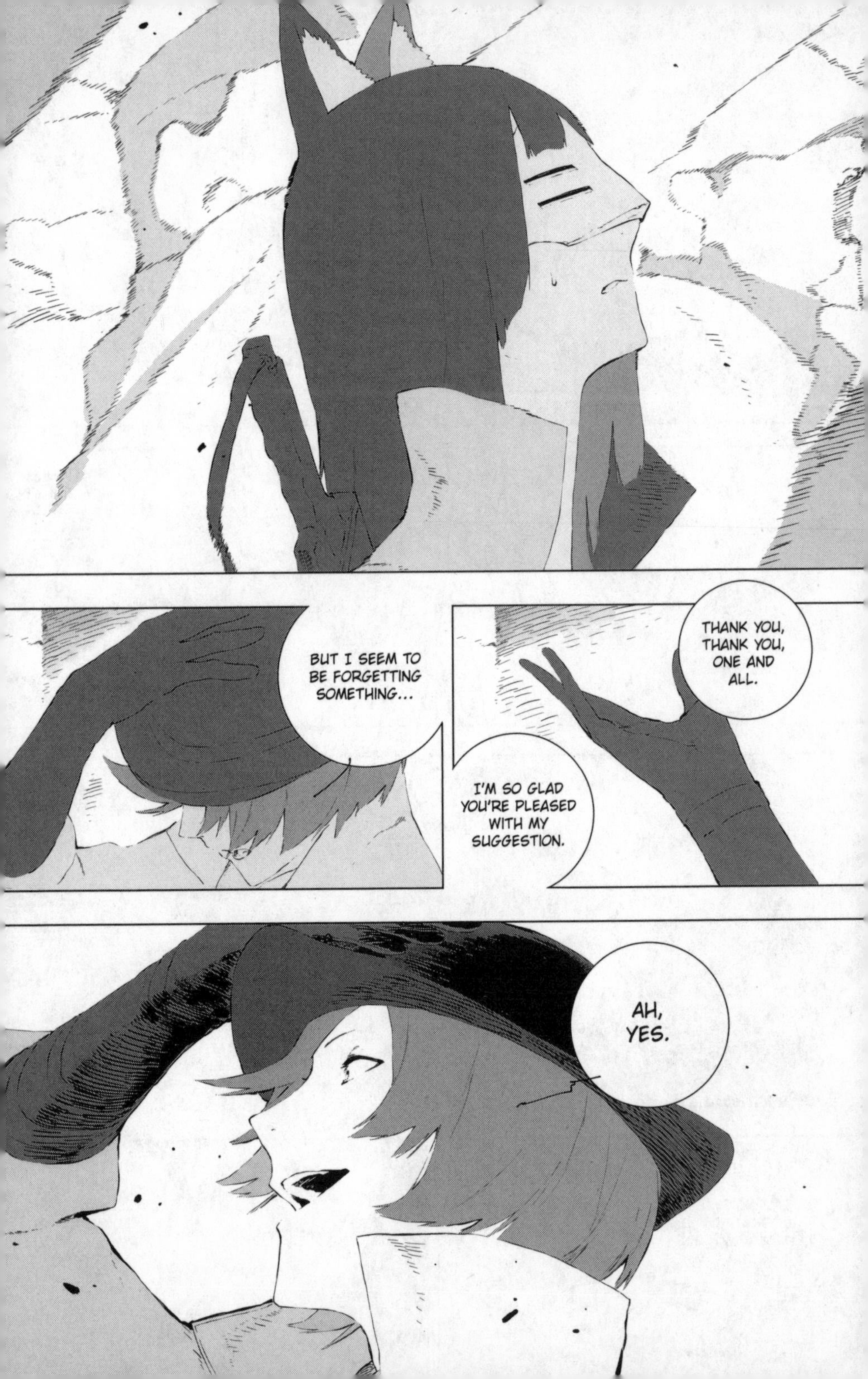
THANK YOU, THANK YOU, ONE AND ALL.
I'M SO GLAD YOU'RE PLEASED WITH MY SUGGESTION.
BUT I SEEM TO BE FORGETTING SOMETHING...
AH, YES.

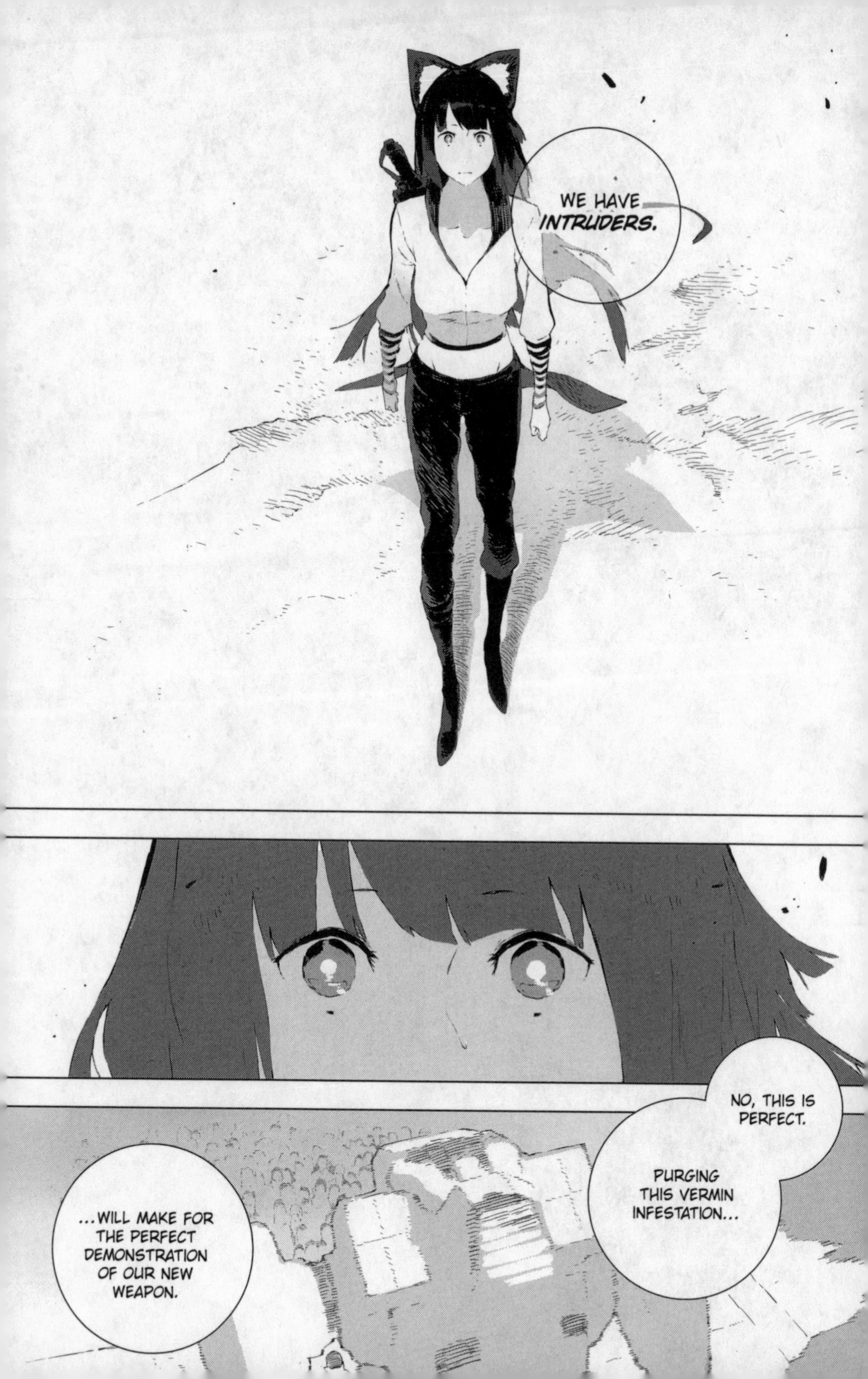
WE HAVE *INTRUDERS.*
NO, THIS IS PERFECT.
PURGING THIS VERMIN INFESTATION...
...WILL MAKE FOR THE PERFECT DEMONSTRATION OF OUR NEW WEAPON.

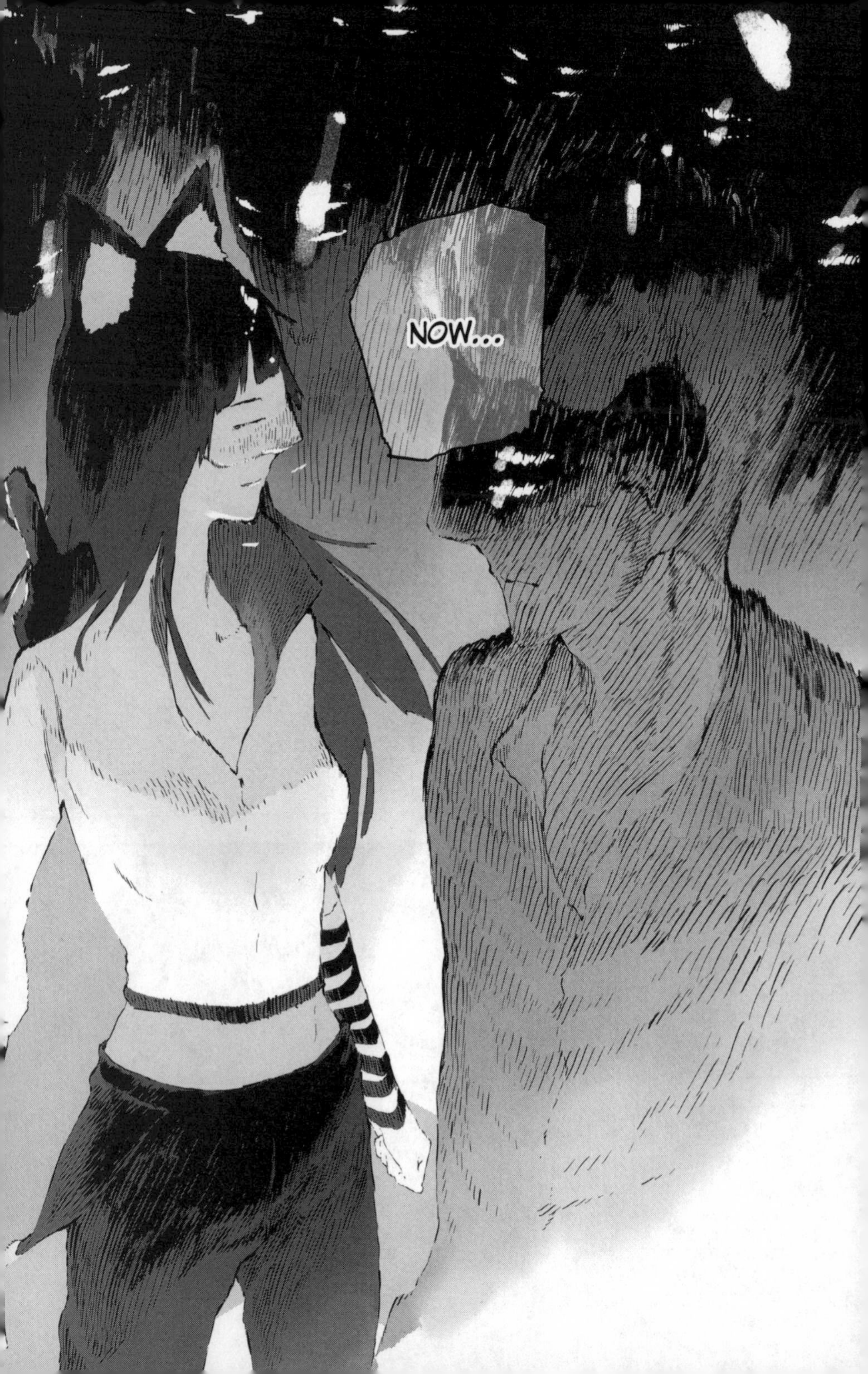
NOW...

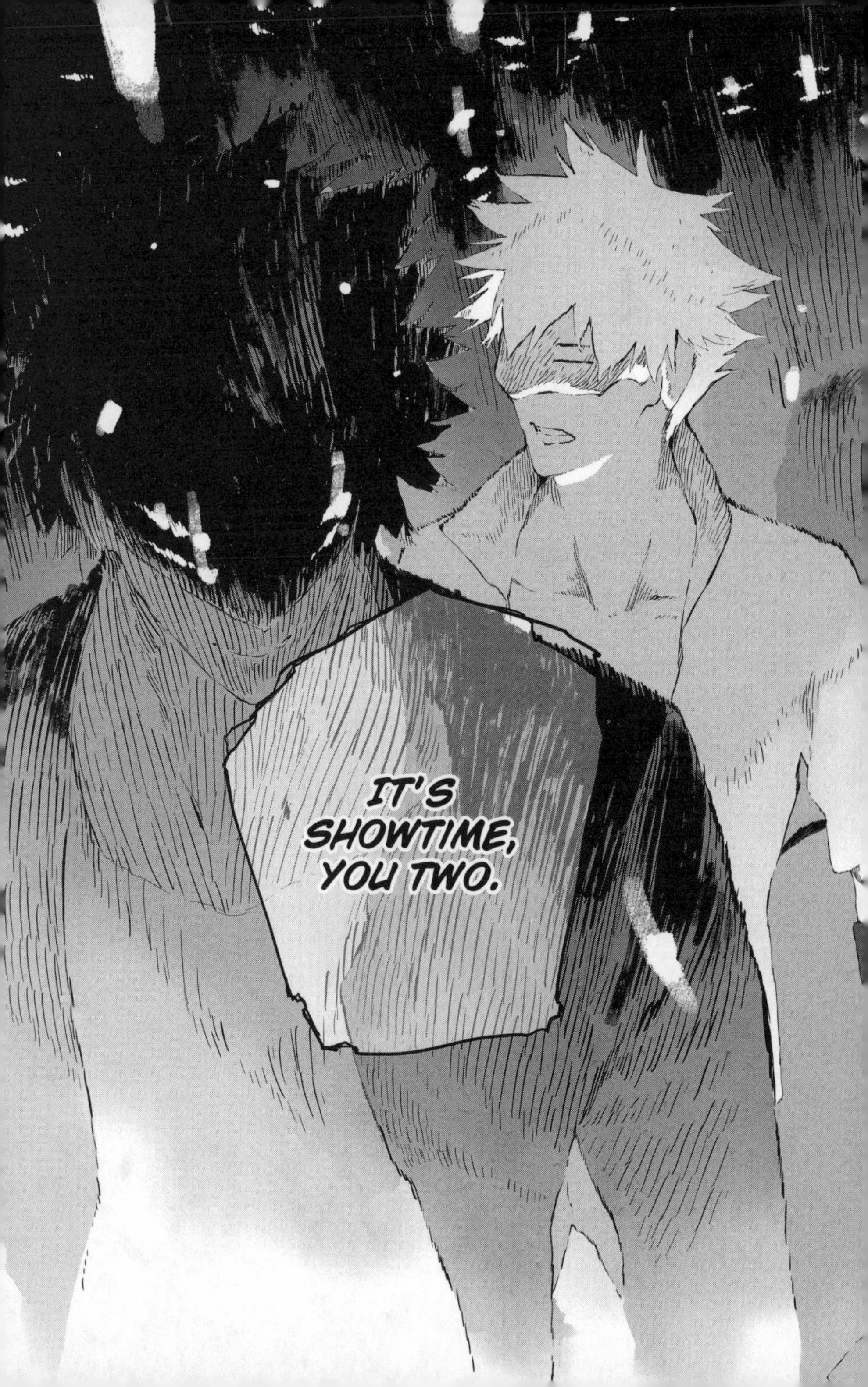
IT'S SHOWTIME, YOU TWO.

RWBY

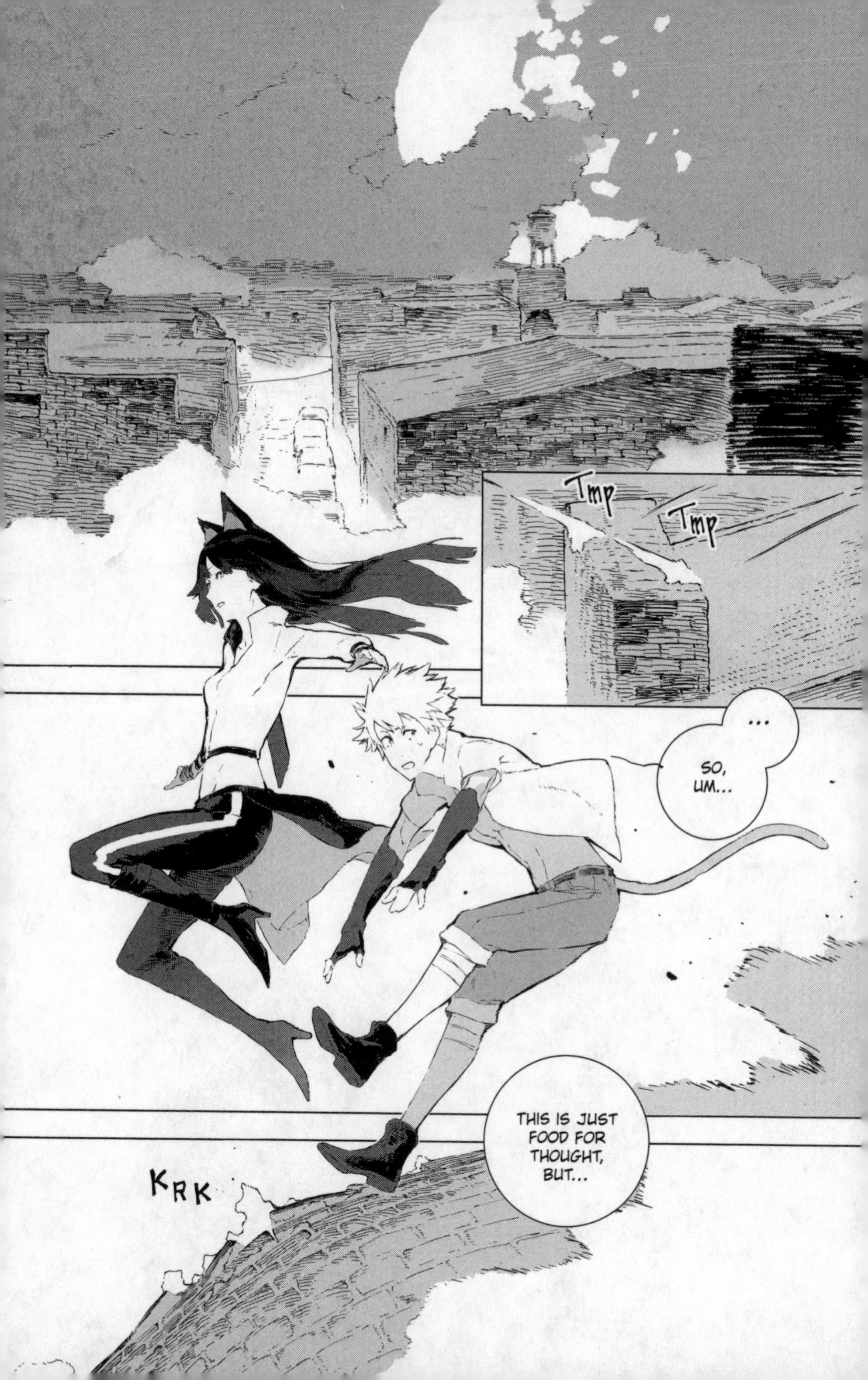
Tmp
Tmp
...
SO, UM...
THIS IS JUST FOOD FOR THOUGHT, BUT...
KRK

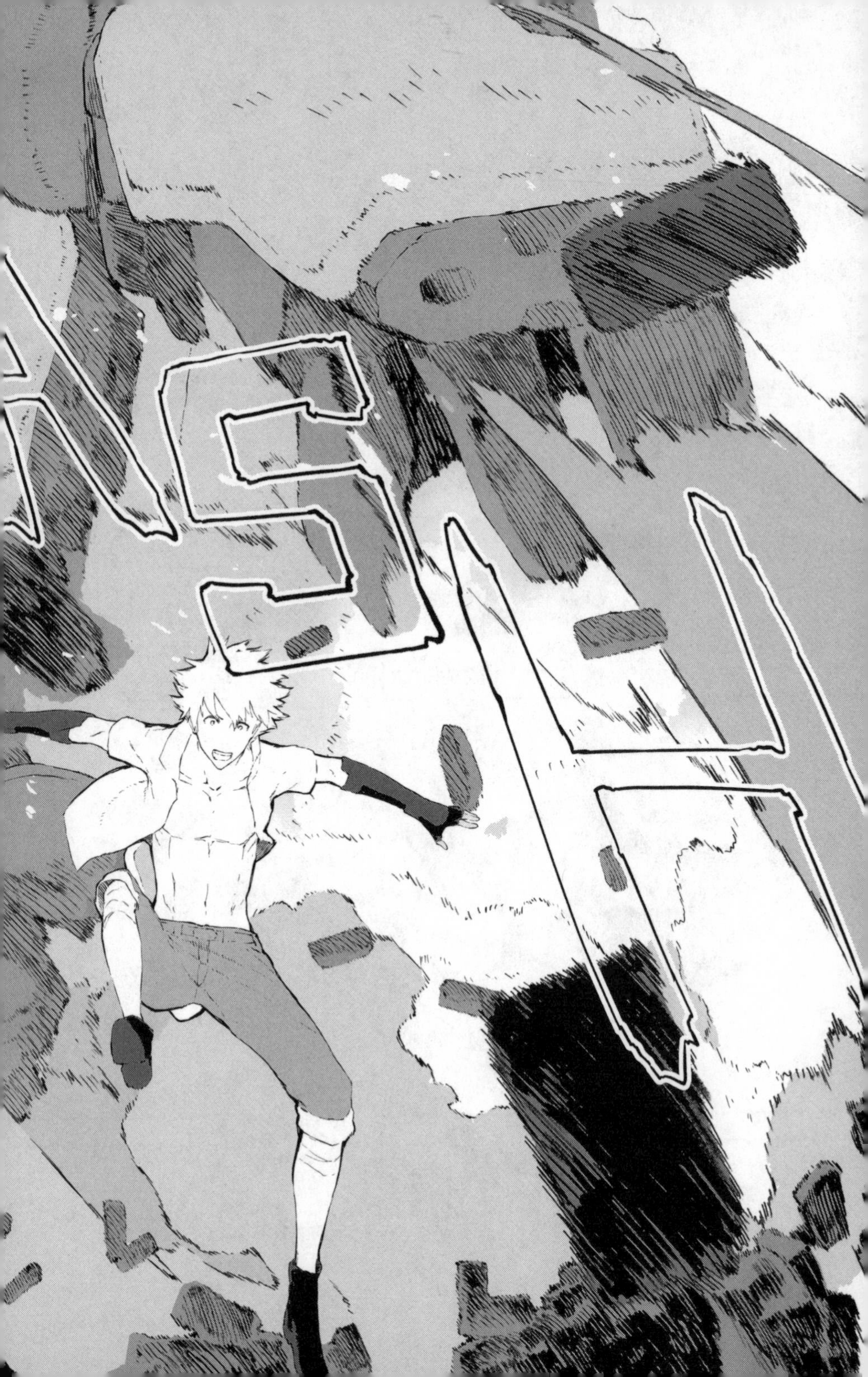

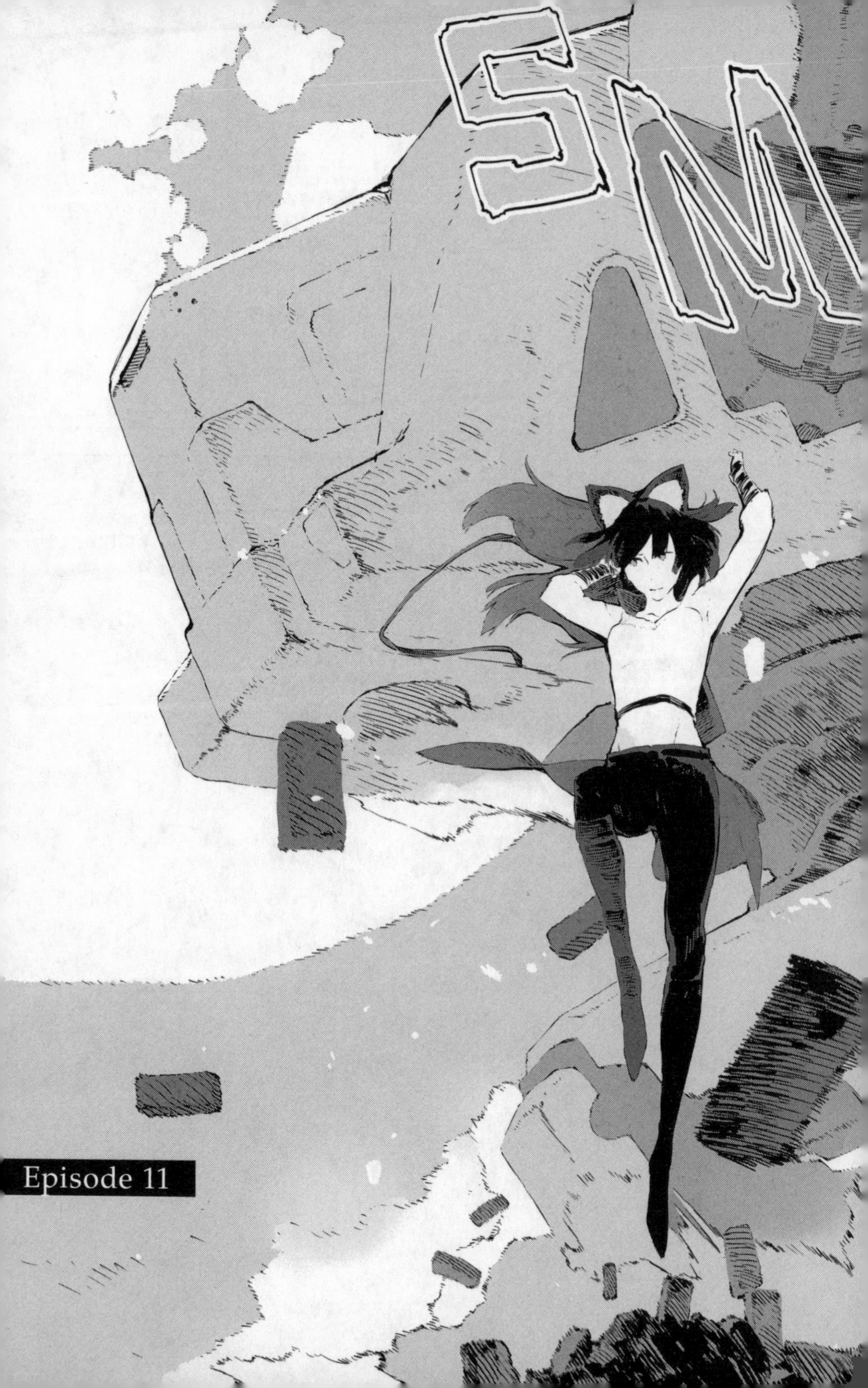
SM
Episode 11

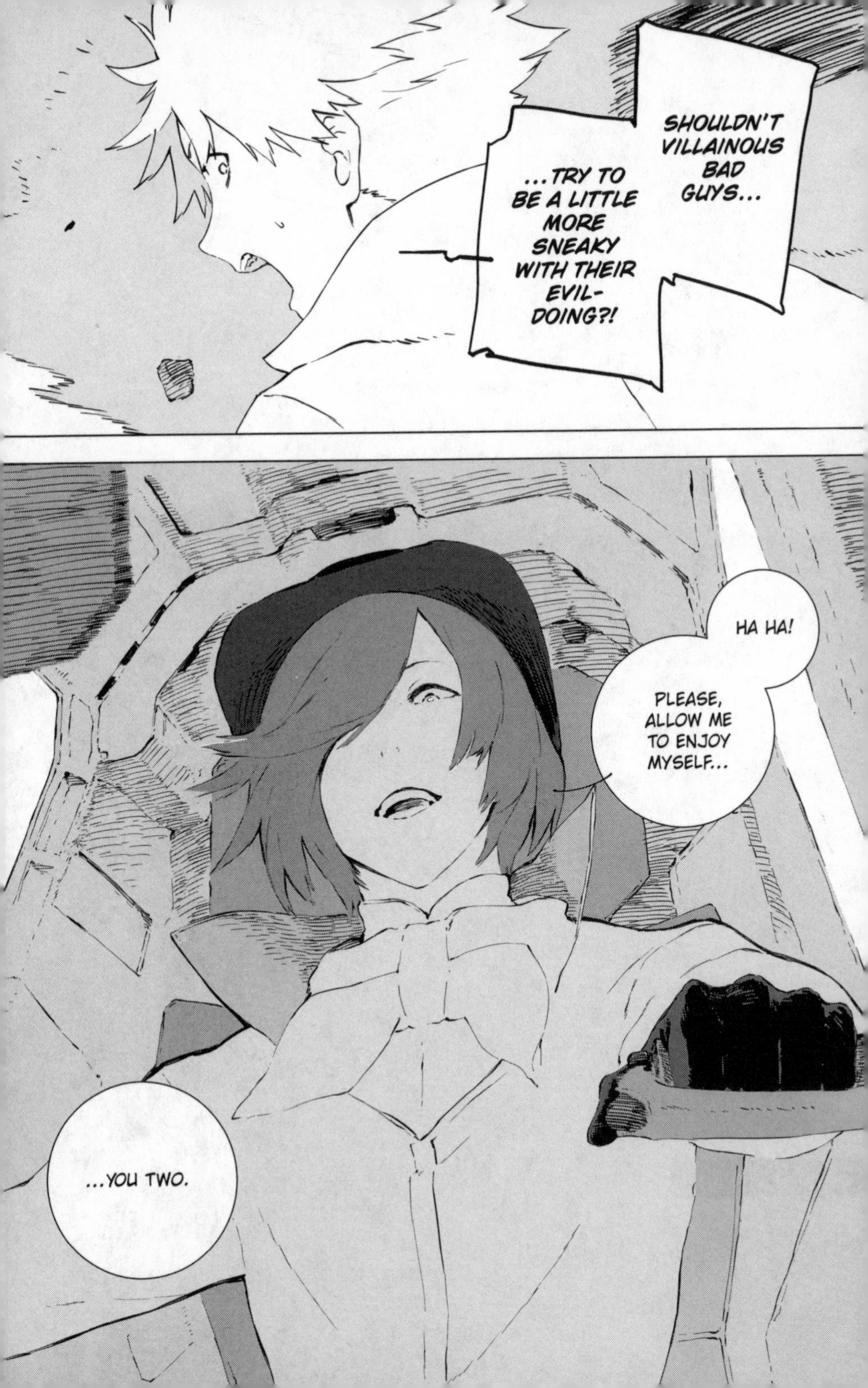
SHOULDN'T VILLAINOUS BAD GUYS...
...TRY TO BE A LITTLE MORE SNEAKY WITH THEIR EVIL-DOING?!
HA HA!
PLEASE, ALLOW ME TO ENJOY MYSELF...
...YOU TWO.

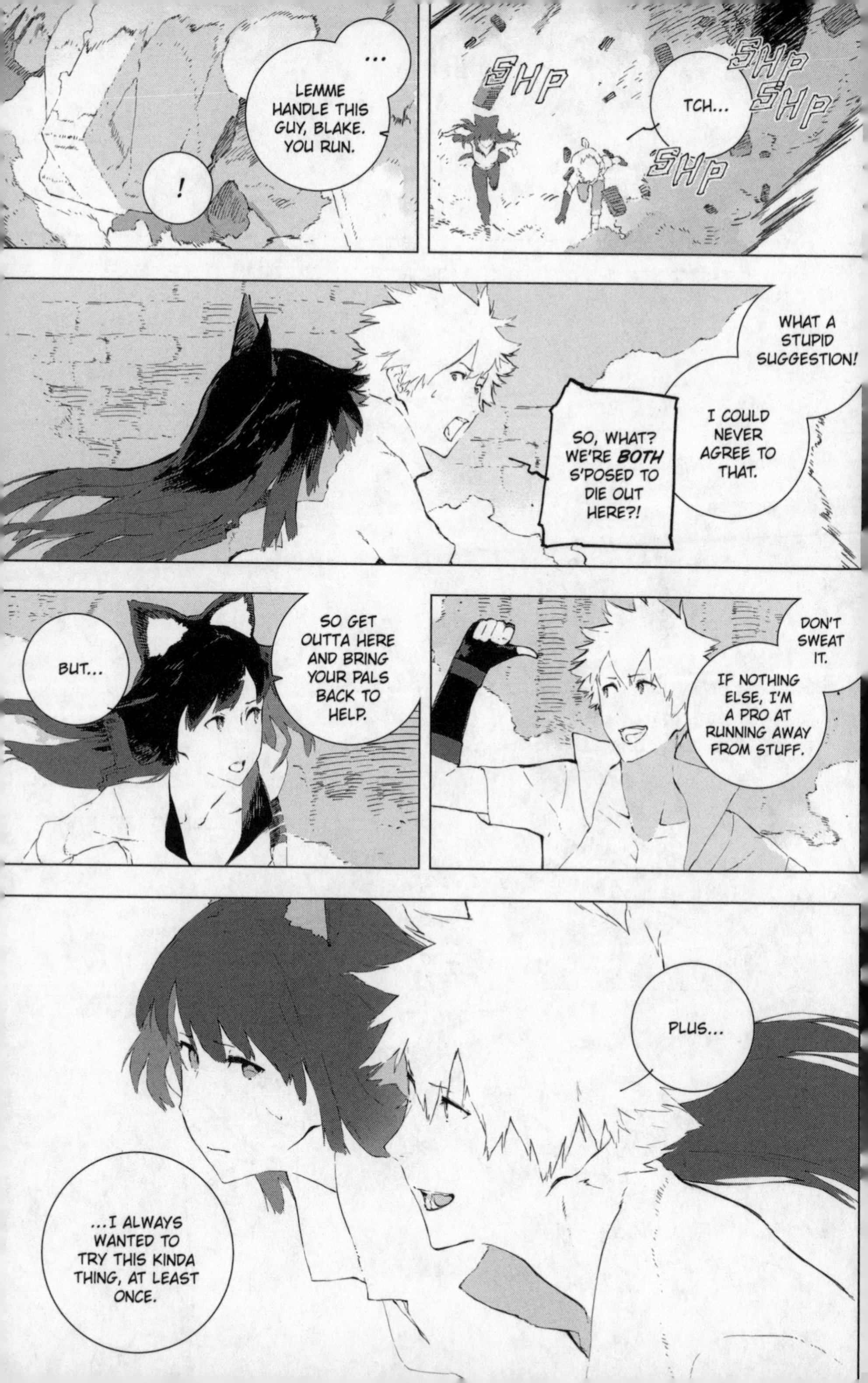
SHP SHP
TCH...
SHP
SHP
...
LEMME HANDLE THIS GUY, BLAKE. YOU RUN.
!
WHAT A STUPID SUGGESTION!
I COULD NEVER AGREE TO THAT.
SO, WHAT? WE'RE **BOTH** S'POSED TO DIE OUT HERE?!
DON'T SWEAT IT.
IF NOTHING ELSE, I'M A PRO AT RUNNING AWAY FROM STUFF.
SO GET OUTTA HERE AND BRING YOUR PALS BACK TO HELP.
BUT...
PLUS...
...I ALWAYS WANTED TO TRY THIS KINDA THING, AT LEAST ONCE.

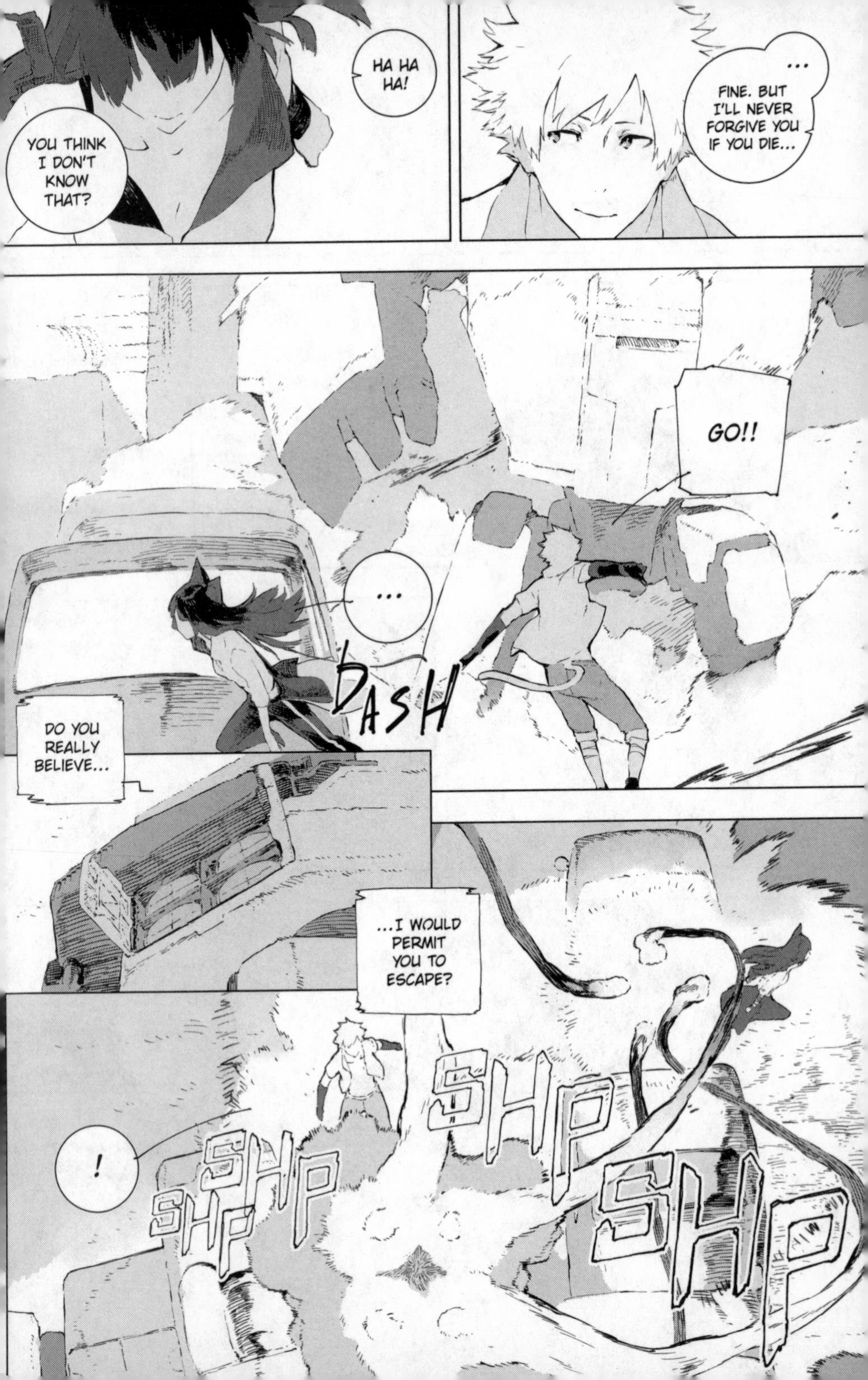
...
FINE. BUT I'LL NEVER FORGIVE YOU IF YOU DIE...
HA HA HA!
YOU THINK I DON'T KNOW THAT?
GO!!
...
DASH
DO YOU REALLY BELIEVE...
...I WOULD PERMIT YOU TO ESCAPE?
SHP
SHP
!
SHP
SHP
SHP

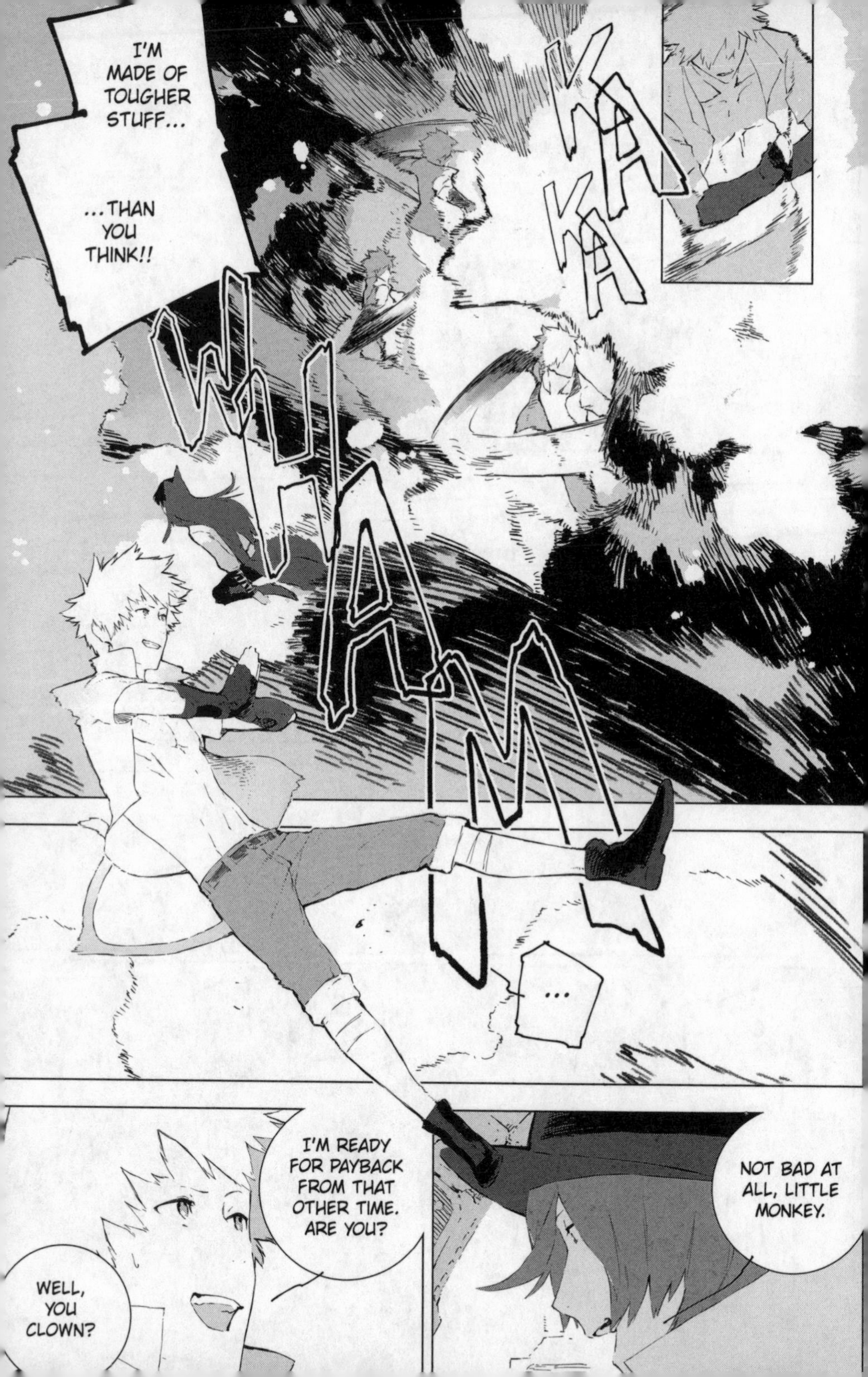
KAKA
I'M MADE OF TOUGHER STUFF...
...THAN YOU THINK!!
WHAM
...
NOT BAD AT ALL, LITTLE MONKEY.
I'M READY FOR PAYBACK FROM THAT OTHER TIME. ARE YOU?
WELL, YOU CLOWN?

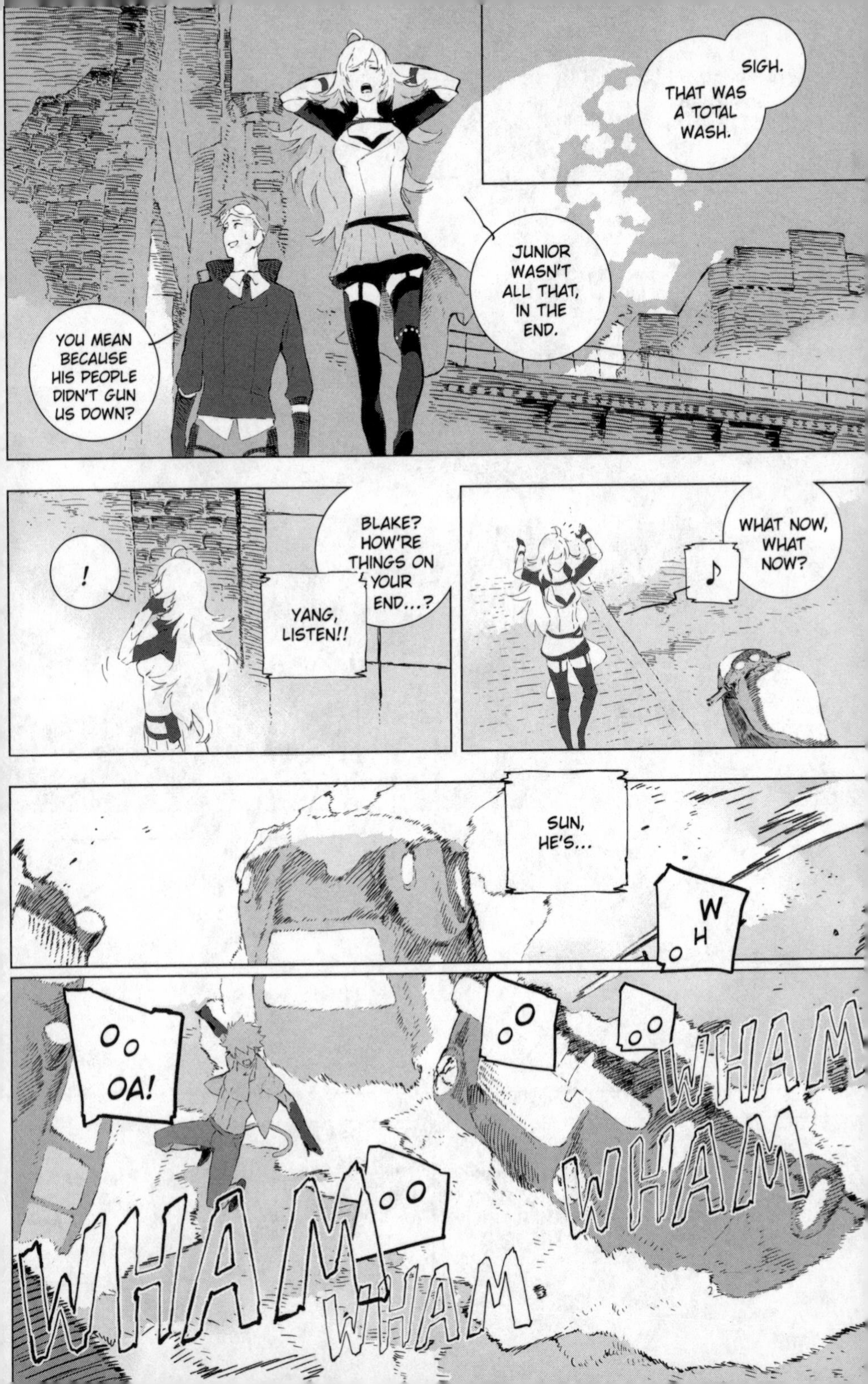
SIGH. THAT WAS A TOTAL WASH.
JUNIOR WASN'T ALL THAT, IN THE END.
YOU MEAN BECAUSE HIS PEOPLE DIDN'T GUN US DOWN?
WHAT NOW, WHAT NOW?
♪
BLAKE? HOW'RE THINGS ON YOUR END...?
YANG, LISTEN!!
!
SUN, HE'S...
WHO
OO
OO
OO
OOOA!
WHAM
WHAM
WHAM
WHAM

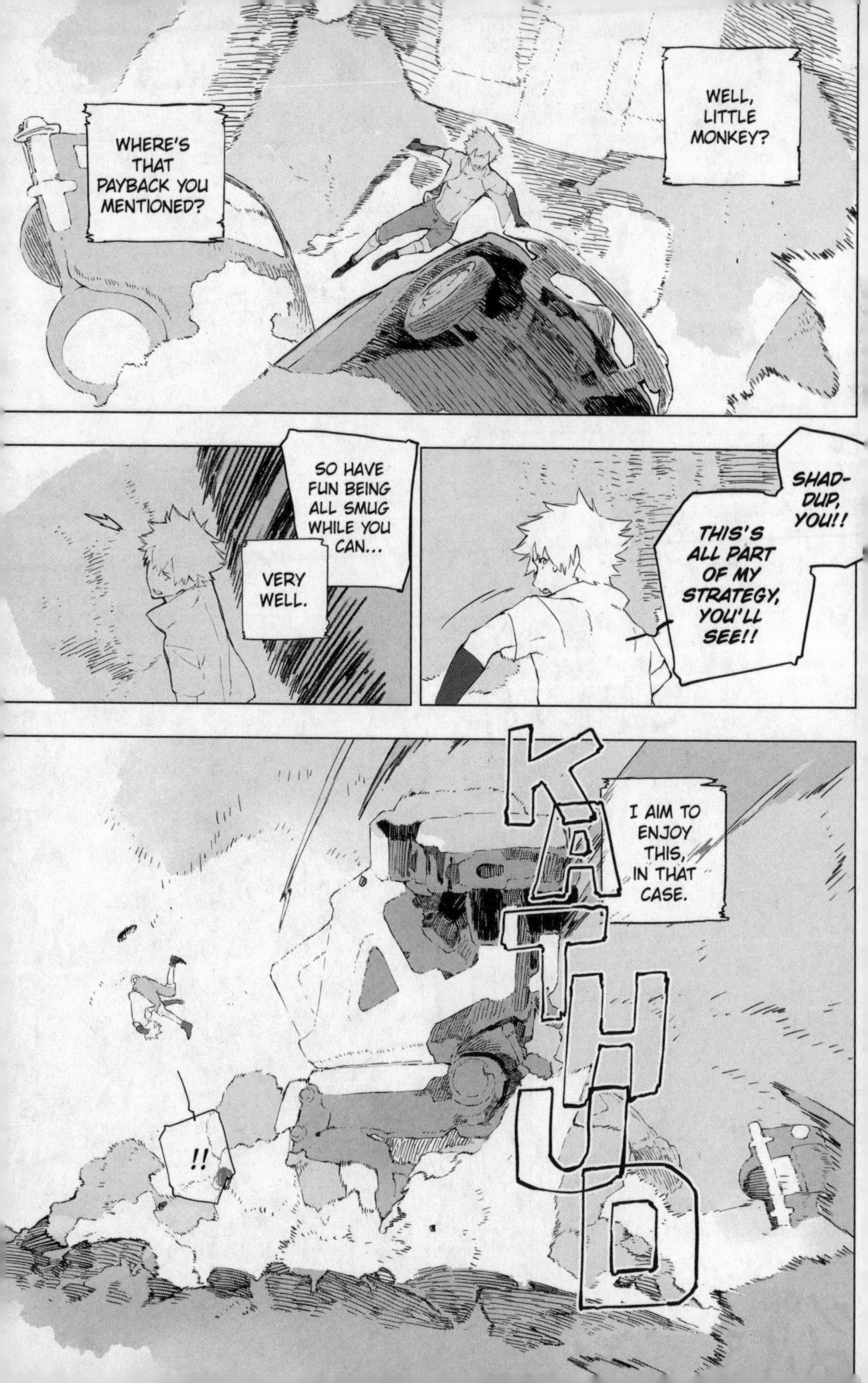
WELL, LITTLE MONKEY?
WHERE'S THAT PAYBACK YOU MENTIONED?
SHAD-DUP, YOU!!
THIS'S ALL PART OF MY STRATEGY, YOU'LL SEE!!
SO HAVE FUN BEING ALL SMUG WHILE YOU CAN...
VERY WELL.
I AIM TO ENJOY THIS, IN THAT CASE.
KATHUD
!!

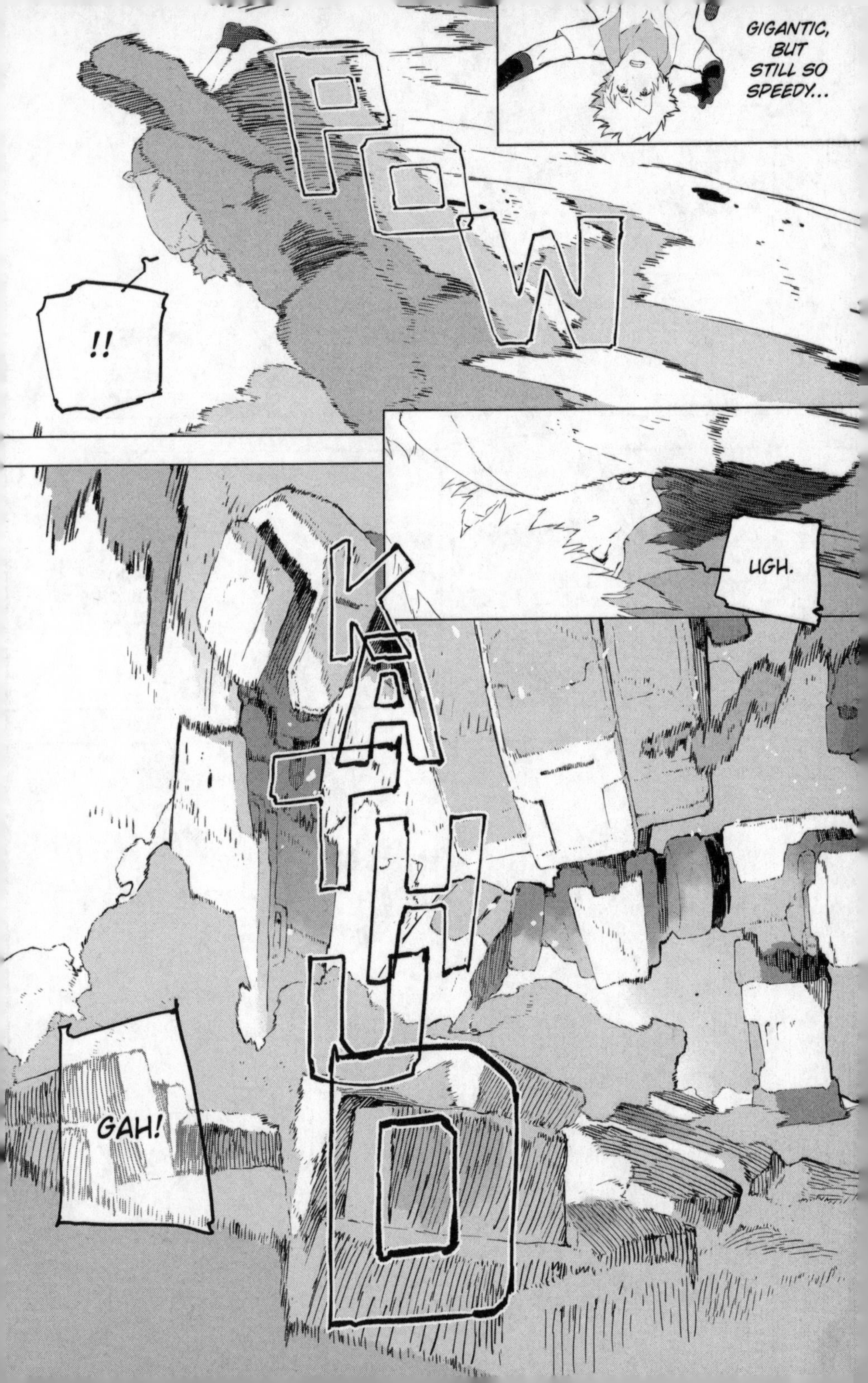
GIGANTIC, BUT STILL SO SPEEDY...
POW
!!
UGH.
KATHUD
GAH!

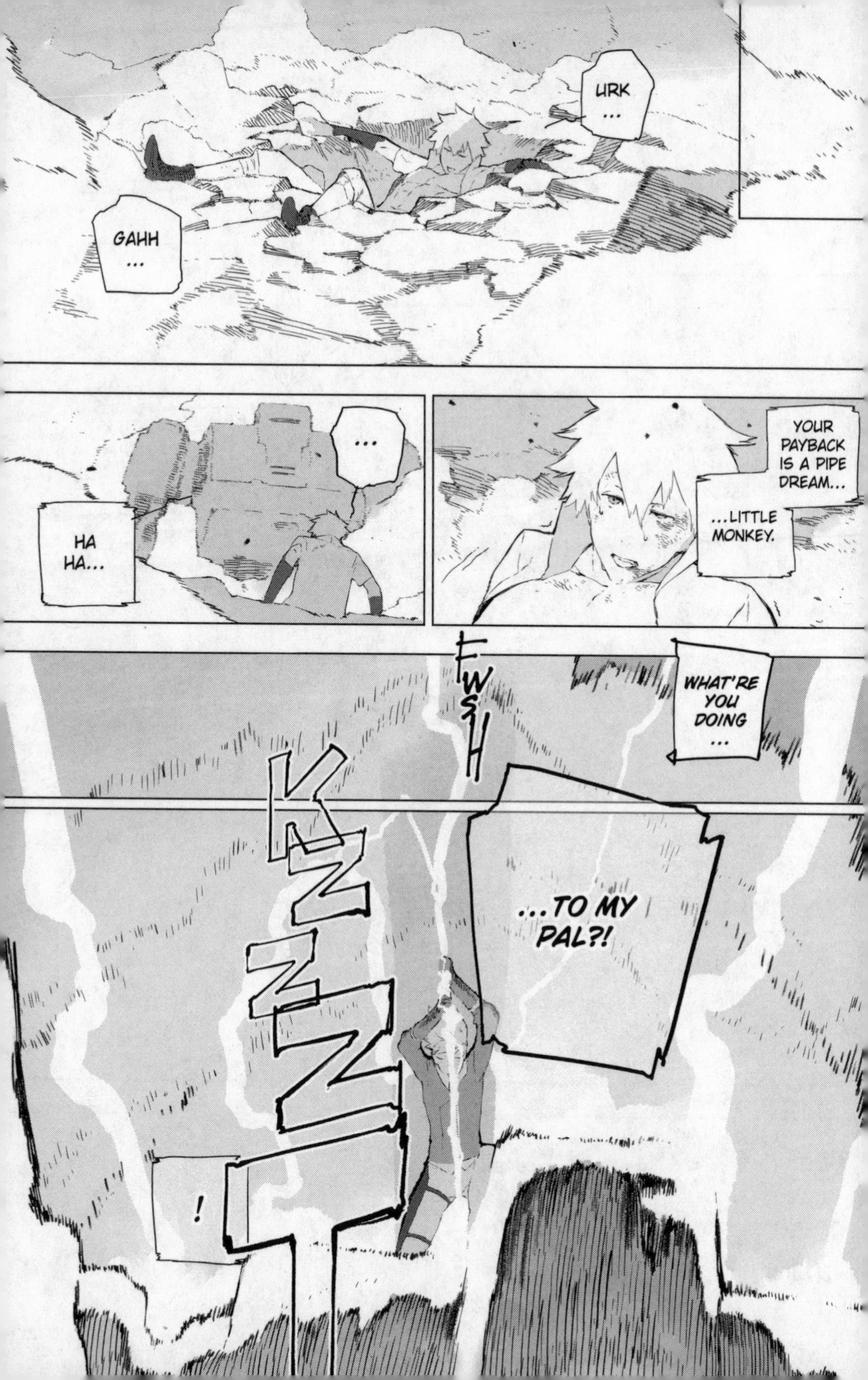
URK
...
GAHH
...
YOUR PAYBACK IS A PIPE DREAM...
...LITTLE MONKEY.
...
HA HA...
WHAT'RE YOU DOING...
FWSH
...TO MY PAL?!
KZZZT
!

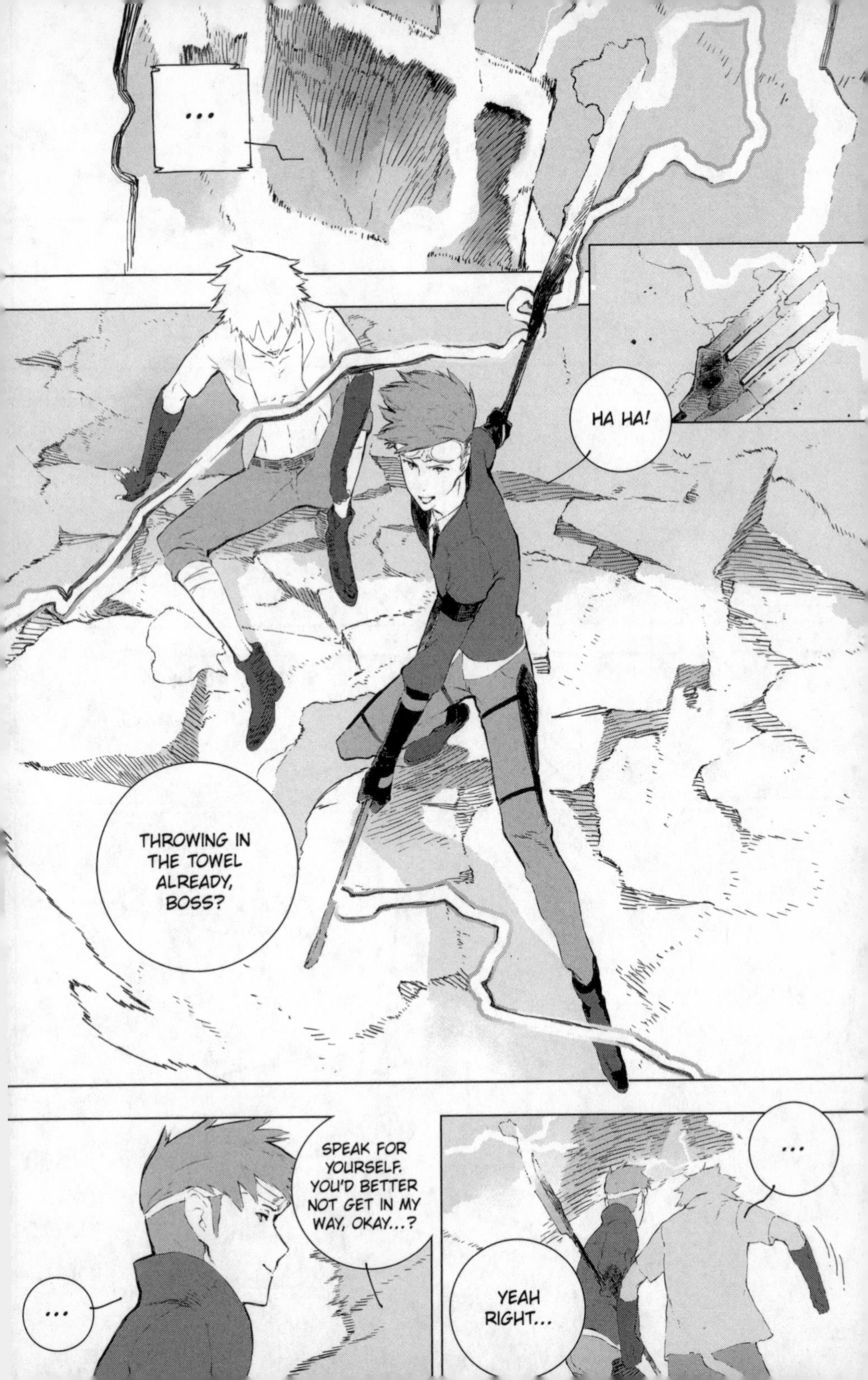
...
HA HA!
THROWING IN THE TOWEL ALREADY, BOSS?
...
YEAH RIGHT...
SPEAK FOR YOURSELF. YOU'D BETTER NOT GET IN MY WAY, OKAY...?
...

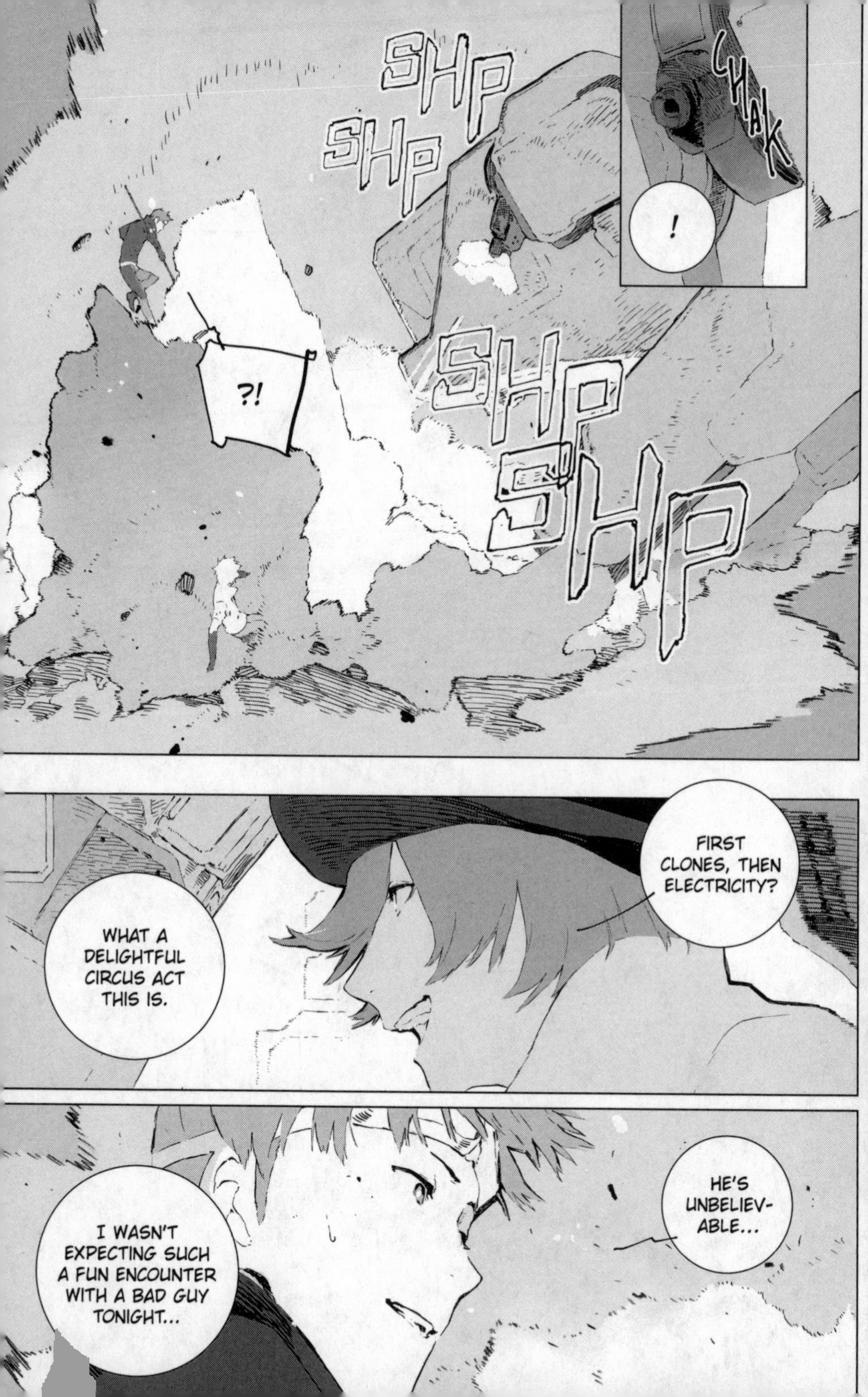
CHAK
!
SHP
SHP
?!
SHP
SHP
SHP
FIRST CLONES, THEN ELECTRICITY?
WHAT A DELIGHTFUL CIRCUS ACT THIS IS.
HE'S UNBELIEV-ABLE...
I WASN'T EXPECTING SUCH A FUN ENCOUNTER WITH A BAD GUY TONIGHT...

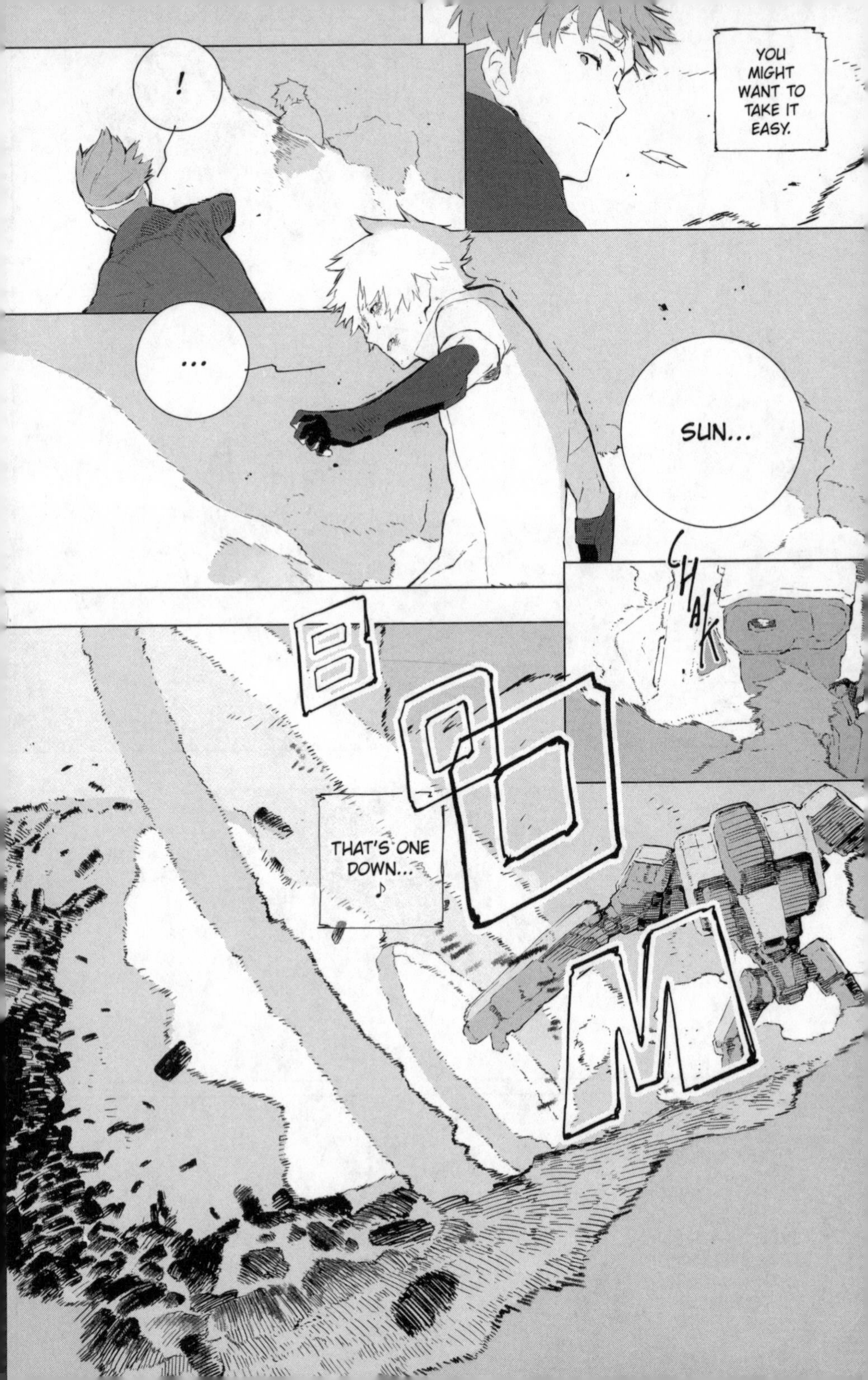
YOU MIGHT WANT TO TAKE IT EASY.
!
SUN...
...
CHAK
BOOM
THAT'S ONE DOWN... ♪

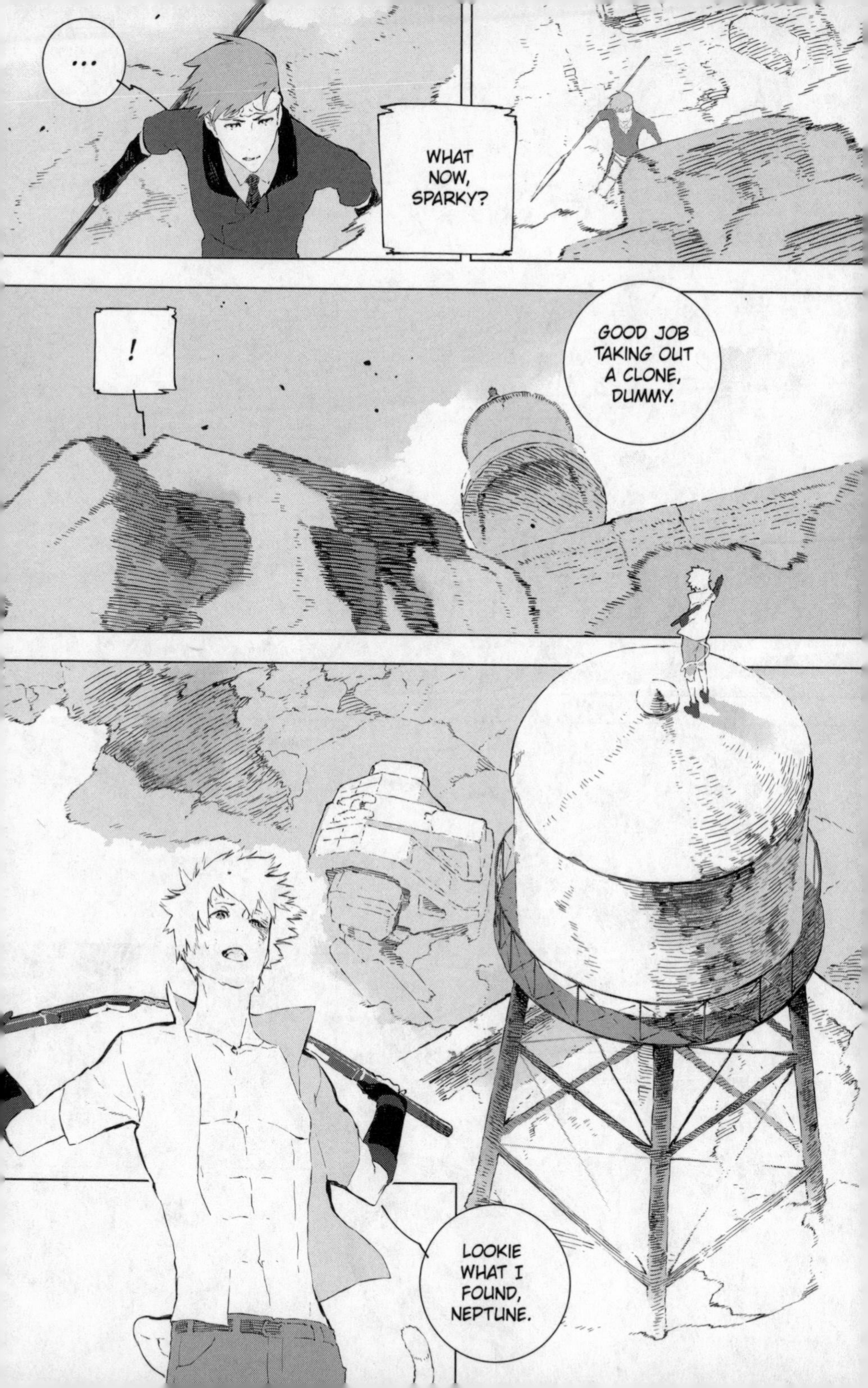
WHAT NOW, SPARKY?
...
GOOD JOB TAKING OUT A CLONE, DUMMY.
!
LOOKIE WHAT I FOUND, NEPTUNE.

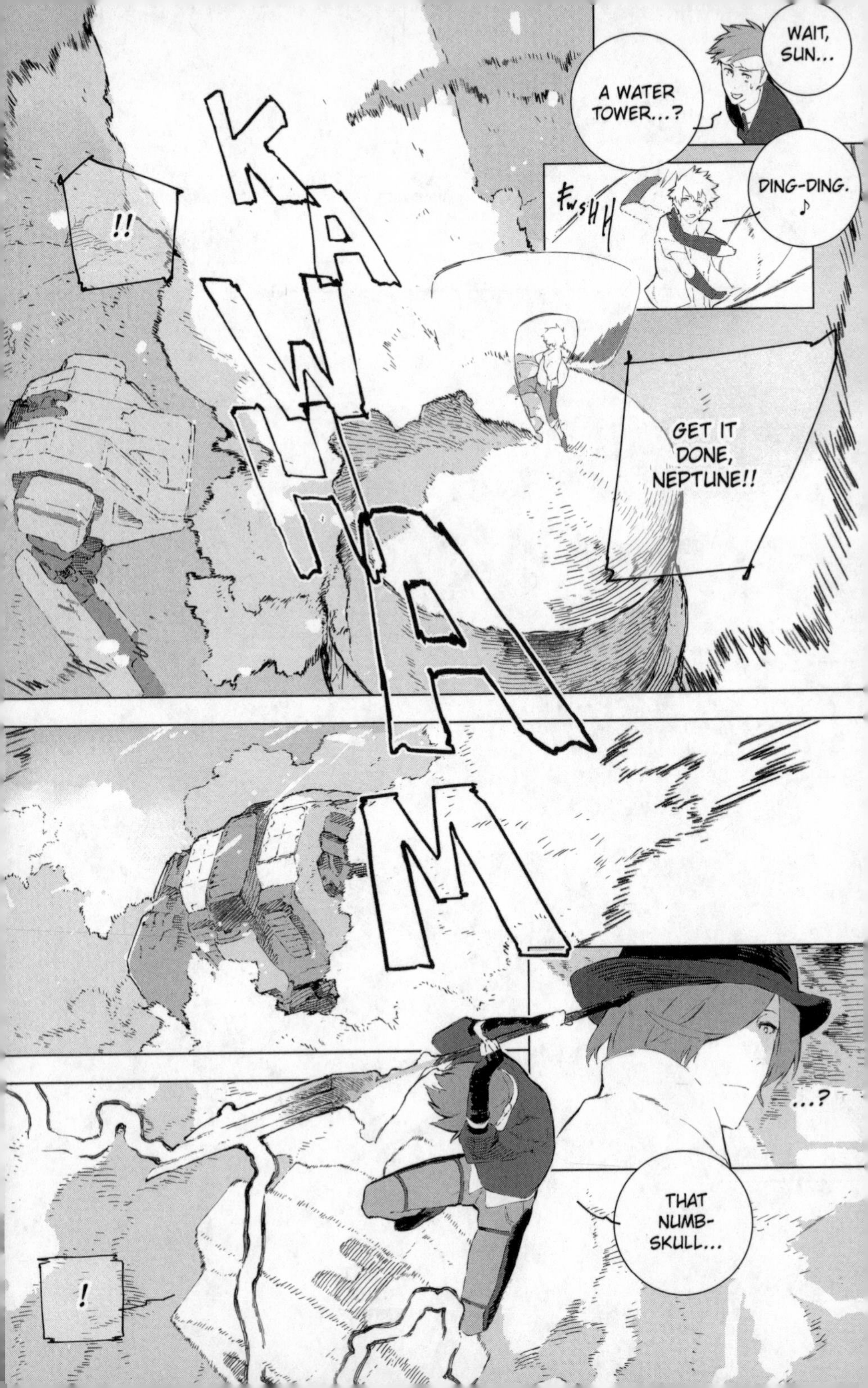
WAIT, SUN...
A WATER TOWER...?
DING-DING. ♪
FWSHH
GET IT DONE, NEPTUNE!!
!!
KAWHAAM
...?
THAT NUMB-SKULL...
!

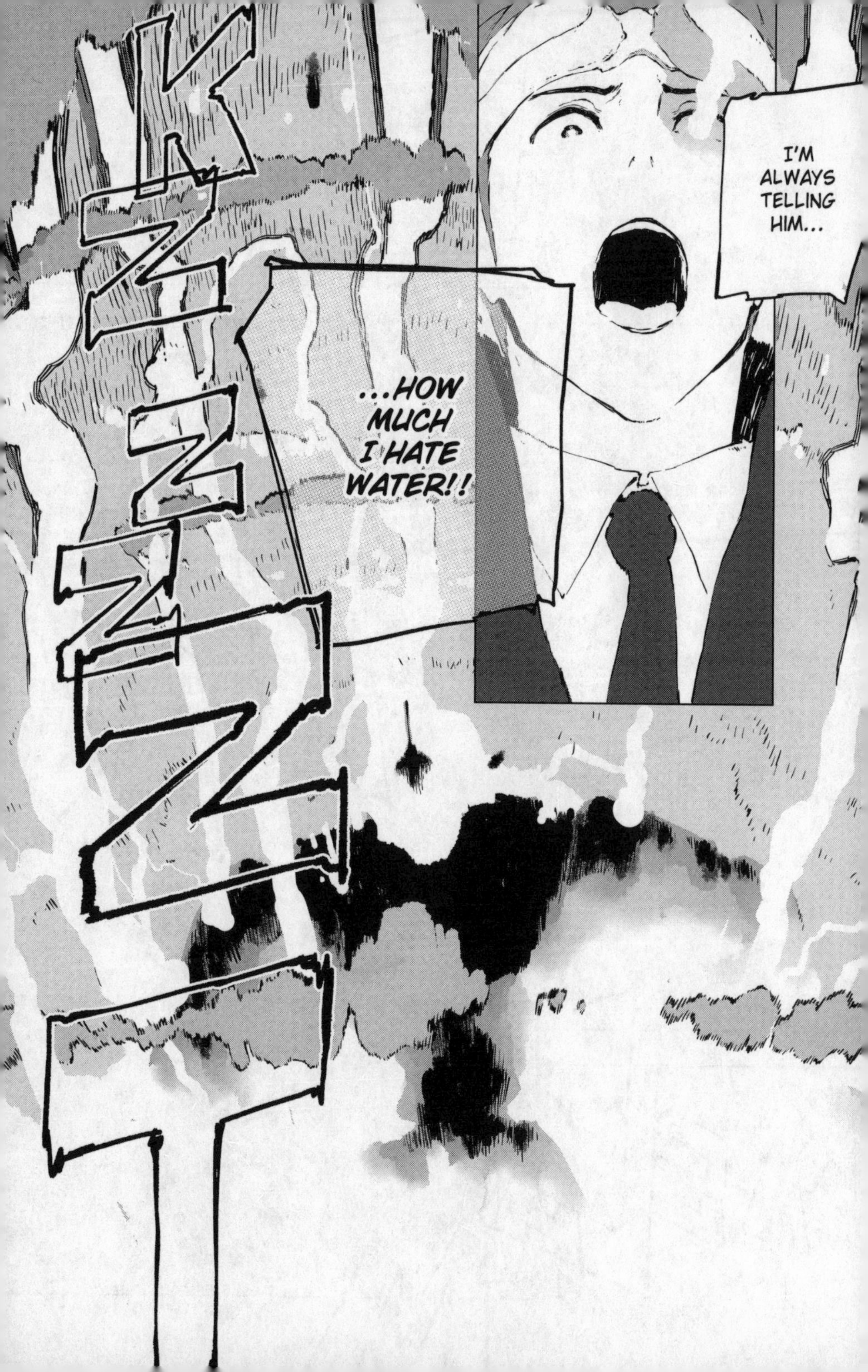
I'M ALWAYS TELLING HIM...
...HOW MUCH I HATE WATER!!
KNNNNT

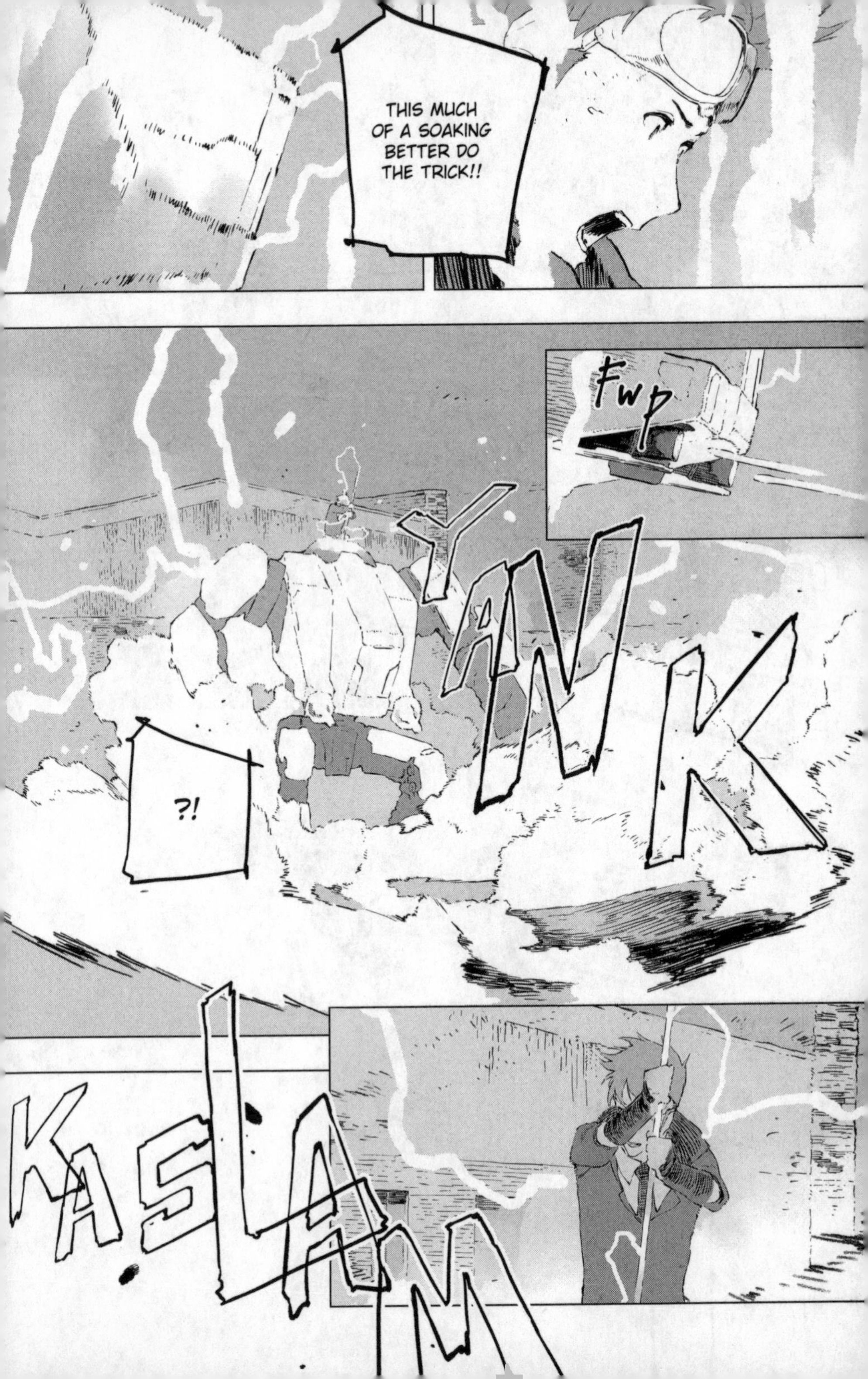
THIS MUCH OF A SOAKING BETTER DO THE TRICK!!
FWP
YANK
?!
KASLAM

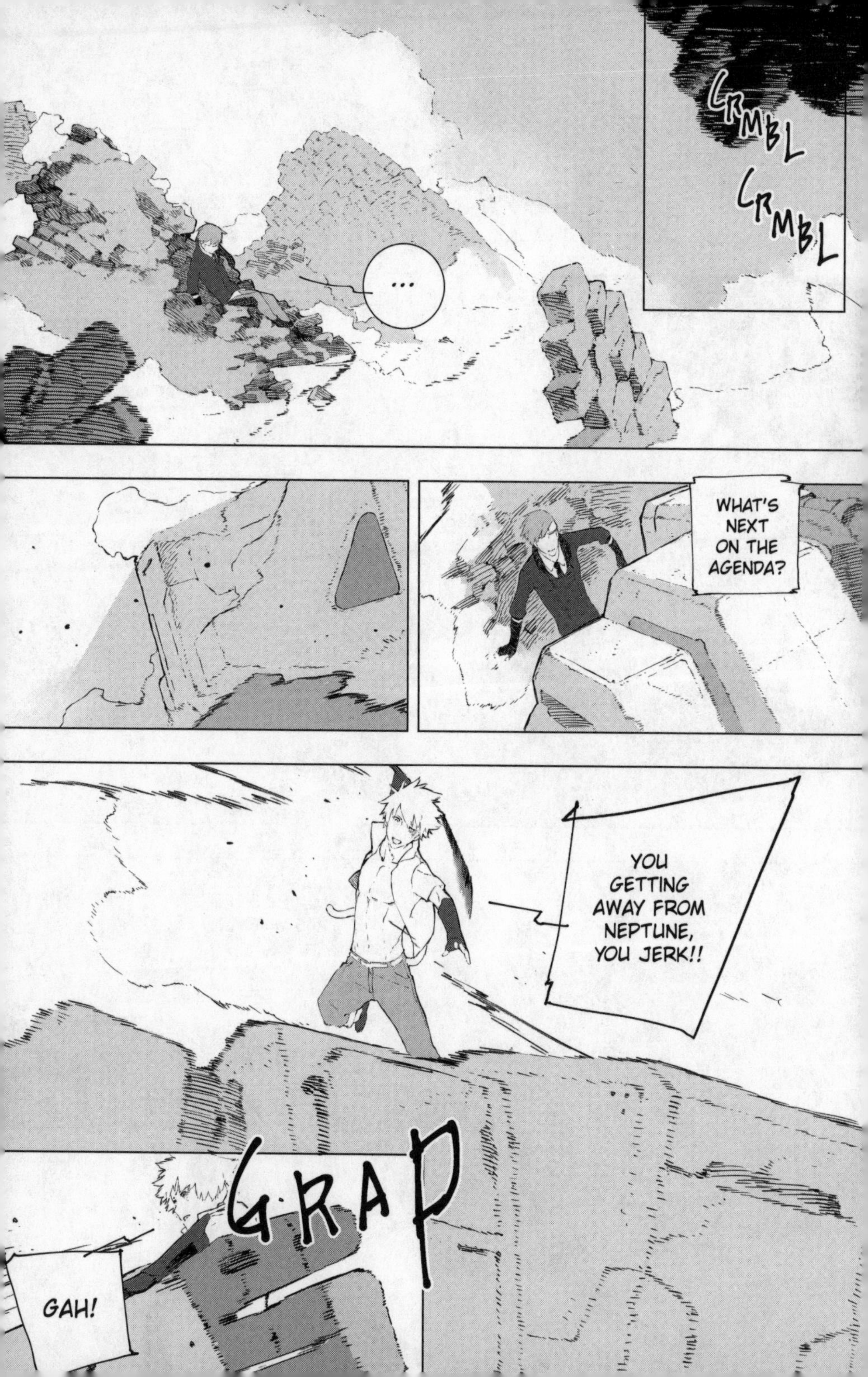
CRMBL
CRMBL
...
WHAT'S NEXT ON THE AGENDA?
YOU GETTING AWAY FROM NEPTUNE, YOU JERK!!
GRAP
GAH!

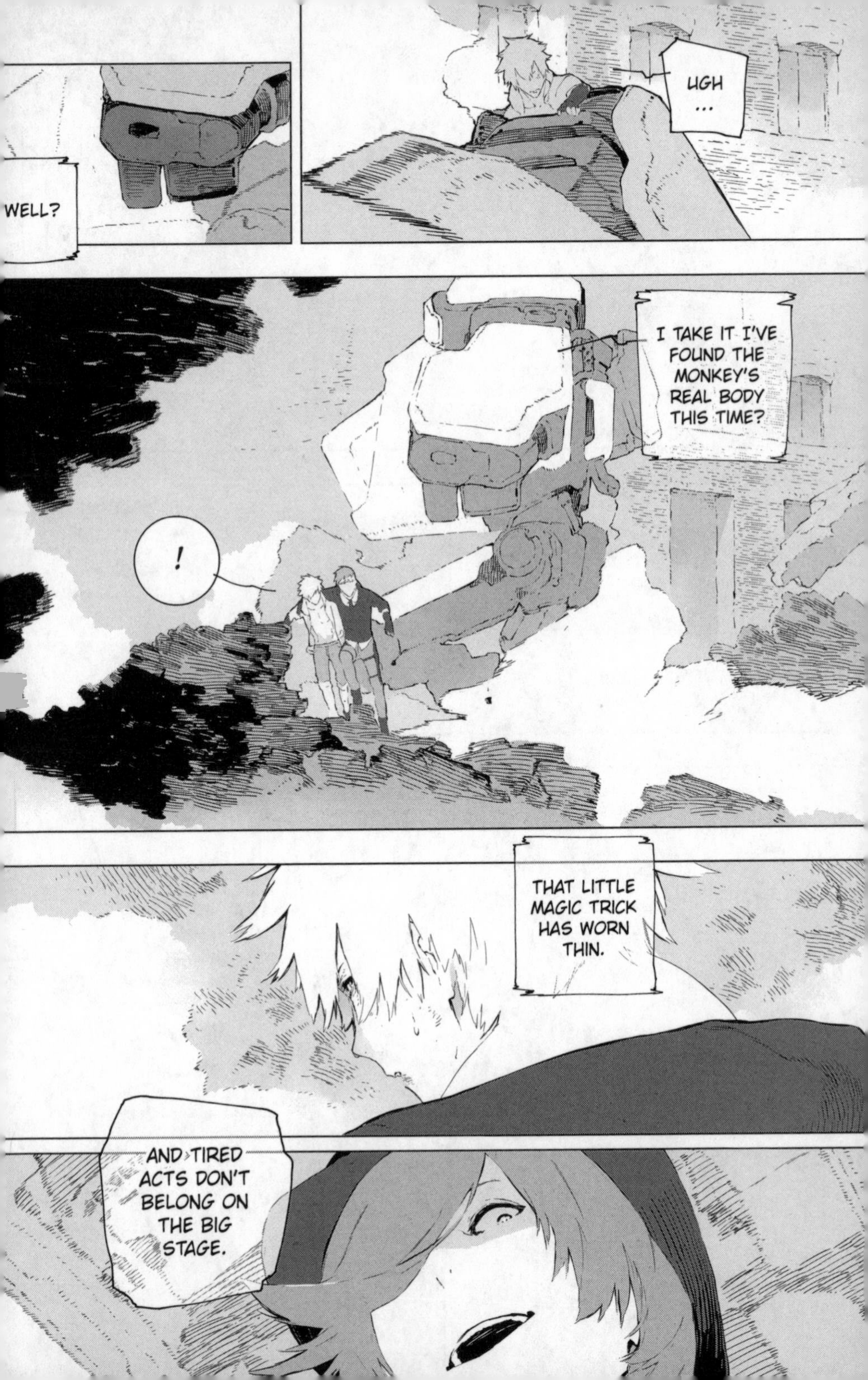
UGH ...
WELL?
I TAKE IT I'VE FOUND THE MONKEY'S REAL BODY THIS TIME?
!
THAT LITTLE MAGIC TRICK HAS WORN THIN.
AND TIRED ACTS DON'T BELONG ON THE BIG STAGE.

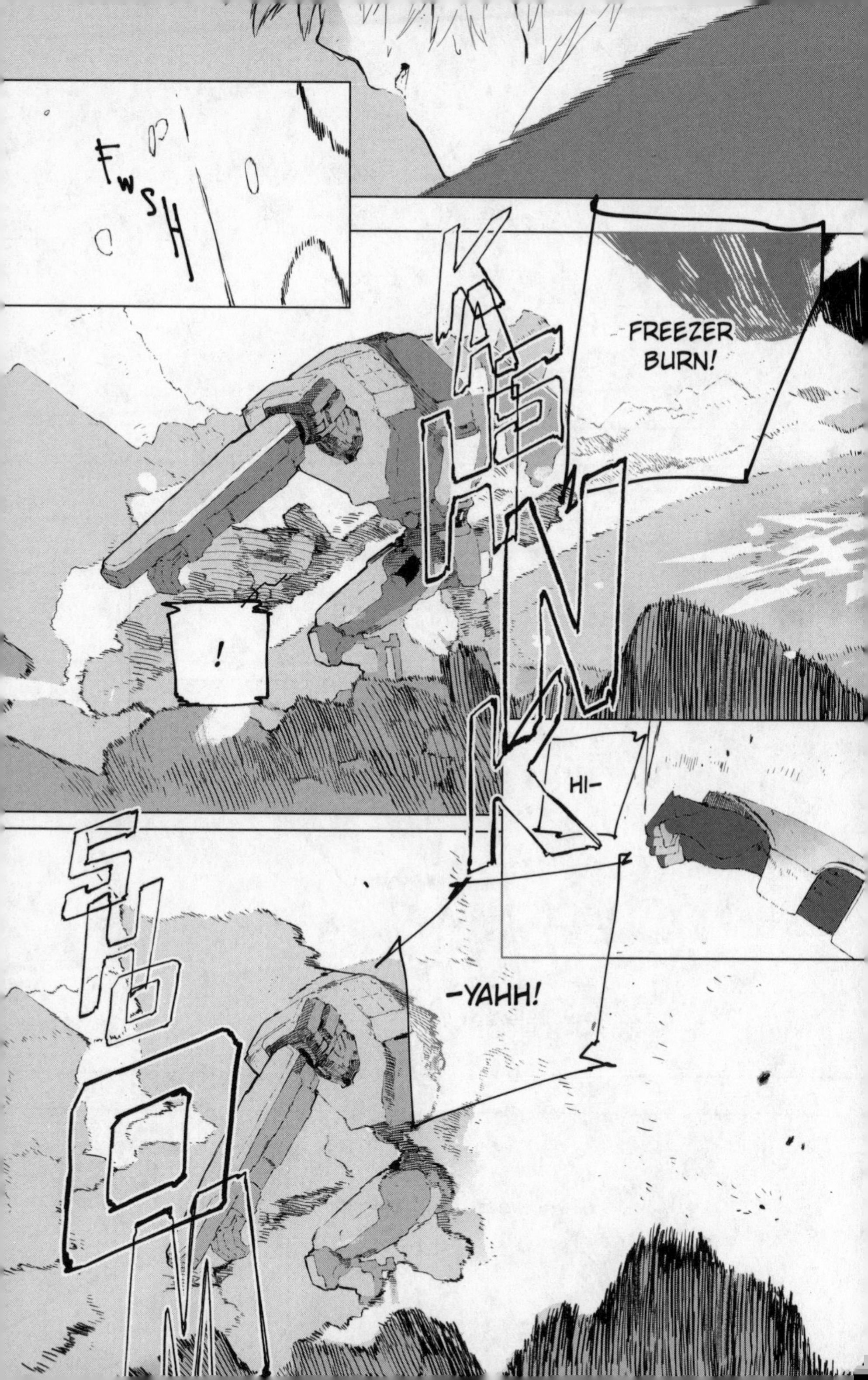
FWSH
FREEZER BURN!
!
HI-
-YAHH!

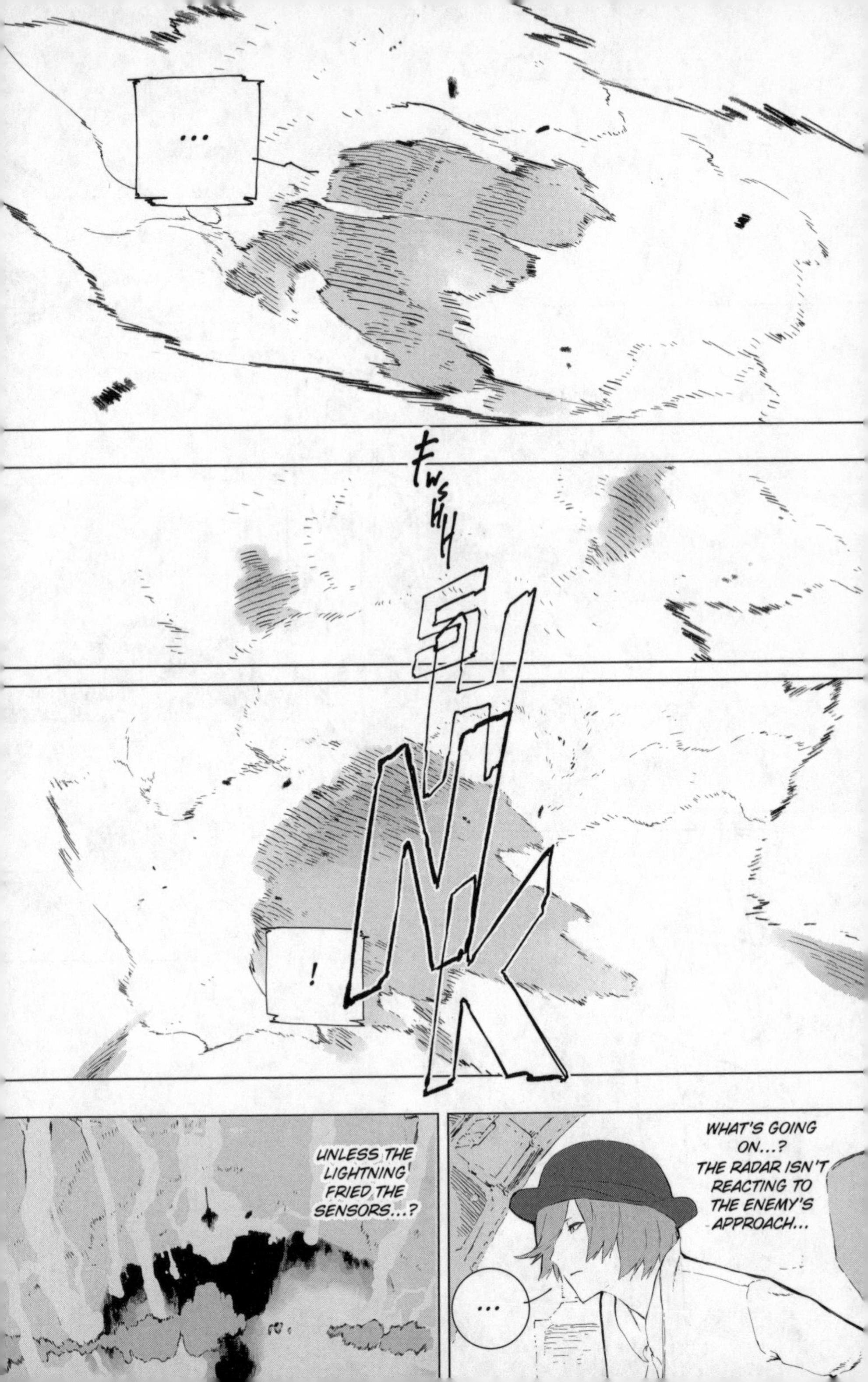
...
FWSHH
SHUNK
!
WHAT'S GOING ON...? THE RADAR ISN'T REACTING TO THE ENEMY'S APPROACH...
...
UNLESS THE LIGHTNING FRIED THE SENSORS...?

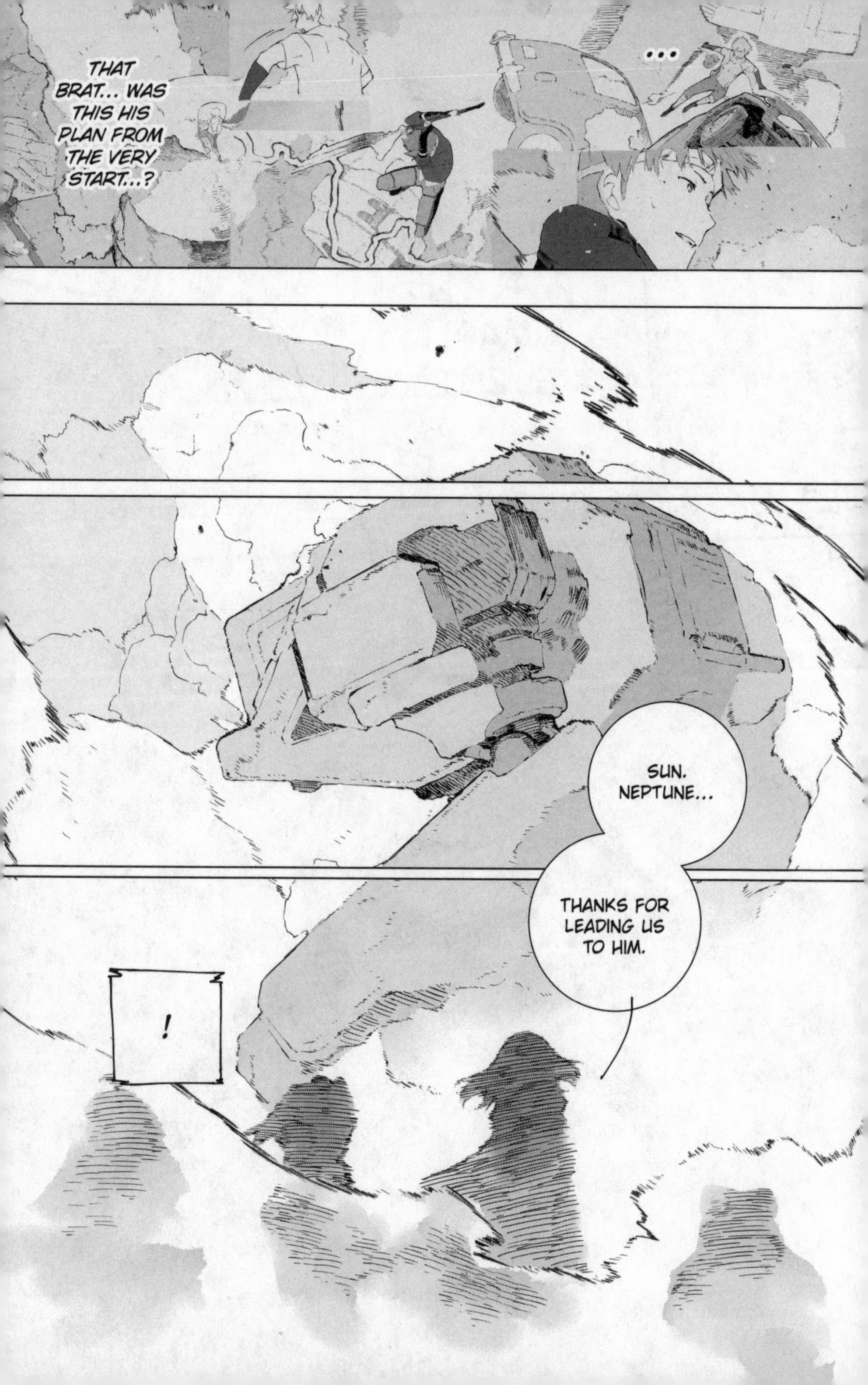
...
THAT BRAT... WAS THIS HIS PLAN FROM THE VERY START...?
SUN. NEPTUNE...
THANKS FOR LEADING US TO HIM.
!

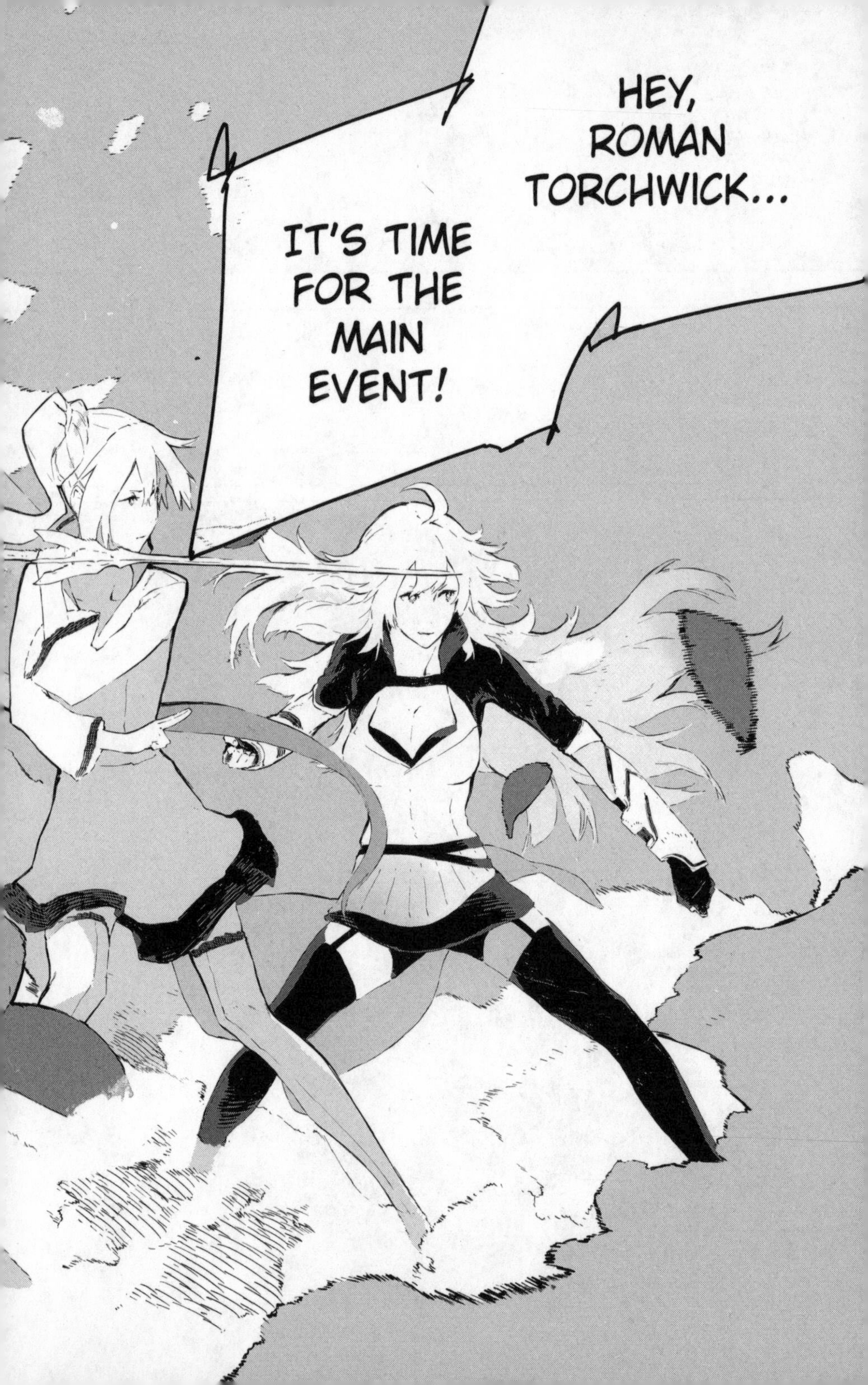
HEY, ROMAN TORCHWICK...
IT'S TIME FOR THE MAIN EVENT!

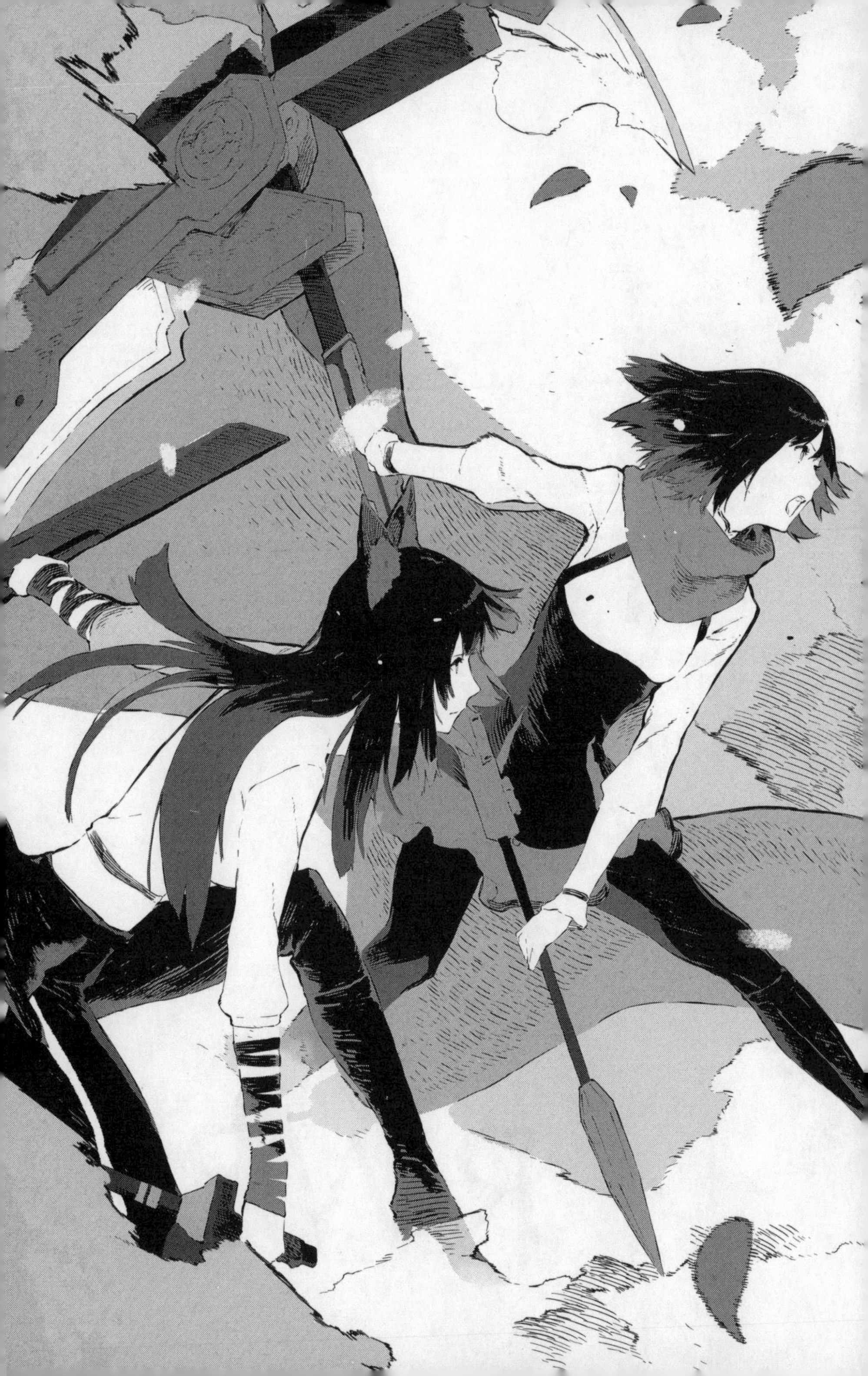

RWBY

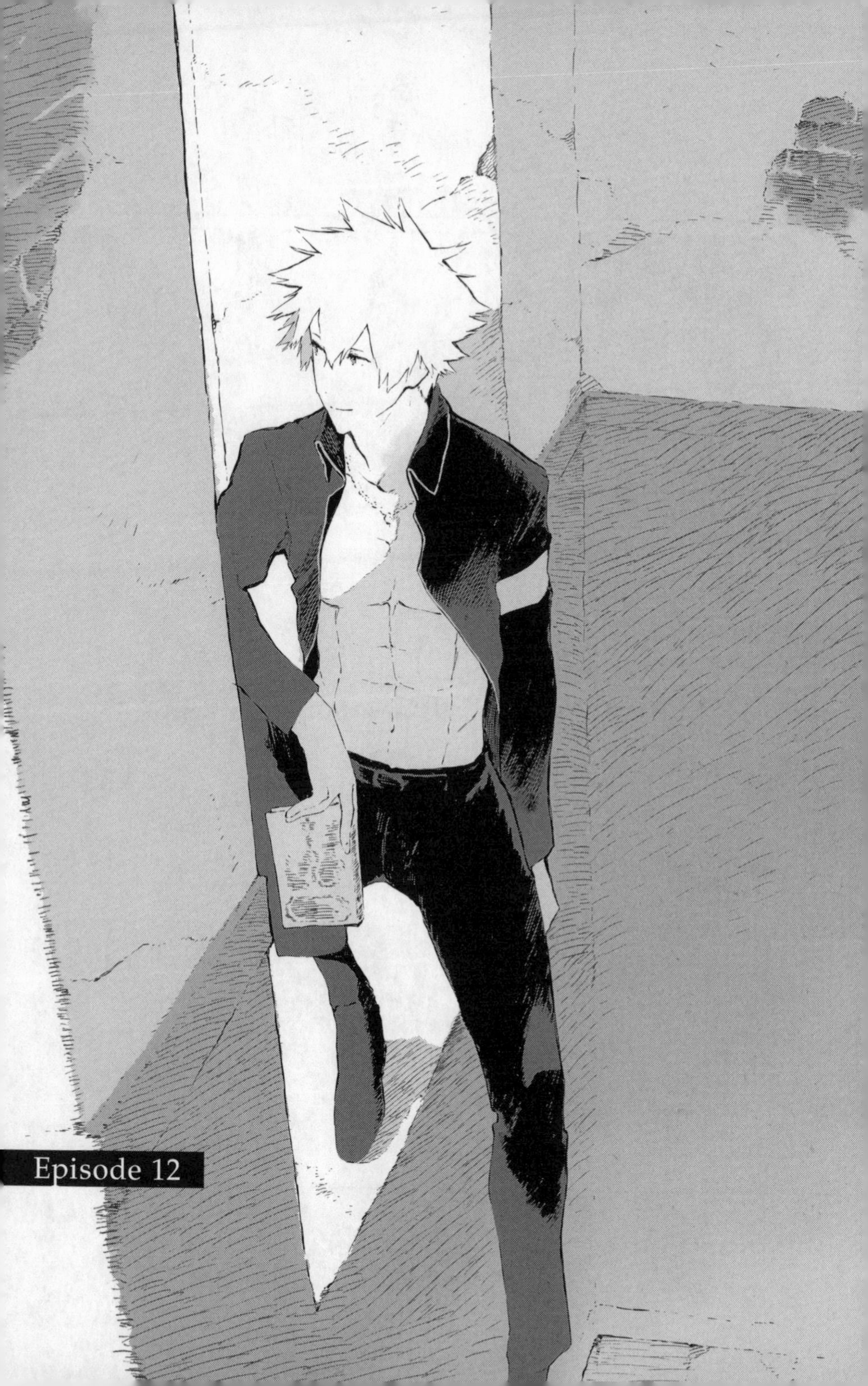

Episode 12

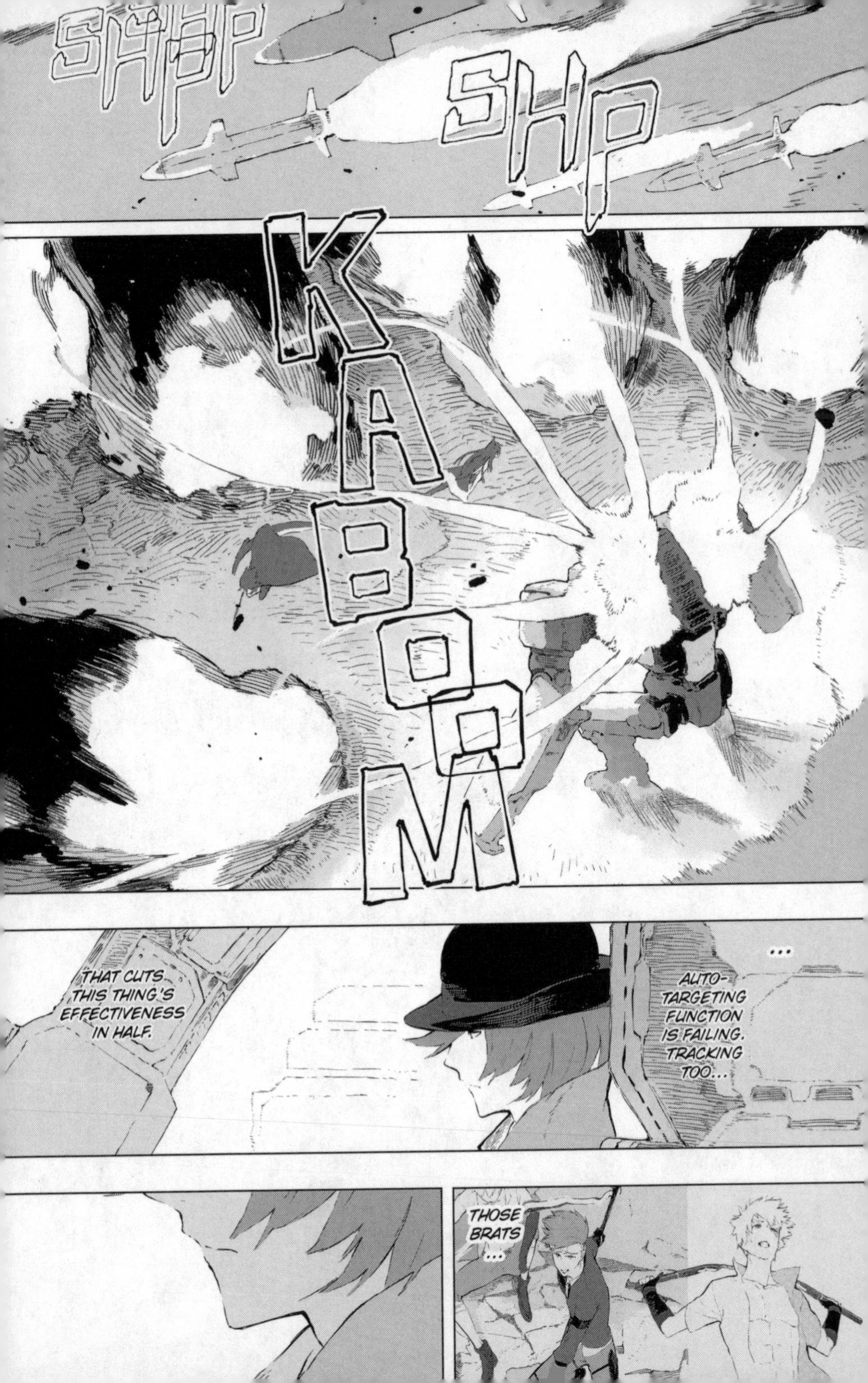
SHP
SHP SHP
KABOOM
...
AUTO-TARGETING FUNCTION IS FAILING. TRACKING TOO...
THAT CUTS THIS THING'S EFFECTIVENESS IN HALF.
THOSE BRATS...

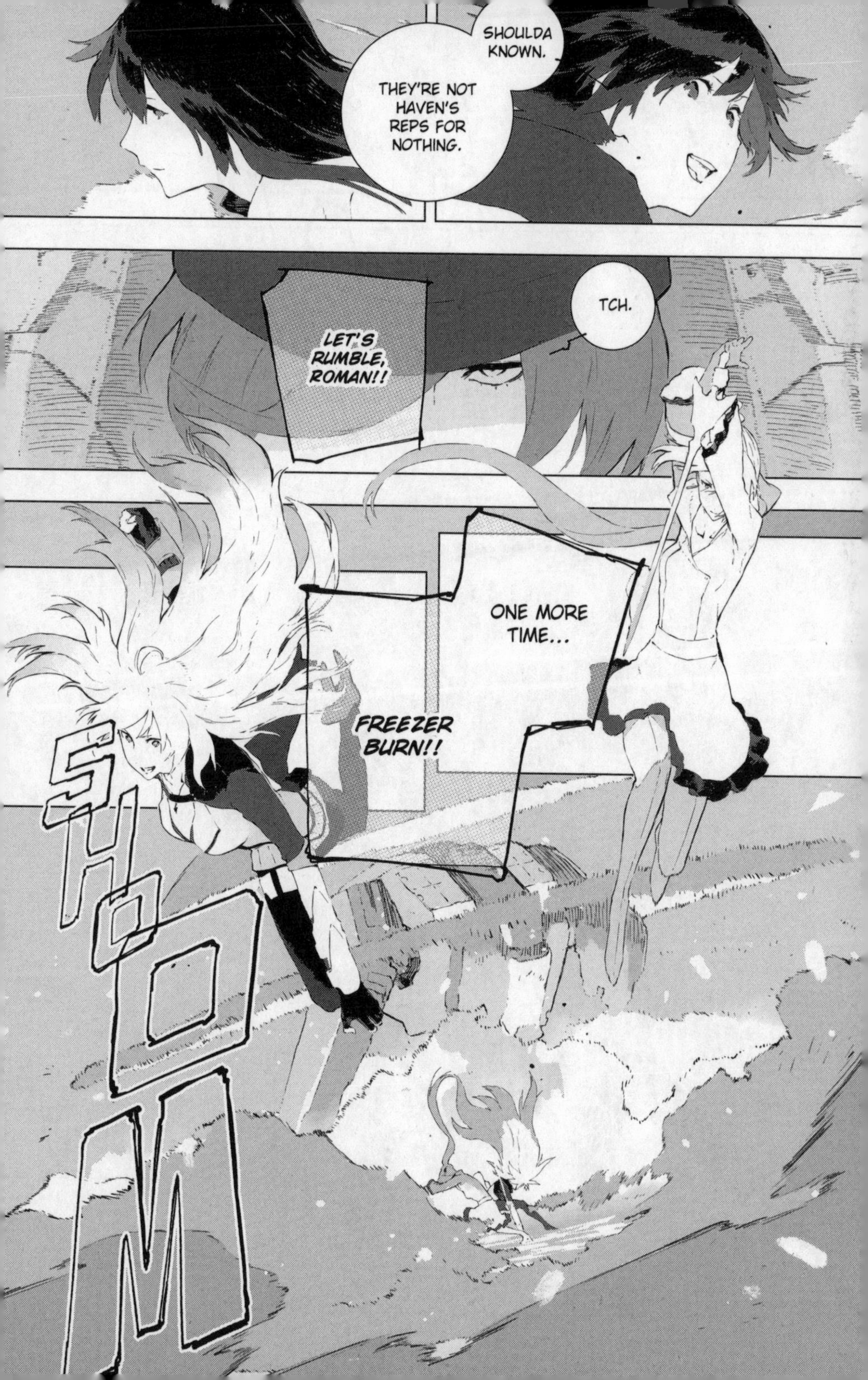
SHOULDA KNOWN.
THEY'RE NOT HAVEN'S REPS FOR NOTHING.
TCH.
LET'S RUMBLE, ROMAN!!
ONE MORE TIME...
FREEZER BURN!!
SHOOM

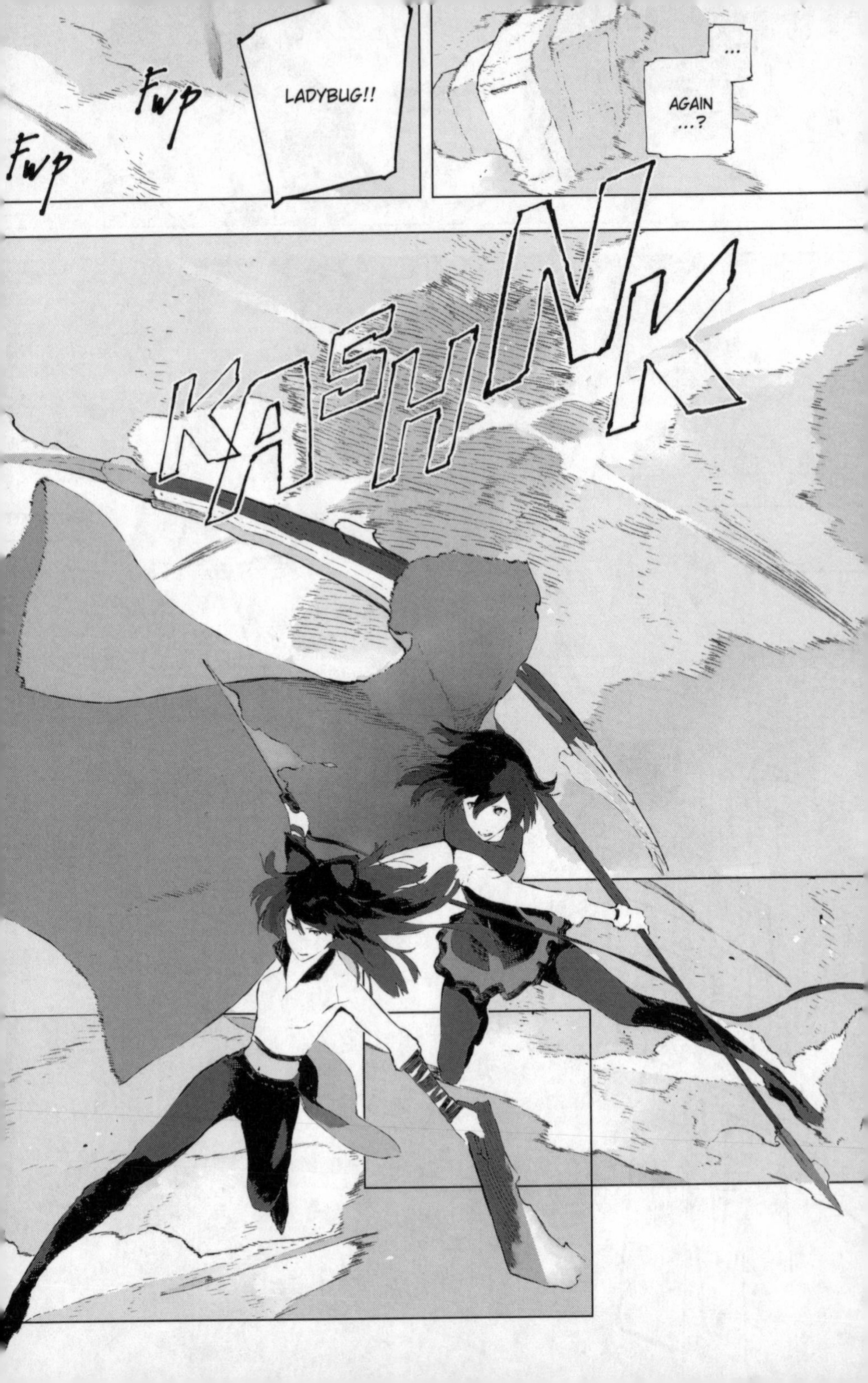
...
AGAIN ...?
LADYBUG!!
Fwp
Fwp
KASHINK

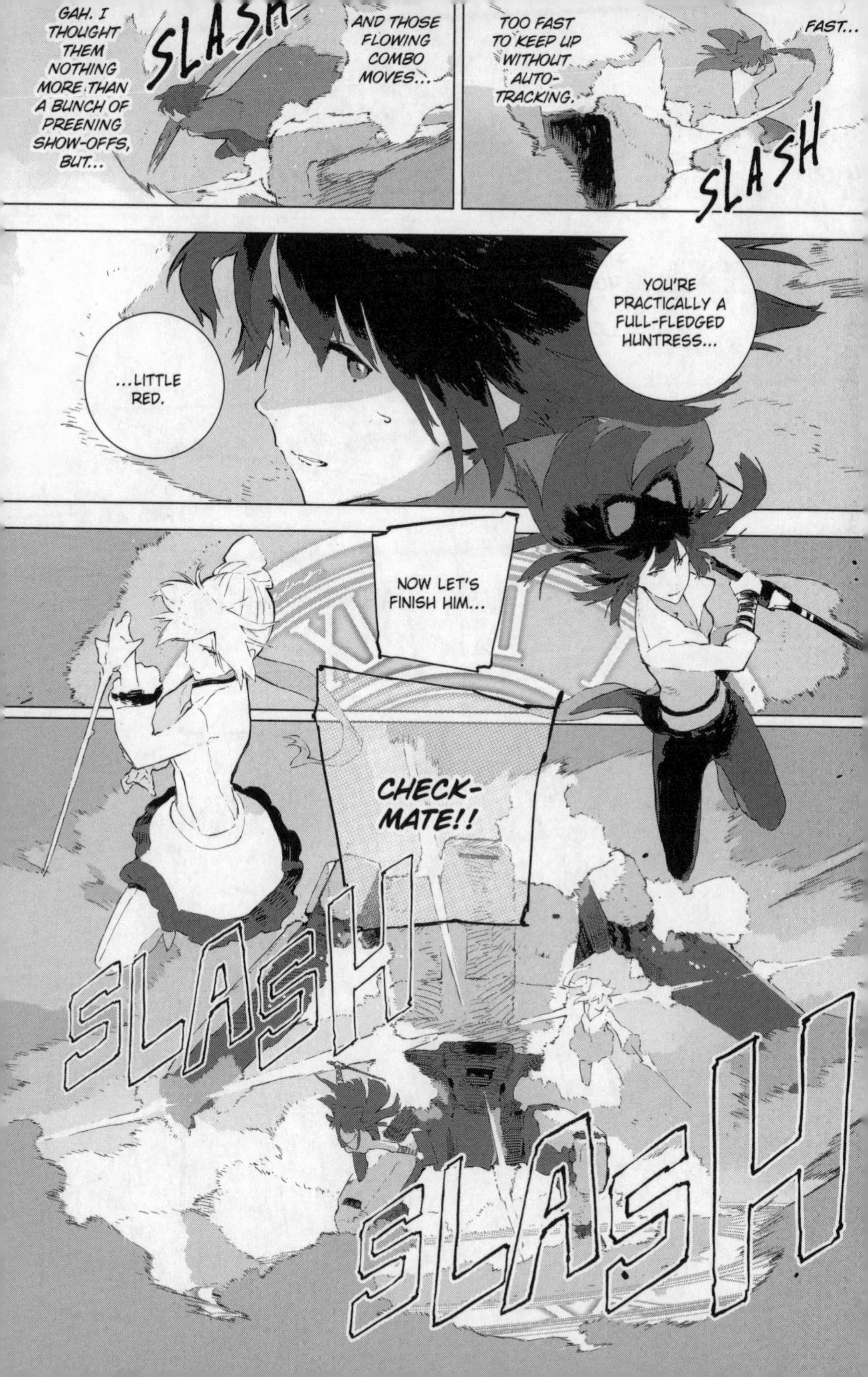
FAST...
TOO FAST TO KEEP UP WITHOUT AUTO-TRACKING.
SLASH
AND THOSE FLOWING COMBO MOVES...
SLASH
GAH. I THOUGHT THEM NOTHING MORE THAN A BUNCH OF PREENING SHOW-OFFS, BUT...
YOU'RE PRACTICALLY A FULL-FLEDGED HUNTRESS...
...LITTLE RED.
NOW LET'S FINISH HIM...
CHECK-MATE!!
SLASH
SLASH

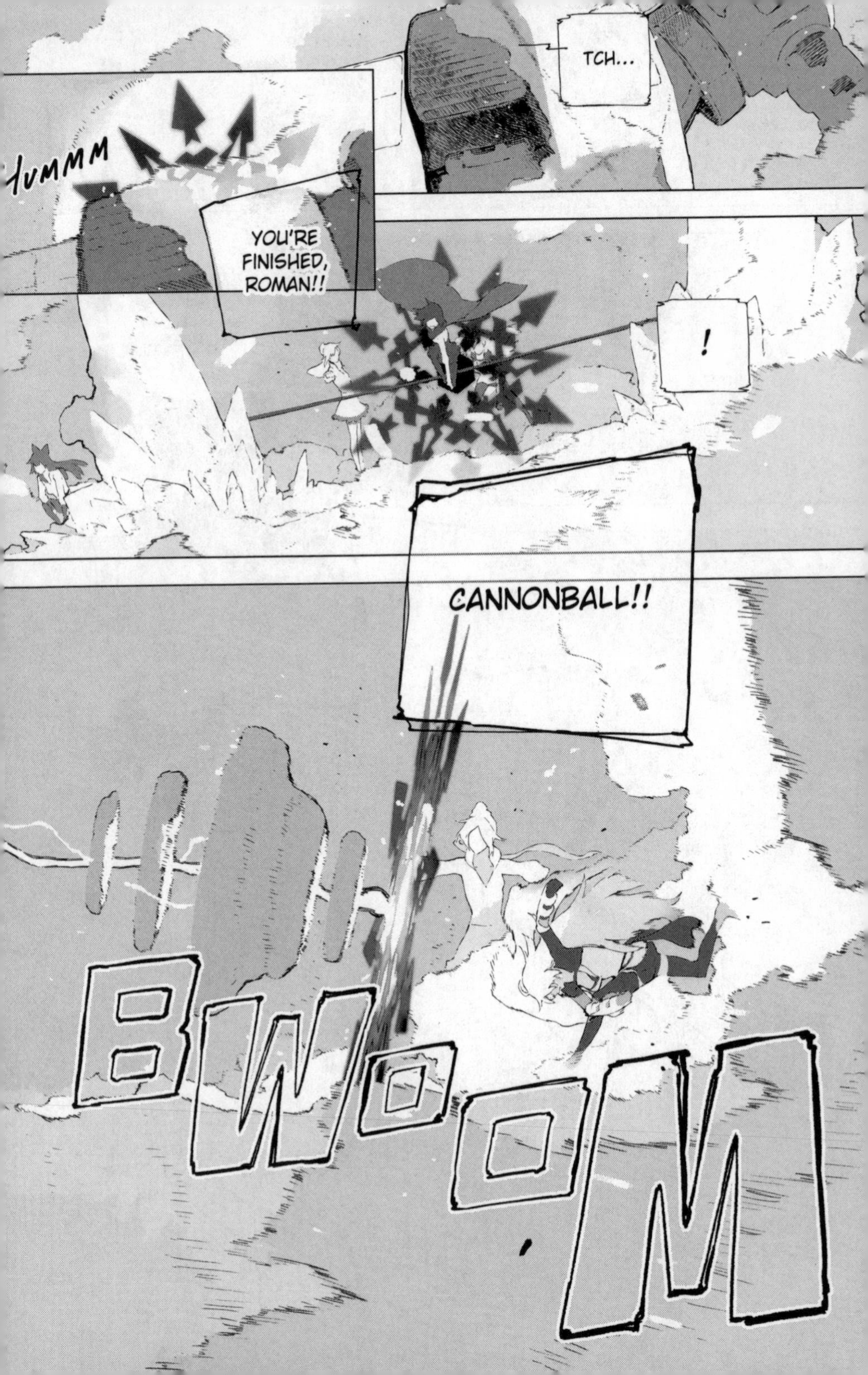
TCH...
HUMMM
YOU'RE FINISHED, ROMAN!!
!
CANNONBALL!!
BWOOM

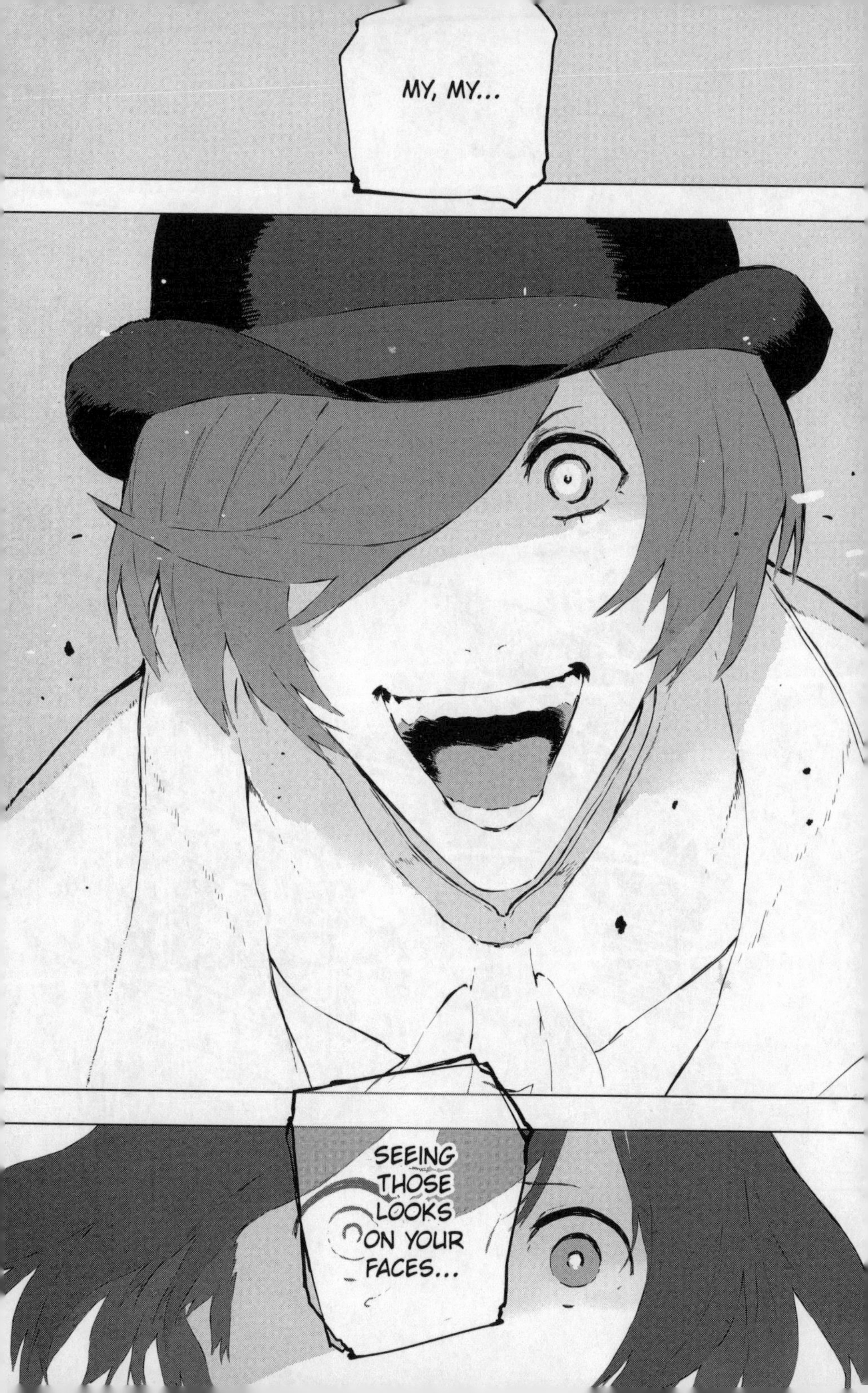
MY, MY...
SEEING THOSE LOOKS ON YOUR FACES...

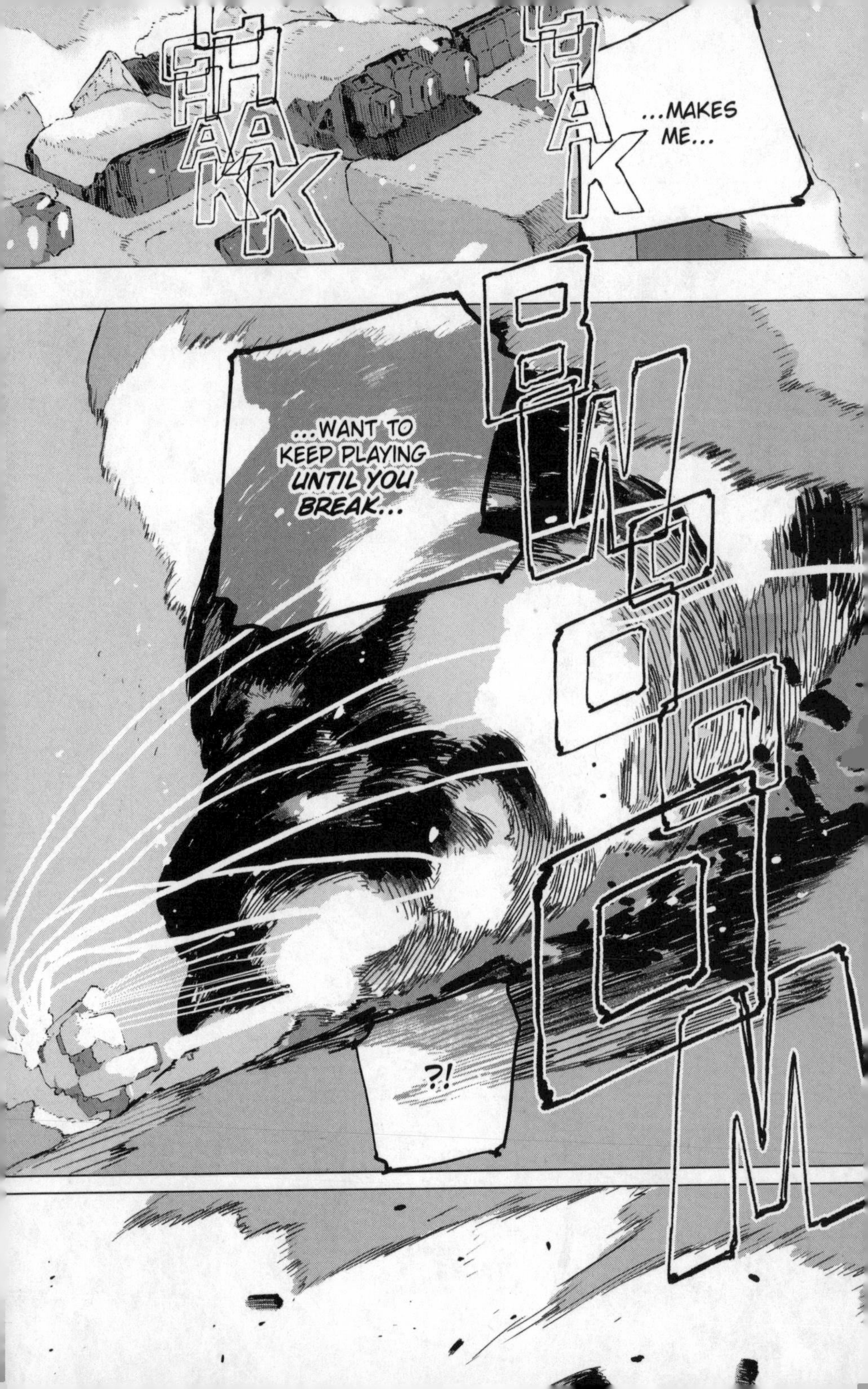
...MAKES ME...
CHAK
CHAAKK
...WANT TO KEEP PLAYING UNTIL YOU BREAK...
BOOOOM
?!

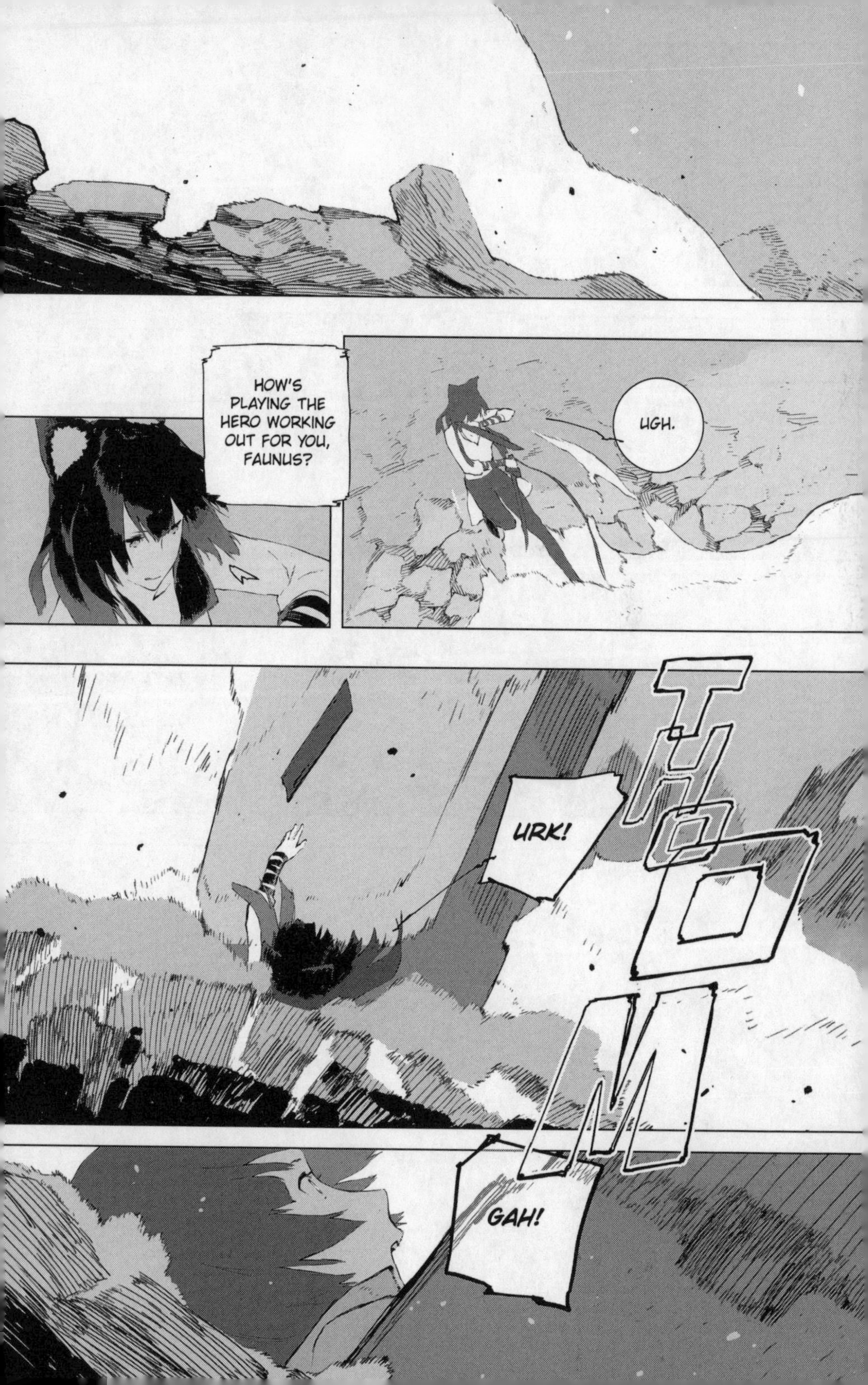
UGH.
HOW'S PLAYING THE HERO WORKING OUT FOR YOU, FAUNUS?
THOOM
URK!
GAH!

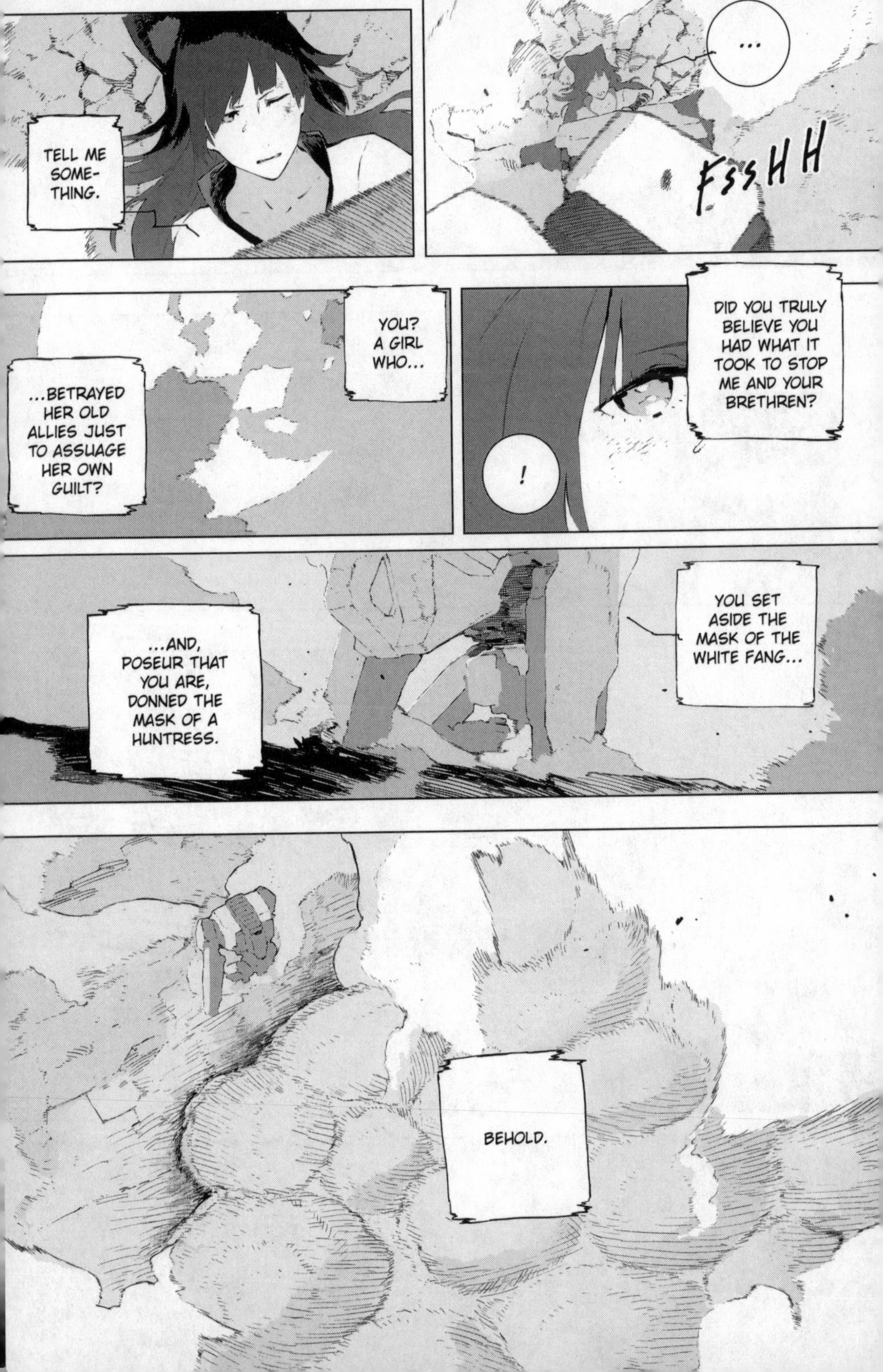
...
FSSHH
TELL ME SOMETHING.
DID YOU TRULY BELIEVE YOU HAD WHAT IT TOOK TO STOP ME AND YOUR BRETHREN?
!
YOU? A GIRL WHO...
...BETRAYED HER OLD ALLIES JUST TO ASSUAGE HER OWN GUILT?
YOU SET ASIDE THE MASK OF THE WHITE FANG...
...AND, POSEUR THAT YOU ARE, DONNED THE MASK OF A HUNTRESS.
BEHOLD.

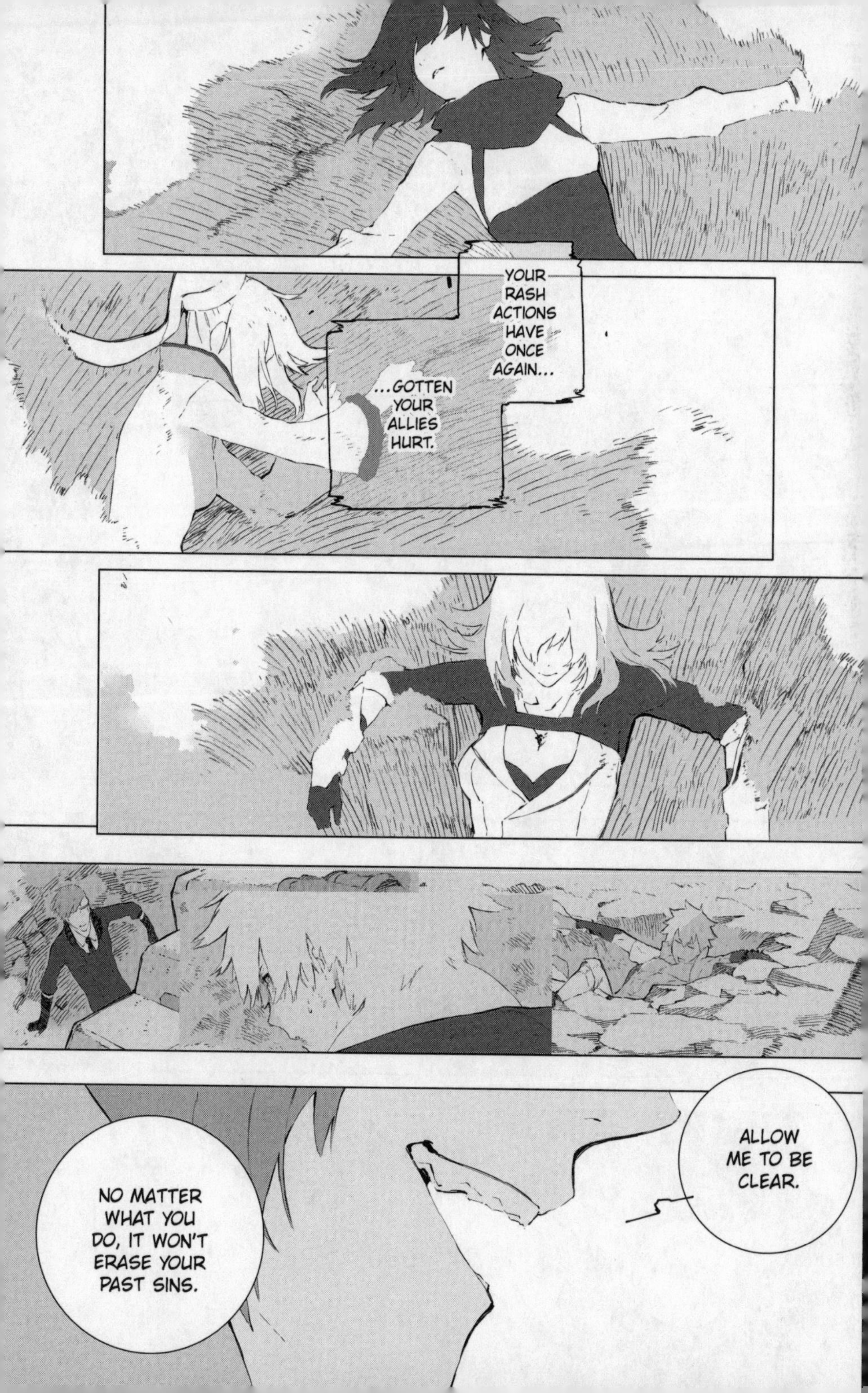
YOUR RASH ACTIONS HAVE ONCE AGAIN...
...GOTTEN YOUR ALLIES HURT.
ALLOW ME TO BE CLEAR.
NO MATTER WHAT YOU DO, IT WON'T ERASE YOUR PAST SINS.

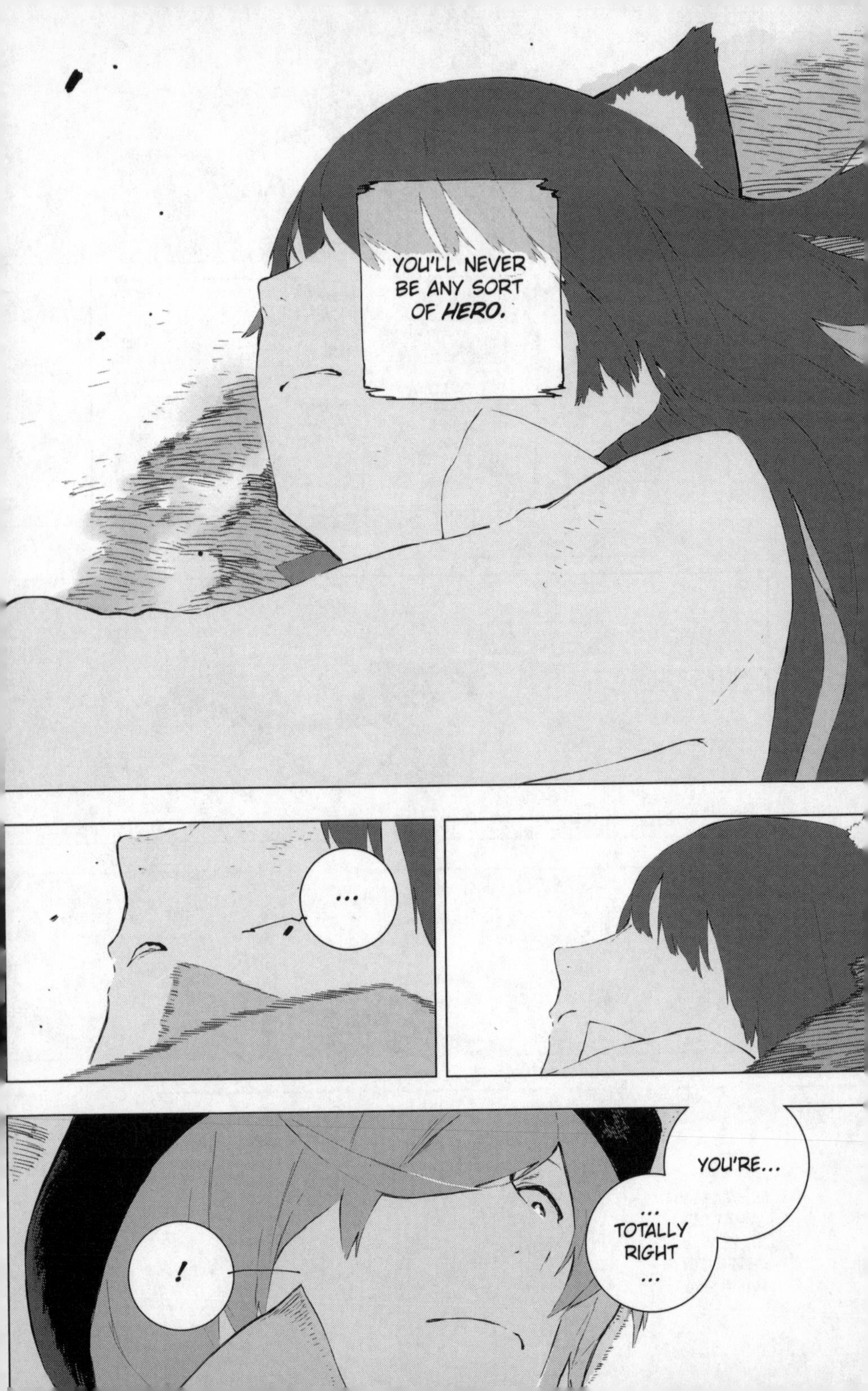
YOU'LL NEVER BE ANY SORT OF HERO.
...
YOU'RE...
... TOTALLY RIGHT ...
!

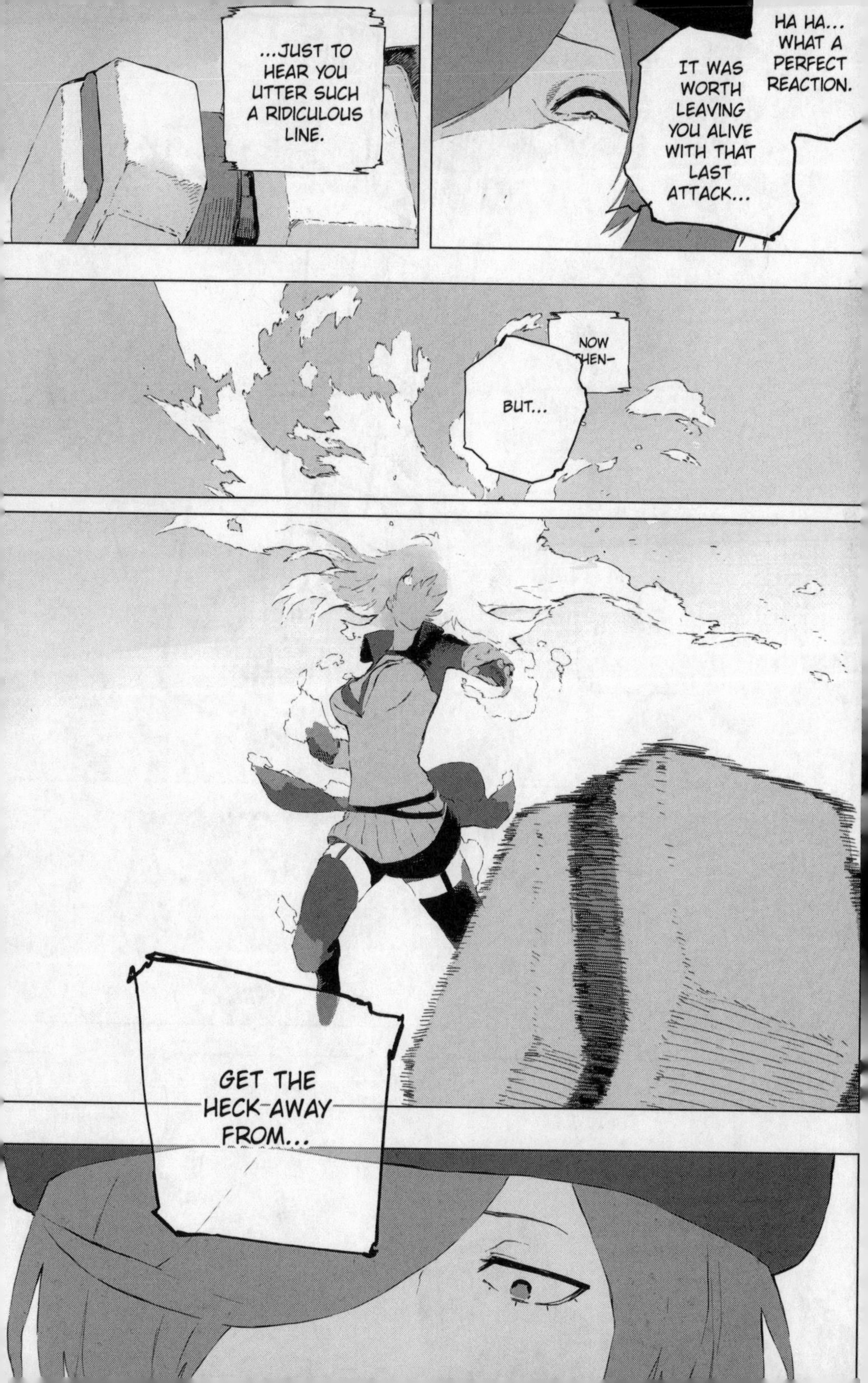
HA HA... WHAT A PERFECT REACTION.
IT WAS WORTH LEAVING YOU ALIVE WITH THAT LAST ATTACK...
...JUST TO HEAR YOU UTTER SUCH A RIDICULOUS LINE.
NOW THEN—
BUT...
GET THE HECK AWAY FROM...

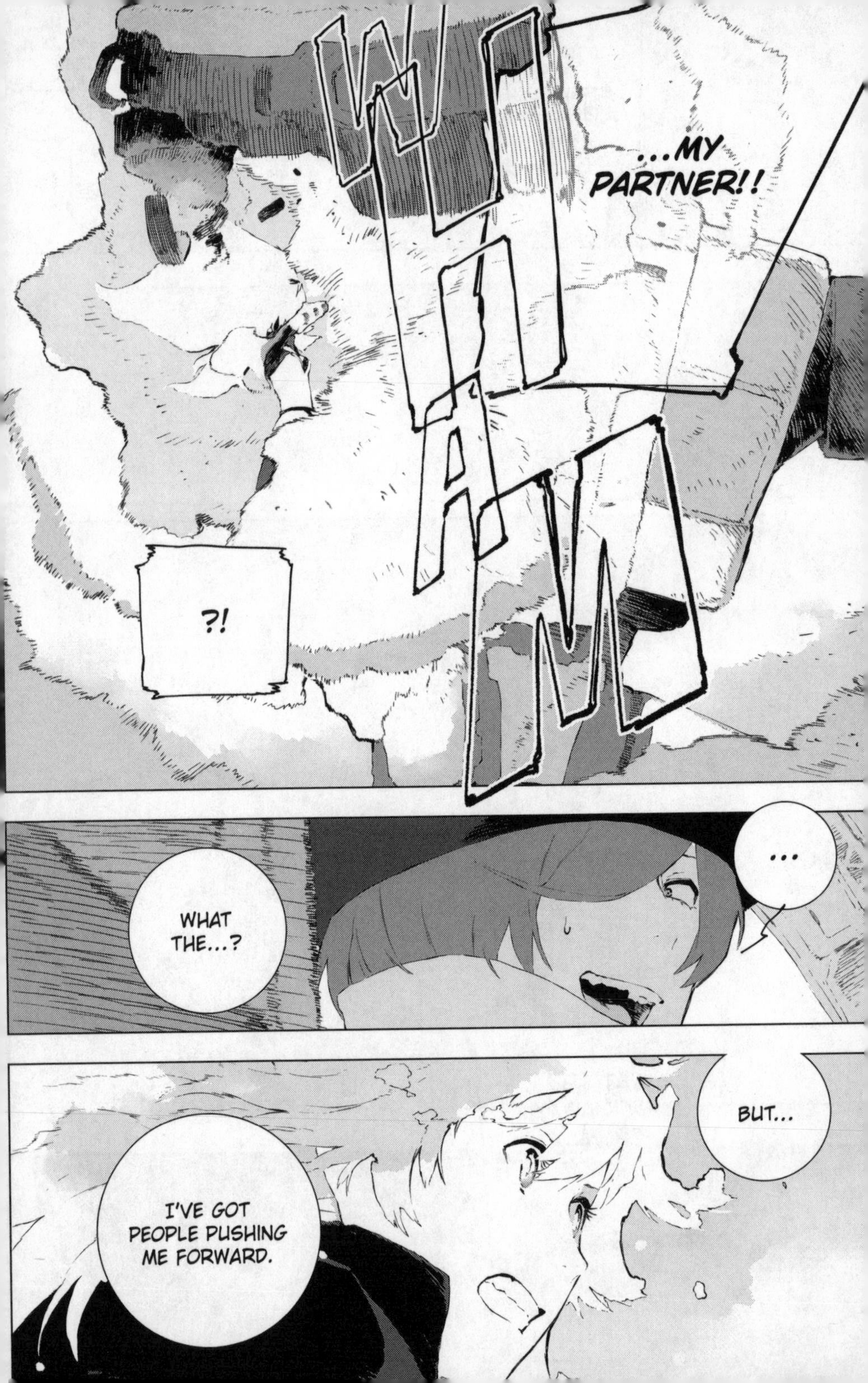
...MY PARTNER!!
WHAM
?!
...
WHAT THE...?
BUT...
I'VE GOT PEOPLE PUSHING ME FORWARD.

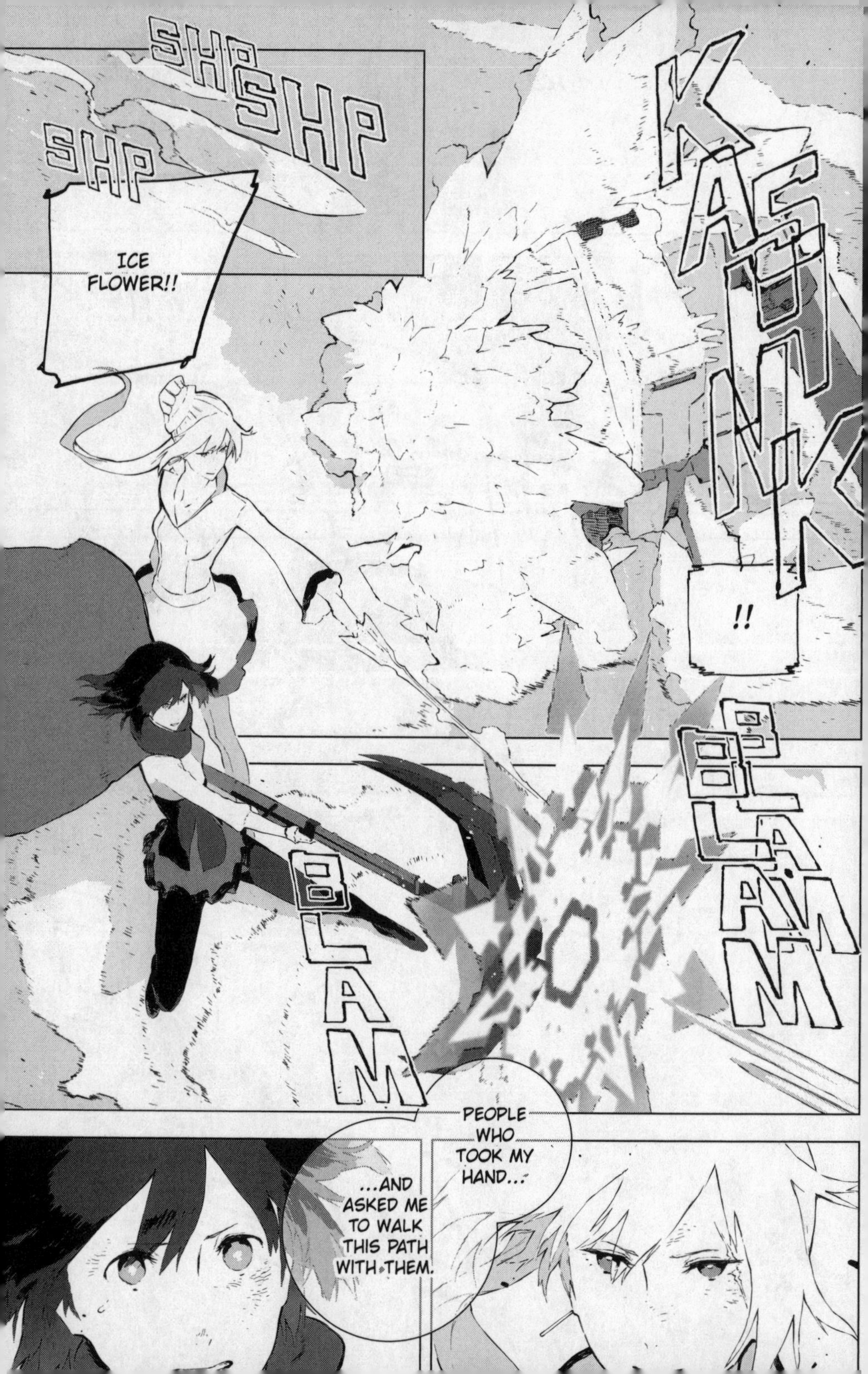
KASHUNK
!!
SHP SHP SHP
ICE FLOWER!!
BLAAM
BLAM
BLAM
PEOPLE WHO TOOK MY HAND...
...AND ASKED ME TO WALK THIS PATH WITH THEM.

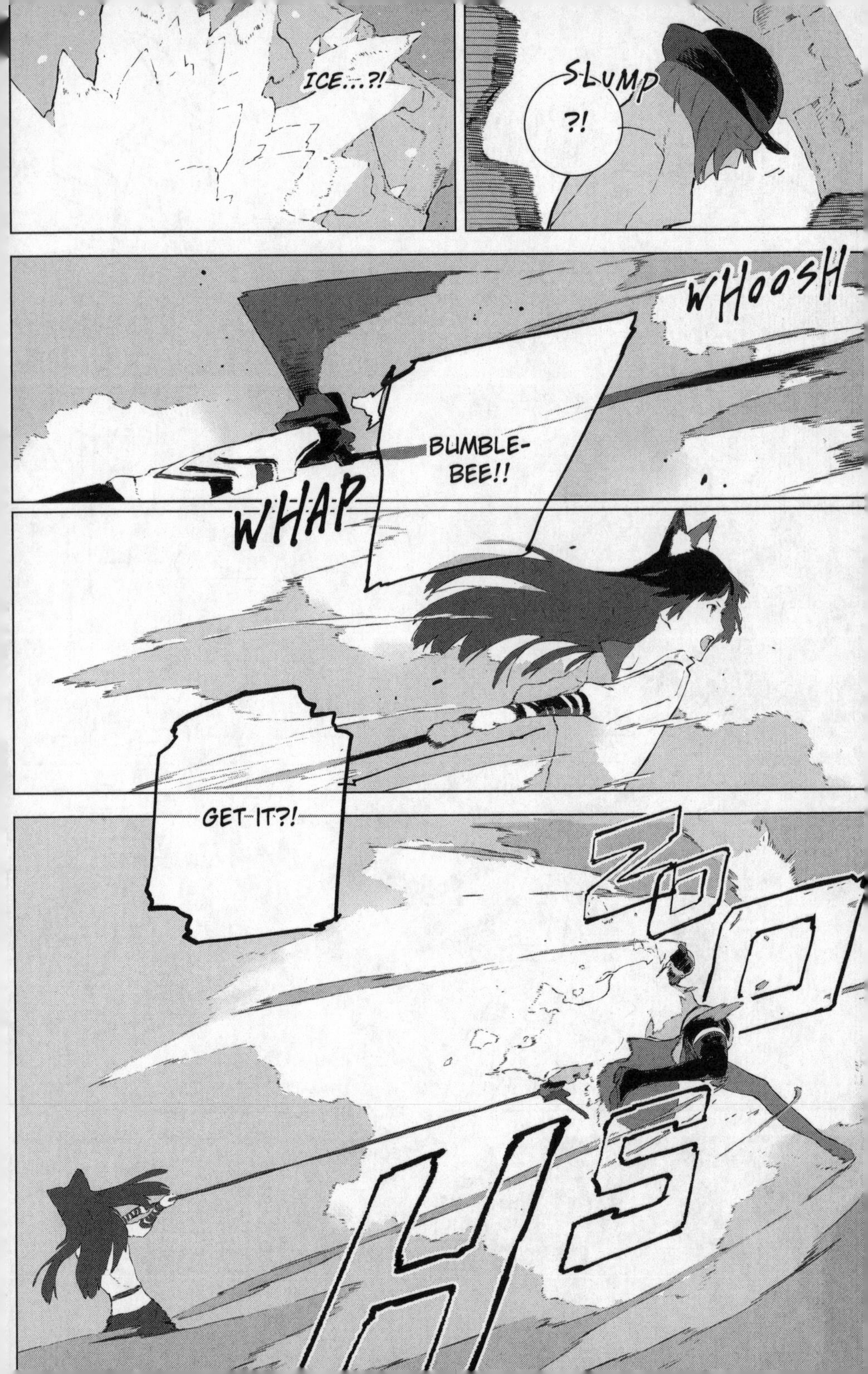
SLUMP
?!
ICE...?!
WHOOSH
BUMBLE-BEE!!
WHAP
GET IT?!

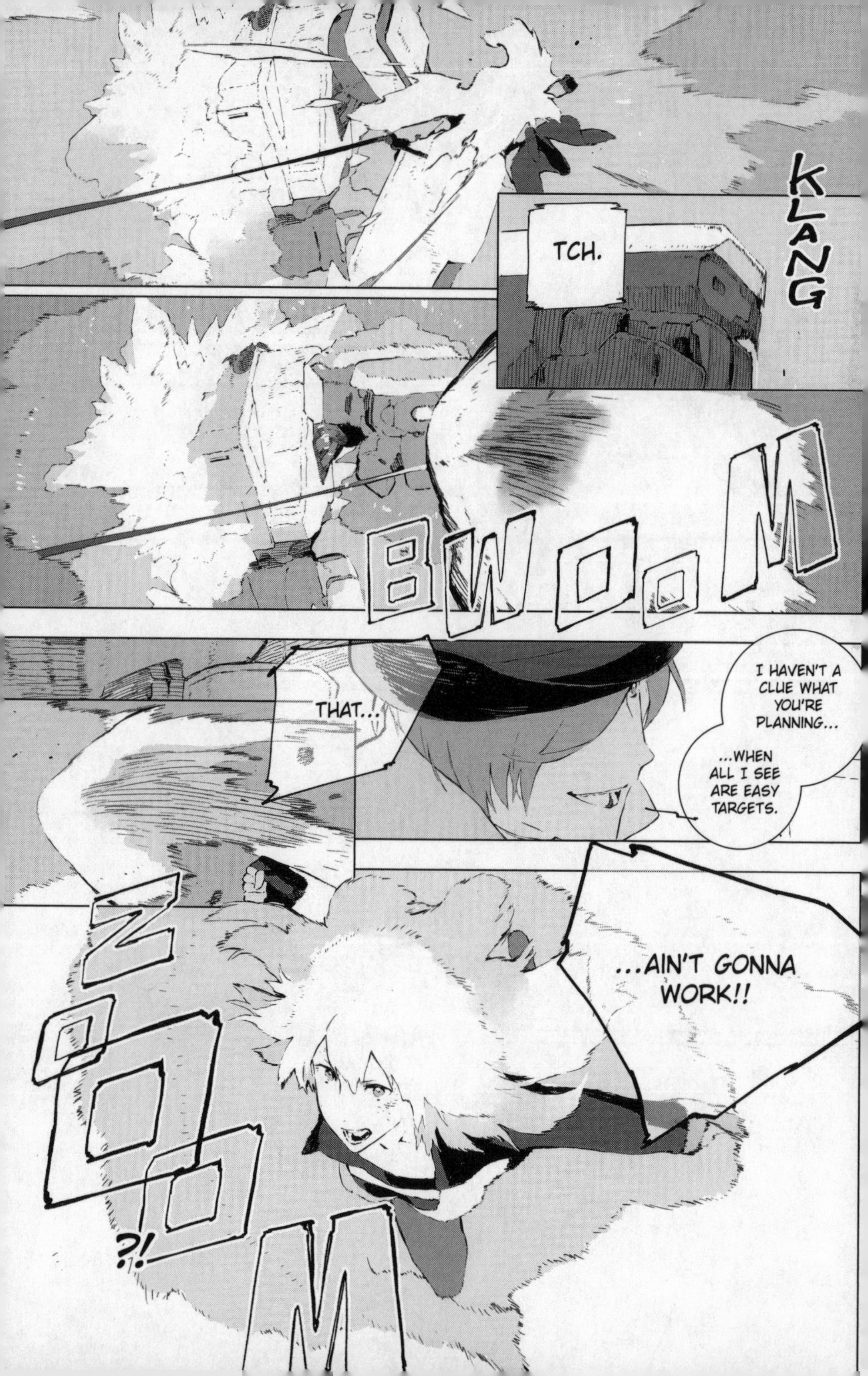
KLANG
TCH.
BWOOM
I HAVEN'T A CLUE WHAT YOU'RE PLANNING...
...WHEN ALL I SEE ARE EASY TARGETS.
THAT...
...AIN'T GONNA WORK!!
?!
ZOOM

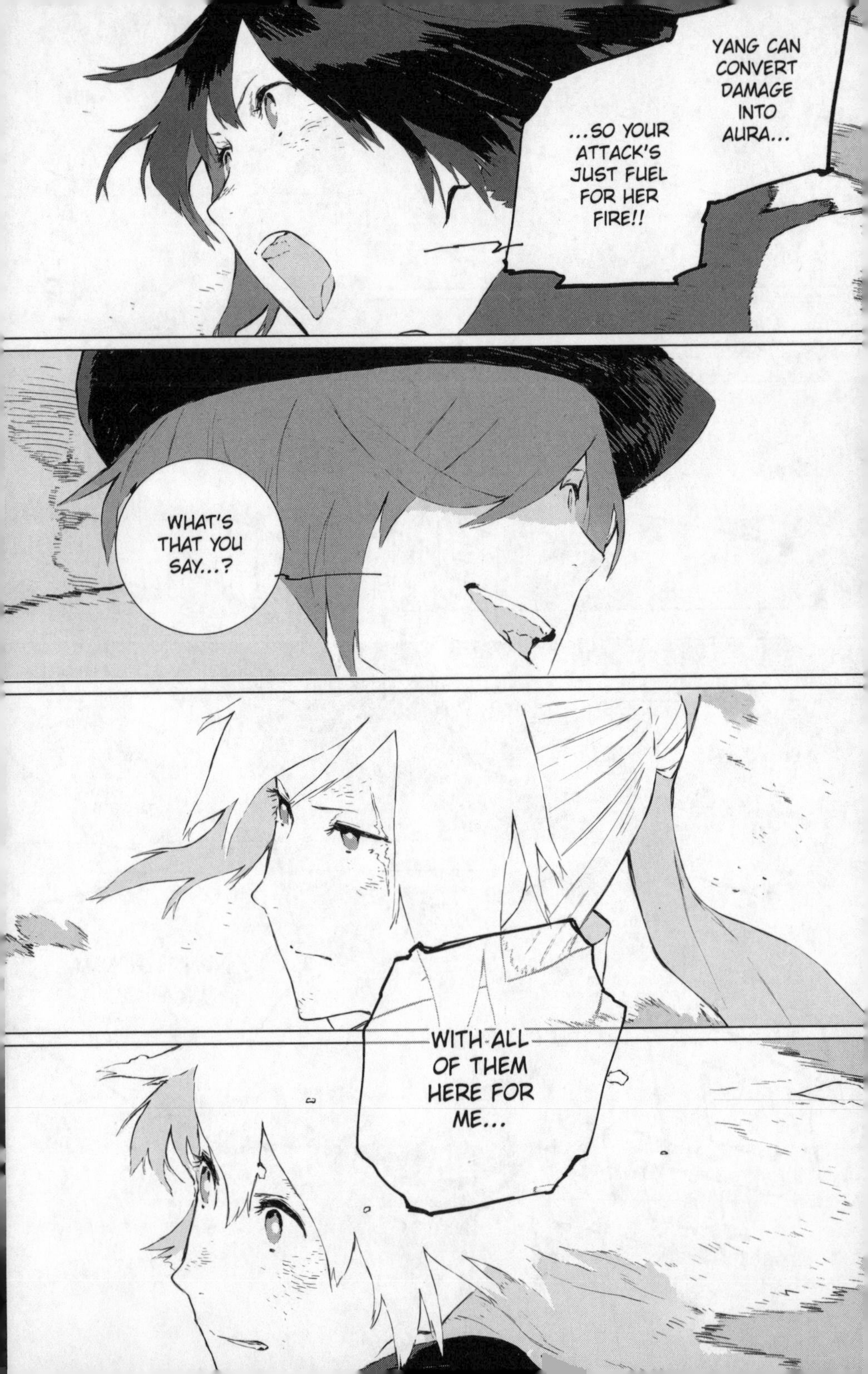
YANG CAN CONVERT DAMAGE INTO AURA...
...SO YOUR ATTACK'S JUST FUEL FOR HER FIRE!!
WHAT'S THAT YOU SAY...?
WITH ALL OF THEM HERE FOR ME...

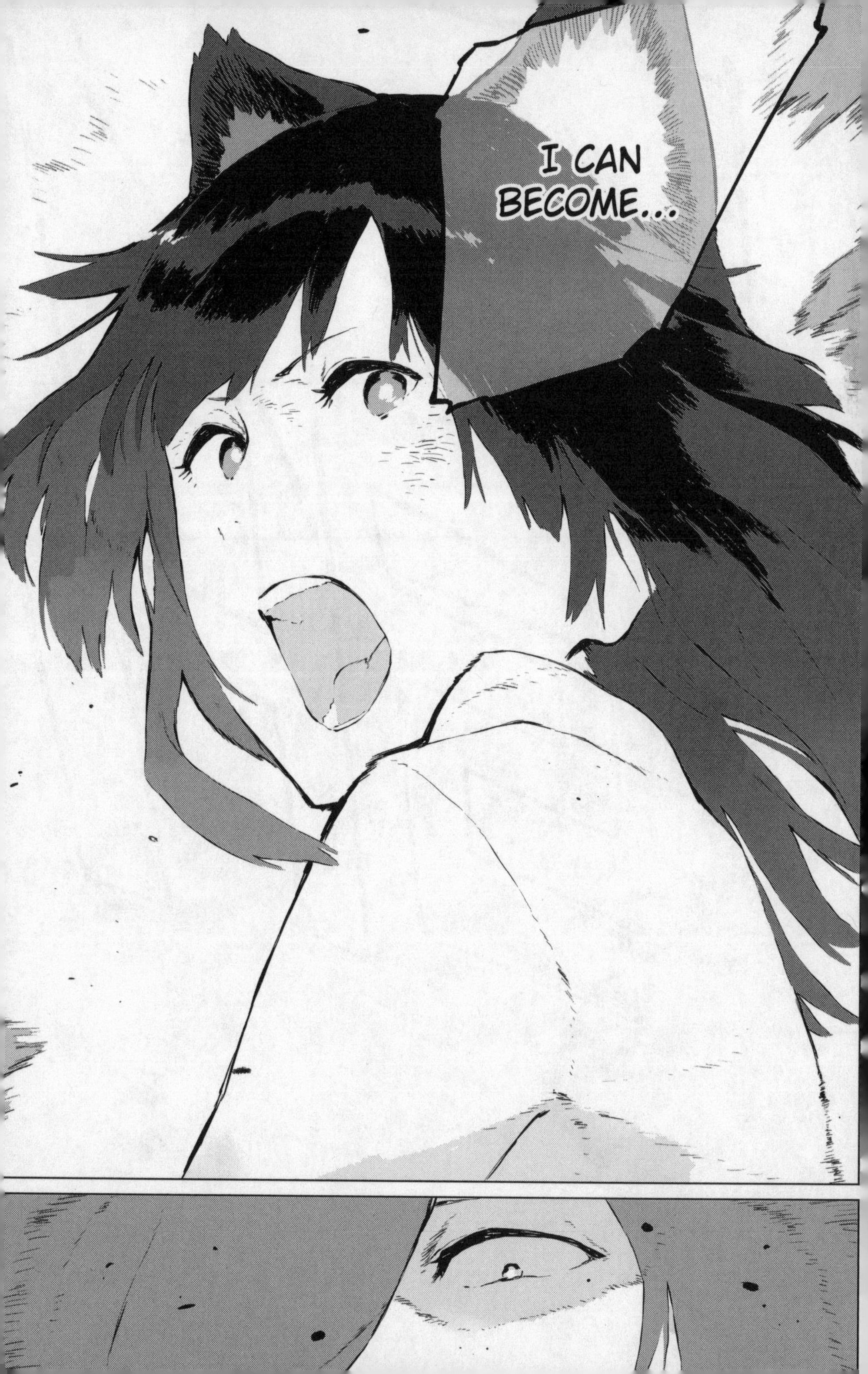
I CAN BECOME...

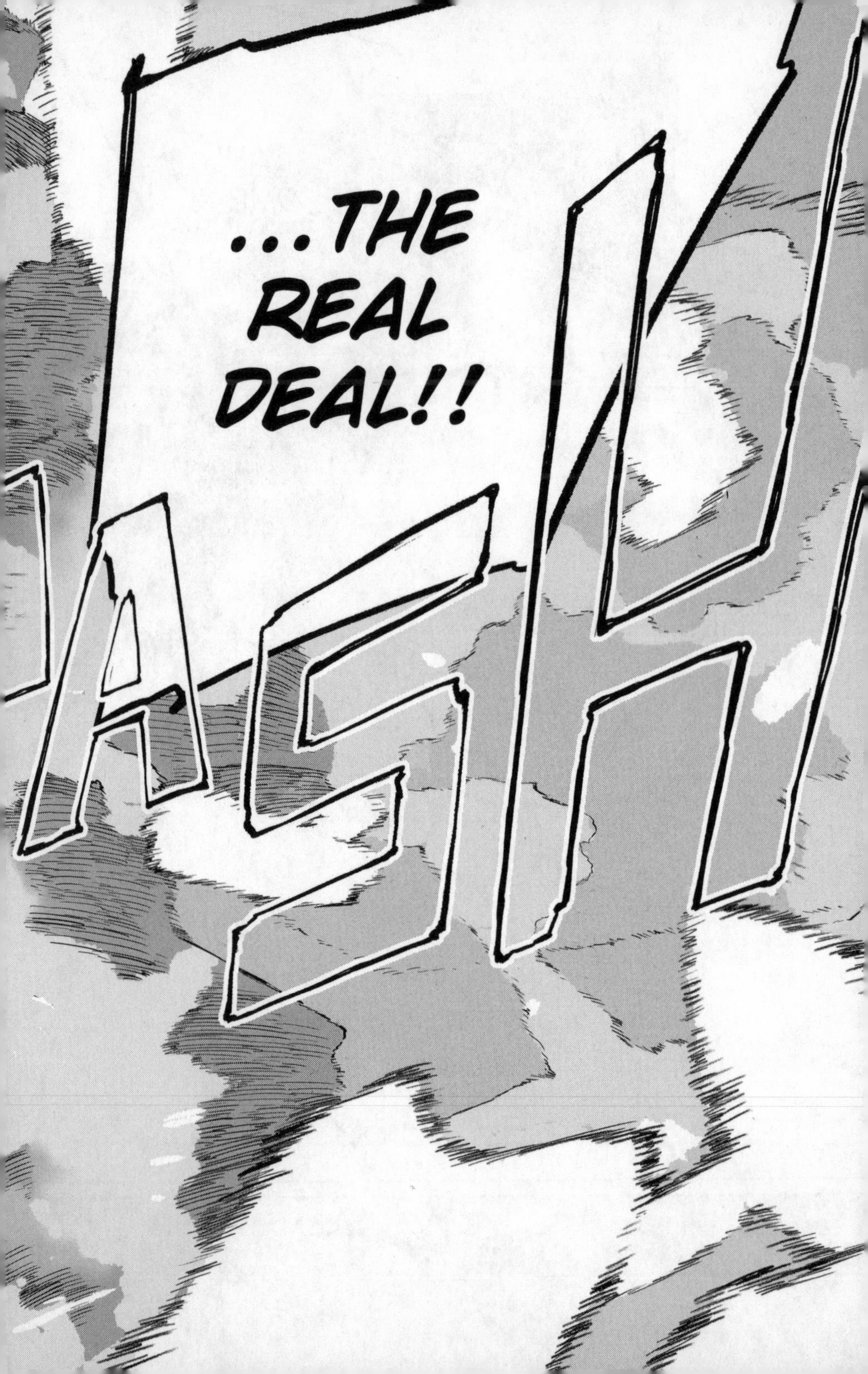
...THE REAL DEAL!!
ASH

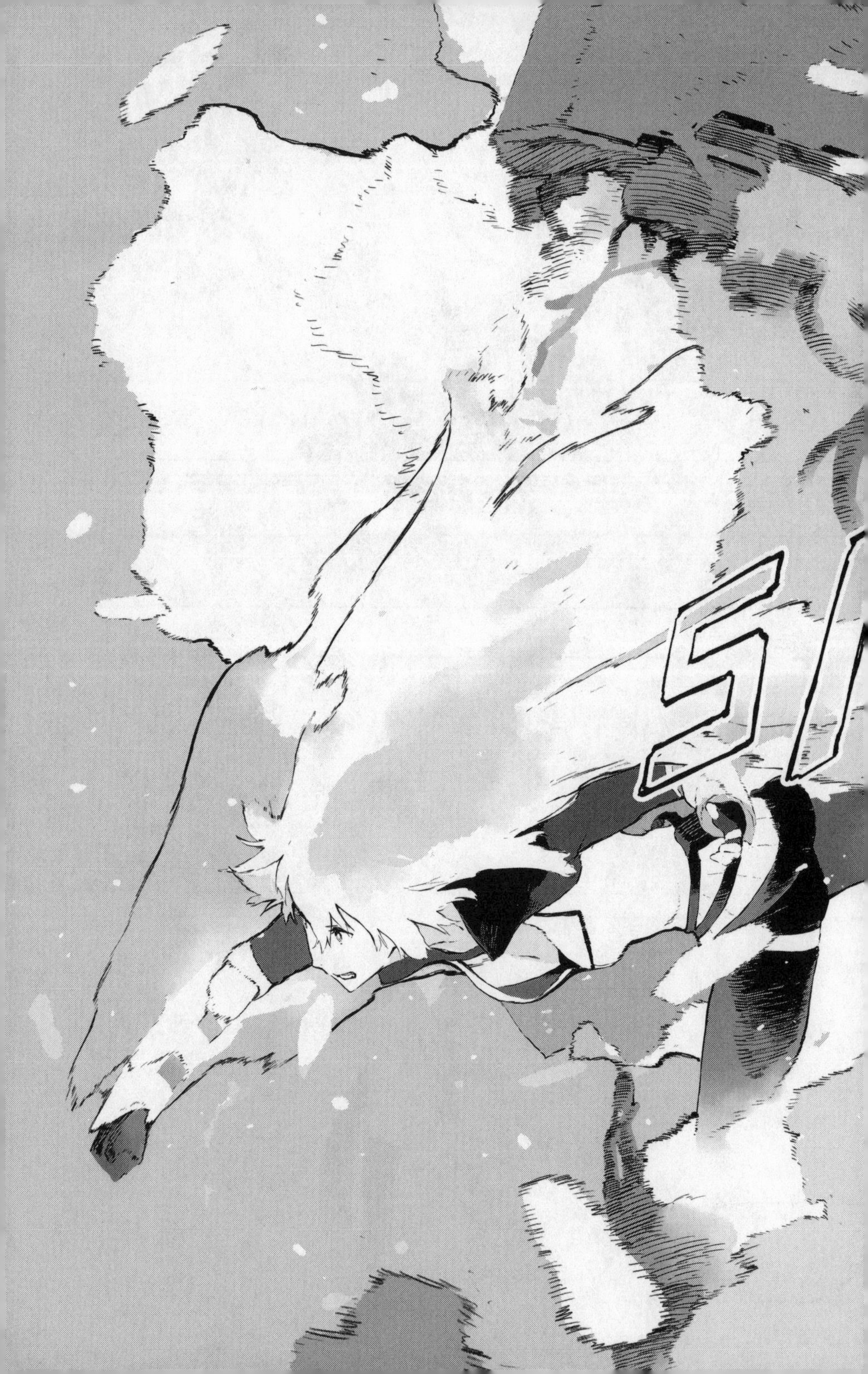

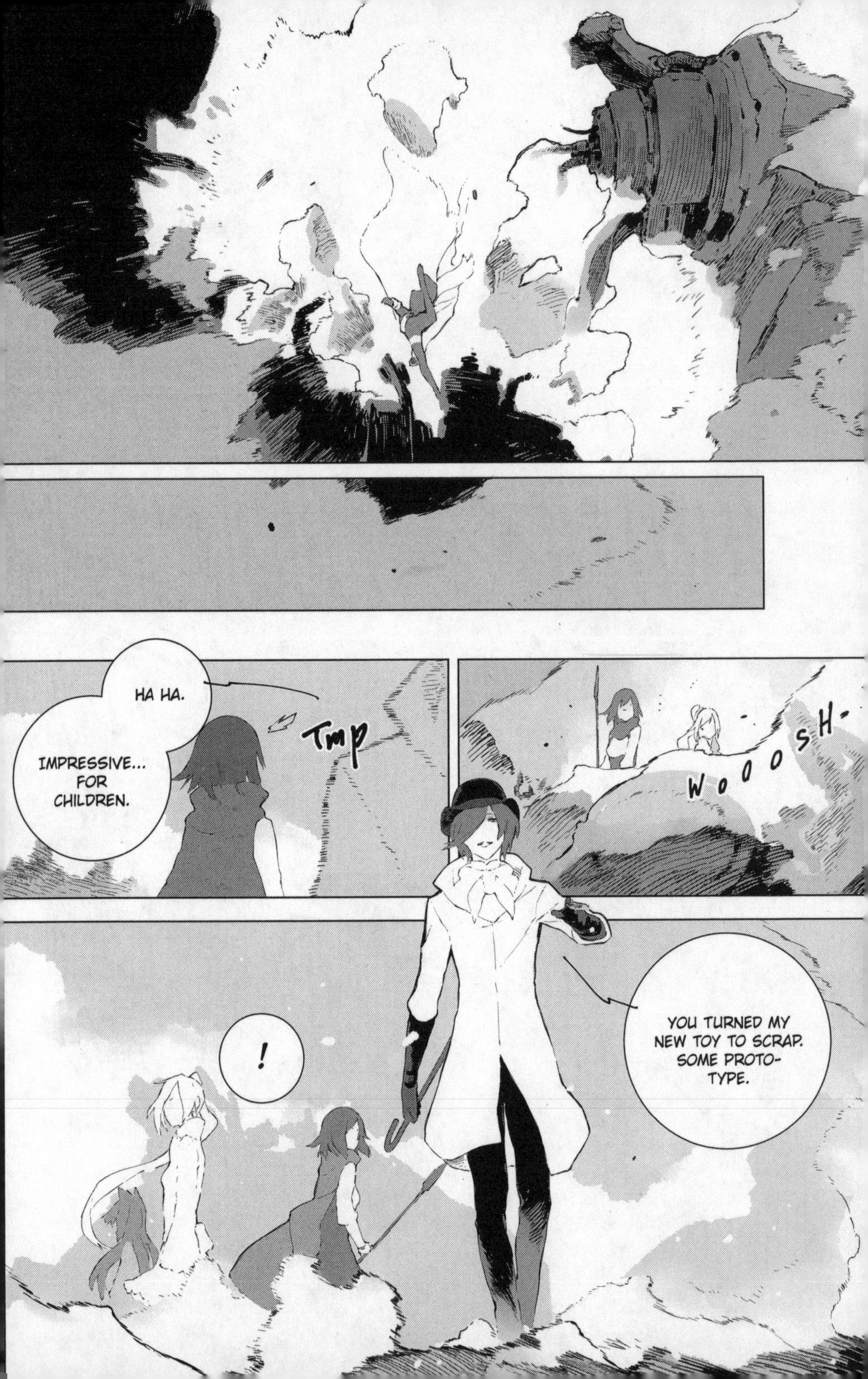
-WOOOSH-
HA HA.
IMPRESSIVE... FOR CHILDREN.
Tmp
YOU TURNED MY NEW TOY TO SCRAP. SOME PROTO-TYPE.
!

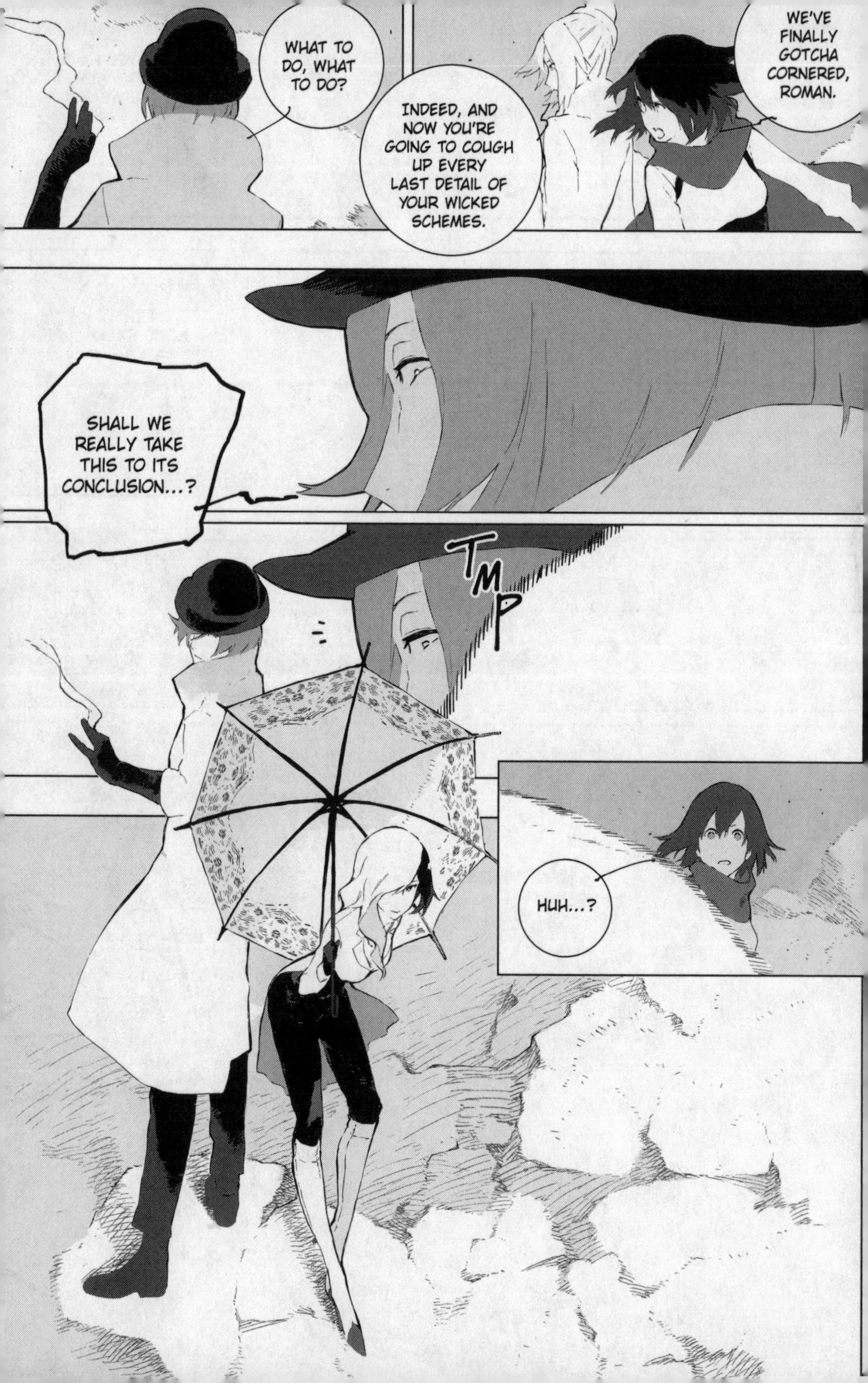
WE'VE FINALLY GOTCHA CORNERED, ROMAN.
INDEED, AND NOW YOU'RE GOING TO COUGH UP EVERY LAST DETAIL OF YOUR WICKED SCHEMES.
WHAT TO DO, WHAT TO DO?
SHALL WE REALLY TAKE THIS TO ITS CONCLUSION...?
TMP
HUH...?

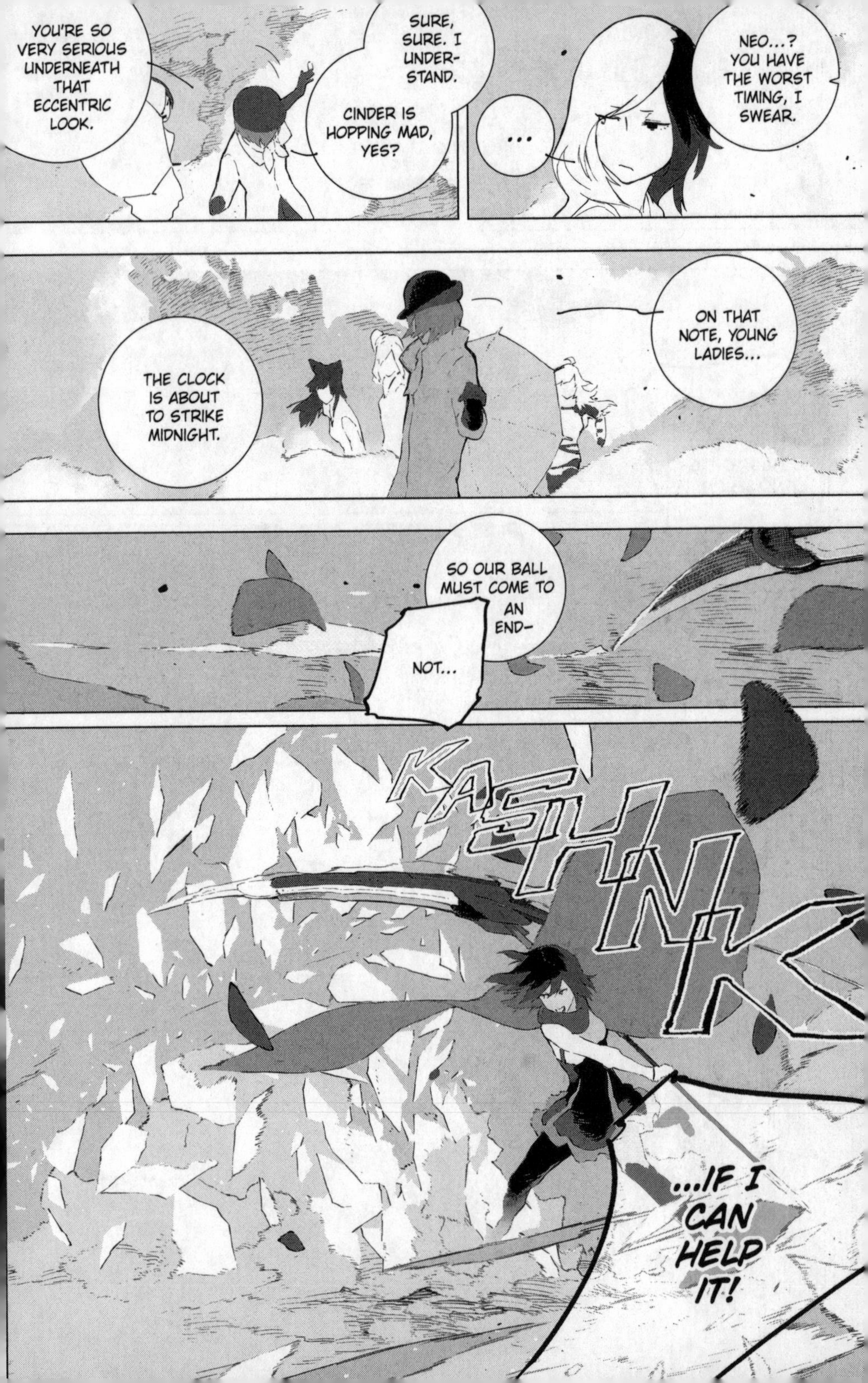
NEO...? YOU HAVE THE WORST TIMING, I SWEAR.
...
SURE, SURE. I UNDER-STAND.
CINDER IS HOPPING MAD, YES?
YOU'RE SO VERY SERIOUS UNDERNEATH THAT ECCENTRIC LOOK.
ON THAT NOTE, YOUNG LADIES...
THE CLOCK IS ABOUT TO STRIKE MIDNIGHT.
SO OUR BALL MUST COME TO AN END-
NOT...
KASHNK
...IF I CAN HELP IT!

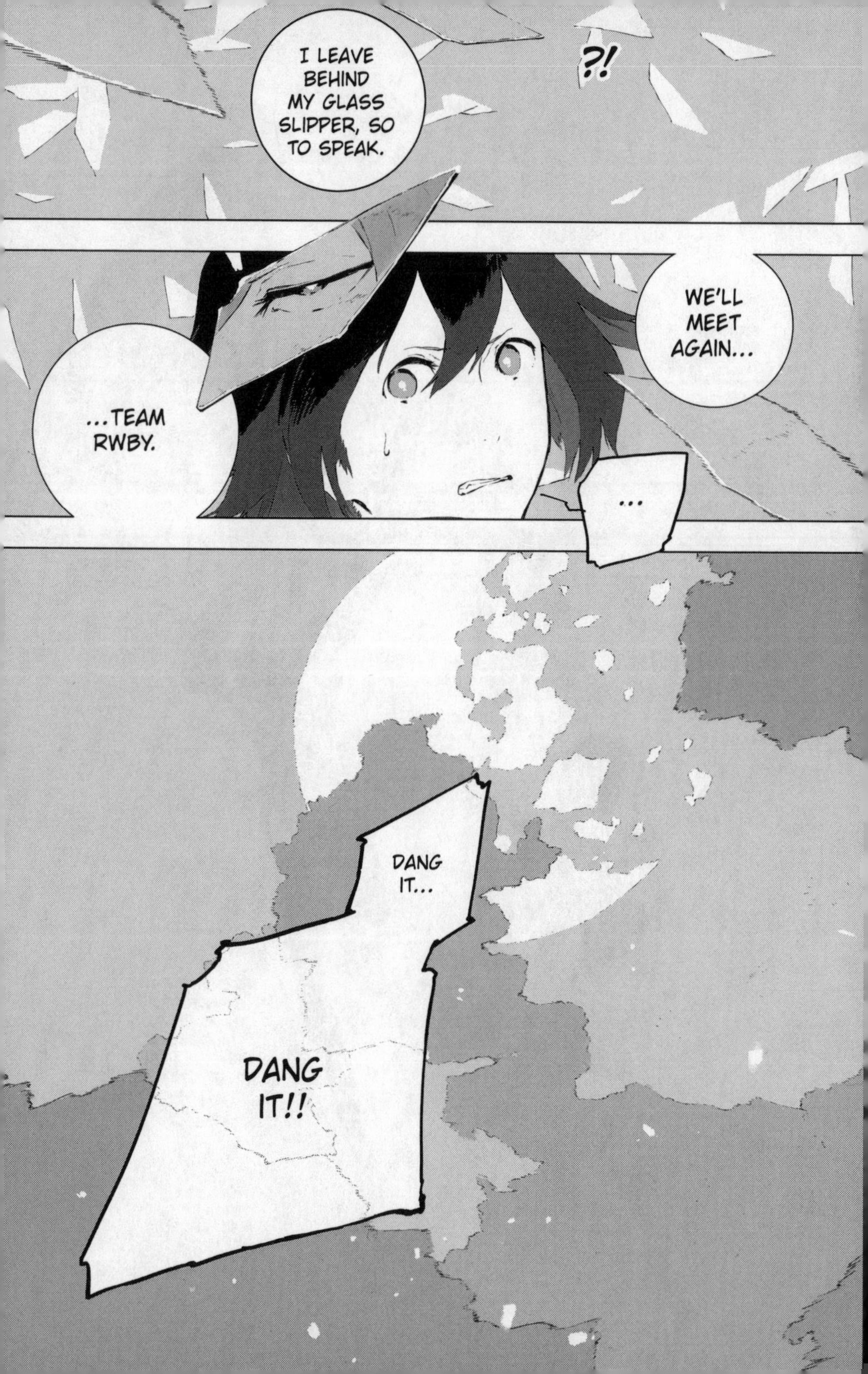
I LEAVE BEHIND MY GLASS SLIPPER, SO TO SPEAK.
?!
WE'LL MEET AGAIN...
...TEAM RWBY.
...
DANG IT...
DANG IT!!

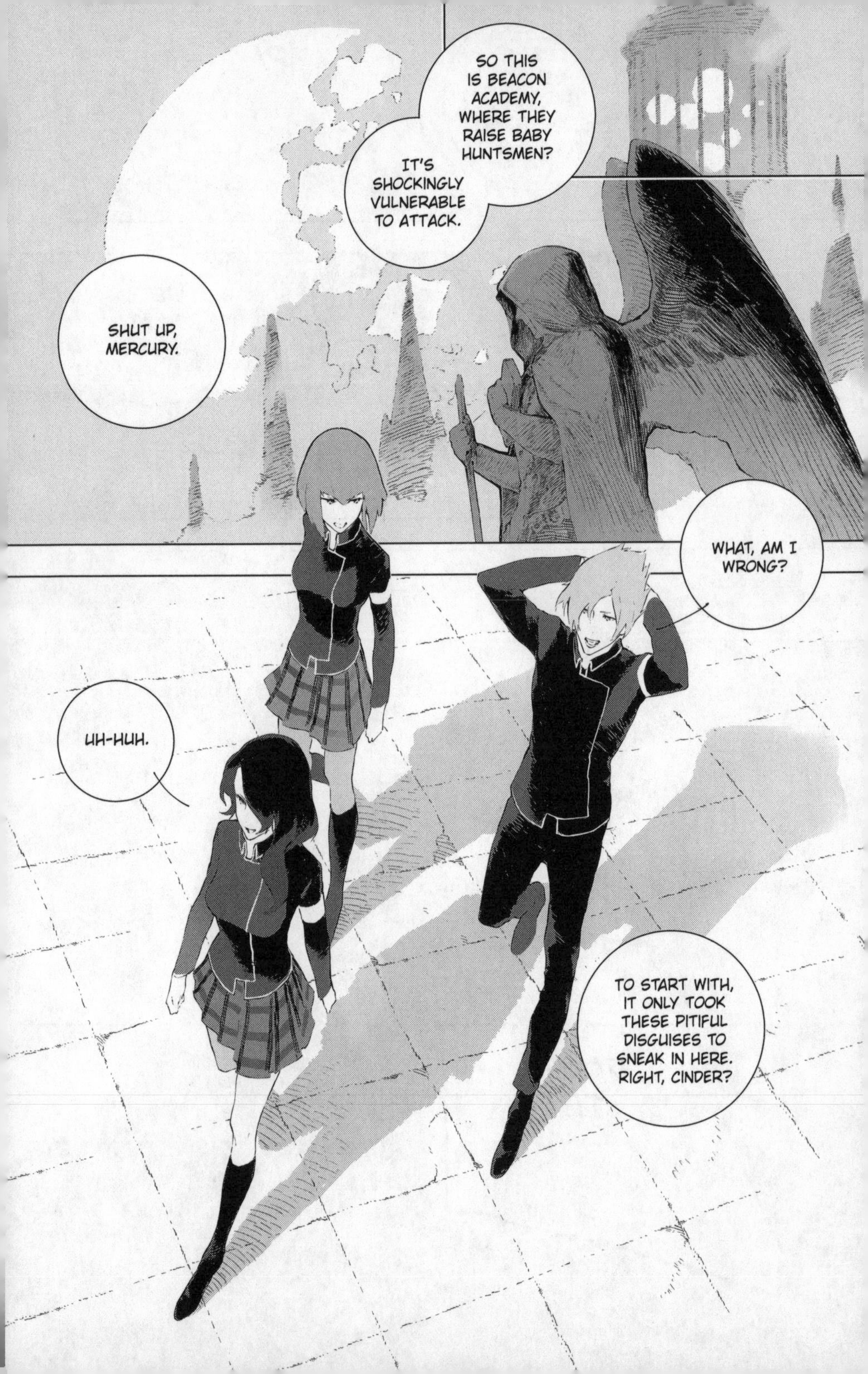
SO THIS IS BEACON ACADEMY, WHERE THEY RAISE BABY HUNTSMEN?
IT'S SHOCKINGLY VULNERABLE TO ATTACK.
SHUT UP, MERCURY.
WHAT, AM I WRONG?
UH-HUH.
TO START WITH, IT ONLY TOOK THESE PITIFUL DISGUISES TO SNEAK IN HERE. RIGHT, CINDER?

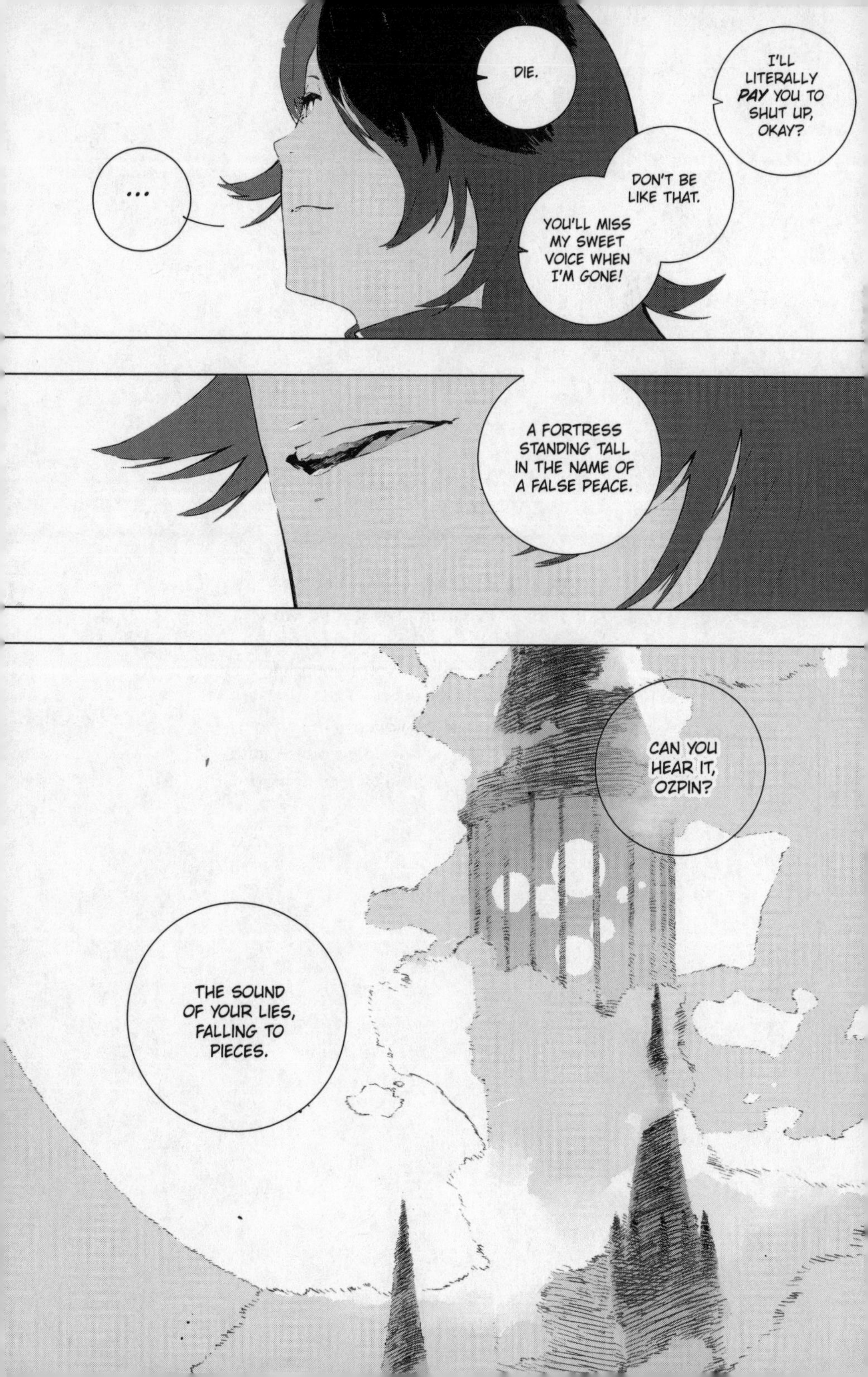
I'LL LITERALLY PAY YOU TO SHUT UP, OKAY?
DIE.
DON'T BE LIKE THAT.
YOU'LL MISS MY SWEET VOICE WHEN I'M GONE!
...
A FORTRESS STANDING TALL IN THE NAME OF A FALSE PEACE.
CAN YOU HEAR IT, OZPIN?
THE SOUND OF YOUR LIES, FALLING TO PIECES.

BUNTA KINAMI was born in Ibaraki Prefecture in Japan, and started drawing manga after he noticed that his friends enjoyed drawing. His favorite series include *Dogs: Bullets & Carnage* by Shirow Miwa and *Nausicaä of the Valley of the Wind* by Hayao Miyazaki. He began his professional career with *RWBY: The Official Manga*.

RWBY
THE OFFICIAL MANGA

VOLUME 2
VIZ SIGNATURE EDITION

STORY AND ART BY
BUNTA KINAMI

ORIGINAL STORY BY
MONTY OUM & ROOSTER TEETH PRODUCTIONS

TRANSLATION **Caleb Cook**
LETTERING **Evan Waldinger**
DESIGN **Shawn Carrico**
EDITOR **David Brothers**

RWBY THE OFFICIAL MANGA
© 2018 Rooster Teeth Productions, LLC
© 2018 by Bunta Kinami
All rights reserved.
First published in Japan in 2018 by SHUEISHA Inc., Tokyo.
English translation rights arranged by SHUEISHA Inc.

The stories, characters and incidents mentioned
in this publication are entirely fictional.

Printed in the U.S.A.

Published by VIZ Media, LLC
P.O. Box 77010
San Francisco, CA 94107

10 9 8 7 6 5 4 3 2 1
First Printing, March 2021

VIZ MEDIA
viz.com

VIZ SIGNATURE
vizsignature.com

PARENTAL ADVISORY
RWBY: THE OFFICIAL MANGA
is rated T for Teen and is
recommended for ages 13 and up.
This volume contains violence.

ratings.viz.com

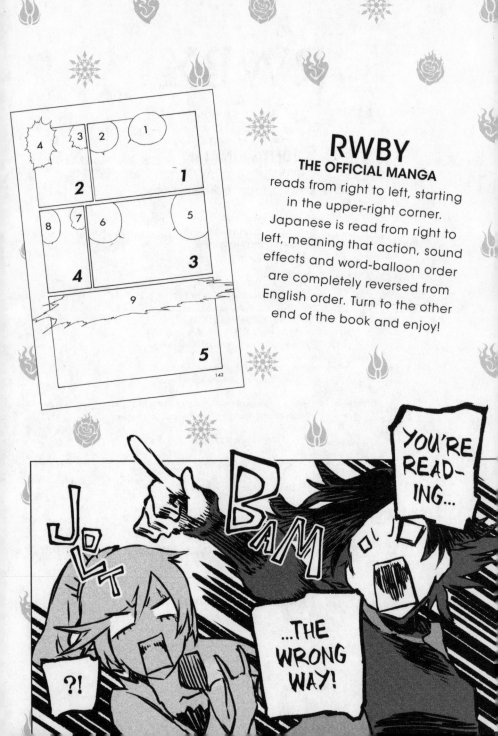

RWBY

THE OFFICIAL MANGA

reads from right to left, starting in the upper-right corner. Japanese is read from right to left, meaning that action, sound effects and word-balloon order are completely reversed from English order. Turn to the other end of the book and enjoy!

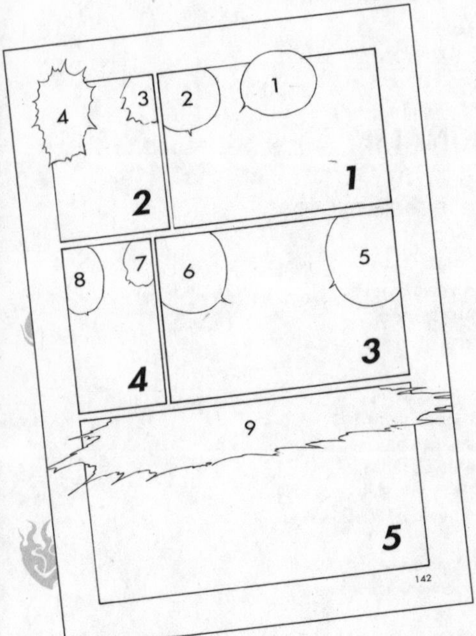
1
2
3
4
1
2
5
6
7
8
3
4
9
5
142

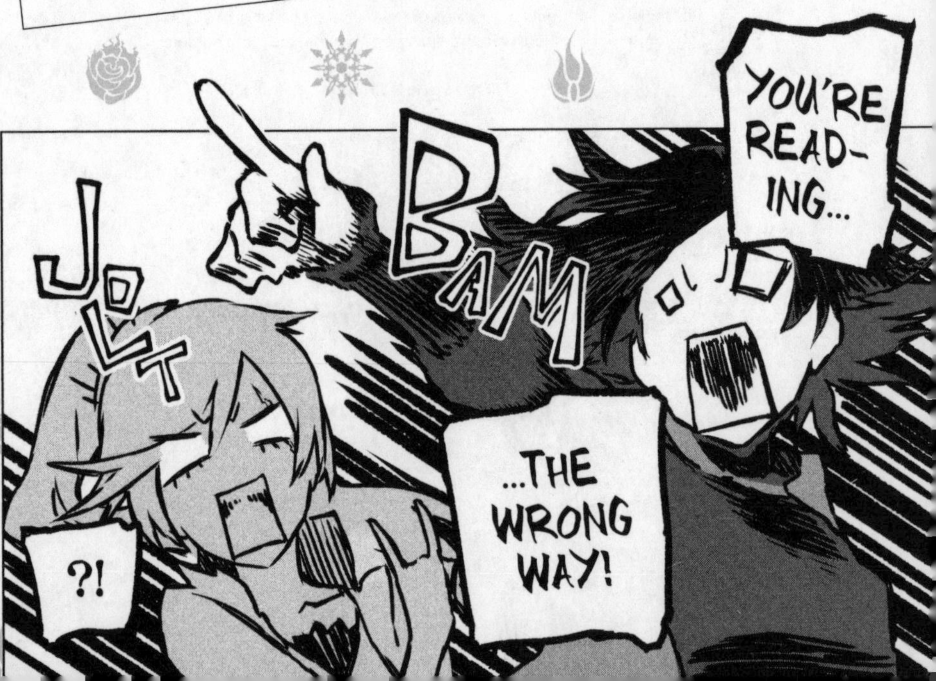
YOU'RE READING...
BAM
JOLT
...THE WRONG WAY!
?!